Fruit Jars

A Collectors' Manual

Julian Harrison Toulouse

Reprint of the 1971 Printing jointly published by Thomas Nelson, Inc.
and Everybodys Press

Fruit Jars: A Collector's Manual

ISBN-10: 1-930665-66-0
ISBN-13: 978-1-930665-66-8

Library of Congress Control Number: 2004116280

THE BLACKBURN PRESS
P. O. Box 287
Caldwell, New Jersey 07006 U.S.A.
973-228-7077
www.BlackburnPress.com

To my wife

Ethel Evelyn Tyer Toulouse

who would "put up" from 300 to 400
jars of food each year
so that we could eat during the winter
while we both worked and both attended
Iowa State University
in the early 1920s.

Introduction

This is a book that grew out of the fruit-jar collections of many friends. When I first became interested in fruit-jar chronology and sent a list of one hundred jar names to friends for verification, I assumed that it was a fairly complete list and was quite pleased with it. When my friends sent me back rubbings and other information that brought the total jar list to just over two hundred, I was amazed that there were so many. By the end of another four months my list grew to the astounding number of three hundred fifty. After a three-month, six-thousand-mile trip in which my wife and I visited over a dozen major collections, the list grew to six hundred fifty fruit-jar names, variations having the same name and fitments such as caps and liners—and I was flabbergasted. Since then the list has grown to over eleven hundred!

My friends have made many useful suggestions that I have tried to follow: to show all possible rubbings they sent me—and this totals seven hundred; to include something about the history of the fruit-jar development, about the glass-making of that day, using the glass-makers and their fruit jars as an index; and to make observations about shapes, patent history, changing styles, and definitions such as I have used in talks before bottle clubs.

For each entry I have tried to answer those questions that a fruit-jar collector asks: how old, how sealed, how made, what colors, what lettering or other design, and by whom made. These I have tried to answer to the best of my ability from nearly forty years' connection with the glass-container industry, both in using and in manufacture.

The patent research, turning up copies of nearly two hundred patents, while still failing to find another forty, was most lucrative. Not only did it develop material for the chapter on "Using the Jars," but it also supplied the information I sought about the construction of the sealing devices for many of the jars, for the purposes of classification. With the illustrations from the patents, collectors may now be able to match up the lucky find of a cap or lid with a jar already owned, and may, as I have done, enable one to remake the wire clip that so long ago rusted away.

Several amusing, yet informative, things turned up in the patent search. Many jars were drastically changed between patent and actual glass-making. Many patents contained remarks about the times, the use of the jars, and not-always-kind references to their competitors' designs. Some jars bore, not the true patent date of the sealing device that they employed, but a prior date for a previous patent—perhaps in order to establish some sort of age-preference in the minds of the company's housewife-customers. Some jars bear patents dates that are not the normal Tuesday issuance dates of the Patent Office Gazette, on whose publication all patents of the week date. Some jars are almost "billboards" of many patent dates—whether they apply or not. It is also interesting to trace the improvement in ideas as the years progressed.

A great deal of history is bound together in these pages, not the least of which is the rise and the fall of fruit-jar companies and fruit-jar ideas. Since the true collector is, perforce, a historian in order to gain the fullest appreciation of the bits of glass that make up his collection, it is my hope that these pages will make the collection of fruit jars an even more interesting, informative, and rewarding avocation.

Julian Harrison Toulouse
Hemet, California

December, 1967

Reference Texts and Acknowledgments

In most respects a fruit jar speaks for itself: approximately when it was made, what means it used for sealing its contents, what glass-making techniques were used, what lettering or designs it carried, and, less often, who made it. Sometimes it carried patent dates that assist in estimating the age, and the trade mark or monogram of the company that made it.

In the case of modern companies my own work and contacts in the glass industry since 1926, especially the friends in the industry I met while I was Chief of the Glass Container Division of the War Production Board, have given me great assistance in obtaining data concerning company beginnings and mergers of recent times in the glass industry.

For dates in modern times I have relied on two general sources: The annual issues of the *Glass Factory Directory* (Budget Publishing Company, Pittsburgh, Pennsylvania), which began in 1924; and the companies themselves, which have generously answered my questions about their history.

For dates previous to 1900, I have relied heavily on three sources, as will appear in the Glossary with the first word of each reference, together with a page number:

"Knittle": *Early American Glass*, by Rhea Mansfield Knittle, Garden City Publishers, Garden City, New York, 1927.

"McKearin": *American Glass*, by George S. McKearin and Helen McKearin, Crown Publishers, New York City, 1941.

"Stevens": *Early Canadian Glass*, by Gerald Stevens, The Ryerson Press, Toronto, Ontario, 1960. In particular, these texts have furnished the dates for many of the older glass factories.

I have consulted, also, but not referenced: Stevens' *In a Canadian Attic*, The Ryerson Press, Toronto, Ontario, 1963; and the McKearins' *Two Hundred Years of American Blown Glass*, Crown Publishers, New York City, 1949.

I am particularly indebted to Mr. Gerald Stevens, Research Associate at the Royal Ontario Museum, Toronto, for many per-

sonal communications about Canadian glass; and to Mr. Don H.
Kennedy, Jr., of Toronto, and to Mr. William M. Hart of Sarnia,
Ontario, for the many rubbings and much information about
Canadian fruit jars. Miss Helen McKearin has given me much in
personal communications, also.

I also wish to name those collectors who have contributed much
information, jar rubbings, and advice, without which this book
could not have been written:

John Algeo	Jerry Eastin	Marilyn Loofbourrow
Glenn Austin	June Eastin	Don Mericle
Bruce Aschenbrenner	Helen M. Eaton	Ula Nims
George Aschenbrenner	Lewis F. Gaynr	Frank Peters
Kenneth Axom, Sr.	Marifred Green	J. E. Pfeiffer
George W. Baker	Jerry Hutter	Adele Reed
Lucy Brichage	May Jones	V. C. Schrantz
Gretta M. Chandler	Don H. Kennedy, Sr.	Robert Soules
Dean Davenport	Alberta Kerr	Jerry Tenbuckel
Nora Davenport	Alex Kerr	John Tibbetts
Barbara Davidson	William Kerr	Joe Wenger

Explanatory Note

This is an explanation of the method of showing information in this book. In describing a jar the following order of furnishing data is followed:

1. An estimation of the date, or dating interval, from exact dates, patents, company life, or other information when available, or from the best estimate based on the manufacturing technique, workmanship, and design.

2. How the jar is sealed, since many collectors have never seen the seals, lids, or caps used on their jars.

3. How the jar was made, its shape and color.

4. What the glass-maker calls "decoration"—the lettering and designs on the side, front, back, bottom, and lid, by separate lines from top to bottom. Script lettering or other lower-case letters are shown in lower case; gothic, block, and italic letters are shown in capitals. The lettering of a single line is separated by single quotation marks; 'THE' and 'Gem' means that the word "THE" appears as a line above the word "Gem," the latter in script.

5. The maker, if known, his location, and period of activity. If the jar was made for a jobber or retailer, his name is given, if known.

6. Remarks about the maker or the patent, or comparisons with other jars, in an effort to add to the interest about a jar.

The names of jars are entered into the Glossary alphabetically, with an added section for non-alphabetical jars. In general, what appears to be the most important word is chosen, with cross indexing in cases where the choice is not clear. The choice is not always a noun; a "strong" modifier, such as a company name or class, is often used. For this reason, ATLAS MASON appears under ATLAS; MASON FRUIT JAR and MASON'S PATENT under MASON rather than under the nouns, "jar" and "patent."

9

Contents

Introduction   5
Reference Texts and Acknowledgments   7
Explanatory Note   9
Contents   *10*
GLOSSARY OF FRUIT JARS   *13*
MEN WHO MADE FRUIT-JAR HISTORY   *340*
   Robert Arthur   *341*
   John Landis Mason   *342*
   Salmon B. Rowley   *347*
   Lewis R. Boyd   *350*
   Henry W. Putnam   *352*
   Albert G. Smalley   *355*
   Frank C. Ball   *357*
   C. N. Brady   *361*
   Alexanler Hewitt Kerr   *363*
USING THE JARS   *368*
   Canning Peaches on the Farm   *377*
   Home Canning of Fruits and Vegetables   *378*
   Home and Farm Canning   *378*
   Canning Fruits and Vegetables at Home   *379*
   Home Canning   *380*
   Home Canning of Fruits, Vegetables and Meats   *381*
   Home Canning of Fruits and Vegetables   *381*
   Hot Pack   *382*
   Modified Hot Pack   *383*
   Cold Pack   *383*
   Open Kettle   *383*
   Low Temperature Packing of Certain Fruits   *384*
   Acidified Vegetable Pack   *384*

Boiling Water-Bath   *384*
Steaming   *385*
Oven Canning   *385*
Pressure Cooking   *385*
DATING THE FRUIT JAR   *387*
CHANGING STYLES IN NAMES AND DECORATION   *391*
THE SHAPE OF THE MASON JAR   *393*
PATENT CHRONOLOGY   *398*
FRUIT-JAR SEALS   *412*
  Early Cork Stoppers and Wax-Dipped Covers   *413*
  The Wax Sealer   *414*
  Stoppers   *419*
  The Helix and Its Forms as Sealing Tighteners   *426*
  Continuous Screw-Thread Shoulder Seals   *427*
  Continuous Screw-Thread Top Seals   *432*
  Continuous Screw-Thread Combination
     Top and Bead Seals   *441*
  All-Glass Screw Caps   *444*
  Helical Lugs on the Jar Neck   *449*
  Helical Slots in the Neck of the Jar   *457*
  Helical Ramps on the Lid   *459*
  Plain Lugs with a Helical Yoke or Cap   *462*
  The Toggles   *464*
  Toggle with the Hinged Lid   *464*
  The Lightning Series of Toggles   *465*
  The Everlasting Toggles of Abramson   *468*
  The Kivlan Series of Twin Toggles   *469*
  Spring Bails   *471*
  Spring Clips   *473*
  The Levers   *482*
  The Cam Levers   *483*
  Simple Levers   *486*
  The Clutch Levers   *489*
  Friction-Held Cover Caps   *491*
  Thumbscrews for Tightening Seals   *493*

Rubber Bands as Fastening Devices   *496*
One-Use Seals   *498*
Protection of Contents   *499*
Protection from Metallic Tastes   *499*
Venting Air from the Jar   *501*
Protection from Air by Immersion   *504*
Wrenches   *507*
Patented Jar Shapes and Design Features   *509*
Diaphragms   *510*
Compression Bands Circling Finish and Cap   *510*
FRUIT-JAR MANUFACTURERS AND THEIR JARS   *512*
DEFINITIONS AND TERMS   *524*
GLASSMAKING IN FRUIT JARS   *536*

Glossary of Fruit Jars

A

"A" with MASON'S PATENT, NOV. 30th, 1858

Circa 1900-15
Mason shoulder seal
Machine-made round, in green tint
Side: 'MASON'S' arched over 'A,' followed
  by 'PATENT,' 'Nov. 30TH,' and '1858'
Maker unknown

A & C

Circa 1880
Probably a glass lid, straddling the ground
  lip to seal on a slanting surface surround-
  ing it, and held by a clip
Handmade round, ground lip, in green
Side: in large letters: 'A & C'
Maker unknown

A B C

Circa 1880-1900
Glass lid Lightning closure, old shoulder
  style
Handmade round, ground lip, in aqua
Side: 'A B C' in large, double-outlined capi-
  tals
Maker unknown

A B G A MASON IMPROVED

Circa 1920
Glass lid and screw-band top seal
Machine-made round, in aqua
Side: three lines: 'MASON,' 'IMPROVED,'
  and 'A B G A'

(BOTTOM)

Bottom and lid: A B G A in four corners of a cross, with 'MADE IN U. S. A.' in the top arc of a circle above, and 'TRADE MARK' in an drooped arc below

Maker unknown

ACME (1)

Circa 1920-30 because of beaded neck design

Lightning beaded neck closure, glass lid

Machine-made rounded square quart, in flint

Side: a shield with 'ACME' slanting upward, five stars above, and alternate stippled bars below

Acme Glass Co., Olean, N.Y., 1902-30

Purchased by Olean Glass Co., later by Thatcher Glass Mfg. Co.

ACME (2)

The pint has three stars in a smaller shield

ADLER [German for "Eagle"]

Modern

Glass lid with hinge attached on one side and snap lock on other

Machine-made round in flint

Side: bare

Lid: 'ADLER CONSERVENGLAS'

Bottom: 'HEYE,' 'DRP 142521,' and 'DRP 261889'

Hermann Heye Glasfabrik, Bremen, Germany

ADVANCE

Circa 1880-1900

Glass lid and metal clamp to two helical neck lugs

Handmade round, ground lip, in light green

Side: a monogram of "J" and "W," with 'ADVANCE' lettered through it. Above: 'TRADE MARK' arched, and below: 'PAT. APL'D. FOR' completing the circle

Maker unknown

AGEE QUEEN

Circa 1921

Glass lid with Kivlan 1921 twin toggle

Machine-made rounded square, in flint

Side: 'AGEE' in extremely large letters, with the 'A' even larger, and the "GEE" underlined; below it 'QUEEN'

Bottom: H – A trade mark only

Made by Hazel Atlas Glass Co., Wheeling, W. Va., for Kivlan & Onthank, Boston, Mass., glass and pottery jobbers

AGEE is probably a coined word, from the first initials of Albert G. Smalley, founder of the firm, and until 1919 senior partner in the firm, Smalley, Kivlan & Onthank

AGNEW (1)

Circa 1854-66

Groove-ring wax sealer, after Arthur patent No. 12,153, Jan. 2, 1855

Handmade round, pressed laid-on-ring, in light green

Side: bare

Bottom: 'JOHN AGNEW & SON' in a circle

John Agnew & Son, Pittsburgh, Pa., 1854-66 (McKearin, p. 604)

Was: Chambers & Agnew, 1842-54

Became: Agnew & Son, 1866-76; Agnew & Co., 1876-92

AGNEW (2)

Same except only "A" on the bottom

AGNEW (3)

Circa 1876-92
Blown wax sealer
Handmade round, ground lip, in light green.
The wide shoulder was pressed down while still on the blow pipe, to form a circular depression. A similar wax sealer was patented Sept. 18, 1860
Side: bare
Bottom: 'AGNEW & CO.' in a circle
Agnew & Co., Pittsburgh, Pa., 1876-92

A G W L

Circa 1860-70
Groove-ring wax sealer
Handmade round, pressed laid-on-ring, in aqua; very crudely made
Bottom: "A G W L PITTS PA" forming a circle
Maker may be the American Glass works, founded in Pittsburgh about 1865 as a window-glass house. It was not unusual for window-glass makers to make bottles and jars, especially from the first third of the pot in which the glass was too seedy for sheet glass. The company operated until about 1905. (McKearin, p. 611)

AIRTIGHT (1)

Circa 1858-63
Blown and tooled wax sealer, the bulbous neck being collapsed into a bead and worked upward to form the groove
Handmade round, barrel-shaped, showing hoops and staves, in green

Side: 'POTTER & BODINE' above 'AIR-TIGHT FRUIT JAR'

Potter & Bodine, Philadelphia, Pa., 1855-63 (operated Bridgeton Glass works, Bridgeton, N.J.) (McKearin, p. 602)

AIRTIGHT (2)

Same as (1) except 'POTTER & BODINE' in front, 'AIRTIGHT FRUIT JAR' on back

AIRTIGHT (3)

Same as (1) except 'POTTER & BODINE'S,' 'AIRTIGHT,' 'FRUIT JAR,' and 'PHILAD^A' in four lines on front, and 'PATENTED APRIL 13th' over '1858' on the back

POTTER & BODINE'S

AIRTIGHT

FRUIT JAR

PHILAD^A

AIRTIGHT (4)

Same as (1) except made after 1870 since 'COHANSEY' replaces 'POTTER & BODINE'

Bottom: 'COHANSEY' across a diameter, 'GLASS MF'G CO' in a half circle above it

Jars have not been found carrying the name: 'J. &. F. BODINE,' who operated the company 1863-70

The basic patent for these first four AIRTIGHT jars was No. 19,954 issued to Joseph Borden, Bridgeton, N.J., April 13, 1858

AIRTIGHT (5)

Similar groove-ring jar, but lettered 'COHANSEY' and 'PAT. MARCH 20, 1877'

See NE PLUS ULTRA for another AIRTIGHT jar

ALL RIGHT (1)

Circa 1868-75

Glass lid with heavy clip over the top, hooking into helical neck grooves which are serrated along top edge

Handmade round, ground lip, in green

Side: 'ALL' and 'RIGHT' over 'PAT^D JAN 28TH 1868' in three heavy cut lines

Bottom: 'PAT NOV 26 67," a basic Hero patent for shape

Hero Glass Works, Philadelphia, Pa., 1856-84, Lockport, N.Y., 1869-72

The Lockport Journal of July 13, 1870, described operations at the Lockport plant, with mention that the ALL RIGHT was being made in a small way. Hero's 1878 letterheads omits the ALL RIGHT

Patent No. 73,724 was issued to W. L. Imlay for this jar

A LL

R I C H T

(FRONT)

PAT^D J A N 2 8TH I 8 6 8

(BACK)

ALL RIGHT (2)

Same except patent date moved to the back, and lighter cut letters

ALMY

Circa 1880

Mason shoulder seal

Handmade round, ground lip, in light blue-green

Side: 'ALMY' in an arched line

Bottom: 'PATENTED DEC. 25, 1877'

Winslow Glass Works, Winslow, N.J., owned by Hay & Co.

Patent No. 198,528 was issued to Theodore F. Woodward, of Winslow, and assigned to Hay & Co.

ALSTON, THE

Circa 1901
Metal lid and wire clip
Handmade round, ground lip, in flint
Side: in script: 'The' above 'Alston'
Maker unknown

AMAZON SWIFT SEAL (1)

Circa 1910-20
Lightning closure, lever wire held by dimples in the neck
Machine-made round, in green
Side: in oval outline: 'AMAZON' and 'SWIFT SEAL' in two lines
Maker unknown

AMAZON SWIFT SEAL (2)

Same except 'PAT'D JULY 14, 1908' added below oval

AMERICAN FRUIT JAR

Circa 1890-1900
Glass lid with old neck design Lightning finish
Handmade round, ground lip, in olive-green
Side: 'AMERICAN' in large, doubly outlined letters, in an arch over an eagle carrying a streaming flag in its talons. Below the eagle: 'FRUIT JAR' in doubly outlined letters. The top line of the letters follow a sagging arc; the bottom line is straight
Maker unknown. The AMERICAN, the FEDERAL, and the COMMONWEALTH were seen in the half-gallon size, all with a side plated, removable panel carrying the letters and interchangeable with each other. The style is indicative of the Albert G. Smalley Co., Boston, Mass., china and glassware jobber

The Alston

AMAZON
SWIFT SEAL

AMERICAN
FRUIT JAR

AMERICAN PORCELAIN LINED

Circa 1885-91

Mason shoulder seal

Handmade round, ground lip, in green and blue tints

Side: a monogram of "N," "A," "G," and "Co." Above it, in two lines: 'THE' above an arched 'AMERICAN'; below it, 'POR-CELAIN LINED' in a drooped arc

North American Glass Co., Montreal, Que., 1885-91 (now Dominion)

ANCHOR

ANCHOR

Circa 1910-20

Glass lid and metal screw-band top seal

Machine-made round, in flint and amethyst (sun-colored ?)

Side: a large fouled anchor above 'ANCHOR'

Maker unknown—not Anchor Hocking Glass Corp.

ANCHOR HOCKING

Since 1937

Mason beaded neck design

Machine-made rounded square, in flint

Side: a large anchor with "H" superimposed, and above in a half circle, 'ANCHOR HOCKING'

Anchor Hocking Glass Corp., Lancaster, Ohio, 1937 to date

ANCHOR HOCKING LIGHTNING

Since 1937

Lightning beaded neck design

Machine-made round, in flint

Side: a large anchor with 'H' superimposed, and below it, 'LIGHTNING'

Anchor Hocking Glass Corp., Lancaster, Ohio, 1937 to date

LIGHTNING

ANCHOR HOCKING MASON

Since 1937
Mason beaded neck design
Machine-made rounded square, in flint
Side: a small anchor with 'H' superimposed.
Above it, 'ANCHOR' and 'HOCKING' in
two slanting lines; below it, 'MASON'
Anchor Hocking Glass Corp., Lancaster,
Ohio, 1937 to date

ANDERSON PRESERVING CO.

Circa 1920-30
Mason beaded neck design
Machine-made round, in flint. Will sun-
color
Side: fruit and vine design circles jar at
top, barred design at bottom
Bottom: in circle: 'ANDERSON PRE-
SERVING C⁰,' with 'CAMDEN' and
'N.J.' in center
Diamonds on bottom may be trade mark of
Diamond Glass Co., Royersford, Pa.,
1888 to date

ATHERHOLT/FISHER & CO.

Age uncertain—circa 1860-90
Plug or stopper fitting inside tapered finish
Handmade round, pressed laid-on-ring
tooled in shape of an inverted "V," with
smooth inside and outside taper and
small inner ledge
Side: 'ATHERHOLT/FISHER & CO.'
arched over 'PHILADᴬ'
Maker unknown

ATLAS EDJ SEAL

An Atlas glass lid for screw-band top seal,
featuring a deep depression to center on
top of beaded neck jar using Mason
shoulder seal

ATLAS E – Z SEAL (1)

Since 1896

Lightning closure, old neck design

Machine-made squat round, in flint, green, blue-green, and amber

Side: two lines: 'ATLAS' and 'E – Z SEAL'

Bottom: "E – Z' and 'SEAL' across the bottom, circled by 'ATLAS' and 'TRADE MARK REG'

Atlas Glass Co., Washington, Pa., 1896-1901, and

Hazel Atlas Glass Co., Wheeling, W. Va., 1902-64

John Algeo, retired Sales Manager for Hazel Atlas tells me that this jar was the initial production of the Atlas Glass Co. in 1896

ATLAS E – Z SEAL (2)

The same except 'ATLAS' in quotation marks

ATLAS E – Z SEAL (3)

Same except 'E – Z' and 'SEAL' in two lines below 'ATLAS'

ATLAS E – Z SEAL (4)

Same except with beaded Lightning neck design, which would date after 1910 and be Hazel Atlas production rather than Atlas

ATLAS E – Z SEAL (5)

Same except with dimple holding lever wire instead of the former tie-wire around the neck. Dates from 1915-20

ATLAS E – Z SEAL (6)

Same except with Hazel Atlas trade mark (H – A), which was first used about 1921

ATLAS E – Z SEAL with moldmaker's error

Same as (2) except SEAL was spelled SEAE

Mrs. Marifred Green tells me that she found a few pages from the June, 1910, *Ladies' World* in her mother's cookbook, including an ad by Hazel Atlas: "The greatest improvement yet made in fruit containers is ATLAS E – Z SEAL JAR – ALL GLASS"

ATLAS
E – Z
SEAE

ATLAS GOOD LUCK (1)

Circa 1920-35
Lightning beaded neck design
Machine-made rounded square, in flint and aqua
Side: large four-leaved clover. Above it: 'ATLAS' in a half circle; below it; 'GOOD LUCK,' continuing the circle
Hazel Atlas Glass Co., Wheeling, W. Va., 1902-64

ATLAS GOOD LUCK (2)

Same, except made after 1921, since the Hazel Atlas trade mark is on the bottom

ATLAS IMPROVED MASON (1)

Circa 1896
Glass lid and metal screw-band top seal
Machine-made round, in dark green
Side: three lines: 'ATLAS' arched over 'IMPROVED' and 'MASON'
Hazel Atlas Glass Co., Wheeling, W. Va., 1902-64, and
Atlas Glass Co., Washington, Pa., 1896-1901

ATLAS IMPROVED MASON (2)

Same but in lighter green and aqua, and probably made after 1910 and by Hazel Atlas only

ATLAS H – A MASON (1)

Circa 1920

Mason beaded neck design

Machine-made rounded square, in flint

Side: large "H" over "A," the trade mark adopted about 1921, with 'ATLAS' above it, and 'MASON' below

ATLAS H – A MASON (2)

Same except the trade mark is small and enclosed in a circle

ATLAS H – A MASON (3)

Same as (2) except the area within the circle is stippled

ATLAS MASON IMPROVED

Circa 1900-10

Glass lid and metal screw-band top seal

Machine-made round, in green and blue-green

Side: four lines: 'ATLAS' slightly arched over 'MASON,' 'IMPROVED,' and 'PAT'D'

Hazel Atlas Glass Co., Wheeling W. Va., 1902-64

ATLAS MASON'S PATENT (1)

Circa 1900-10

Mason shoulder seal

Handmade round, ground lip, in aqua

Side: three lines: 'ATLAS,' 'MASON'S,' arched, and 'PATENT'

Hazel Atlas Glass Co., Washington, Pa., 1902-64, and

Atlas Glass Co., Washington, Pa., 1896-1901

This jar is unusual since Atlas is supposed to have used only machines, but it could have been made in one of the old Hazel Glass plants

ATLAS MASON'S PATENT (2)

Same except machine-made in blue-green

ATLAS MASON'S PATENT NOV. 30th, 1858

Circa 1900

Mason shoulder seal

Machine-made tapered-shoulder round, in blue-green

Side: five lines: 'ATLAS,' 'MASON'S,' arched, 'PATENTS,' 'NOV 30ᵀᴴ,' and '1858'

Hazel Atlas Glass Co., Wheeling, W. Va., 1902-64, and

Atlas Glass Co., Washington, Pa., 1896-1901

ATLAS SPECIAL

Circa 1910-30

Mason shoulder seal

Machine-made squat round, in green and aqua

Side: 'ATLAS' arched over 'SPECIAL'

Hazel Atlas Glass Co., Wheeling, W. Va., 1902-64

ATLAS SPECIAL MASON (1)

Circa 1910-30

Mason shoulder seal

Machine-made squat round, in green and aqua

- ATLAS -
MASON'S
PATENT

ATLAS
MASON'S
PATENT
NOV 30ᵀᴴ
1858

ATLAS
SPECIAL

ATLAS
SPECIAL
MASON

Side: three lines: 'ATLAS' arched over
'SPECIAL' and 'MASON'
Hazel Atlas Glass Co., Wheeling, W. Va.,
1902-64

ATLAS SPECIAL MASON (2)

Same except with beaded neck style Mason
finish

-ATLAS-
STRONG SHOULDER
MASON

ATLAS STRONG SHOULDER MASON

Circa 1915

Mason beaded neck style, and one of the
first to have this construction which
would take either a shoulder seal (on the
bead) or a top seal on the new machine-
made surface. It enabled greater
strength in the shoulder by eliminating
the sharp angles formerly at the sealing
ring
Machine-made round, in flint, aqua, and
light green
Side: three lines: 'ATLAS,' 'STRONG
SHOULDER,' and 'MASON'
Hazel Atlas Glass Co., Wheeling, W. Va.,
1902-64

ATLAS
WHOLEFRUIT
JAR

ATLAS WHOLEFRUIT JAR (1)

Circa 1910

Lightning wide-mouth finish, old shoulder
style
Machine-made wide-mouth round, in flint
Side: three lines: 'ATLAS' over 'WHOLE-
FRUIT' (slanting) and 'JAR'
Hazel Atlas Glass Co., Wheeling, W. Va.,
1902-64

ATLAS WHOLEFRUIT JAR (2)

Same, except beaded Lightning finish
adopted shortly after 1910

ATLAS WHOLEFRUIT JAR (3)

Same except dimple Lightning finish used
about 1920

ATMORE & SON

Circa 1920-35
Glass lid and metal screw-band top seal
Machine-made wide-mouth round, in green
Bottom: 'ATMORE & SON' and 'PHILA-
DELPHIA' forming a circle, with
'MINCEMEAT' across the diameter
Maker unknown
Bottom has the Miller machine "valve
mark"

AUTOMATIC SEALER, THE

Circa 1890-1905
Glass lid with spring-wire bail held by tie
wire on neck
Handmade round, ground lip, in green
Side: three lines: 'THE,' 'AUTOMATIC,'
and 'SEALER'
Maker unknown

B

"B" in a shield, with MASON PATENT NOV 30th 1858

Circa 1885-1900
Mason shoulder seal
Handmade round, very crude ground lip,
in flint and sun-colored
Side: "B" in a small shield, followed by
'MASON' (arched), 'PATENT,' 'NOV
30TH,' and '1858' in four lines
Maker unknown

BAKER BROS.

Circa 1860
Groove-ring wax sealer
Handmade round, pressed laid-on-ring, in
blue-green
Bottom: 'BAKER BROS., BALTO., MD.'
in a circle
Baker Bros. & Co., Baltimore, Md., 1853-
1905 (?)

BALL (1)

Circa 1890
Mason shoulder seal
Handmade round, ground lip, in green
Side: only the word, 'Ball' in slanting script
Ball Bros. Co., Muncie, Ind., 1888 to date

BALL (2)

Same except underlined by finial from the
final "l"

BALL, THE

Circa 1890
Lightning closure, old neck style, but with
metal lid
Handmade round, ground lip, in light green
Side: 'The Ball,' in straight line script, over
'PAT. APL'D FOR'
Ball Bros. Co., Muncie, Ind., 1888 to date

BALL DELUXE JAR

Circa 1930
Lightning closure, dimple neck design
Machine-made round, in flint
Side: three lines: 'BALL,' 'DELUXE,' and
'JAR' in block letters. The deeply cut
lettering is almost prismatic
Ball Bros. Co., Muncie, Ind., 1888 to date
Ball acquired this jar when it purchased the
Pine Glass Co. in 1929

BALL DELUXE JAR with moldmaker's error

The second "L" in BALL had been cut as an "E" and then repaired by peening out the unwanted part of the letter

BALL
DELUXE
JAR

BALL ECLIPSE (1)

Circa 1925
Lightning closure, dimple neck style
Machine-made rounded square, in flint
Side: 'Ball,' in script, over 'ECLIPSE'
Ball Bros. Co., Muncie, Ind., 1888 to date

BALL ECLIPSE (2)

Same, except 'ECLIPSE' is in italics

BALL ECLIPSE WIDE MOUTH (1)

Same as BALL ECLIPSE except 'ECLIPSE' and 'WIDE MOUTH' appear in italics below 'Ball' in script

BALL ECLIPSE WIDE MOUTH (2)

Same except as a round jar, and probably older

BALL IDEAL (1)

Circa 1915-20
Lightning closure, old neck style
Machine-made round, in green and flint
Side: 'Ball,' in slanting script, above 'IDEAL'
Ball Bros. Co., Muncie, Ind., 1888 to date

BALL IDEAL (2)

Same as (1) except beaded neck style
Lightning closure, circa 1920

BALL IDEAL (3)

Circa 1930-62, when discarded
Lightning closure, dimple neck style
Machine-made rounded square, in flint

Ball

IDEAL

PAT`D JULY 14 1908

PROPERTY OF

SOUTHERN

METHODIST

ORPHANS

HOME

WACO, TEXAS

Side: 'Ball,' in slanting script, above 'IDEAL,' in block letters, and 'PAT'D JULY 14, 1908'
Ball Bros. Co., Muncie, Ind., 1888 to date

BALL IDEAL (4)

Same, except patent date is on the back

BALL IDEAL (5)

Same as (4) except 'MADE IN U S A' as third line on front

BALL IDEAL (6)

Same except half gallon square flint lettered on back: 'PROPERTY OF,' 'SOUTHERN,' 'METHODIST,' 'OR-PHANS,' 'HOME,' and 'WACO, TEXAS'

BALL IDEAL with moldmaker's error

The "9" in the patent date, JULY 14, 1908, was cut backwards

BALL IMPROVED (1)

Circa 1910-22
Glass lid and metal screw-band top seal
Machine-made round, in green and aqua
Side: 'Ball,' in slanting script, above 'IM-PROVED'
Ball Bros. Co., Muncie, Ind., 1888 to date
Ball Brothers inform me that this jar was made in green until about 1915 for domestic use, and until 1922 for export

BALL IMPROVED (2)

Same except tall wide-mouth with almost no neck and shoulder

BALL IMPROVED MASON PATENT

Circa 1900
Glass lid and metal screw-band top seal

Machine-made round, tapered-shoulder, in blue-green

Side: four lines: 'Ball,' in slanting script, 'IMPROVED,' 'MASON,' and 'PATENT'

Ball Bros. Co., Muncie, Ind., 1888 to date

BALL IMPROVED MASON PATENT 1858

The date, '1858,' is added as a fifth line to 'Ball' 'IMPROVED' 'MASON' 'PATENT'

BALL IMPROVED MASON PATENT 1858 with moldmaker's error

The "R" in IMPROVED is unfinished and appears as IMPPOVED

BALL JAR MASON'S PATENT NOV 30th 1858, THE

Circa 1890

Mason shoulder seal

Handmade round, ground lip, in aqua and light green

Side: six lines: 'THE BALL' (arched), 'JAR,' 'MASON'S' (arched), 'PATENT,' 'NOV 30$\underline{TH}$,' and '1858'

Ball Bros. Co., Muncie, Ind., 1888 to date

Ball used these gothic or block letters styles until 1892 or 1893 or later, then italics, and script before 1900. There were exceptions later, as the gothic BALL DE-LUXE JAR

BALL MASON (1)

Circa 1895-1910

Mason shoulder seal

Handmade round, slightly barrel-shaped, ground lip, in green and blue

Side: 'Ball,' in script, above 'MASON,' in block letters. The finial from the second "l" ends in a large slanting loop, which is

IMPPOVED
MASON
PATENT
1858

THE BALL
JAR
MASON'S
PATENT
NOV 30 TH
1858

MASON

(BASIS OF 3-L RUMOR)

one of several that give rise to the story
that there were Ball jars spelled "Balll"

Ball Bros. Co., Muncie, Ind., 1888 to date

BALL MASON (2)

Same, except that the shoulder is well
rounded, while the rest of the body of
the jar is a straight cylinder

BALL MASON (3)

Same as (2) except that the shoulder is
only slightly rounded and flattened on
top

BALL MASON (4)

Same, except machine-made, circa 1900-20

BALL MASON, THE

Circa 1900-10

Mason shoulder seal

Machine-made round, in light green

Side: 'Mason,' in slightly slanting script,
with the initial stroke of the "M" a small
circle enclosing "THE" in block letters.
Above is 'Ball,' in matching script, without a finial and smaller than usual

Ball Bros. Co., Muncie, Ind., 1888 to date

Except for the word "Ball" the lettering is
exactly the same as a jar lettered "The
Mason," and since there is some indication that the word "Ball" was added by
another workman, perhaps Ball Brothers
acquired this mold from a company that
they had purchased, and relettered it

BALL MASON'S PATENT (1)

Circa 1900-20
Mason shoulder seal
Machine-made round, in green
Side: three lines: 'Ball,' in slanting script
with a straight line finial from the last
"l," over 'MASON'S' and 'PATENT' in
small block letters
Ball Bros. Co., Muncie, Ind., 1888 to date

BALL MASON'S PATENT (2)

Circa 1900-20
Mason shoulder seal
Machine-made round, in flint
Side: three lines: 'Ball,' in slanting script,
'MASON'S,' arched, and 'PATENT'
Ball Bros. Co., Muncie, Ind., 1888 to date

BALL MASON'S PATENT 1858 (1)

Circa 1895-1900
Mason shoulder seal
Handmade round, ground lip, in green
Side: four lines: 'Ball,' in horizontal script,
with finial underline from the last "l,"
over 'MASON'S,' arched, 'PATENT,' and
'1858'
Ball Bros. Co., Muncie, Ind., 1888 to date

BALL MASON'S PATENT 1858 (2)

Same except the underline is not connected to the last "l"

BALL MASON'S PATENT 1858 (3)

Same except the word "Ball" is in crudely cut script on back of the jar

(FRONT)

(BACK)

BALL MASON'S PATENT 1858 (4)

Same as (1) except machine-made in flint, circa 1910-25

BALL MASON'S PATENT 1858 (5)

Same as (4) except slightly different lettering style, in aqua

BALL MASON'S PATENT 1858, THE (1)

Circa 1890

Mason shoulder seal

Handmade round, ground lip, in aqua and light green

Side: four lines: 'THE BALL,' 'MASON'S,' 'PATENT,' and '1858,' all in block letters

Ball Bros. Co., Muncie, Ind., 1888 to date

BALL MASON'S PATENT 1858, THE (2)

Circa 1895-1905
Mason shoulder seal
Handmade round, ground lip, in aqua
Side: four lines: 'The Ball,' in horizontal script without underline, above 'MASON'S,' 'PATENT,' and '1858'
Ball Bros. Co., Muncie, Ind., 1888 to date

BALL MASON'S PATENT 1858, THE, with mold repair

Same, except the "N" in PATENT shows welding and recutting

BALL MASON'S PATENT NOV 30th 1858 (1)

Circa 1890-1905
Mason shoulder seal
Handmade round, ground lip, in aqua
Side: five lines: 'Ball,' in horizontal script not underlined, 'MASON'S,' arched, 'PATENT,' 'NOV 30ᵀᴴ,' and '1858'
Ball Bros. Co., Muncie, Ind., 1888 to date

BALL MASON'S PATENT NOV 30th 1858 (2)

Same except 'Ball' in slanting script on back, possibly an acquired mold

BALL MASON'S PATENT NOV 30th 1858 (3)

Same except 'Ball' in horizontal script on back

BALL MASON'S PATENT NOV 30th 1858 (4)

Circa 1890. Similar to (1) except 'BALL' in block-lettered arch

BALL MASON'S PATENT
NOV 30th 1858 (5)

Circa 1890. Same as (1) except BALL in straight line block letters

BALL MASON'S PATENT
NOV 30th 1858 (6)

Circa 1910-20

Mason shoulder seal

Machine-made round, in green and aqua

Side: five lines: 'Ball,' in slanting script, 'MASON'S,' arched, 'PATENT,' 'NOV 30th,' and '1858.' "Ball" is heavily underlined

Ball Bros. Co., Muncie, Ind., 1888 to date

BALL MASON'S PATENT
NOV 30th 1858 (7)

Similar to (6) except the script "Ball" ends in a finial curving below the name, forming a loop

BALL MASON'S PATENT
NOV 30th 1858 (8)

Similar to (7) except the finial is a straight line

BALL "N" MASON'S PATENT
NOV 30th 1858 (1)

Circa 1904-13

Mason shoulder seal

Machine-made round, in aqua

Side: six lines: 'Ball,' in slanting script, 'N,' 'MASON'S,' 'PATENT,' 'NOV 30th,' and '1858'

Ball Bros. Co., Muncie, Ind., 1888 to date

The design was probably acquired by Ball when they bought the Port Glass Company, Belleville, Ill., in 1904 and operated the plant until 1913

BALL "N" MASON'S PATENT NOV 30th 1858 (2)

Same except 'Ball Brothers' in script on back

BALL PERFECT MASON (1)

Circa 1900-15

Mason shoulder seal

Machine-made round, in flint and light green

Side: three lines of gothic capitals, with lines successively indented: 'BALL,' 'PERFECT,' and 'MASON'

Ball Bros. Co., Muncie, Ind., 1888 to date

This may be the oldest "PERFECT MASON" since Ball used gothic before script

BALL
PERFECT
MASON

BALL PERFECT MASON (2)

Same as (1) except lines not indented

BALL PERFECT MASON (3)

Circa 1915

Mason shoulder seal

Machine-made round, in flint and sun-colored

Side: three lines: 'Ball,' in slanting script, 'PERFECT,' and 'MASON'

Ball Bros. Co., Muncie, Ind., 1888 to date

Ball
PERFECT
MASON

BALL PERFECT MASON (4)

Circa 1915

Mason shoulder seal

Machine-made round, in flint and green tint

Side: 'BALL,' in italics, above 'PERFECT' and 'MASON'

Ball Bros. Co., Muncie, Ind., 1888 to date

BALL
PERFECT
MASON

BALL PERFECT MASON (5)

Circa 1920
Mason beaded seal
Machine-made round, in blue
Side: 'BALL,' in italics, above 'PERFECT'
and 'MASON'
Ball Bros. Co., Muncie, Ind., 1888 to date

BALL PERFECT MASON (6)

Differs from (3) by having 'Ball' in heavy
script without underline

BALL PERFECT MASON (7)

Circa 1935
Mason beaded neck seal
Machine-made round in flint, green, and
blue-green
Side: 'Ball,' in slanting script with straight
line finial under the name, above 'PER-
FECT' and 'MASON.' A feature of this
jar is a series of vertical ridges for grip-
ping—an idea based on BROCKWAY
SURGRIP, made by Brockway Glass Co.
which Ball purchased in 1935. See
BROCKWAY
Ball Bros. Co., Muncie, Ind., 1888 to date

BALL PERFECT MASON (8)

Same as (7) except jar is a flattened round
in shape

BALL PERFECT MASON (9)

Differs from (7) in having the added lettering, 'MADE IN U S A' below other
lettering, as a fourth line

BALL PERFECT MASON (10)

Differs from (7) in having cup and ounce
measurements blown in the mold

BALL SANITARY SURE SEAL (1)

Circa 1908-22

Lightning closure with dimpled neck design

Machine-made round, in green, blue, and blue-green

Side: three lines: 'Ball,' in slanting script, 'SANITARY,' and 'SURE SEAL'

Ball Bros. Co., Muncie, Ind., 1888 to date

BALL SANITARY SURE SEAL (2)

Same, except 'PAT'D JULY 14 1908' added below rest of lettering

See also BALL SURE SEAL and SURE SEAL

BALL SCULPTURED PATTERN MASON JAR

Modern

Mason beaded neck seal furnished with two-piece metal closure

Machine-made tall wide-mouth round, in flint

Bottom: 'Ball,' in small script letters, followed by 'SCULPTURED PATTERN MASON JAR,' all in a circle

Ball Bros. Co., Muncie, Ind., 1888 to date

BALL SPECIAL (1)

Circa 1910

Mason shoulder seal

Machine-made tall round, in blue-green

Side: 'Ball,' in slanting script, over 'SPECIAL'

Ball Bros. Co., Muncie, Ind., 1888 to date

BALL SPECIAL (2)

Same except with Mason beaded neck seal, circa 1915-20

BALL SPECIAL (3)

Same as (2) except also lettered 'MADE IN U S A' as bottom line

BALL SPECIAL (4)

Same as (3) except 'MADE IN U S A' on back

BALL SPECIAL WIDE MOUTH

Circa 1920-30

Mason beaded neck design, in wide-mouth style

Machine-made round, in flint

Side: three lines: 'Ball,' in slanting script, over 'SPECIAL' and 'WIDE MOUTH'

Ball Bros. Co., Muncie, Ind., 1888 to date

BALL SPECIAL WIDE MOUTH MASON

Circa 1910-15

Mason shoulder seal in wide-mouth style

Machine-made round, in green and blue-green

Side: four lines: 'Ball,' in slanting script with a straight line finial extending from name, over 'SPECIAL,' 'WIDE MOUTH,' and 'MASON'

Ball Bros. Co., Muncie, Ind., 1888 to date

This is older than BALL SPECIAL WIDE MOUTH preceding

BALL STANDARD (1)

Circa 1888-1912

Groove-ring wax sealer

Handmade round, pressed laid-on-ring, in blue-green

Side: 'Ball,' in slanting script, over 'STANDARD'

Ball Bros. Co., Muncie, Ind., 1888 to date

BALL STANDARD (2)

This jar has been reported as machine-made, but has not been verified. It is likely that Ball dropped this jar when they closed out their hand operations about 1912

BALL SURE SEAL (1)

Circa 1908-22
Lightning dimple neck design
Machine-made round, in green, blue, and blue-green
Side: 'Ball,' in slanting script, over 'SURE SEAL,' in very large letters, and 'PAT'D JULY 14 1908'
Ball Bros. Co., Muncie, Ind., 1888 to date

BALL SURE SEAL (2)

Same as (1), but without patent date

BALL SURE SEAL (3)

Same as (1) except 'SURE SEAL' in much smaller letters

BALL SURE SEAL (4)

Same as (1) except 'SURE' and 'SEAL' on separate lines

BALTIMORE GLASS WORKS

Circa 1860
Stopper finish for WILLOUGHBY STOPPLE patented in 1859
Handmade round, pressed laid-on-ring, in aqua
Side: 'BALTIMORE' arched over 'GLASS WORKS'
The owner at that time was Baker Bros. & Co., which also produced the BAKER BROS. wax sealer. The Baltimore Glass

works had been built about 1799 and passed through several ownerships before its closing about 1915

BANNER (1)

Circa 1920-40
Lightning dimple neck design
Machine-made round, in flint
Side: 'BANNER' across a circle formed by 'TRADE MARK' above, and 'WARRANTED' below
Ball Bros. Co., Muncie, Ind., as a private mold design for Fisher-Bruce of Philadelphia, Pa.

BANNER (2)

Same in wide-mouth design, and 'W M' in the circle below BANNER

BANNER (3)

Same except 'REG U S PATENT OFFICE' added below the circle

BANNER (4)

Similar jar except for the following lettering:
Side: a hanging banner, supported by a bar across the top, and carrying a geometric device with three lines: 'TRADE MARK,' in a drooping arc, 'BANNER,' in letters slanting backwards, and 'REGISTERED,' arched

B B G M Co (1)

Made only in 1886-87
Glass lid and metal screw-band top seal
Handmade round, ground lip, in aqua and green
Side: a monogram of "B B G M Co" with the two B's intersecting the outer legs of the M as well as the inner legs

Lid: repeats the monogram, with 'BALL BROTHERS GLASS MANUFACTUR-ING CO.' and 'BUFFALO, N.Y.' circled around the monogram

Ball Brothers Glass Manufacturing Co., Buffalo, N.Y., 1886-87

These early jars are often called the "Buffalo" jars. See *Fruit Jars to Satellites,* by Edmund Ball, for early company history in a booklet issued by Ball Bros. Co., 1957

B B G M Co (2)

Same except that the B's intersect only the inner legs of the M

B B G M Co (3)

Same as (1) except the word 'MASON' arched above the monogram

B B G M Co (4)

Same as (1) except 'Mason's' arched above the monogram, and 'PATENT,' 'Nov. 30th,' and '1858' in three lines below

B B G M Co PORCELAIN LINED

Circa 1886-87 only

Mason shoulder seal

Handmade round, ground lip in green

Side: different monogram from B B G M Co (2), in which the B's do not interlace the outer legs of the M, with 'PORCE-LAIN' arched above and 'LINED' in a straight line below

Ball Bros. Glass Manufacturing Co., Buffalo, N.Y., 1886-87

BEACH&CLARRIDGE

BOSTON MASS

MASON'S

IMPROVED

BEACH & CLARRIDGE MASON'S IMPROVED

Circa 1890-1900
Glass lid and metal screw-band top seal
Handmade wide-mouth round, in green
Front: 'BEACH & CLARRIDGE'
Back: three lines: 'BOSTON, MASS,' 'MASON'S' (arched), and 'IMPROVED'
Maker unknown
Beach & Clarridge was a flavoring- and extract-maker who advertised extensively in the *National Bottlers' Gazette* from 1886 to 1908

BEACH & CLARRIDGE Co.

Similar to the above, except that the only lettering was 'BEACH & CLARRIDGE Co.'

BEAVER (1)

Circa 1897
Glass lid and metal screw-band top seal
Handmade round, ground lip, in light green and flint
Side: a beaver facing right, with log and branch, over 'BEAVER'
Beaver Flint Glass Co., Toronto, Ont., 1897-1948

BE AVER

BEAVER

BEAVER (2)

Same, except Beaver only in outline

BEAVER (3)

Same, but very rare, in amber

BEAVER (4)

Same, but exceedingly rare, with beaver facing left

BEAVER (5)

The word 'BEAVER' without other decoration

BEAVER (6)

Circa 1910-20

Similar to (1) except machine-made, in flint

For information about this jar and company, see Stevens: *Early Canadian Glass*, p. 86

BEE HIVE

Circa 1920-30

Glass lid and metal screw-band top seal

Machine-made round, in blue tint

Side: a conical "straw" beehive in a background of bees and flowers, and resting on a table. Divided, near opposite sides: 'TRADE' and 'MARK.' Below: 'BEE HIVE,' in double-outlined letters

Dominion Glass Co., Montreal, Que., 1913 to date

BENNETT'S No. 1

Circa 1900-10

Mason shoulder seal

Machine-made round, in flint

Side: 'BENNETT'S' over 'No. 1.' On one specimen another name had been in the mold but had been peened out and could not be read

Maker unknown

Apparently this more modern jar had no relation to the Edwin Bennett of the 1860s, unless the jar was a revival of the old name by a continuation of the same company

BENNETT'S No. 2

Circa 1860-70

Stopper-like seal with serrations, vertically, at the lower inside of the stopper well

Handmade round, pressed laid-on-ring, in light green

Side: 'BENNETT'S' over 'No. 2'

Possibly the Franklin Flint Glass Co., Philadelphia, Pa., 1861-1930, in which Edwin Bennett was a partner 1863-67. (McKearin, p. 610)

BENNETT'S

N₀ 2

BENNETT'S No. 2 with moldmaker's error

The "2" is cut backwards

Edwin Bennett of Baltimore, Md., obtained Patent No. 16,139, for a wax sealer, on Dec. 2, 1856. This may have been the original BENNETT'S No. 1

Gillinder & Bennett received Patent No. 49,256, Aug. 8, 1865, which probably replaced Bennett's No. 2 with an all-glass screw cap

Bernardin

MASON

BERNARDIN MASON (1)

Between 1932 and 1938

Mason beaded neck style

Machine-made round, in flint

Side: 'Bernardin,' in upward slanting script, over 'MASON'

Bottom: in circle: 'W. J. LATCHFORD GLASS CO., LOS ANGELES'

Made by the W. J. Latchford Glass Co., Los Angeles, Cal., 1932-38, for the Bernardin Bottle Cap Co., Evansville, Ind., mid-1850s to date, who furnished a two-piece metal lid and screw-band cap for it

BERNARDIN MASON (2)

Same except rounded square. On back: 'EXCELLENT FOR JELLIES'

BERNARDIN MASON (3)

Same as (2) except bottom lettered 'LATCHFORD MARBLE GLASS CO., LOS ANGELES,' the glass company name from 1938 to 1957. Now the Latchford Glass Company

BEST (1)

Circa 1922, since in Dominion catalog of that date
Glass lid and metal screw-band top seal
Machine-made squat round, in flint and green
Side: 'BEST' in an arch
Bottom: 'D' in a diamond
Dominion Glass Co., Montreal, Que., 1913 to date

BEST, THE (1)

Circa 1870-80
Glass stopper, threaded for internal thread in jar neck, with glass extensions, or bosses, to take lever for tightening and loosening
Handmade round, pressed laid-on-ring, in green
Front: 'THE BEST' in one line
Back: 'L L S'
Lid: 'PATENTED AUG 18th 1868'
Patent No. 81,296 was issued to F. Rohrbacher and F. Hormann of Philadelphia for this seal

BEST, THE (2)

Same, but without patent date

BEST FRUIT KEEPER, THE

Circa 1896

Glass lid held by spring clip, inserted from the side, tightening by rotating on helical lugs

Handmade round, pressed laid-on-ring, in green

Side: 'The Best,' in script, over 'FRUIT KEEPER'

Lid: 'PAT. MAY 5th, 1896'

Maker unknown

Patent No. 559,564 was issued to Jacob Bonshire, of Yorktown, Ind., on May 5, 1896

BEST WIDE MOUTH (1)

Circa 1922

Glass lid and metal screw-band

Machine-made squat round, in flint and green

Side: 'Best' in slanting script, over 'WIDE MOUTH'

Dominion Glass Co., Montreal, Que., 1913 to date

BEST WIDE MOUTH (2)

Same as (1) except an added line 'MADE IN CANADA'

BEST WIDE MOUTH (3)

Same as (2) except rounded square

BOLDT MASON

Circa 1900-15

Mason shoulder seal

Machine-made round, in green

Side: 'BOLDT MASON'

Charles Boldt Glass Co., Cincinnati, Ohio, 1900-15

BOLDT MASON JAR

Circa 1912-27

Mason shoulder seal

Machine-made round, in green

Side: two lines: 'BOLDT' and 'MASON JAR'

Charles Boldt Glass Co., Cincinnati, Ohio, 1900-19; Charles Boldt Glass Manufacturing Co., Cincinnati, Ohio, and Huntington, W. Va., 1919-28

BORDEN'S CONDENSED MILK CO.

Circa 1880-1900

Glass lid and metal screw-band top seal

Handmade hexagonal pint, ground lip, in flint

Lid: 'BABY'

Side: 'BORDEN'S' and 'CONDENSED' on one panel in two lines; 'MILK' and 'COMPANY' on another panel, all in rough, double-outlined letters

Maker unknown

See also MAINE CONDENSED MILK CO. for identical jar

BOSCO DOUBLE SEAL (1)

Circa 1915-30

Lightning closure, old neck contour

Machine-made round, in flint

Side: 'BOSCO' over 'Double seal,' in slanting script

Bottom: 'P C' in a divided rectangle

Pacific Coast Glass Co., San Francisco, Cal.; 1925-30, and possibly by its predecessor, the Pacific Coast Glass Works, 1902-24

BOSCO is a coined name and could not be traced

BOSCO DOUBLE SEAL (2)

Same, except as a beaded style Lightning design

See also DOUBLE SEAL without the word BOSCO

BOYD MASON (1)
[Note: Boyd, not Boyds]

Circa 1915-20

Mason beaded seal

Machine-made round, in flint and green

Side: 'Boyd' in script, with ribbon finial from the "d" containing the word 'MASON'

Bottom: 'I P G Co'

Illinois Pacific Glass Co., San Francisco, Cal., 1902-30

Probably also by the Illinois Glass Company, of which it was a unit

BOYD MASON (2)

Same jar but without maker's trade mark. Either the Illinois Glass Co. or the Illinois Pacific Glass Co.

BOYD MASON (3)

Same, without the ribbon finial, and with 'MASON' in block letters

BOYDS MASON, GENUINE (1)
[Note Boyds; possessive, but without apostrophe]

Circa 1900-10

Mason shoulder seal

Handmade round, ground lip, in green

Side: 'GENUINE' above a script 'Boyds,' followed by 'MASON'

Illinois Pacific Glass Co., San Francisco, Cal., 1902-30, and Illinois Glass Co., Alton, Ill., 1873-1929. Trade marks not shown

BOYDS MASON, GENUINE (2)

Same as (1) except later, since machine-made, in flint

BOYDS MASON, GENUINE (3)

Same as (2) but having the Illinois Glass Co. trade mark on the bottom, "I G Co" in a diamond, as used about 1906-1910

BOYDS MASON, GENUINE (4)

Same as (2) but with Illinois Pacific Glass Co. (1902-30) trade mark, "I P G Co.," on the bottom

GENUINE

Boyds

MASON

I P G Co

BOYDS MASON

Circa 1890-1900
Mason shoulder seal
Handmade round, ground lip, in green
Side: 'Boyds,' in script, over 'MASON'
Illinois Glass Co., Alton, Ill, 1873-1929
This mold was originally lettered 'GENU-INE' 'MASON,' but "GENUINE" had been peened out and "Boyds" substituted

Boyds

MASON

BOYD PERFECT MASON (1)

Circa 1910
Mason shoulder seal
Machine-made round, in flint

Side: three lines: 'BOYD,' arched, 'PER-
FECT,' and 'MASON,' all in block letters
Illinois Pacific Glass Co., San Francisco,
Cal., 1902-30, and Illinois Glass Co., Al-
ton, Ill., 1873-1929

BOYD PERFECT MASON (2)

Same except 'BOYD' is in a straight line

BOYD PERFECT MASON (3)

Same except 'BOYD' in a straight line of
italics

BRELLE JAR

Circa 1912-20
Glass lid held by a clip
Machine-made wide-mouth round, in flint
Side: 'Brelle,' in script, over 'JAR'
Lid: in circle: 'THE BRELLE FRUIT JAR
MFG. Co., SAN JOSE, CAL.' around
'PAT. OCT. 29' and '1912'
Maker unknown. Brelle was a jobber. Brelle
Glass Co., 1913-16.

BRELLE JAR, THE

Same as BRELLE JAR with "THE" added
on same line

BRIGHTON

Circa 1885-1900
Glass lid held by toggle resembling the
EVERLASTING Seal
Handmade round, ground lip, in flint
Side: 'BRIGHTON'
Lid: 'CLAMP PAT. MARCH 30th, 1886'

Maker unknown

Patent No. 339,083, by Hermann Buchholz of Pittsburgh, Pa., issued on Mar. 30, 1886, was for a toggle closely resembling the EVERLASTING of twenty years later

BROCKWAY CLEAR-VU MASON (1)

Circa 1925-36

Mason beaded neck seal

Machine-made round, in flint

Side: 'Brockway,' in script, and 'CLEAR-VU' in two slanting lines above 'MASON'

Brockway Glass Co., Brockway, Pa., 1907 to date

This jar was discontinued in 1936

BROCKWAY CLEAR-VU MASON (2)

Same, but last years of production, since bottom has the Brockway trade mark, a "B" in a circle

BROCKWAY SUR-GRIP MASON

Circa 1932-33 only

Mason beaded neck seal

Machine-made round, in flint. Vertical bars spaced around the body of the jar

Side: 'Brockway,' in slanting script, over 'SUR-GRIP' and 'MASON'

Brockway Glass Co., Brockway, Pa., 1907 to date

Brockway received Design Patent No. D44,443 on July 25, 1932 and registered SUR-GRIP as a trade mark on July 7, 1932. The patent was sold to Ball Brothers early in 1933 and Brockway retired from fruit-jar making. Ball added the gripping feature to their PERFECT MASON

BROUGH, J. H., & CO.

Circa 1880-1900

Glass stopper sealed with a cork-ring side seal

Handmade round, ground lip, in light green

Side: four lines surrounding a swan: 'J. H. BROUGH & C⁰,' and 'FINE TABLE SALT,' both arched over the swan, 'TRADE MARK' (divided), and 'LIVERPOOL,' in a drooped arc below the swan

Maker unknown

BROWN & Co., GEO. D.

Circa 1870

Broad, squared neck bulge, probably for glass lid and clip

Handmade round, ground lip, in olive green

Side: 'GEO. D. BROWN & C⁰' in an arch

Maker unknown

Finish shape resembles drawing in Patent No. 76,915, April 21, 1868, by A. J. H. Hilton and the PURITAN, which was a ramp-lid design

BULACH

Modern Swiss jar

Glass lid top seal, in dark brown, held by a wire clip which is centered in a groove on the lip, and is sprung under a squared ledge on the finish

Machine-made tall round, in green glass (contrasting with the glass lid)

Side: bare

Lid: 'BULACH,' for which there are three known variations in design

Glashutte Bulach, St. Prex, Switzerland

  BULACH   BULACH

BURLINGTON, THE

Circa 1876
Glass lid and metal screw-band top seal
Handmade round, ground lip, in flint and green
Side: four lines: 'THE,' 'BURLINGTON,' 'B. G. Co' and 'R'D 1876'
Burlington Glass Co., (also Burlington Glass Works), Hamilton, Ont., 1875-99. Now part of Dominion Glass Co., for which see Stevens: *Early Canadian Glass*, p. 30

THE
BURLINGTON
B.G.Co
R'D 1876

BURNHAM & Co., C.

Circa 1860
Crude cast-iron lid with threads to engage two bulbous neck projections. Top seal on ground lip. No evidence of inner protection of contents from iron of lid
Handmade round, ground lip, in green
Side: three lines: 'C BURNHAM & Co' arched over 'MANUFACTURERS' and 'PHILAD^A'
Lid: 'FRIDLE & CORNMAN'S PATENT, OCT. 20, 1859,' in a circle
Maker unknown
Patent No. 25,894 was actually issued Oct. 25, 1859 (not Oct. 20, as on lid) and to William Fridley (not Fridle as on lid) and Frederick Cornman, of Carlisle, Pa.

C BURNHAM & Co
MANUFACTURERS
PHILAD^A

c

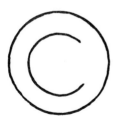

CHATTANOOGA

MASON

"C" in a circle (1)

Modern

Mason beaded seal

Machine-made flattened round, in flint

Side: a large "C" in a circle over 'CHATTANOOGA' and 'MASON'

Chattanooga Glass Co., Chattanooga, Tenn., 1901 to date

This jar is a continuation of the LAMB MASON, and probably made at the former Lamb Glass Co. plant in Mt. Vernon, Ohio, since it merged with Chattanooga in 1963

"C" in a circle (2)

Same, except round in shape

"C" with MASON'S PATENT NOV 30th 1858

Circa 1880-90

Mason shoulder seal

Handmade round, ground lip, in green and blue tint

Side: five lines: 'MASON'S' arched over 'C,' 'PATENT,' 'NOV 30TH,' and '1858'

Attributed to Craven Brothers Glass Co., Salem, N.J., 1879-95, which later became the Salem Glass Works

CALCUTT'S (1)

Circa 1893

All-glass screw cap using internal helical lugs within the cap for three-point contact with the jar threads. "Milled" gripping edges and shoulder seal

Handmade round, ground lip, in green
Cap: 'PAT APRIL 11 and NOV 7, 1893' in
circle, 'CALCUTT'S,' across diameter
Maker unknown

CALCUTT'S (2)

Circa 1870-90
Glass lid and wire-clip closure
Handmade round, pressed laid-on-ring, in
green
Side: 'CALCUTT'S'
Maker unknown

CANADA

Circa 1910-25
Mason shoulder seal
Machine-made round, in green. Very thin
for Canadian glass
Side: a compass, with "E," "W," "N," and
"S." Above it: 'CANADA,' arched; below:
'TRADE MARK'
Maker unknown

CANADIAN JEWEL

Late jar, discontinued in 1960
Glass lid and metal screw-band top seal
Machine-made round, in flint
Side: 'Canadian,' in script slanting upward,
over 'JEWEL' and 'MADE IN CANADA'
Bottom: "C" in a triangle
Consumers Glass Co., Toronto, Ont., 1917
to date
See also JEWEL JAR

CANADIAN KING

Circa 1920-40
Lightning adjustable neck design
Machine-made wide-mouth rounded square,
in flint

WIDE MOUTH
ADJUSTABLE

Side: a shield with 'Canadian' and 'King,' in two lines of ascending script. Above the shield, arched, 'MADE IN CANADA,' and below the shield in two lines, 'WIDE MOUTH' and 'ADJUSTABLE'
Probably by Dominion Glass Co., Montreal, Que., 1913 to date
Jars marked MADE IN CANADA generally date from about 1920

CANADIAN

MASON

JAR

MADE IN CANADA

CANADIAN MASON JAR

Modern—as of 1966 the only fruit jar made by Consumers
Mason beaded neck design
Machine-made rounded square, in flint
Side: four lines: 'CANADIAN,' 'MASON,' in double-outlined letters, slanted, 'JAR,' and 'MADE IN CANADA'
Bottom: "C" in a triangle
Consumers Glass Co., Toronto, Ont., 1917 to date

CANADIAN
SURE SEAL
MADE IN CANADA

CANADIAN SURE SEAL

Circa 1920-40
Mason beaded neck design
Machine-made round, in flint
Side: three lines: 'CANADIAN,' 'SURE SEAL,' slanting, and 'MADE IN CANADA'
Consumers Glass Co., Toronto, Ont., 1917 to date
See also SURE SEAL, BALL SURE SEAL, and BALL SANITARY SURE SEAL

THE CANTON
DOMESTIC
FRUIT JAR

CANTON DOMESTIC FRUIT JAR, THE (1)

Circa 1890
Glass lid with high wing and notch for spring-wire bail. The bail hooks into dimples in the neck of the jar, and has an

oxbow loop on each side to develop
spring action. It is not a Lightning
Handmade round, ground lip, in flint
Side: 'THE CANTON' in half circle above
'DOMESTIC' and 'FRUIT JAR' com-
pleting the circle below it
Canton Glass Co., Canton, Ohio, 1883-93;
moved to Marion, Ind., 1894 and sold to
National Glass Co. in 1899 and closed.
Opened by new company in 1904, closed
in 1905
Patent No. 418,266 was issued to David
Barker, who assigned it to the Canton
Glass Co. of Canton, Ohio, on Dec. 31,
1889

CANTON DOMESTIC FRUIT JAR (2)

The shape of the dimples were changed to
form an ear

CASSIDY

Circa 1880-90
Glass lid and spring-wire clip
Handmade round, ground lip, in flint
Side: 'CASSIDY' in an arched line
Maker unknown

C C Co

Circa 1900
Glass lid and spring-wire bail
Handmade round, ground lip, in green
Side: with the letters in vertical line: 'C,'
'C,' and 'Co'

Maker unknown

An imperfectly blown second "C" may have been meant for a "G," but the spring-wire bail is different from that of the CANTON, whose maker's initials would be C G Co. See also C G Co, below

C C No. 2

Circa 1880

Groove-ring wax sealer

Handmade round, pressed laid-on-ring, in apple green

Bottom: in circle: 'C C No. 2 MILW'

Chase Co., No. 2 (or Chase Valley Co., No. 2), Milwaukee, Wis., 1880-81. Became Wisconsin Glass Company

C F G Co

These initials were reported without other information, and may have been misread for C F J Co (or a moldmaker's error) for Consolidated Glass Co.

C F J Co monogram

Appearing in several styles, this was the trade mark of the Consolidated Glass Co., of New Brunswick, N.J., a combination made up from the Jersey City Glass Works, the New York Metal Screw Company, the Mason Manufacturing Co., Payne & Co., and others, to market the Mason Jar and the zinc cap fitting it. Consolidated registered this trade mark on May 29, 1871, and registered the name IMPROVED on May 23, 1871. From 1867 to 1871 it appears to have used a "C" on the bottom of the jar. About 1882 Hero seems to have acquired its assets, so far as fruit-jar making was concerned

C F J Co MASON'S IMPROVED (1)

Circa 1871-82
Glass lid and metal screw-band top seal
Handmade round, ground lip, in green
Side: 'MASON'S' arched over a monogram
  of "C F J Co," followed by 'IMPROVED'
Maker unknown

C F J Co MASON'S IMPROVED (2)

Same except 'CLYDE, N.Y.' on the back
The Clyde Glass Works, Clyde, N.Y., 1868-
  85; reopened 1895-1912. Clyde opened as
  a cylinder window-glass factory in 1827
  and started making bottles in 1868. It
  was the principal Consolidated jar supplier, since Consolidated did not make its
  jars, and Clyde seems to be the only Consolidated supplier to identify itself. Consolidated did operate a small pot furnace
  plant later in order to make its opal cap
  liners

C F J Co MASON'S IMPROVED (3)

Similar to (2) except that 'CLYDE N.Y.'
  appears on the front

C. F. J. Co MASON'S IMPROVED (4)

No maker identification, but lid reads 'REG
  MAY 23, 1871,' the date that the name
  IMPROVED was copyrighted

C F J Co MASON'S IMPROVED (5)

Same except 'MASON'S IMPROVED' on
  the front and a large 'C F J Co' trade
  mark on back. The lid reads: 'TRADE
  MARK,' 'MASON'S IMPROVED,' and
  'REG MAY 23, 1871'
Mason patented several glass lid and metal
  screw-band top seal jars, the most successful of which was that of Sept. 24,

IMPROVED

CLYDE, N.Y.

IMPROVED
(FRONT)

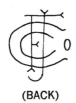

(BACK)

1872, but all jars were greatly modified when made into glass. Patent No. 131,-695 of Sept. 24, 1872, includes the bit of metal on the side of the cap, and the lever design which engaged it in order to tighten and loosen the cap. The bit of metal was a piece of rod placed in a vertical position, and Hero promptly patented the same idea with a horizontally placed bit of rod

C F J Co MASON'S IMPROVED BUTTER JAR

Circa 1870-80

Glass lid and metal screw-band top seal

Handmade round, ground lip, in light green

Side: 'MASON'S' arched over the C F J Co monogram. Below, in two lines, 'IMPROVED' and 'BUTTER JAR'

Lid: 'REG MAY 10, 1870,' but the lid has the patented 1872 metal bit for the tightening lever

Maker unknown. There were several of these butter jars, generally used to hold butter water tight for spring-house cooling and ice-chests

C F J Co MASON'S PATENT NOV 30th 1858 (1)

Circa 1870-82

Mason shoulder seal

Handmade round, ground lip, in green, amber, and "black"

Front: 'MASON'S' arched over the C F J Co monogram, followed by 'PATENT,' 'NOV 30TH,' and '1858'

Back: 'CLYDE N Y'

Clyde Glass Works, Clyde, N.Y., 1868-86 and 1895-1912

C F J Co MASON'S PATENT NOV 30th 1858 (2)

Same, but without the CLYDE identification on back

C F J Co MASON'S PATENT NOV 30th 1858 (3)

Same as (2) but with D446 on the bottom. This identifies D446 as a Consolidated mold number, and it is listed elsewhere under "D" since it appears without the monogram

C G Co

Circa 1890
Mason shoulder seal
Handmade round, ground lip, in aqua
Side: a monogram of "C G Co"
Canton Glass Co., Canton, Ohio, 1883-93;
    Marion, Ind., 1893-99, 1904-05

C G Co MASON'S PATENT NOV 30th 1858

Circa 1890
Mason shoulder seal
Handmade round, ground lip, in green and
    aqua
Side: 'MASON'S' arched over a monogram
    of "C G Co," followed by 'PATENT,'
    'NOV 30ᵀᴴ,' and '1858'
Canton Glass Co., Canton, Ohio, 1883-93;
    Marion, Ind., 1893-99, 1904-5

CHAMPION SYRUP

Circa 1890-1900
Mason shoulder seal
Handmade round, ground lip, in aqua
Side: three lines: 'CHAMPION SYRUP'
    arched over 'REFINING CO.' and 'IN-
    DIANAPOLIS'
Maker unknown

THE
CHAMPION
PAT. AUG. 3, 1869

CHAMPION, THE

Circa 1869

Glass lid held by yoke and thumbscrew applying pressure through a thin metal sheath (see below)

Handmade round, ground lip, in green

Side: three lines: 'THE,' 'CHAMPION,' and 'PAT. AUG 3, 1869'

Maker unknown

Patent No. 94,452 was issued to W. S. Thompson of Rochester, N.Y., on Aug. 31, 1869, for an all-glass lid having a thin metal sheath over the threads and following the thread contour in order to reduce the friction in glass-to-glass contact. It may have not been successful, but the jar was usable with the regular cap

MRS. CHAPIN'S

MAYONNAISE

BOSTON, MASS.

CHAPIN'S MAYONNAISE, MRS.

Circa 1920-25

Lightning closure with glass bosses, Drey patent for Schram, holding the lever wire. This is the only commercial jar seen using it

Machine-made round, in flint

Side: three lines: 'MRS. CHAPIN'S' arched over 'MAYONNAISE' and 'BOSTON, MASS.'

Schram Glass Mfg. Co., St. Louis, Mo., 1902-25

CHEF (1)

Circa 1930

Lightning closure, old neck style

Machine-made rounded square, in flint

Side: 'CHEF' above the figure of a chef, with ribbon scrolls on either side, with 'TRADE' and 'MARK,' surrounded by double outline, arched

Owens Illinois Glass Co., Toledo, Ohio,
1929 to date
Hazel Atlas Glass Co., Wheeling, W. Va.,
1902-64
Used by Berdan & Co., wholesale grocers

CHEF (2)

Same except 'BERDAN & Co TOLEDO,
O.,' with scrolls, added below figure

CHEF (3)

Same as (1), except adjustable Lightning
finish and word "TIGHT"

CHEF (4)

Same as (1) except lettering in oval outline
instead of a square

CHRISTMAS MASON

A name given because the old German let-
tering, with bars vertically through
'MASONS' had knobbed ends resembling
lights
Circa 1885-1900
Mason shoulder seal
Handmade round, ground lip, in green
Side: 'MASONS' arched over 'PATENT,'
'NOV 30th,' and '58.' In addition to the
bar illumination of MASONS other letters
were barbed along their sides

C J Co

May be a misreading of "G" of the Gilchrist
Jar initials "G J Co."

CLARKE FRUIT JAR CO (1)

1886-89 only
Glass lid and stamped sheet-metal cam
lever, hinged to wire bail
Handmade round, ground lip, in green and
blue-green

CLARKE

FRUIT JAR CO

CLEVELAND,O.

Side: three lines: 'CLARKE,' 'FRUIT JAR CO,' and 'CLEVELAND, O.'

Lever: stamped 'PAT MAY 17, 1885'

Clarke Fruit Jar Co., Cleveland, Ohio, 1886-89

The patent was not found. Clarke managed the Boston Store in Cleveland, which does not denote glass-house experience

CLARKE FRUIT JAR CO (2)

Same except lever stamped 'PAT MAR 17, 1885.' This was found as Patent No. 314,- 109, issued to William Clarke

CLARK'S

PEERLESS

CLARK'S PEERLESS (1)

Circa 1882-98

Lightning closure, old neck style

Handmade round, ground lip, in green and aqua

Side: 'CLARK'S' arched over 'PEERLESS'

Bottom: 'SALEM'

Holz, Clark & Taylor, Salem, N.J., 1862-79

Leased to John Gayner who operated until 1898, then purchased plant and incorporated as Gayner Glass Works in 1898. The jar was produced during Gayner's leasing since the Lightning was not invented until 1882

CLARK'S PEERLESS (2)

Same except machine-made

This jar's origin was first solved when Jerry Tenbuckel found a LEOTRIC jar with CLARK'S PEERLESS partly peened out. Until then it was not known which Salem and which Clark were involved. LEOTRIC had been identified with Gayner of Salem, N.J.

CLARK'S PEERLESS (3)

Same except 'REG T M No. 43288' in circle on bottom. This confirmed the Gayner identification, since the same number appears on the LEOTRIC jar

CLARK'S PEERLESS (4)

Same except that the name is enclosed in a circle

CLEAR-VU

See BROCKWAY

CLEVELAND FRUIT JUICE Co. (1)

Circa 1930-40
Lightning closure, beaded neck design
Machine-made round, in flint
Bottom: 'CLEVELAND FRUIT JUICE Co.' with Hazel Atlas trade mark
Hazel Atlas Glass Co., Wheeling, W. Va., 1902-64

CLEVELAND FRUIT JUICE Co. (2)

Same, except without the Hazel Atlas trade mark, possible in the 1920s

CLIMAX (1)

Circa 1910-30
Lightning closure, beaded neck design
Machine-made round, in flint and green
Side: 'CLIMAX' across the diameter of a circle formed by 'TRADE MARK,' above, and 'REGISTERED,' below
Ball Bros. Co., Muncie, Ind., 1888 to date, for Fisher-Bruce, Philadelphia, Pa.

CLIMAX (2)

Same except Lightning dimple neck design

CLYDE (1) [CLYDE GLASS WORKS]

Circa 1895

Lightning closure, old neck style

Handmade round, ground lip, in flint and light green

Lid: 'CLYDE GLASS WORKS, CLYDE, N.Y.' in circle

Clyde Glass Works, Clyde, N.Y., 1868-85; 1895-1912

This jar made after the 1895 reopening of the factory, which apparently had to close when Consolidated retired from the fruit-jar field in 1882

CLYDE (2) [CLYDE MASON]

Either circa 1882-85 or after 1895

Mason shoulder seal

Handmade round, ground lip, in green

Side: 'CLYDE' over 'MASON'

Clyde Glass Works, Clyde, N.Y., 1868-85; 1895-1912

The jar could have been made during the brief period that Clyde operated after losing the Consolidated business, or after the reopening, since it represents an individual effort by Clyde

CLYDE (3) [THE CLYDE]

Similar to (1) except 'The Clyde' in slanting script

CLYDE (4) [CLYDE IMPROVED MASON]

Circa 1882-85 or after 1895

Glass lid and metal screw-band top seal

Handmade round, ground lip, in green

Side: three lines: 'CLYDE,' 'IMPROVED,' and 'MASON'

Clyde Glass Works, Clyde, N.Y., 1868-85; 1895-1912

CLYDE LIGHTNING

Circa 1895
Lightning closure, old-style neck design
Handmade round, ground lip, in green
Side: 'CLYDE' over 'LIGHTNING'
Clyde Glass Works, Clyde, N.Y., 1868-85;
1895-1912

COHANSEY (1)

Circa 1870
Flared finish, as for corks
Handmade barrel-shaped round, outlining
hoops and staves as in the AIRTIGHT.
Lip is flared and fire-polished. Light blue
Side: 'COHANSEY'
Bottom: 'COHANSEY' across a diameter,
with 'GLASS MF'G. Co' circling top side
Cohansey Glass Mfg. Co., Philadelphia,
Pa., 1870-1900
See also AIRTIGHT, NE PLUS ULTRA,
and POTTER & BODINE. The Bodines
who operated the plant at Bridgeton, N.J.
named their company for a local Indian
chief of that name

GLASS MF'G. Co
COHANSEY
(ON 1)

COHANSEY (2)

Circa 1870
Glass lid top seal, held by heavy wire
formed to fit jar threads, with an end
curved to press on top center of lid
Handmade barrel-shaped round, showing
hoops and staves, ground lip, in aqua
Side: 'COHANSEY,' spaced two letters to
the stave
Lid: in half circle: 'PAT. MAR. 10th, 1868'
Cohansey Glass Mfg. Co., Philadelphia, Pa.,
1870-1900

COHANSEY

This was Wm. L. Imlay's Patent No. 75,-275. The jar was first known as the VALVE JAR and sold by the Valve Jar Co., of Philadelphia, Pa., probably before J. & F. Bodine renamed their company in 1870

COHANSEY (3)

Circa 1872-95

Glass lid top seal, with wire circling edge of lid and having first two, and later three, loops engaging as many helical lugs serrated beneath

Handmade, barrel-shaped round, showing hoops and staves, ground lip, in aqua

Side: 'COHANSEY,' spaced two letters to a stave

Lid: in half circle: 'PAT. JULY 16th, 1872' Some lids carried two dates: 'Pat. MAR. 10th, 1868 & JULY 16th, 1872' in a circle. The lids were interchangeable—the wire changed

Cohansey Glass Mfg. Co., Philadelphia, Pa., 1870-1900

Patent No. 129,235, July 16, 1872 was by Charles G. and Wm. L. Imlay

This seal was placed on plain round jars for both P. LORILLARD & CO. and JOHNSON & JOHNSON

COHANSEY (4)

Circa 1876-1900

Glass lid top seal, held by cup-shaped metal cap whose indentations engaged helical lugs on the neck of the jar. Very modern in appearance

Handmade tapered-shoulder round, ground lip, in aqua

Side: 'COHANSEY' in an arch

Lid: 'PAT. JAN. 18, 1876'

Cohansey Glass Mfg. Co., Philadelphia, Pa., 1870-1900

Patent No. 172,289 was issued to John Young, of Amsterdam, N.Y.

COHANSEY (5)

Circa 1877

Wax sealer with groove, but not Arthur type

Handmade barrel-shape with hoops and staves as in the AIRTIGHT. The groove is tooled by collapsing a blown bulge, pinching it together and then tooling upward into a groove. In green

Side: 'COHANSEY'

Bottom: 'COHANSEY' across the diameter of a circle formed by 'GLASS MFG C°' and 'PAT MAR 20, 77'

Cohansey Glass Mfg. Co., Philadelphia, Pa., 1870-1900

(WAX SEALER)

COLBURN'S FOUNTAIN STOPPLE JAR

Circa 1860

Stopper lip will take the WILLOUGHBY STOPPLE, which see

Handmade round, tooled laid-on-ring, in green

Side: four lines: 'COLBURN'S' arched over 'FOUNTAIN,' 'STOPPLE,' and 'JAR'

Maker unknown

This jar finish is often mistaken for a plain cork finish

COLUMBIA (1)

Circa 1896-1900

Glass lid with two spiral ramps on top to tighten a solid metal yoke which is

COLUMBIA

hooked under a plain finish ledge, when jar lid or yoke is rotated

Handmade round, ground lip, in flint, green, and aqua

Side: 'COLUMBIA'

Lid: 'PAT DEC 29, 1896'

Cumberland Glass Co., Bridgeton, N.J., 1896-1920; purchased in 1920 by the Illinois Glass Co., Alton, Ill., 1873-1929

COLUMBIA (2)

Same jar but with both 'COLUMBIA' and patent date on lid

See JOHNSON & JOHNSON for a square COLUMBIA in cobalt blue, for which Cumberland was a specialist

COMMONWEALTH FRUIT JAR

Circa 1890-1900

Glass lid with old neck design Lightning finish

Handmade round, ground lip, in olive green

Side: 'Commonwealth,' in rising script, between 'FRUIT' above it, and 'JAR' below it, separated by a scroll and a linear finial

Maker unknown. The AMERICAN, the FEDERAL, and the COMMONWEALTH were seen in the half-gallon size, all with one side plated for a removable panel carrying the lettering, and interchangeable with each other. Since the glass lid and the Lightning finish was most popular in the Commonwealth of Massachusetts (of the four commonwealths — Massachusetts, Pennsylvania, Virginia, and Kentucky), I feel that this was an early Albert G. Smalley jar

CONSERVE JAR

Circa 1890-1900
Lightning closure, old-style neck design
Handmade round, ground lip, in flint
Side: 'CONSERVE' arched over 'JAR'
Maker unknown

CORONA, IMPROVED

Circa 1940-60
Mason beaded neck design
Machine-made round, in flint
Side: 'IMPROVED' over a double-outlined 'CORONA,' slanting upwards, over 'MADE IN CANADA'
Bottom: "C" in a triangle, 'CORONA,' and 'TRADE MARK REG'D'
Consumers Glass Co., Toronto, Ont., 1917 to date

CORONA JAR

Circa 1920-30
Mason beaded neck design
Machine-made round, in flint
Side: three lines: 'CORONA,' 'JAR,' and 'MADE IN CANADA'
Bottom: "C" in a triangle
Consumers Glass Co., Toronto, Ont., 1917 to date

CORONA JAR, IMPROVED

Circa 1940-60
Mason beaded neck design
Machine-made round, in flint
Side: four lines: 'IMPROVED,' 'CORONA,' at a slant, 'JAR,' and 'MADE IN CANADA'
Consumers Glass Co., Toronto, Ont., 1917 to date

CROWN

There are many designs of the crown that appear on certain fruit jars made in Canada, of which I show twenty-one of the sixty or more. At first one may not see the differences that add much to the collecting of these jars. This one design evolved greatly during the over fifty years in which it has been used in one Canadian glass factory or another. I do not show those variations of the same design that are probably due only to mold-cutting.

The question is of variation. All have crosses surmounting them, but that is the chief similarity. Shape varies from very modern straight lines to heart shaped, either shallowly depressed on top, or very deeply cut. The pedestal on which the cross rests may be short, or tall, or absent. One CROWN uses an orb as a pedestal. The tiara, or mid-portion between headband and cross, may also have a cross, or not. The fleurs-de-lis may be well defined, or briefly shown. There may be one, two, or three headbands, and these may or may not be ornamented by symbols for ermine, diamonds, other jewels, or simply gadrooned or cross-hatched. Usually, but not always, the crown may be bordered on top and sides by jewels on short stems, and the numbers of jewels vary

CROWN

CROWN (1)

Circa 1870-80
Glass lid and zinc screw-band top seal
Handmade round, ground lip, in blue tint
Crown is relatively tall and narrow, heart shaped with shallow top indentation,

jeweled along top and sides. Pedestal is
long, topped by a cross formée. A second cross is on the tiara, between two
fleurs-de-lis. Two unadorned headbands.
'CROWN' below
Attributed to the Hamilton Glass Works,
Hamilton, Ont., 1865-93. Probably one of
the oldest CROWNS. See Stevens: *Early
Canadian Glass*, p. 20

CROWN (2)

Circa 1870-90
Glass lid and metal screw-band top seal
Handmade round, ground lip, in blue tint
Crown is broad and in "stylized" modern
straight lines, with shallow top, very
short pedestal with cross formée. Tiara
almost absent, being only two fleurs-de-
lis, sharply defined. One headband, with
diamonds and dotted jewels. No jewels
along edges. 'CROWN' below
Because of style, may be North American
or Excelsior—see CROWN (7)

CROWN (3)

Differs from (2) only in being smaller and
relatively taller. Probably by the same
maker

CROWN (4)

Circa 1880-90
Glass lid and metal screw-band top seal
Handmade round, ground lip, in blue tint
Crown is deeply indented heart shaped,
filled with a large pedestal holding a
cross formée. Tiara has only two fleurs-
de-lis with orb in center instead of a
cross. Three unadorned headbands. No
jeweled outline. 'CROWN' below
Also attributed to Hamilton Glass Works,
Hamilton, Ont., 1865-93, but doubtful

IMPERIAL

1/2 GAL

IMPERIAL

Qt

CROWN

CROWN (5)

Circa 1880-90

Glass lid and metal screw-band top seal

Handmade round, ground lip, in blue tint

Crown is deeply indented heart shaped, without pedestal, but topped by a cross formée. Tiara with two short fleurs-de-lis and a cross formée with bottom wing missing. Jewels border top and sides. Three headbands: top one bare, middle dotted with jewels, and lower with diamonds and dots alternating. Above it is 'CROWN' and below is 'IMPERIAL' and '1/2 GAL'

May also be by Hamilton Glass Works, Hamilton, Ont., 1865-93

CROWN (6)

Similar to (5) except that the pedestal is defined and the fleurs-de-lis are little more than symbolic and somewhat shortened. An orb replaces the cross in the tiara. 'CROWN' above, a stretched-out 'IMPERIAL' and 'Qt' below

CROWN (7)

Circa 1885-91

Glass lid and metal screw-band top seal

Handmade round, ground lip, in aqua and blue tint

Similar to (2) and (3) in its squared lines, and crown is in double outline. Cross formée on top is supported by an orb on a pedestal, very large and long. Tiara has stylized fleurs-de-lis, central cross minus lower wing, with partial crosses shown at the outline in profile. Many jewels line top and sides. Two headbands: top one dotted and lower one

dashed, or "ermined." 'CROWN' below

North American Glass Co., Montreal, Que., 1885-91. See Stevens: *Early Canadian Glass*, p. 124

This is the first CROWN of this series to be positively identified as to maker, and it is also one of the most elaborate

CROWN (8)

Circa 1900-1910

Glass lid and metal screw-band top seal

Machine-made round, in green

Heart shape is shallowly indented on top, with pedestal and slightly misshapen cross formée. Tiara has fleurs-de-lis in realistic design, and a central cross formée without a lower wing. Jeweled outline along top and sides. Three headbands: top gadrooned, center ermined, and bottom with a line of connected diamonds. 'CROWN' below

Maker not identified

A feature of this CROWN is the broad "O"

CROWN (9)

Very similar to (8) except lettered 'CROWN' above, with 'IMPERIAL' and 'Qt' below

CROWN (10)

Similar to (8) except only the lower headband is decorated, and with a diamond and dot design. IX on design probably refers to the serial number of the mold in a set of identical molds made at one time

CROWN (11)

Similar to (9) except the style of the fleurs-de-lis is changed, and all headbands are decorated: upper gadrooned, center dotted, and lower with diamonds and dot design

Attributed to Jefferson Glass Co., Toronto, Ont., 1913-25, and if correct may also identify (9), (10), and possibly (8) as Jefferson through the similarity of the "O" in CROWN, and by the type of pedestal. 'CROWN' is above; 'IMPERIAL' and 'Qt' below

CROWN (12)

Very similar to (11) in the broad "O," but the "C" differs. The crown is heart shaped with a shallow indentation on top, supporting a cross formée on a pedestal. Sides and top jeweled. Another cross in the tiara, but the fleurs-de-lis are only symbolic in style. Top headband is ornamented with a zig-zag design, while the middle and lower bands are dotted. 'CROWN' below. B3 is a mold serial number

Back: 'THE T. EATON CO. LTD,' '190 YONGE STREET,' and 'TORONTO, CAN.'

Jefferson Glass Co., Toronto, Ont., 1913-25, which dates it

CROWN (13)

Similar to (12) except Eaton's address is given as 'TORONTO and WINNEPEG,' omitting street address. This jar cannot date before the 1906 opening of the Winnepeg store, and not before 1913 if Jefferson. The only different detail of the crown from (12) is the ermined top headband

CROWN (14)

Somewhat smaller crown than (13) but identified as Eaton by the "E" in a tilted square, or diamond, on back. The chief change in the crown is the gadrooned upper headband, dotted center band, and diamond and dot design on the lower band. 2 is a mold serial number in a set of molds

CROWN (15)

A radically different crown design than (12), (13), and (14), yet identified with Eaton through the diamond-E trade mark, this time on the bottom. The crown is deeply heart shaped, with a pedestal filling the center and supporting a cross formée. Tiara has fleur-de-lis design more resembling (5) and (6), as does the deep-cut heart. Cross in center of tiara. Upper headband bare, middle dotted, and lower with diamond-dot design. 'CROWN' below

More a Hamilton design than a Jefferson, and may be a very early Eaton

CROWN (16)

Crown has the Jefferson type of shallow heart shape, pedestal, and a somewhat deformed cross formée, together with heavy jewels around top and sides. Tiara has Jefferson type symbolic fleur-de-lis design and center deformed cross. Top headband plain, middle dotted, and lower with dash-dot design. 'CROWN' below has broad "O." D1 is a serial number

Probably Jefferson, 1913-25

CROWN (17)

Smaller than (16) but similar in most details. The upper headband is cross-hatched, and the lower has a connected-diamond design. The "O" in the 'CROWN' below the figure is not broad. 4X is a serial number
Possibly Jefferson

CROWN (18)

Similar to (17) in most respects except that the bottom headband is a diamond-dot design. 'CROWN' below and 'IMPERIAL' above. Mold serial number 5X
Possibly Jefferson

CROWN (19)

Similar to (18) except lettered only 'CROWN' below. Mold serial number 6
Possibly Jefferson

CROWN (20)

Returns to the deep pedestal, even showing highlights as if reflections, and more realistic fleurs-de-lis of earlier crowns. Cross on tiara is very small. Top headband zig-zag, middle dotted, and lower with diamond-dot design. Above is 'CROWN' and below is 'IMPERIAL' over '1/2 GAL'

CROWN (21)

Made since 1920, since it has 'MADE IN CANADA' over the crown. Few jewels along top and sides. Small pedestal. Symbolic fleurs-de-lis on both sides of a large cross formée on tiara. Upper two headbands not separately defined at the ends, and similar to (19) and (20); top bare, middle dotted, and lower band with diamond-dot design. 'MADE IN CANADA' above, and 'CROWN' below

CROWN CORDIAL & EXTRACT

Circa 1885
Lightning closure, old neck design
Handmade round, ground lip, in flint and
    light green
Side: 'CROWN CORDIAL & EXTRACT
    CO.' arched over 'NEW YORK'
Bottom: 'PUTNAM' and 'LIGHTNING'
Maker unknown

CROWN, IMPROVED

Circa 1900-1913
Glass lid and metal screw-band top seal
Machine-made round, in pale green
Side: two lines: 'Improved' over 'Crown,'
    both in slanting script, much resembling
    the Sydenham GEM's
Possibly the Sydenham Glass Co., Wallaceburg, Ont., 1894-1913

CROWN MASON (1)

Circa 1910
Mason beaded neck design
Machine-made rounded square, in flint,
    with three vertical ribs on each of the
    three sides, much like the later BROCKWAY SUR-GRIP and the BALL PERFECT MASON

Side: a very crudely lettered 'CROWN' (with a larger "C") slanted over 'MASON'

Maker unknown

This jar probably introduced to practical operation the beaded seal neck design first shown in Patent No. 234,842 of Nov. 30, 1880, by W. E. Andrew. On the CROWN MASON it enabled a top seal with the advantages of machine production of a smooth top. The rest of the industry soon followed suit, although there was question for a time as to just how smooth the machine-made thread-top could, or should, be

CROWN MASON, IMPROVED

Same as the CROWN MASON except for 'CROWN' in heavy, slanted letters and for a somewhat changed bead design probably in an effort to improve the smoothness of the top. Efforts to seal on the top surface were not successful until the more flexible metal lids in 1915

CROWN, WHITE

See WHITE CROWN MASON and WHITE CROWN CAP

CRYSTAL (1)

Circa 1873-80

Mason shoulder seal, with all-glass threaded cap. Compare with the earlier CAL-CUTT and the later SIMPLEX

Handmade round, ground lip, in pale aqua

Side: 'CRYSTAL' in arched design

Bottom: 'PAT NOV 26 67 & FEB 4 73.' (These are Hero dates)

Hero Glass Works, Philadelphia, Pa., 1856-84

The name "Crystal" is included on Hero's 1878 letterhead

The November 26, 1867 patent date (Hero seldom even punctuated dates) is Design Patent No. D2,840 by Salmon B. Rowley, Hero's owner, and it covered the shape of the jars that Hero made, and to many of his other jars not so made, with a sloping shoulder. He seems to have been making trade-capital of the easier broken squared shape of the Mason shoulder seal. Patent No. 135,430 of Feb. 4, 1873, was by Henry Howson, assigned to Rowley, and covered the making of the glass lid and the threads in the jar mold

CRYSTAL (2)

McKearin, *American Glass*, p. 610, lists the Independent Glass Co., of Pittsburgh, 1862-1900 (See also CANTON) as advertising "crystal glass fruit jars, air tight glass tops." The word "Crystal" may not have been used as a jar name, but of a quality or glass color

CRYSTAL JAR

Circa 1879

Mason shoulder seal with all-glass threaded cap

Handmade round, ground lip, in flint and amethyst (sun-colored ?)

Side: 'CRYSTAL' arched over 'JAR'

Maker believed to be Consolidated Fruit Jar Co., New Brunswick, N.J., 1867-82

CRYSTAL JAR C G

Circa 1878

Mason shoulder seal and all-glass lid

Handmade round, ground lip, in flint

Side: 'CRYSTAL' arched over 'JAR,' be-

neath which are the initials 'C G'

Lid: 'PATENTED DEC. 17, 1878'

Probably Consolidated Fruit Jar Co., New Brunswick, N.J., 1867-82

The only cover patent of this date is that of G. L. Harrison, No. 211,011, which is not directly applicable. "C G" may stand for Consolidated Glass

CRYSTAL JAR, MASON'S

Circa 1878

Mason shoulder seal with all-glass lid

Handmade round, ground lip, in flint

Side: 'MASON'S' arched over 'CRYSTAL' and 'JAR'

Consolidated Fruit Jar Co., New Brunswick, N.J., 1867-82

This is probably Consolidated's answer to the CRYSTAL of Hero's Rowley, or vice versa

CRYSTALVAC

Circa 1925-38

Closure not identified

Machine-made rounded square, in amber

Side: "CRYSTALVAC"

Back: 'H and H' with the H's doubly outlined

Bottom: '3 RIVERS'

3 Rivers Glass Co., Three Rivers, Tex., 1925-38

Note: The glass company always used the figure 3, while the town spelled out Three. See also: RIVERS, 3

CUNNINGHAM & IHMSEN

Circa 1868-79

Groove-ring wax sealer

Handmade round, pressed laid-on-ring, in green

Side: 'CUNNINGHAM & IHMSEN,' dimly
cut

Bottom: '1868'—could be the date of first
manufacture

Cunningham & Ihmsen, Pittsburgh, Pa.,
1865-79. Was Cunningham & Jackson,
1845-65 and became Cunninghams & Co.,
1879-1909. The latter is plural to denote
the three Cunninghams. One of them,
Dominick O. Cunningham, formed his
own separate company, the D. O. Cunningham Glass Co., 1882-1931

CUNNINGHAMS & Co.

A wax sealer similar to CUNNINGHAM &
IHMSEN, and probably a continuation
of it. This name on bottom only. Made
after 1879

See D O C for D. O. Cunningham Glass
Co. wax sealer

CURTIS & MOORE

Circa 1890-1900

Lightning closure, old neck design

Handmade round, ground lip, in flint

Side: a monogram of "C" and "M" flanked
by 'TRADE' and 'MARK.' Above is
'CURTIS & MOORE,' arched, and below
is 'BOSTON, MASS.,' arched

Maker unknown

D

D446 MASON'S PATENT NOV 30th 1858

Circa 1871-82

Mason shoulder seal

Handmade round, ground lip, in green

Side: 'MASON'S' arched over 'D446,' followed by 'PATENT,' 'NOV 30$\underline{\text{TH}}$,' and
'1858'

Probably the Clyde Glass Works, Clyde, N.Y., 1868-85; 1895-1912, for the Consolidated Fruit Jar Co., New Brunswick, N.J. Identification is because D446 appears on a jar also having Consolidated's trade mark. Dates are the copyright date for the trade mark and that of Consolidated's closing

D446 MASON'S PATENT NOV 30th, 1858, with moldmaker's error

Same in all details except that the "6" is upside down

DAISY, THE (1)

Circa 1880-1900

Lightning closure, old neck design

Handmade round, ground lip, in flint and sun-colored

Side: three lines: 'THE,' 'DAISY,' and, in a drooped arc, 'F. E. WARD & CO.'

Lid: 'PAT APRIL 25, 1882' (Lid may not be original—Lightning lids were largely interchangeable)

Maker unknown

DAISY, THE (2)

Same design except machine-made in aqua circa 1910. The lettering is enclosed in a circle

DAISY JAR, THE

Circa 1880-1900

Closure uncertain—probably a glass lid and clip or yoke

Handmade round, ground lip, in flint and sun-colored

Side: 'THE DAISY' arched over 'JAR'

Maker unknown

DALBEY'S FRUIT JAR (1)

Circa 1858

Metal lid with three thumbscrews, tightening a collar held by a removable shim in a circular depression in the neck of the jar

Handmade round, ground lip, in blue-green

Side: 'DALBEY'S' arched over 'FRUIT JAR' and 'PAT NOV 16 1858'

Maker unknown

Patent No. 22,066, issued Nov. 16, 1858, to R. M. Dalbey of Mount Washington, Ohio, was the first of the thumbscrew closing jars. The collar could be removed by slipping the shim from the slightly dished neck

DALBEY'S
FRUIT JAR
PAT NOV 16 1858

DALBEY'S FRUIT JAR (2)

Circa 1866

Glass lid held by yoke engaging paired helical lugs on jar neck. Lugs serrated below to prevent yoke slippage

Handmade round, ground lip, in green

Side: four lines: 'PATENTED,' 'BY,' 'R. M. DALBEY,' and 'JUNE 6TH 1866'

Maker not verified on jar but could be William McCully of Pittsburgh, Pa., who placed Dalbey's name and this patent date on their MAGIC FRUIT JAR

PATENTED
BY
R. M. DALBEY
JUNE 6TH 1866

DANDY, THE (1)

Circa 1885

Glass lid and single wire bail, hooked into a neck wire having loops on opposite sides. The lid had two notches; one on top for full holding tension, and the other part way up the top to give reduced tension in order to allow the escape of air during the boiling or cooking operation of canning

TRADE MARK

THE DANDY

Handmade tall round, ground lip in light blue and amber

Side: 'TRADE MARK' arched over 'THE DANDY'

Maker unknown. The jar was made for the Gilberds Butter Tub Co., of Jamestown, N.Y., after Patent No. 328,115 issued to James Gilberds, Oct. 13, 1885. The original patent design called for dimples about halfway down the side of the jar, into which the bail would be hooked, but this was unworkable, so he substituted the neck tie wire. The same patent was the basis of GILBERDS IMPROVED JAR

DANDY, THE (2)

A jar has been found having a DANDY lid, a plain jar, and held by a CANTON-type spring-wire bail into slanting grooves in the neck. It is probably a plain CANTON jar with a substitute lid

DARLING, THE

THE DARLING

Circa 1880-1900

Glass lid and metal screw-band top seal

Handmade round, ground lip, in blue tint

Side: a monogram of the letters "A," "D," and "M," whose order is not known. Below the monogram is: 'THE DARLING'

Maker unknown. Any combination of the letters does not seem to be the initials of any glass company. See next jar for an indication that THE DARLING is Canadian

DARLING IMPERIAL, THE

Monogram of the same letters except for the addition of a character that may be an ampersand. Below the monogram, in two lines: 'THE DARLING' and 'IMPERIAL'

THE DARLING
IMPERIAL

DECKER DEPENDABLE FOOD

Circa 1910-20

Mason shoulder seal

Machine-made round, in flint

Side: three lines in a diamond within a circle: 'DECKER,' 'DEPENDABLE,' and 'FOOD,' followed by 'JACOB E. DECKER & SON' and 'MASON CITY, IOWA'

Hazel Atlas Glass Co., Wheeling, W. Va., 1902-64, and

Ball Bros. Co., Muncie, Ind., 1888 to date

DECKER
DEPENDABLE
FOOD

JACOB E DECKER & SON
MASON CITY, IOWA

DECKER'S IOWANA (1)

Circa 1930

Lightning closure, beaded neck design

Machine-made round, in flint

Side: two lines: 'DECKER'S' and 'IOWANA'

Hazel Atlas Glass Co., Wheeling, W. Va., 1902-64, and

Ball Bros. Co., Muncie, Ind., 1888 to date

DECKER'S IOWANA (2)

Circa 1930

Lightning dimple neck design

Machine-made round, in flint

Side: In a circle: 'DECKER'S' along the top arc, 'IOWANA' across the center diameter, and 'MASON CITY, IOWA,' following the lower arc, and with 'PAT'D JULY 14 1908' at lower side-wall

Ball Bros. Co., Muncie, Ind., 1888 to date

DECKER'S
IOWANA
MASON CITY, IOWA.

PAT'D JULY 14 1908

DECKER'S VICTOR

Circa 1930

Lightning closure, beaded neck style

Machine-made round, in flint

Side: three lines within a rough circle: 'DECKER'S,' as the top arc, 'Victor,' in script, slanting across diameter, and 'MASON CITY, IOWA,' the bottom arc

Hazel Atlas Glass Co., Wheeling, W. Va., 1902-64, and

Ball Bros. Co., Muncie, Ind., 1888 to date

Jacob Decker & Son is a meat packer

DEWEY, JR., S. B.

Circa 1859

Finished for the WILLOUGHBY STOP-PLE (which see) of Jan. 4, 1859

Handmade round, pressed laid-on-ring, in aqua

Side: five lines: 'S. B. DEWEY J^R' arched over 'N^O 65,' 'BUFFALO ST.,' in a drooped arc, 'ROCHESTER,' and 'N.Y.'

Maker unknown

The WILLOUGHBY STOPPLE expanded a rubber ring by squeezing it between two plates by action of a thumbscrew

DEXTER (1)

Circa 1865

Glass lid and metal screw-band top seal

Handmade round, ground lip, in green and aqua

Side: 'DEXTER' in a background of fruits and vegetables

Maker unknown, but may be the Franklin Flint Glass Works, Philadelphia, Pa., 1861-1930

See also FRANKLIN and FRANKLIN-DEXTER

Some jars bear a patent date of Aug. 8, 1865, which was Patent No. 49,256 issued to William T. Gillinder and Edwin Bennett. It shows a thick glass lid and metal screw-band—not the all-glass cap shoulder seal often attributed to this jar; but see also the FRANKLIN-DEXTER FRUIT JAR

DEXTER (2)

Same except only the name DEXTER without background decoration

DEXTER

D G Co as a monogram

Circa 1890-1900
Glass lid and metal screw-band top seal
Handmade squat round, ground lip, in flint
Side: a large, elaborate, monogram of "D G Co"
Diamond Glass Co., Montreal, Que., 1891-1901, or
Dominion Glass Co., Montreal, Que., 1887-98; purchased by Diamond, and not the present Dominion formed by the merger of Diamond (Flint) Glass Co., and the Sydenham Glass Co. in 1913

DIAMOND FRUIT JAR

Circa 1915-20
Lightning closure, beaded neck design
Machine-made round, in flint or sun-colored
Bottom: a large diamond, with the word 'DIAMOND' divided to follow above the two top edges, 'FRUIT' and 'JAR' along the lower two edges, and with 'TRADE MARK' across the center
Maker unknown

DIAMOND FRUIT JAR, IMPROVED

Circa 1915-1920

Lightning closure, old neck design

Machine-made round, in flint and sun-colored

Bottom: a large diamond, with 'DIA-MOND' and 'FRUIT JAR' along the two upper sides, 'TRADE' and 'MARK' along the lower two sides, and 'IMPROVED' across the center

Maker unknown

Note that in this instance IMPROVED meant a change in sealing style, but not to the glass lid and metal screw-band

DICTATOR, THE

Circa 1855-69

Groove-ring wax sealer

Handmade round, pressed laid-on-ring, in green

Side: 'THE DICTATOR' in an arch

Bottom: 'Wm. McCULLY' and 'PITTS-BURGH'

William McCully & Co., Pittsburgh, Pa., 1832-85

See McKearin, p. 600 and Knittle, p. 320

DICTATOR D with moldmaker's error

Circa 1869-85

Metal disc and rubber gasket, held by spring clip

Handmade round, pressed laid-on-ring, in green and blue

Front: 'DICTATOR' arched over 'D'

Back: three lines: 'PATENTED,' arched above 'D. I. HOLCOMB,' across the diameter and 'DEC 1LTH 1869' (note upside-down "7" which should be a "4") completing the circle below

Bottom: 'Wm. McCULLY' and 'PITTS-BURGH'

William McCull, & Co., Pittsburgh, Pa., 1832-85

Patent No. 97,920 was issued to D. I. Holcomb of Henry County, Iowa, for this design. Without the patent description the jar could be easily mistaken for a wax sealer

(NOTE "7")

DILLON

Circa 1890-1900

Groove-ring wax sealer

Handmade round, pressed laid-on-ring, in light blue-green

Bottom: in a circle: 'DILLON & CO., FAIRMOUNT, IND.' It may also read 'DILLON G CO.' as the "&" or "G" is uncertain

Dillon Glass Co., Fairmount, Ind., 1890's.

D O C

Circa 1882

Groove-ring wax sealer

Handmade round, pressed laid-on-ring, in green

Side: 'D O C'

D. O. Cunningham Glass Co., Pittsburgh, Pa., 1882-1931

Do not confuse with Cunningham & Ihmsen or Cunninghams & Co. (which see), although Dominick O. Cunningham and his father withdrew from the latter (the plural indicates the three brothers who founded the company) to form D. O. Cunningham in 1882

D O C

DODGE–SWEENEY & Co.

Circa 1890-1900

Glass lid and metal screw-band top seal

Handmade wide-mouth round, ground lip, in green

Side: 'CALIFORNIA' across the diameter of a circle formed by 'DODGE–SWEENEY & Co.,' above and 'BUTTER,' below

Lid: 'MASON'S IMPROVED' and 'PAT MAY 10, 1870'

Maker unknown

DOMINION

Circa 1886-98

Glass lid and metal screw-band top seal

Handmade round, ground lip, in flint

Side: 'DOMINION' in an arch

Dominion Glass Co., Montreal, Que., 1886-98

Do not confuse this, the *old* Dominion Glass Co., which was purchased by Diamond Glass Company, with the *new* Dominion Glass Co., which was formed in 1913 by merger of Diamond and Sydenham Glass Co.

DOMINION MASON (1)

Circa 1915-20

Mason shoulder seal

Machine-made round, in flint

Side: 'Dominion,' in rising script, over 'MASON'

Dominion Glass Co., Montreal, Que., 1913 to date

DOMINION MASON (2)

Circa 1920 and later

Same except 'MADE IN CANADA' is added as a third line

DOMINION MASON (3)

Same as (2) except "D" in a diamond added on bottom—Dominion trade mark

DOMINION WIDE MOUTH SPECIAL (1)

Circa 1915-20

Mason shoulder seal

Machine-made wide-mouth round, in flint

Side: 'Dominion' and 'Wide Mouth,' in two lines of rising script, above 'SPECIAL'

Dominion Glass Co., Montreal, Que., 1913 to date

DOMINION WIDE MOUTH SPECIAL (2)

Same, except using a Mason beaded finish, and having added 'MADE IN CANADA' on the side, and the "D" in a diamond (Dominion trade mark) on the bottom

DOOLITTLE

Circa 1901

Glass lid held by two spring clips permanently mounted on the lid, and tightening by rotating to bring an arm under a finish ledge

Handmade wide-mouth round, pressed laid-on-ring, in flint

Front: 'DOOLITTLE'

Lid: 'Doolittle,' in script, with patent dates in a circle: Jan. 2, 1900, June 12, 1900, Dec. 3, 1901, and Dec. 24, 1901

Maker unknown

Due to the wide mouth, pints are very squat shaped

Doolittle had troubles, and his Patent No. 689,543 of Dec. 24, 1901, aired them— breakage and cost. His Patent No. 640,-182 of Jan. 2, 1900, had two heavy clips riveted into ears in the glass cap and they could not even be assembled without undue breakage. His Patent No. 651,500, of June 12, 1900, retained the riveting but tried to reduce breakage by a supporting tie wire between the two ears. The final patent changed from riveting to clips loosely held in small depressions rather than in complete holes through the glass

DOUBLE SAFETY (1)

Circa 1905

Lightning closure, old neck design

Machine-made round, in flint

Side: 'Double' and 'Safety' in two lines of slanting script

Bottom: 'A. G. SMALLEY & Co., BOSTON, MASS.' in a circle

Maker unknown, since Smalley was a jobber and had his bottles and jars made for him by several glass companies in successive years

DOUBLE SAFETY (2)

Circa 1907

Same as (1) except bottom lettered 'SMALLEY, KIVLAN & ONTHANK, BOSTON, MASS.,' which was the company name after 1907

DOUBLE SAFETY (3)

Circa 1909

Glass lid, retained by twin wire toggles rising from opposite sides of the neck and hooking over edge of lid. Held by neck tie wire

Machine-made round, in flint

Side: 'Double' and 'Safety,' in two lines of slanting script

Bottom: 'PAT FEB 23, 1909' in a small circle and 'SMALLEY, KIVLAN & ON-THANK, BOSTON, MASS.' in a large circle around the date

Various makers since Smalley, Kivlan & Onthank were jobbers

Patent No. 913,214, Feb. 23, 1909, was by John Kivlan, his first of three versions of the twin-toggle idea

DOUBLE SAFETY (4)

Lightning closure similar to (2) except only the initials "S, K & O" on the bottom

DOUBLE SAFETY (5)

Circa 1920. Converted to a Lightning adjustable design, and with "K & O" on the bottom, for Kivlan & Onthank, 1919 successors to Smalley, Kivlan & Onthank

DOUBLE SEAL (1)

Circa 1910-20

Lightning closure, old-style neck design

Machine-made round, in flint (and sun-colored)

Side: 'Double Seal' in slanting script

Probably the Pacific Coast Glass Works, San Francisco, Cal., 1902-24, since they made the BOSCO DOUBLE SEAL

DOUBLE SEAL (2)

Circa 1920-30

Lightning closure, beaded neck design

Machine-made round, in flint

Side: 'Double Seal' in slanting script

Pacific Coast Glass Works, San Francisco, Cal., 1902-24, and

Pacific Coast Glass Co., San Francisco, Cal., 1924-30

See also BOSCO DOUBLE SEAL

DREY EVER SEAL

Circa 1910-20

Lightning closure, old neck design

Machine-made round, in flint

Side: 'Drey,' in script, above 'EVER' and 'SEAL' in two more lines

Schram Glass Mf'g. Co., St. Louis, Mo., 1906-25. Ball Brothers purchased Schram in 1925. See also SCHRAM

DREY IMPROVED EVER SEAL (1)

Circa 1920-25

Lightning closure, beaded neck design

Machine-made round, in flint

Side: four lines: 'Drey' and 'Improved,' both in script, above 'EVER' and 'SEAL'

Schram Glass Mf'g. Co., St. Louis, Mo., 1906-25

DREY IMPROVED EVER SEAL (2)

Circa 1920-25

Lightning closure, lever wire held by glass bosses on neck

Machine-made round, in flint

Side: four lines: 'Drey,' in script, above 'EVER' and 'SEAL,' with 'IMPROVED' to the left of the latter

Schram Glass Mf'g. Co., St. Louis, Mo., 1906-25

Leo A. Drey and James L. Hiett received Patent No. 1,352,119 for this design on Sept. 7, 1920

DREY IMPROVED EVER SEAL (3)

Same except 'PAT^D 1920' on bottom

DREY IMPROVED EVER SEAL (4)

Same except 'PAT SEPT 7 1920' on back

DREY IMPROVED EVER SEAL (5)

Same as (1) except lettered in three lines: 'Drey,' in script, 'IMPROVED,' and 'EVER SEAL'

DREY MASON (1)

Circa 1910-20
Mason shoulder seal
Machine-made round, in light green
Side: 'Drey,' in script, above 'MASON,' in block letters
Schram Glass Mf'g. Co., St. Louis, Mo., 1906-25
The half-gallon shoulder is tapered—others not

DREY MASON (2)

Circa 1920
Same except beaded neck design and in flint

DREY PERFECT MASON (1)

Circa 1910
Mason shoulder seal
Machine-made round, in green
Side: three lines: 'Drey,' in script, over 'PERFECT' and 'MASON'
Schram Glass Mf'g. Co., St. Louis, Mo., 1906-25

DREY PERFECT MASON (2)

Circa 1920
Same except beaded neck design and in flint

DREY SQUARE MASON (1)

Circa 1920-25
Mason beaded neck style
Machine-made rounded square, in flint
Side: 'Drey,' in script, above 'SQUARE,' in very square slanting letters, and 'MASON.' A carpenter's square extends along the right of the letters and above 'MASON'
Schram Glass Mf'g. Co., St. Louis, Mo., 1906-25

DUNKLEY (1)

Circa 1898
Glass lid and spring-steel band, of a shape to contact the lid in its center, and gripping under a ledge of the finish
Machine-made round, in flint
Bottom: 'PAT$^{\underline{D}}$ SEPT 20, 98' forming a flat-topped inner circle, with 'DUNKLEY' circled above and 'KALAMAZOO' below
Maker unknown. Dunkley was a preserves manufacturer
Patent No. 610,897 of Sept 20, 1898, by S. J. Dunkley calls for the details given

DUNKLEY (2)

Circa 1901
Same, except that "KALAMAZOO" is omitted on the bottom, replaced by 'APL. 30, 01' (added to 'DUNKLEY' and 'PAT$^{\underline{D}}$ SEPT 20, 98'). The second patent was No. 673,048, by S. J. Dunkley, for a spring-clip band centering on a small depression in the center of the lid

DU PONT

Circa 1907-15
Mason shoulder seal
Handmade round, ground lip, in green
Front: four lines: 'MASON'S,' arched,

'PATENT,' 'NOV 30ᵀᴴ,' and '1858'
Back: 'DU PONT' in an oval
Maker unknown
It is not known why DU PONT used or
sold the jar. It was made some time between the earliest known use of the trade
mark, in 1907, and the advent of the
beaded Mason neck design circa 1915

DUR FOR (French for "STRONG HEART")

Modern French Jar
Glass lid, attached to one side by a wire
hinge and with a snap-wire seal on the
other side
Machine-made round, in dark green
Lid: 'DUR' and 'FOR,' 2 lines within a
rough circle
Manufactures des Glaces et Produits Chi-
miques de Saint Gobain, Chauney et
Ciney, France

DURHAM

Circa 1910-20
Lightning closure, old neck design
Machine-made round, in light green
Side: 'DURHAM'
Maker unknown

DYSON'S PURE FOOD (1)

Circa 1915
Glass lid and metal screw-band top seal
Machine-made round, in flint
Side: 'DYSON'S,' arched over a large cross,
resembling the HERO CROSS except
for rounded contour at the root of the
indentations. Below the cross, 'PURE
FOOD' and 'PRODUCTS'
Bottom: "D" in a diamond
Dominion Glass Co., Montreal, Que., 1913
to date

DYSON'S PURE FOOD (2)

Circa 1920

Lids have been found bearing the "D" in a diamond trade mark, and 'MADE IN CANADA,' indicating a jar made after 1920

E

"E" in a tilted square

See CROWN (14) and (15)

EACLE

EAGLE (1)

Circa 1860-65

Glass lid and spring-steel band clip

Handmade round, pressed laid-on-ring, in green and blue-green

Side: 'EAGLE'

Bottom: 'PAT DEC 17 61'

Patent No. 33,938 was issued to N. S. Gilbert of Lockport, N.Y. It called for a glass lid held by an elaborate locking mechanism not found with this jar. On Nov. 4, 1862, another patent, not yet seen, was issued—it may have called for the more simple spring clip

The jar was possibly made at the Hitchen's factory (Lockport Glass Works, Lockport, N.Y., 1840-69) because Hero bought that factory and acquired its assets, which may have included this jar since Hero shows this patent date on known Hero jars

EAGLE (2)

Similar to (1) except that when found had a handmade yoke and thumbscrew. This may or may not have been original equipment, and there is no clue

EAGLE (3)

Circa 1868

Glass lid, clamp unknown

Handmade round, pressed laid-on-ring, in green

Side: 'EAGLE' across the diameter of a circle formed by 'PAT DEC 28TH 1858' above, and 'REIS^D JUNE 16TH 1868' below

Maker unknown

A patent, No. 22,433 by John K. Jenkins on Dec. 28, 1858, for a wax compound, and No. 78,976 by L. Lehman on June 16, 1868, for a hinged lock, do not seem to apply. No others were found

EAGLE (4)

Circa 1860

Groove-ring wax sealer

Handmade round, pressed laid-on-ring, in blue-green

Side: 'EAGLE'

Maker unknown

EARLE'S PATENT

See NATIONAL PRESERVE JAR

EASI-PAK MASON, METRO

Circa 1942-46 only, according to Metro Glass

Mason beaded neck design

Machine-made round, in flint

Side: three lines: 'METRO,' 'EASI-PAK,' in slanted capitals, and 'Mason'; "METRO" and "Mason" in heavy letters

Metro Glass Co., Jersey City, N.J., 1949 to date

Metro Glass Bottle Co., 1935-49; a Knox Glass Associate

METRO

EASY PAK

EASY

CO

TRADE MARK

VACUUM

JAR

EASY-PAK, METRO

Same except without the word MASON, METRO is in double-outlined letters, and EASY instead of EASI

EASY VACUUM JAR (1)

Circa 1893

Glass lid and three-position wire clamp for slanting side seal

Handmade tall round, in flint

Side: a large "V" with "J" superimposed on the left leg and "C" on the right; 'TRADE' and 'MARK' flanking it; above: 'EASY' in an arch; below: 'VACUUM' and 'JAR'

Bottom: monogram repeated, with 'PAT JULY 11, 1893'

San Francisco & Pacific Glass Co., San Francisco, Cal., 1879-1901

Patent No. 501,418, July 11, 1893, was issued to Franz Guilleaume and Ewald Goltstein of Bonn, Germany. A round rubber ring fitted a half-circle depression around the slanting finish and was compressed by the cap

Goltstein was later the inventor of one of the two ideas (Landsberger the other) that went into the making of the LANDS-BERGER, and then the ECONOMY jars

EASY VACUUM JAR (2)

Some versions of this jar have an indentation in the neck to hold a spring clip

EATON

See CROWN (12) and (13)

ECLIPSE

See BALL ECLIPSE

ECLIPSE, THE

Circa 1860-70
Groove-ring wax sealer
Handmade, pressed laid-on-ring, in green
Side: 'THE' over 'ECLIPSE'
Maker unknown

ECLIPSE WAX SEALER

Same except 'WAX SEALER' added as a
third line

ECONOMY (1)

Circa 1903-09
Metal lid with attached heat-softenable
gasket, held by spring clip during proc-
essing
Machine-made round, in flint (will sun-
color)
Side: 'Economy,' in slanting script, above
'TRADE MARK,' also slanting
Bottom: 'KERR GLASS MANUFACTUR-
ING Co., PORTLAND, ORE.' in a circle
Illinois Pacific Glass Co., San Francisco,
Cal., 1902-30, who made the jar from
1903 to 1909, and
Hazel Atlas Glass Co., Wheeling, W. Va.,
1902-64, who made the jar from 1906 to
1909
There is evidence that the jar was produced
in 1903 as the LANDSBERGER (which
see) by Julius A. Landsberger, holder of
Patent No. 731,793, June 23, 1903, for
the spring clip, and assignee of Patent
No. 730,760 by Ewald Goltstein, June 9,
1903, for the heat-softenable gasket.
Landsberger evidently sold Kerr the
fruit-jar rights, then became one of the
founders of the Phoenix Company, who
made the caps

THE

ECLIPSE

ECONOMY (2)

Same except 'PAT JUNE 9, 1903' on the side

ECONOMY (3)

Same as (1) except showing 'PAT JUNE 9, 1903' and '& JUNE 23, 1903' on the side in two lines

TRADE MARK

(PORTLAND)

(PORTLAND)

ECONOMY jars will differ greatly according to the underlining of the word "ECONOMY," from two to four or five lines, sometimes converging to a common point, sometimes converging but not joining at a point. Generally the more elaborate lettering is on older jars, and in later years only two lines were used. The June 9, 1903, date appears in several locations. 'PORTLAND' appeared in the bottom lettering until 1909. 'TRADE MARK' was sometimes omitted

See KERR ECONOMY for later jars, after the company office was moved to Chicago, Ill., and manufacturing started briefly at Altoona, Kan., to be followed by moving the factory and office to Sand Springs, Okla. A very few ECONOMY jars were produced with the lettering of the Chicago address before the name was changed to KERR ECONOMY

ECONOMY WAX SEALER

Circa 1858

Groove-ring wax sealer

Handmade round, pressed laid-on-ring, in dark blue-green

Side: four lines: 'ECONOMY,' arched, 'SEALER,' 'PAT$^{\underline{D}}$ SEPT 13,' and '1858'

Maker unknown

September 13th was not a patent-issue date, and no patent was found

ECONOMY WAX SEALER with moldmaker's error

Same except date is given as 1885

E D J SEAL

See ATLAS E D J SEAL

E G Co monogram

See EXCELSIOR; and Stevens: *Early Canadian Glass,* p. 128

E H E MASON'S PATENT NOV 30th 1858

Circa 1890-1900
Mason shoulder seal
Handmade round, ground lip, in green
Side: 'MASON'S,' arched, 'PATENT,' 'NOV 30th,' and '1858.' E H E near heel
Edward H. Everett Glass Co., Newark, Ohio, 1885-1904. Was Ohio Bottle Company in 1904, then part of American Bottle Co. merger in 1905

EIRE

Appears on a dealer's want-list, and may be a misprint for ERIE

ELECTRIC (1)

Circa 1900-10
Lightning closure, old neck style
Handmade round, ground lip, in aqua
Side: 'TRADE MARK' arched over 'ELECTRIC'
Gayner Glass Works, Salem, N.J., 1898-1957 (after leasing in 1879)

ELECTRIC (2)

Circa 1910
Lightning closure, old neck style
Machine-made round, in green

TRADE MARK
ELECTRIC

Electric
TRADE MARK

Side: 'Electric,' in rising script, over 'TRADE MARK'

Gayner Glass Works, Salem, N.J., 1898-1957

ELECTRIC FRUIT JAR

Circa 1890-1900

Glass lid and clamp, and somewhat similar to the PURITAN and the GEO. D. BROWN & Co.

Handmade round, ground lip, in aqua

Side: a globe, with 'ELECTRIC' arched above and 'FRUIT JAR' circling below

John Gayner, lessee, then owner, Broadway Glass Works, Salem, N.J., 1879-98 (formerly Holz, Clark & Taylor)

Gayner Glass Works, Salem, N.J., 1898-1957

ELECTROGLAS, N W

Between 1950 and 1955 only

Mason beaded neck design

Machine-made round, in flint

Side: 'N W ELECTROGLAS'

Northwestern Glass Co., Seattle, Wash., 1936 to date

ELECTROLUX

Circa 1930-40

Short-height screw finish, not Mason

Machine-made round, in green and flint

Side: 'ELECTROLUX'

Owens Illinois Glass Co., Toledo, Ohio, 1929 to date (1930-38 production)

Armstrong Cork Co., Lancaster, Pa., 1938 to date (1938-40 production)

Used on the Model XII Electrolux vacuum cleaner as a solution jar

EMPIRE (1)

Circa 1859-66

Stopper finish, to take WILLOUGHBY STOPPLE, which see

Handmade round, pressed laid-on-ring, in blue and aqua

Side: 'EMPIRE' in an arch

Empire Glass Co., Cleveland, N.Y., 1852-77

EMPIRE with moldmaker's error

Same except the final "E" not completed

EMPIRE (2)

Circa 1910-20

Lightning closure, old neck design

Machine-made round, in flint and sun-colored

Side: a square panel with a rounded top contains a cross pattée, across two wings of which is 'EMPIRE.' Rest is stippled

Maker unknown

EMPIRE, THE (1)

Circa 1866

Two lugs blown in neck hold a cam lever, retaining a glass lid

Handmade round, ground lip, in light green

Front: two lines: 'THE' and 'EMPIRE'

Back: four lines: 'F. A. BUNNELL'S' arched over 'PAT. No 52,525,' 'FEB 13ᵀᴴ 1866,' and 'SYRACUSE, N.Y.'

Empire Glass Co., Cleveland, N.Y., 1852-77

EMPIRE, THE (2)

Same except patent date on bottom, and without back lettering as (1)

EMPIRE

THE

EMPIRE

(FRONT)

F. A. BUNNELL'S

PAT. No 52,525

FEB 13 ᵀᴴ 1866

SYRACUSE, N.Y.

(BACK)

ENG HUNG CHI

Circa 1930-40

Lightning closure, dimple neck design

Machine-made 12 oz. squat round, in flint

Side: four lines: 'ENG HUNG CHI,' '1332 WAVERLY PLACE,' 'SAN FRANCISCO,' and 'BEAN CAKE,' and with Chinese characters

Bottom: "O" and "I" in a diamond (Owens Illinois trade mark 1929-56)

Owens Illinois Glass Co., Toledo, Ohio, 1929 to date. Probably made at San Francisco or Oakland factories

ENG SKELL CO. (1)

Circa 1905-20

Glass lid and Improved Everlasting seal, a toggle invented in San Francisco in 1905

Machine-made wide-mouth squat round, in flint

Side: 'ENG SKELL CO.' and 'SAN FRANCISCO,' with Chinese characters

Illinois Pacific Glass Co., San Francisco, Cal., 1902-30, who owned the patent for the Everlasting seal

ENG SKELL CO. (2)

Same, except in this half-gallon size, the lettering of ENG SKELL was in the vertical fashion

ERIE FRUIT JAR

Circa 1895-98

Mason shoulder seal

Handmade round, ground lip, in aqua

Side: "E" in a hexagon. Around it a circle of 'ERIE' above and 'FRUIT JAR' below

Probably the Erie Glass Works, Port Colburne, Ont., 1895-98. Little is known of this company, now being researched by Mr. Gerald Stevens of Toronto's Royal Ontario Museum

ERIE LIGHTNING

Circa 1913-25
Lightning closure, old-style neck design
Machine-made round, in flint
Side: 'ERIE' over 'LIGHTNING'
Attributed to Jefferson Glass Co., Toronto, Ont., 1913-25

ERIE
LIGHTNING

ERMEBLOK

Modern European jar
Glass lid is hinged at one side, closed by a wire snap lock on the other as in L'IDEALE, LE PRATIQUE, TRI-OMPHE, and others of European make
Machine-made squat round, in flint
Lid: 'Ermeblok,' in slanting script
Maker unknown

EUREKA (1)

Circa 1865
Friction side-seal, using metal cap pressed down on very slightly tapering finish
Handmade, dip-molded finish, in flint and aqua. The dip molding consisted of pressing the finish portion of the neck of the bottle, reheated at the "glory hole" while being held at the bottom by a "snap tool," into an iron cavity having the desired taper in the circular hole
Side: 'EUREKA,' arched over 'PAT FEB 9th, 1864'
Bottom: in circle, 'EUREKA JAR CO., DUNBAR, W. VA.'

Maker unknown. The Dunbar Chamber of Commerce can report no glass company of that name, but it may have been a jobber

EUREKA (2)

Same except 'PAT FEB 9th & DEC 27th 1864' in circle on side around 'EUREKA'

EUREKA (3)

Same except 'PAT^D DEC 27TH,' and '1864' on side below "EUREKA." '17' is a mold serial number

EURE̲KA (4) [Underlined letters large capitals]

Circa 1900-1910

Glass lid and metal spring clip rotating on Mason-type threads

Side: 'EureKa,' in slanting script. The "E" and the "K" are large capitals; the rest is lower case lettering

Bottom: 'EUREKA JAR CO., DUNBAR, W. VA.' in a circle

Maker unknown, as before

EURE̲KA (5) [Underlined letters large capitals]

Same except bottom reads: 'EUREKA JAR CO., BOSTON, MASS.' in a circle

Patent No. 41,575, Feb. 9, 1864, by Elbridge Harris, of Boston, Mass., shows the finish taper most like the jars throughout the series. Patent No. 45,601, Dec. 27, 1864, by J. F. Griffen, of New York City, shows a less taper, but more of the metal cap detail. The latter patent also shows a standard Mason shoulder seal with the rubber ring with a thumb-tab on the side for easier breaking of the seal, and is perhaps the oldest detail of the Mason jar unchanged to this day

EVERETT

An alternate form of the E H E Mason's Patent Nov. 30th, 1858, already listed. See: E H E

EVERLASTING JAR

Circa 1904

Glass lid held by an "over-the-top" toggle as a clamp

Machine-made round, in flint and sun-colored

Side: 'Everlasting,' in rising script, with 'JAR' in the ribbon finial from the initial "E"

Illinois Pacific Glass Co., San Francisco, Cal., 1902-30

Patent No. 776,162 was issued Nov. 29, 1904, to Edward Abramson, part-owner of the San Francisco & Pacific Glass Co., 1879-1902, with the Illinois Glass Co., Alton, Ill., 1873-1929. While assigning control to Illinois Glass, who then formed Illinois Pacific, he retained interests as shown by this patent

EVERYLASTING JAR, IMPROVED (1)

Circa 1905

Glass lid held by an "over-the-top" cam lever

Machine-made round, in flint

Side: 'IMPROVED' over 'Everlasting,' in script, with 'JAR' on a ribbon finial as before

Illinois Pacific Glass Co., San Francisco, Cal., 1902-30

Patent No. 797,711, August 22, 1905, was issued to Edward Abramson and Edward O. Bennett. It converted the toggle into a cam-lever device. While the toggle lay flat when closed, the cam lever formed a "tent" when closed

EVERLASTING JAR, IMPROVED (2)

Same, except for the following changes:
Lettering placed in an oval panel, all in block letters: 'IMPROVED,' 'EVER-LASTING,' and 'JAR'
Jar shape changed to 10-panel pint and 14-panel quart
Since the two lids and wire sealing devices are interchangeable, collectors will find all combinations of jars, lids, and wire sealing devices

EXCELSIOR (1)

Circa 1880-1890
Glass lid and metal screw-band top seal
Handmade round, ground lip, in aqua
Side 'EXCELSIOR' with a monogram of "E G Co"
Probably the Excelsior Glass Co., St. Johns, Que., 1879 and Montreal, Que., 1880-89. See Stevens: *Early Canadian Glass*, p. 128

EXCELSIOR (2)

Same, without the monogram

EXCELSIOR IMPROVED (1)

Circa 1880-1890
Glass lid and metal screw-band top seal
Handmade round, ground lip, in aqua
Side: 'EXCELSIOR' over 'IMPROVED'
Probably the Excelsior Glass Co., St. Johns, Que., 1879; Montreal, Que., 1880-89

There seems no change to warrant the name IMPROVED; it might be only the recognition that the top seal was generally known as such

EXCELSIOR, IMPROVED (2)

Same except machine-made. This may be an extension of the name by the Diamond Glass Co., successors to Excelsior

F

F A & Co

Circa 1860-62 only

Stopper finish for WILLOUGHBY STOPPLE, which see

Handmade round, pressed laid-on-ring, in green

Bottom: 'F A & Co'

Fahnstock, Albree & Co., Pittsburgh, Pa., 1860-62, who leased the Lorenz factory for two years

F A & CO

FAHNSTOCK, ALBREE & Co.

Same as F A & Co except name spelled in full, in a circle

FAHNSTOCK, FORTUNE & Co.

Circa 1868

Groove-ring wax sealer

Handmade round, pressed laid-on-ring, in green

Bottom: 'FAHNSTOCK, FORTUNE & CO.'

Fahnstock, Fortune & Co., Pittsburgh, Pa., 1868-? (McKearin, p. 612) B. L. Fahnstock and William Fortune built this factory, but soon sold it to Evans, Sell & Co.

F C G Co.

Age uncertain; probably circa 1860-70

Groove-ring wax sealer

Handmade round, pressed laid-on-ring, in amber and blue-green

Bottom: 'F C G Co.'

Maker unknown

Since no glass company known to have these initials has been found, it may be possible that a "P" was mistaken, dimly cut, for "F," and that the initials stand for the Pittsburgh City Glass Co., or Works, the plant name used by Cunninghams & Co., Pittsburgh, 1879-1909, or Cunningham & Ihmsen, 1855-79. It was quite common to have both a company name and a factory name

FEDERAL FRUIT JAR

Circa 1890-1900

Glass lid with old neck design Lightning finish

Handmade round, ground lip, in olive-green

Side: 'FEDERAL' in doubly outlined letters, in an arch, with "F" very large and "L" larger than the rest. Below the arch is a draped flag carrying a cross of St. George with five superimposed stars visible. Below the flag: 'FRUIT JAR' with the top outline of the letters in a sagging arc and the bottom outline straight. The flag was not identified

Maker unknown. The AMERICAN, COMMONWEALTH, and FEDERAL fruit jars were seen in the half-gallon size, all with one side plated for a removable panel carrying the lettering, and interchangeable with each other. The style is indicative of Albert G. Smalley Co., Boston, Mass., jobber of china and glassware

FINK & NASSE

Circa 1876-1900

Glass lid held by Cohansey's helical wire closure

Handmade round, ground lip, in green

Side: all in double-outlined letters in oval outline: 'FINK' along upper contour, '&' and 'NASSE' arching through the center, and 'S̲T̲ LOUIS' along the lower contour

Bottom: 'COHANSEY GLASS MANU-FACTURING CO., PHILAD̲A̲' in a circle

Cohansey Glass Manufacturing Co., Philadelphia, Pa., 1870-1900

The patent for this finish was No. 172,289, by John Young, Jan. 18, 1876. See CO-HANSEY for details

FLACCUS CO., E. C. (1)

Circa 1890

Mason shoulder seal, small diameter, with SIMPLEX all-glass cap

Handmade round, very roughly ground, in opal glass

Side: an *elk's* head and antlers with 'TRADE' and 'MARK' flanking it and with flowers, stems, and leaves as decorations above the head. 'E. C. FLACCUS CO' on a ribbon scroll below, with decoration of flowers, stems, and leaves at the bottom. Compare the STEERSHEAD, which have a similar design

Probably made by Hazel Glass Co., 1886-1902, and then located at Washington, Pa., for E. C. Flaccus, a Wheeling, W. Va., food broker and manufacturer

FLACCUS, E. C. (2)

Several similar jars have been found in green glass, differing only in minor details of the decorations. Elk's head continued

E. C. FLACCUS (3)

Same as (2), except the elk's head replaced by a steer's head

FLETT, W. & J. (1)

Circa 1896-1900

Glass lid held by a heavy wire shaped to fit Mason-like threads

Handmade round, ground lip, in blue tint

Side: an animal's head in a gadrooned circle. Above it is 'W. & J. FLETT,' and below it is 'LIVERPOOL'

Bottom: 'REDFEARN BROS., LIVERPOOL AND BARNSLEY' in a circle

Redfearn Bros., Barnsley Works, Yorks., England, 1862 to date, for a customer

FLETT, W. & J. (2)

Circa 1880

Stopper finish, closed by glass stopper holding cork or rubber side seal ring

Handmade round, ground lip, in blue tint

Rest of details similar to W. & J. FLETT (1)

FLICKINGER [Shown only by initials J. H. F. as a ligature, or joining together of letters as a monogram]

Circa 1885-1900
Lightning closure, old neck design
Handmade round, ground lip, in light green
Side: a monogram in the form of a ligature, joining the upright portions of "J" and "F" with a crossbar to form "H"
Unknown maker, for J. H. Flickinger Packing Co., pioneer San Jose, Cal., orchardist and food packer. Flickinger was once interested in glass making as a partner in the ill-starred Campbell Glass Co., Oakland, Cal., 1885 only. It is doubted that the jar was made by Campbell

FLICKINGER (2)

Same, except 'PUTNAM' on bottom

FOREST CITY BAKING POWDER

FOREST CITY
BAKING POWDER
GORMAN ECKERT & CO
LONDON

Circa 1880-95
Glass lid and metal screw-band top seal
Handmade round, ground lip, in light blue
Side: four lines: 'FOREST CITY,' 'BAKING POWDER,' 'GORMAN ECKERT & CO,' and 'LONDON'
Attributed to the Hamilton Glass Co., Hamilton, Ont., 1865-93
London, Ont., was known as the Forest City

FORSTER JAR, THE

THE
FORSTER
JAR

Circa 1910-20
Glass lid and metal screw-band top seal
Heavy machine-made round, in flint
Side: three lines: 'THE,' 'FORSTER,' and 'JAR'
Forsters Glass Co., St. Helens, Lancs., Eng., 1902 to date

FOSTER

See SEALFAST

FRANK

Circa 1860

Groove-ring wax sealer

Handmade round, pressed laid-on-ring, in green

Bottom: in a circle around a diamond (perhaps the earliest use of this popular symbol by a glass house): Wm. FRANK & SONS, PITTSBURGH'

William Frank & Sons, Pittsburgh, Pa., 1858-66. (Dates from personal communication by William Frank's grandson)

FRANKLIN FRUIT JAR

Circa 1865

Mason shoulder seal

Handmade round, ground lip, in blue-green and aqua

Side: 'FRANKLIN' above, and 'FRUIT JAR' below, forming a circle

Maker unknown, unless the Franklin Flint Glass Co., Philadelphia, Pa., 1861-1930, who may also have made the DEXTER

FRANKLIN-DEXTER FRUIT JAR (1)

Circa 1865

Mason shoulder seal, small diameter for all-glass cap

Handmade round, ground lip, in green

Side: 'FRANKLIN' above, and 'FRUIT JAR' below, forming a circle, with 'DEXTER' across the diameter

Lid: in circle: 'PAT OCT 24 1882'

Possibly the Franklin Flint Glass Co., Philadelphia, Pa., 1861-1930

See also: FRANKLIN and DEXTER

The only patent found for this date was No. 266,375, by Anton Luger. It was for a hinged lid and its application is doubtful

FRANKLIN-DEXTER FRUIT JAR (2)

With larger finish diameter for standard Mason shoulder seal

FRUIT GROWERS TRADE CO.

Circa 1900-15

Glass lid, clamp uncertain

Machine-made oval, in aqua and green

Side: a triangle made from a nesting of four triangles, flanked by 'TRADE' and 'MARK.' Above, in an arch: 'FRUIT GROWERS TRADE'; below 'C⁰'

Bottom 'PAT FEB 13 1893' but machine manufacture suggests later date

Maker unknown

FRUIT GROWERS TRADE CO. with moldmaker's error

Same, but a lid on which the "9" of "1893" of the same patent date is cut backward has been found

FRUIT-KEEPER (1)

Circa 1880-1900

Glass lid with a cam lever eccentrically moving two wire loops to cross over lid and hook under finish

Handmade round, ground lip, in aqua

Side: 'FRUIT-KEEPER' in half circle above 'C G Co.' as a monogram

Canton Glass Co., Canton, Ohio, 1883-93; Marion, Ind., 1893-99 and 1904-5

See also CANTON DOMESTIC

FRUIT-KEEPER (2)

Same, except also with 'J H S Co.' on bottom, for J. Hungerford Smith Co. of Albany, N.Y., extensive users of glass jars for packing fine fruits for the hotel trade. See also: TRUE FRUIT, with a J H S Co. monogram and a glass lid spelling out J. Hungerford Smith Co. in full.

G

THE

GAYNER

GLASS-TOP

GAYNER GLASS-TOP, THE

Circa 1915
Lightning closure, dimple neck design
Machine-made round, in flint
Side: three lines: 'THE,' 'GAYNER,' and 'GLASS-TOP'
Gayner Glass Works, Salem, N.J. 1898-1937, and
Gayner Glass Co., 1937-54, Salem, N.J.

GEM and THE GEM

Since the first was THE GEM, followed by GEM and then by other modifications, as NEW GEM, IMPROVED GEM, and the like, we will begin out of alphabetical order with THE GEM in order to preserve chronology. Those made by Hero, if not otherwise labeled, will be recognized by the list of patent numbers and dates also shown for Hero, which habitually listed every number it could on the lid or on the bottom of the jar, or both. In an occasional return to modesty, Hero used only "PAT NOV 26 67" on the jar, which may almost be considered a Hero trade mark

GEM, THE (1)

Circa 1856

Blown-wax sealer, with jar formed in mold with almost a flat top, then with the finish pushed downward, while hot, to form a shallow depression circling the finish. The first GEM patents were for the lids to be used with it, and Hero became a lid specialist

Handmade round, ground lip, in green and aqua

Side: two lines: 'THE' and 'GEM'

Hero Glass Works, Philadelphia, Pa., 1856-84, becoming

Hero Fruit Jar Co., Philadelphia, Pa., 1884-1909

This is the original GEM

**THE
GEM**

GEM, THE (2)

Same, except 'THE GEM' on one line

THE GEM

GEM, THE (3)

Circa 1869

Glass lid and metal screw-band top seal

Handmade tapered-shoulder round, in green and blue-green

Side: 'THE GEM' on one line

Bottom: 'PAT NOV 26 67'

Hero Glass Works, Philadelphia, Pa., 1856-84

The date identifies the maker. This was Salmon B. Rowley's Design Patent No. 2,840, which covered the tapered shoulder as a matter of strength

The lid found with this jar carried ten patent dates, of which "JUNE 19, 1869" was the latest

GEM, THE (4)

Same but the more common bottom lettering (without the word PAT as was most common with Hero) 'NOV 26 67,' often in scrawling script

THE GEM

(FRONT)

(BACK)

GEM, THE (5)

Circa 1871

Glass lid and metal screw-band top seal

Handmade round, ground lip, in aqua and green

Front: 'THE GEM'

Back: a monogram of "H G W" in heavy letters

Bottom: "NOV 26 67" and "FEB 7 71"

The "H G W" monogram was used by the Hero Glass Works from the 1860s to 1882, when the unlettered cross was adopted as a trade mark. When the company name changed to Hero Fruit Jar Co., in 1884, its new initials were placed in the wings of the cross

Hero Glass Works, Philadelphia, Pa., 1856-84

M. R. Bissel received Patent No. 111,607 on Feb. 7, 1871, for a method of grinding the lip flush with the sealing surface so that the glass lid could be made more shallow. He assigned it to Rowley

G E M

GEM, THE (6)

Same as (5) except with much finer lettering

GEM, THE (7)

Circa 1868

Similar to (5) but with bottom dates shown: 'NOV 26 67,' 'DEC 17 67,' and 'REIS SEPT 1 68,' in a circle

GEM, THE (8) [with Hero unlettered cross]

Circa 1882-84 only
Similar to (3) except the Hero unlettered cross is on the back

THE GEM
(FRONT)

(BACK)

GEM, THE (9) [with Consolidated monogram]

Circa 1882-84
Glass lid and metal screw-band top seal
Handmade round, ground lip, in aqua
Side: 'THE GEM' arched over the Consolidated monogram of C F J Co.
Hero Glass Works, Philadelphia, Pa., 1856-84
This jar is one of the indications that Hero had taken over the Consolidated assets about 1882, since it combines the Hero-owned GEM with the Consolidated-owned monogram. Other evidence was found that indicated that it was Hero that did the taking-over
The lid was a Hero lid with nine known Hero patent dates. Of course, any lid may be suspect in that it may have been combined later, but the fact that it fit this jar is meaningful

GEM, THE (10) [Hourglass]

Similar to (3) except the back has an hourglass-shaped shield without lettering. It is similar to its use on a MASON'S PATENT NOV 30th 1858 with Hero patent dates on the bottom, and to one jar which has the hourglass without any other decoration

THE GEM
(FRONT)

(BACK)

THE GEM
RUTHERFORD&Co.

GEM, THE (11)

Circa 1873
Glass lid and metal screw-band top seal
Handmade round, ground lip, in blue
Side: 'THE GEM' in large letters, above 'RUTHERFORD & Co.'
Lid: 'RUTHERFORD & Co., HAMILTON, ONT.' in circle
Hamilton Glass Works, Hamilton, Ont., 1865-93. The jar dates from the year George Rutherford took over as proprietor (George Rutherford & Co.) in 1873. His name or company name was more often used until acquired by Diamond Glass Company, of Montreal, in 1893

THE GEM

RUTHERFORD&Co.

GEM, THE (12)

Same as (11) except 'THE GEM' is in much smaller lettering

GEM (1)

Circa 1867-82
Glass lid and metal screw-band top seal
Handmade round, ground lip, in blue-green
Side: 'GEM' in very heavy letters
Bottom: "PAT NOV 26 67"
Hero Glass Works, Philadelphia, Pa., 1856-84

GEM (2)

Circa 1882-84 only
Glass lid and metal screw-band top seal
Handmade round, ground lip, in green
Side: an unlettered Hero Cross, above 'GEM' in bold letters
Hero Glass Works, Philadelphia, Pa., 1856-84

GEM (3)

Circa 1884 and later
Glass lid and metal screw-band top seal
Handmade round, ground lip, in green
Side: a lettered Hero cross, above 'GEM'
in lighter letters than (2)
Hero Fruit Jar Co., Philadelphia, Pa., 1884-
1909

GEM (4)

Circa 1885
Glass lid and metal screw-band top seal
Handmade round, ground lip, in blue-green
Side: a very large 'GEM' above 'RUTHER-
FORD & CO.'
Hamilton Glass Works, Hamilton, Ont.,
1865-93
Note that earlier Rutherford called it "THE
GEM"

GEM, IMPROVED (1)

Circa 1868
Glass lid and metal screw-band top seal
Handmade round, ground lip, in green
Side: two lines: 'IMPROVED' above 'GEM'
Bottom: several Hero patent dates, the
latest being June 9, 1868
Hero Glass Works, Philadelphia, Pa., 1856-
84
This use of "IMPROVED" is two years be-
fore Consolidated registered it in con-
nection with a similar jar as the IM-
PROVED MASON

GEM, IMPROVED (2)

Circa 1915
Glass lid and metal screw-band top seal
Machine-made round, in flint and (rare) in
amber

Side: three slanting lines: 'Improved' and 'Gem,' in script, and 'TRADE MARK REG'D,' in block letters, all in the style of the Sydenham GEMS before the Sydenham-Diamond merger

Dominion Glass Co., Montreal, Que., 1913 to date

GEM, IMPROVED (3)

Same except for quotation marks around 'Gem'

GEM, IMPROVED (4)

Circa 1920

Glass lid and metal screw-band top seal

Machine-made round, in flint

Side: 'Improved,' in slanting script, followed by 'GEM' and 'MADE IN CAN-ADA' in block letters

Dominion Glass Co., Montreal, Que., 1913 to date

GEM, NEW (1)

Circa 1910

Glass lid and metal screw-band top seal

Machine-made round, in flint

Side: 'NEW' in seriffed, small block letters, above 'Gem' in very large script

Sydenham Glass Co., Wallaceburg, Ont., 1894-1913

GEM, NEW (2)

Circa 1915

Same as (1) except for a "D" in a diamond on the bottom

Dominion Glass Co., Montreal, Que., 1913 to date

(SIDE)

(BOTTOM)

GEM, WALLACEBURG

Circa 1905-13
Glass lid and metal screw-band top seal
Machine-made round, in flint
Side: 'WALLACEBURG' in small block
    letters, above a large script 'Gem'
Sydenham Glass Co., Wallaceburg, Ont.,
    1894-1913

GEM, 1908

Probably circa 1908
Glass lid and metal screw-band top seal
Machine-made round, in flint
Side: '1908' above a large script 'Gem'
Sydenham Glass Co., Wallaceburg, Ont.,
    1894-1913

GEM BUTTER JAR

Circa 1880-1900
Glass lid and metal screw-band top seal
Handmade   extra - wide - mouth   round,
    ground lip, in green
Side: two lines of rather old-style lettering:
    'GEM' and 'BUTTER JAR'
May be Hero Fruit Jar Co., Philadelphia,
    Pa., 1884-1909

GENUINE MASON (1)

Circa 1900-10
Mason shoulder seal
Machine-made round, in flint and light
    green
Side: 'Genuine,' in slanting script, above
    'MASON' in ribbon finial from the final
    "e"
Heel: 'I P G Co'
Illinois Pacific Glass Co., 1902-30

GENUINE MASON (2)

Slightly different style than (1) and without "I P G Co" identification

It was a jar of this style that was found with "GENUINE" peened out, and "Boyd" cut in script in its place. See BOYD MASON

GENUINE MASON (3)

Same as (1) except MASON in block letters but not on ribbon

G G Co

Circa 1935-45

Mason beaded neck style

Machine-made rounded square, in flint

Side: a monogram of "G G Co" in a wreath and ribbons

Back: three lines: 'GENERAL GROCERY Co.,' 'MANUFACTURERS,' and 'PORTLAND, ORE.'

Bottom: "O" and "I" interlacing a diamond

Owens Illinois Glass Co., Toledo, Ohio, 1929 to date

GILBERDS JAR

Circa 1883-85

Glass lid held by heavy wire passing completely around the jar, held at bottom by a groove, and on lid by *one* notch at the top

Handmade round, ground lip, in green

Side: 'GILBERDS' and 'JAR,' the upper and lower arcs of a circle around a five-pointed star

Maker unknown. For Gilberds Butter Tub Co., Jamestown, N.Y.

James Gilberds received Patent No. 282,188 for this seal and jar on July 31, 1883. It combined the Van Vliet (1881) all-around wire feature with a glass lid and a notch, or "stop" on top of the lid in place of the thumbscrew

GILBERDS IMPROVED JAR

Circa 1885

Glass lid with *two* notches, held by wire as in GILBERDS JAR

Handmade round, ground lip, in aqua and green

Side: 'GILBERDS' and 'JAR' above and below a five-pointed star as in the GILBERDS JAR. 'IMPROVED' is lettered across the star. A misplaced apostrophe appears below the S in Gilberds' name

Maker unknown

Patent No. 328,115, issued to James Gilberds on Oct. 13, 1885, had two features. One called for a second notch, half way up the crown of the glass lid, as a position of less tension, to allow air to escape during the boiling operation of canning. The other, with great modification, became THE DANDY, which see

GILLAND & Co.

Circa 1880-1900

Glass stopper, with cork ring as seal

Handmade very heavy round, ground lip, in light green

Side: 'GILLAND & Co.'

Back: 'LT'D., LONDON'

Bottom: 'S Y G B Co.'

South Yorkshire Glass Bottle Co., Yorks., Eng., dates unknown

G J [Gilchrist Jar]

Circa 1895

Mason shoulder seal, with inverted dome-shaped inner liner within wide-mouth zinc cap

Handmade wide-mouth round, in flint

Side: "G" and "J" interlaced as a monogram for Gilchrist Jar

Elmer Glass Works, Elmer, N.J., dates uncertain, for the Gilchrist Jar Co., Wilkes Barre, Pa.

Patent No. 536,870 was issued to Ruth A. Gilchrist on Apr. 2, 1895, and Design Patent D24,337 was issued to her on May 28, 1895. Both covered details of the shape of the inverted domed liner, which had the purpose of holding solid portions of the jar's contents below the liquid level, as well as to displace liquid during the act of sealing, so that liquid ran over the lip and excluded all air

Ruth A. Gilchrist and the Elmer Glass Works were sued because her jar infringed on a patent. They lost and both were bankrupted

G J Co (1)

Same as G J except "Co" also added. The "C," as well as the "o" within it, were within the "G," and intersected the rising stem of the "J"

G J Co (2)

Same as (1) except with neither "C" or "o" intersecting the "J." The "C" lay within the "G" to the left of the "J," and the "o" to the right of the "J"

G J Co MASON'S PATENT NOV 30th, 1858

Circa 1895

Mason shoulder seal

Handmade round, ground lip, in light green

Side: the G J Co monogram (1) below 'MASON'S,' arched, and above 'PATENT,' 'NOV 30$^{\underline{TH}}$' and '1858'

Elmer Glass Works, Elmer, N.J., dates unknown. For Gilchrist Jar Co., Wilkes Barre, Pa.

G J MASON'S PATENT NOV 30th, 1858

Same as G J Co MASON'S PATENT NOV 30th 1858, except only the letters "G" and "J" in the monogram

G with A and R as a monogram

An alternate monogram used by Ruth A. Gilchrist (the order of letters is R A G) and the Gilchrist Jar Co.

GLASSBORO TRADE MARK

Circa 1880-1900

Mason shoulder seal

Handmade round, ground lip, in deep green

Side: 'TRADE' and 'MARK' forming a circle below 'GLASSBORO,' arched

Whitney Brothers, Glassboro, N.J., 1837-87, and

Whitney Glass Works, Glassboro, N.J., 1887-1918

GLASSBORO IMPROVED

Circa 1880-1900

Glass lid and metal screw-band top seal

Handmade round, ground lip, in green and aqua

GLASSBORO TRADE MARK IMPROVED

Side: 'GLASSBORO' arched above 'TRADE' and 'MARK' which form a circle, and with 'IMPROVED' below

Whitney Brothers, Glassboro, N.J., 1837-87, and

Whitney Glass Works, Glassboro, N.J., 1887-1918

GLASS TOP

See both KERR GLASS TOP and GAYNER GLASS TOP

GLENHAVEN

Reported on a dealer's want-list, but not verified as a jar name

GLENNY

Reported on a dealer's want-list, but not verified as a jar name

GLENSHAW

MASON

GLENSHAW

Circa 1959-66 only

Mason beaded neck style

Machine-made round, in flint

Side: 'GLENSHAW' above a squared "G" in a square, above 'MASON'

Bottom: "G" in a square

Glenshaw Glass Co., Glenshaw, Pa., 1894 to date

See also MALLINGER and G SQUARE MASON

GLIDE

After the owner had reported this name to me, he found that it was a commercial jar and, in his words, he "put the axe to it." Hence, no description

GLOBE

Circa 1880

Glass lid, held by hemispherical cam moving in a socket, held by bail

Handmade round, ground lip, in green, flint, and amber

Side: 'GLOBE'

Lid: 'PAT MAY 25, 1880'

Maker unknown

GLOCKER

Circa 1911

Glass lid and metal clamp

Machine-made squat round, in blue-green

Side: five lines: 'GLOCKER' and 'TRADE MARK' arched above 'SANITARY,' 'PAT. 1911,' and 'OTHERS PENDING.' The "O" and "K" of GLOCKER are enlarged for emphasis of OK

Lid: repeats side lettering, except TRADE MARK

Maker unknown

GLOCKER
TRADE MARK
SANITARY
PAT. 1911
OTHERS PENDING

GLOCKER
PAT 1911
OTHERS PENDING
SANITARY

GOLDEN STATE (1)

Circa 1910

Metal lid with small screw threads

Machine-made wide-mouth round, in flint and sun-colored. Smaller sizes squat because of wide mouth

Side: "S" in a small triangle, flanked by 'PAT'D' and 'DEC. 20$\underline{TH}$ 1910' on left, and 'OTHER' and 'PATENTS PEND-

GOLDEN-STATE
PAT. DEC. 20TH 10 /S\ PATENTS PENDING
MASON

ING,' on right. 'GOLDEN STATE' arched above, 'TRADE' over the triangle and 'MARK' and 'MASON,' in a drooped arc, below the triangle

Bottom: 'SAN FRANCISCO' and 'BEN SCHLOSS'

Illinois Pacific Glass Co., San Francisco, Cal., 1902-30

Patent No. 979,183 was issued to Francis J. Mackin on Dec. 20, 1910, and assigned to Ben Schloss. Its feature was a grooved top with the object of preventing small cracks or crizzles in manufacture. These would allow air leakage in use. Mackin theorized that they would not form on the inner wall of the top groove. The patent called for a crimped metal lid, but in practice was changed to the small-threaded metal screw cap

GOLDEN STATE (2)

Same as (1) except 'BEN SCHLOSS MANUFACTURING CO.' and 'SAN FRANCISCO' in a circle on bottom

GOLDEN STATE (3)

Same as (1) except 'BEN SCHLOSS MFG. CO.' and 'SAN FRANCISCO' in a circle on bottom

GOLDEN STATE (4)

Same as (1) but without "TRADE" and "MARK"

GOLDEN STATE IMPROVED

Circa 1915

Mason shoulder seal

Machine-made round, in flint

Side: 'IMPROVED' over same design as in GOLDEN STATE (1), except patent date omitted

Bottom: bare
Illinois Pacific Glass Co., San Francisco,
Cal., 1902-30
Ben Schloss operated a pottery

GOOD HOUSE KEEPERS MASON JAR (1)

Circa 1935-46
Mason beaded neck design
Machine-made round, in flint
Side: four lines: 'GOOD,' 'HOUSE,' 'KEEPERS,' and 'MASON JAR'
Bottom: "O" and "I" in a diamond, and 'CUPPLES CO., ST. LOUIS'
Owens Illinois Glass Co., Toledo, Ohio, 1929 to date

GOOD
HOUSE
KEEPERS
MASON   JAR

GOOD HOUSE KEEPERS MASON JAR (2)

Same except rounded square shape

GOOD HOUSE KEEPERS REGULAR MASON

Circa 1935-46
Mason beaded neck design
Machine-made rounded square, in flint
Side: six lines: 'GOOD,' 'HOUSE,' 'KEEP-ERS,' "R" within a circle, 'REGULAR,' and 'MASON'
Owens Illinois Glass Co., Toledo, Ohio, 1929 to date

GOOD
HOUSE
KEEPERS
®
REGULAR
MASON

GOOD HOUSE KEEPERS WIDE MOUTH MASON

Circa 1935-46
Mason beaded neck design
Machine-made round, in flint
Side: six lines: 'GOOD,' 'HOUSE,' 'KEEP-

GOOD
HOUSE
KEEPERS
®
WIDE MOUTH
MASON

ERS,' "R" within a circle, 'WIDE MOUTH' and 'MASON'

Owens Illinois Glass Co., Toledo, Ohio, 1929 to date

GREEN MOUNTAIN (1)

Circa 1910

Lightning closure, old-style neck design

Machine-made round, in blue-green

Side: 'GREEN' and 'G. A. Co.' forming a circle, with 'MOUNTAIN' across a diameter

Maker unknown

GREEN MOUNTAIN (2)

Same as (1) except lettering in oval

GREEN MOUNTAIN (3)

Circa 1925

Lightning closure, adjustable neck design

Machine-made round, in flint and sun-colored

Side: in an arched-top square double outline: 'GREEN,' 'MOUNTAIN,' slanting, and 'G A Co.'

Maker unknown

GRIFFEN

Circa 1862

Glass lid, held down by cage-like cast-metal frame which has one or more spring arms toward the top center of the lid, and a ring-yoke having spiral contour to catch under two lugs in the neck

Handmade round, ground lip, in green

Bottom: in circle: 'GRIFFEN'S PATENT' and 'OCT 7 1862'

Maker unknown

John F. Griffen, New York City bottle
jobber, received Patent No. 36,612 on
Oct. 7, 1862, as an improvement over
H. D. Ludlow's Patent No. 33,002 of
Aug. 6, 1861, by adding the spring action
feature of the yoke. Griffen also advertised the EUREKA

GROOVE RING JAR, RAU'S IMPROVED

Groove-ring wax sealer

Handmade round, very smooth laid-on-ring
indicating late manufacture, in light
green

Side: four lines: 'RAU'S IMPROVED,'
and 'PAT. APPLIED FOR,' both lines
arched over 'GROOVE RING,' and 'JAR'

Fairmount Glass Co., Indianapolis, Ind.,
1888 to date

G SQUARE MASON

Circa 1930-40

Mason beaded neck design

Machine-made rounded square, in flint

Side: 'SQUARE' above a "G" in a square
and 'MASON'

Glenshaw Glass Co., Glenshaw, Pa., 1894
to date

H

HAINES

Circa 1870

Always found with a glass lid with two
spiral ramps around the edges on which
a wire yoke could be tightened. But note
the patent description, below

Handmade round, pressed laid-on-ring, in
light green and blue-green. Circular

grooves in lid and on top finish compress gasket material

Side: 'HAINES' arched over 'PATENT,' 'MARCH 1ˢᵀ,' and '1870'

Putnam Flint Glass Works, Putnam, Ohio, 1852-81 (Knittle)

HAINES'S

Same except spelled with an apostrophe and final "S"

HAINES COMBINATION

Same as HAINES except finish has very sharply "squared" profile, for which the meaning is unknown

HAINES IMPROVED

Jar reported, but not verified

Patent No. 100,396, of Mar. 1, 1870, was by Joel Haines, of West Middleburg, Ohio. The patent detailed a metal lid, formed with two spiral ramps on the edges, a sharp edge intended to cut into the rubber gasket, and a wire clip. Every lid so far seen has been of glass, and held by a flat metal clip rather than by wire. The several names for HAINES jars may be due to these changes

HALLE

CLEVELAND, O.

HALLE

Circa 1860-80

Groove-ring wax sealer

Handmade round, pressed laid-on-ring, in green

Side: two lines: 'HALLE' and 'CLEVE-LAND, O.'

Maker unknown

The Halle Brothers Department Store, of Cleveland, started in 1934, has no information about the jar bearing their name. It was probably made before the time of the Clarke Fruit Jar Co., Cleveland, Ohio, 1886-89, but there were other Cleveland glass houses

HAMILTON (1)

Circa 1865-73

Very primitive groove-ring wax sealer

Handmade round, mold blown with flat shoulder which was then tooled downward to form a groove for the wax, ground lip, in blue-green

Side: 'HAMILTON'

Hamilton Glass Works, Hamilton, Ont., 1865-93

Probably before 1873, since George Rutherford added his name when he took over the company in that year

HAMILTON (2)

Circa 1865-73

Glass lid and clamp rotating in two helical lugs in the neck

Handmade round, ground lip, in blue

Side: 'HAMILTON'

Hamilton Glass Works, Hamilton, Ont., 1865-93

HAMILTON GLASS WORKS (1)

Circa 1865-73

Glass lid held by yoke and central thumbscrew, similar to the 1862 MILLVILLE

Handmade round, ground lip, in blue

Front: 'HAMILTON' above 'GLASS WORKS'

Back: 'CLAMP JAR' and '1/2 GAL

Lid: 'HAMILTON GLASS WORKS'

Hamilton Glass Works, Hamilton, Ont., 1865-93

HAMILTON
GLASS WORKS

HAMILTON GLASS WORKS (2)

Circa 1865-73

Same as (1) except in front lettering style: 'HAMILTON' forming the top of an oval; 'GLASS WORKS' the bottom; 'No 3,' presumably a mold identification number, in the center

Do not confuse these jars with those of the Burlington Glass Works, also of Hamilton, Ont. But see also GEM by Rutherford of Hamilton Glass Works

HAMILTON & JONES

Very old pottery jar—age uncertain—possibly circa 1855-60

Top grooved for wax sealing

Wheel-turned, round pottery jar

Side: 'HAMILTON & JONES,' stamped before firing

Hamilton & Jones, Greensboro, Pa., dates unknown

HANSEE'S

See PALACE HOME JAR, HANSEE'S

HARRIS

Circa 1864

Friction side seal for metal cap

Handmade round, with lip reheated and pressed into tapered form in a dip mold, in dark green

Side: 'HARRIS'

Maker unknown

Elbridge Harris received Patent No. 41,575 for this seal on Feb. 9, 1864. The actual shape of the EUREKA jar, as made, followed this patent closer than it does the Dec. 27, 1864, patent that was issued John Griffen, New York bottle jobber, for the EUREKA

HARRIS IMPROVED

No description could be obtained for this jar, nor what made it improved

HARTELL'S GLASS AIR TIGHT COVER

HARTELL'S GLASS

AIRTIGHT COVER

Circa 1858

All-glass cap, fitting three helical lugs blown in jar neck, and sealing as a top seal on the ground lip, by a gasket within the cover

Handmade round, ground lip, in aqua

Lid: 'HARTELL'S GLASS AIR TIGHT COVER' completely circling the side of the cap, and 'PATENTED OCT. 19, 1858' in a circle on top

Maker unknown

Thomas R. Hartell, of Philadelphia, obtained Patent No. 21,831 on Oct. 19, 1858, for the mold that made the pressed cover in glass—not for the cover itself

HASEROT MASON PATENT

THE HASEROT
COMPANY
CLEVELAND
MASON
PATENT

Circa 1910-30

Mason shoulder seal

Machine-made round, in green and aqua

Side: five lines: 'THE HASEROT,' 'COMPANY,' 'CLEVELAND,' 'MASON,' and 'PATENT'

Maker unknown. The Haserot Company, still operating in Cleveland, Ohio, is a food-merchant house, and has no record of the jar

HAWLEY

Circa 1880-1900

Mason shoulder seal

Handmade round, ground lip, in green

Side: no lettering
Bottom: 'HAWLEY GLASS Co., HAW-LEY, PA.' in a circle
Hawley Glass Co., Hawley, Pa., 1872-1931

HAZEL

HAZEL

Circa 1896-1901
Lightning closure, old neck design
Machine-made round, in green, possibly the "Blue" machine
Side: 'HAZEL,' slightly arched
Hazel Glass Co., Washington, Pa., 1886-1902

HAZEL ATLAS E – Z SEAL

Circa 1902-15
Lightning closure, old neck design
Machine-made round, in flint
Side: three lines: 'HAZEL ATLAS' arched above 'E – Z' and 'SEAL'
Hazel Atlas Glass Co., Wheeling, W. Va., 1902-64

HAZEL ATLAS
LIGHTNING
SEAL

HAZEL ATLAS LIGHTNING SEAL (1)

Circa 1902-15
Lightning closure, old neck design
Machine-made round, in light green and amethyst
Side: three lines: 'HAZEL ATLAS' arched above 'LIGHTNING' and 'SEAL'
Hazel Atlas Glass Co., Wheeling, W. Va., 1902-64

HAZEL ATLAS LIGHTNING SEAL (2)

Circa 1915-40
Same as (1) but with Lightning beaded neck design

HAZEL ATLAS TRADE MARK, H over A

Circa 1925

Lightning closure, beaded neck design

Machine-made rounded square, in flint and blue tint

Bottom: Hazel Atlas trade mark, "H over A"

Hazel Atlas Glass Co., Wheeling, W. Va., 1902-64

The trade mark dates from about 1921. This is probably a commercial jar rather than a fruit jar as such

H & D with moldmaker's error

Circa 1910-30

Glass lid and metal screw-band top seal

Machine-made round, in light green. Lid is opal glass

Bottom: 'H & D.' The ampersand is cut backward

Maker unknown

H&D

HELME'S

See RAILROAD MILLS

HERMANN & CO., C.

Circa 1854-86

Stone (pottery) jar for cork stopper and wax seal

Wheel-turned pottery, round

Side: 'C. HERMANN & CO., MILWAU-KEE' stamped and fired

C. Hermann & Co., Milwaukee potters, 1854-86

MALTESE   PATTÉE

FORMEE   HERO

THE HERO CROSS IS UNIQUE

HERO CROSS

The cross used by the Hero Fruit Jar Company has been described variously as a Maltese Cross, as a Cross Pattée, and as a Cross Formée. It is none of these. The Maltese Cross differs in having the wings indented, for which reason it is also known as "the cross of eight points." In the Cross Pattée the indentation between the wings is formed by the arcs of a circle. The Cross Formée has simple angular indentations between the wings

The HERO CROSS is quite different from these. The indentations between the wings are parallel lines, connected at the bottom by a straight crossbar, as an inspection of the drawing will show. Search in books of heraldry disclosed nothing similar, except one military decoration in which the bottom of the indentation was a half-circle. Therefore the Hero Cross is unique unto itself, and seems to have been designed by Hero for the specific purpose

The cross originated about 1882 in the Hero Glass Works, and was lettered in the wings with H F J and Co when the company changed its name to Hero Fruit Jar Company in 1884. H G W was used before 1882

THE
HERO

HERO, THE (1)

Circa 1867
Glass lid and metal screw-band top seal
Handmade round, ground lip, in blue-green
Side: 'THE' above 'HERO'
Bottom: 'PAT NOV 26 67'
Hero Glass Works, Philadelphia, Pa., 1856-82

HERO, THE (2)

Same, except lettered 'THE HERO' on one line

THE HERO

HERO IMPROVED, THE

Circa 1869
Glass lid and metal screw-band top seal
Handmade round, ground lip, in blue-green
Side: three lines: 'THE,' 'HERO,' and 'IMPROVED'
Bottom: patent dates from 1861 to 1869
Hero Glass Works, Philadelphia, Pa., 1856-84

HERO CROSS with "HERO" (1)

Circa 1882
Glass lid and metal screw-band top seal
Handmade round, ground lip, in green, flint, and purple (sun-colored)
Side: 'HERO' arched above an unlettered HERO CROSS
Hero Glass Works, Philadelphia, Pa., 1856-84

HERO CROSS with "HERO" (2)

Same except with lettered cross, circa 1884 and later
Hero Fruit Jar Co., Philadelphia, Pa., 1884-1909

HERO CROSS with "HERO" (3)

Circa 1894
Lightning type closure, differing from Putnam's and with slightly different neck style
Handmade round, ground lip, in green and aqua
Side: 'HERO' arched over the lettered HERO CROSS. The lettering is light and the letters seriffed

Hero Fruit Jar Co., Philadelphia, Pa., 1884-1909

No patent date is given, but HERO came out with a "lightning" version of its own about ten or fifteen years after the Lightning patent and changed designs slightly in order to do so. The lever wire presses at the edge of the lid instead of in the center. A full loop on each side gives the necessary "spring" to the wire. The neck band is composed of two flat pieces of metal whose hooked ends join to form a bearing for the "eye" of the lever wire. The whole design has a "squarish" appearance, contrasting with the round of the Lightning jar

HERO CROSS with "HERO" (4)

Same except more of a Putnam-style neck

HERO CROSS with MASON'S IMPROVED (1)

Circa 1882-84

Glass lid and metal screw-band top seal

Handmade round, ground lip, in aqua

Side: 'MASON'S' arched above an unlettered HERO CROSS, and 'IMPROVED,' below

Bottom: 'PAT NOV 26 67'

Hero Glass Works, Philadelphia, Pa., 1856-84

HERO CROSS with MASON'S IMPROVED (2)

Same as (1) except order is: HERO CROSS, unlettered, above 'MASON'S,' arched, above 'IMPROVED'

HERO CROSS with MASON'S IMPROVED (3)

Same as (1) in order: 'MASON'S' arched above lettered HERO CROSS and 'IM-PROVED' but the lettered cross indicates circa 1884 or later

HERO CROSS with MASON'S IMPROVED (4)

Same order as (2) but with lettered cross of post-1884

HERO CROSS with MASON'S IMPROVED (5)

Same as (3) but with different lettering style, notably the curling right leg of the "R," and general slenderness of letters

HERO CROSS with MASON'S IMPROVED (6)

Same as (3) except HERO CROSS is below both 'MASON'S,' arched, and 'IM-PROVED'

HERO CROSS with MASON'S PATENT NOV 30th 1858

Circa 1882-84

Mason shoulder seal

Handmade round, ground lip, in flint, green, and sun-colored

Side: 'MASON'S' arched over unlettered HERO CROSS, followed by 'PATENT,' 'NOV 30TH,' and '1858'

Hero Glass Works, Philadelphia, Pa., 1856-84

HERO CROSS and C F J Co monogram with MASON'S PATENT NOV 30th 1858 (1)

Circa 1882-84

Mason shoulder seal

Handmade round, ground lip, in green, flint, and sun-colored

Side: the unlettered HERO CROSS above an arched 'MASON'S.' Below it is the "C F J Co" monogram of the Consolidated Fruit Jar Co., followed by 'PATENT,' 'NOV 30$^{\underline{TH}}$,' and '1858'

Hero Glass Works, Philadelphia, Pa., 1856-84

This jar has great significance. It shows that Hero had acquired the right to use the Consolidated trade mark, whose copyright had not yet expired. The position of the cross indicates that it has been added to an existing jar mold already having the Consolidated monogram. This jar is one of the best proofs in a series of related facts. Hero must have dominated since it continued until 1909. Consolidated faded from sight as a jar supplier—it still exists as a metals company. Mason went back to New York. The Clyde Glass Works, which had made Consolidated's jars, failed after several years trying to make and sell fruit jars under its own name. A company with no relation to Mason "borrowed" his name and called itself the "Mason Fruit Jar Co." Hero finally dropped its own line of named jars: PEARL, GEM, HERO, PORCELAIN LINED, etc., and concentrated on the Mason line. But by that time the patents had ran out, and everyone else was making them, also

HERO CROSS and C F J Co monogram with MASON'S PATENT NOV 30th 1858 (2)

Same as (1) except that the C F J Co monogram is in double outline

HERO CROSS with "S" and MASON'S PATENT 1858

Circa 1882-84

Mason shoulder seal

Handmade round, ground lip, in green

Side: HERO CROSS above an arched 'MASON'S' followed by 'S,' 'PATENT,' and '1858.' The cross is unlettered and departs slightly from the usual form. May be early

Hero Glass Works, Philadelphia, Pa., 1856-84

HERO IMPROVED

Circa 1884-90

Glass lid and metal screw-band top seal

Handmade round, ground lip, in light green

Side: 'HERO' above 'IMPROVED'

Hero Fruit Jar Co., Philadelphia, Pa., 1884-1909

HEROINE, THE

Circa 1865-79

Glass lid and metal screw-band top seal

Handmade round, ground lip, in light green

Side: three lines: 'THE,' 'HERO,' and 'INE'

Bottom: 'CUNNINGHAM & IHMSEN, PITTSBURGH, PA.' in a circle, and 'NOV 26 67' in center

Cunningham & Ihmsen, Pittsburgh, Pa., 1865-79

See also CUNNINGHAMS & Co.; D. O. CUNNINGHAM & CO.

This jar must have been made upon license from Hero since it bears the Hero patent date. It is also known that Hero licensed the San Francisco & Pacific Glass Works, hence defining one of their policies

H F G Co

Report of these initials by a collector could not be confirmed. May be confused with H F J Co

H F J Co

See various HERO items, as these are the initials of the Hero Fruit Jar Company

H G W as a monogram

See GEM as these are the initials of the Hero Glass Works, which became the Hero Fruit Jar Co. in 1884

HIGH GRADE, THE, with MASON'S PATENT NOV 30th 1858

Circa 1910-20

Mason shoulder seal

Machine-made round, in flint

Front: four lines: 'THE HIGH GRADE' arched over 'MF'G'D FOR,' 'KINNEY &

LEVAN,' and 'CLEVELAND O.'

Back: 'MASON'S' arched above 'PATENT,' 'NOV 30th,' and '1858'

Maker unknown. Kinney & Levan were glassware jobbers.

HOLZ CLARK & TAYLOR (1)

Circa 1871-80

Glass-faced, metal screw stopper, requiring internal threads on jar

Handmade round, pressed laid-on-ring, in dark green, aqua, and amber

Side: 'HOLZ CLARK & TAYLOR' in an arched semi-circle, across the diameter of which is 'SALEM NJ'

Bottom: 'PAT APPLIED FOR'

Holz, Clark & Taylor, Salem, N.J., 1860s to 1879 when the plant was leased to John Gayner, who eventually purchased it. Incorporated as Gayner Glass Works in 1898

One of the few internal-thread stopper-type seals. See also CLARK'S PEERLESS, LEOTRIC, and ELECTRIC

William Taylor and Charles Hodgetts were granted Patent No. 117,236 on July 18, 1871, not for the threaded-stopper seal, but for a protective ceramic facing on it to protect the food contents. The patent rights were assigned to Louis [Lewis] R. Boyd since the latter had patented his zinc cap inner glass lining only two years before and had prior rights

HOLZ CLARK & TAYLOR (2)

Same except 'THE SALEM JAR' on back

HOLZ CLARK & TAYLOR (3)

Circa 1880
Same as (1) except converted to glass
   stopper held by a metal screw-band. Internal thread abandoned

HOME PACKER

See JEANNETTE HOME PACKER

HOM-PAK

Circa 1940
Mason beaded neck seal
Machine-made round, in flint
Side: 'HOM-PAK'
Bottom: "H" in a triangle
J. T. & A. Hamilton, Pittsburgh, Pa., 1884-
   1944

HOOSIER JAR

Circa 1890-1910
Mason shoulder seal
Handmade heavy round, ground lip, in
   aqua
Side: 'HOOSIER' arched above 'JAR'
Maker unknown

HORMEL FINE FOOD

Circa 1920-35
Lightning closure, beaded neck style
Machine-made round, in flint
Side: 'HORMEL FINE FOOD'
Bottom: H over A trade mark
Hazel Atlas Glass Co., Wheeling W. Va.,
   1902-64

HOUR GLASS

Circa 1870
Glass lid and metal screw-band top seal
Handmade round, ground lid, in green
Side: a large, hour-glass-shaped shield,

(HOUR GLASS—SEE GEM)

with no lettering

Hero Glass Works, Philadelphia, Pa., 1856-84

The jar may be the result of a mold-maker's error in not finishing the cutting on molds for GEM and MASON'S PATENT NOV 30th 1858 since it also appears on certain of both these jars

HOWE, THE

Circa 1888

Class lid top seal, held by single wire whose coiled ends were held by circular depressions in the neck of the jar

Handmade round, ground lip, in light green and aqua

Side: 'THE HOWE,' 'SCRANTON,' and 'PA'

Lid: 'PAT FEB'Y 28/88'

Maker unknown

THE HOWE

SCRANTON

PA

HOWE JAR, THE

Same except 'JAR' added as another line below 'THE HOWE'

H & R

Circa 1860-80

Groove-ring wax sealer

Handmade round, pressed laid-on-ring, in green

Bottom: 'H & R'

Maker unknown

H & R

H & S

Circa 1880-1900

Possible side seal because of bulged finish

Handmade squat round, ground lip, in light green

Side: 'H & S'

Maker unknown

I

IDEAL, LEGRAND

Circa 1900-20
Cup-shaped finish, stopper unknown
Machine-made round, in light green
Side: a monogram of "L I J Co," exact order of letters unknown. Above it, 'LEGRAND IDEAL,' arched; below it, 'VACUUM' and 'JAR' in two lines
Maker unknown

IDEAL, THE

Circa 1880-1900
Mason shoulder seal
Handmade round, ground lip, in flint
Side: 'THE' slightly arched above 'IDEAL,' the latter in seriffed letters
Maker unknown

IDEAL WIDE MOUTH JAR

Circa 1920
Mason beaded neck design
Machine-made wide-mouth round, in flint
Side: a shield with three lines: 'IDEAL,' 'WIDE MOUTH,' and 'JAR.' Below the shield, 'MADE IN CANADA'
Bottom: "D" in a diamond
Dominion Glass Co., Montreal, Que., 1913 to date

L'IDEALE (THE IDEAL)

Modern French jar
Glass lid, hinged on one side, with a snap lock on the other
Machine-made round, in flint
Side 'L'IDEALE'
Manufactures des Glaces et Produits Chimiques de Saint Gobain, Chauney et Ciney, France

I G Co

Circa 1895-1905

Mason shoulder seal

Machine-made very heavy round, probably semi-automatic, in aqua

Bottom: arched 'I G Co'

Illinois Glass Co., Alton, Ill., 1873-1929

This trade mark used until about 1905, then placed in a diamond. Could not have been made before 1895 first semi-automatic machines

I G Co with MASON'S PATENT NOV 30th 1858 (1)

Circa 1906-14

Mason shoulder seal

Machine-made round, in light green

Side: a monogram, consisting of a tall "I," bisected by a nesting of a large "G," a smaller "C," and a still smaller "O." The "I" and "G" are double outlined. Below, in four lines: 'MASON'S' arched above 'PATENT,' 'NOV 30ᵀᴴ,' and '1858'

Illinois Glass Co., Alton, Ill., 1873-1929

The design of the monogram first appeared in their 1906 catalog and was used on fruit jars only until about 1914

I G Co with MASON'S PATENT NOV 30th 1858 (2)

Same except monogram slightly changed. The "C" and "O" do not bisect the "I" —"C" lies within the "G" but to the left of "I" and "O" lies within the "G" and to the right of "I"

IMPERIAL, THE (1)

Circa 1880-85

Glass lid and metal screw-band top seal

Handmade round, ground lip, in blue tint

Side: "E," "G," and "Co" intertwined as a large monogram with doubly outlined letters, with 'THE' arched above it and 'IMPERIAL' arched below it

Excelsior Glass Co., St. Johns, Que., 1879; Montreal, Que., 1880-85. Became North American Glass Co. in 1885

IMPERIAL, THE (2)

Circa 1886

Glass lid having ramps on its edges to engage hooks from a heavy wire half circling from a bead on the jar neck

Handmade round, ground lip, in green

Side: 'THE' above 'IMPERIAL'

Lid: 'PAT APRIL 20th, 1886'

Maker unknown

Patent No. 340,428 was issued to J. L. de Steiger and E. A. de Steiger of La Salle, Ill. The first named was to invent the COLUMBIA JAR ten years later

IMPERIAL BRAND, TRUE'S

Circa 1908-28

Lightning closure, dimple neck design

Machine-made round, in flint and light green

Side: design of crown, wreath, and flags. In three lines below, on draped banner: 'J. W. TRUE,' 'TRUE'S IMPERIAL BRAND,' and 'PORTLAND, ME.'

Maker unknown, but probably jobbed through Smalley, Kivlan & Onthank of Boston, Mass., who used the same flag, crown, and wreath design on their KING and WEARS jars

There is some confusion about the initials. Jonathan True started a food business in 1856, with D. W. True as part owner, and his initials, though not given, may have been "J. W." D. W. True became full owner in 1866, incorporated it in 1882 as "D. W. True," and continued it until his death in 1928

INDEPENDENT

Circa 1882

Mason shoulder seal with all-glass cap

Handmade round, ground lip, in flint and light green

Side: 'INDEPENDENT' in a broad arch

Lid: 'PAT OCT 24 1882'

Independent Glass Co., Pittsburgh, Pa., 1876-?

See McKearin, p. 610. Independent advertised: "crystal clear fruit jars; air tight lids"

See also FRANKLIN-DEXTER whose lids show the same patent date. The only corresponding patent found was by Anton Luger, No. 266,375, but it does not correspond since it was for a *hinged* glass lid

INDEPENDENT JAR

Same as INDEPENDENT except the word "JAR" is added below

I O Co with MASON'S PATENT NOV 30th 1858

Circa 1880-1900

Mason shoulder seal

Handmade round, ground lip, in light green

Side: a monogram, consisting of a large, spindle-shaped "I," in double outline,

MASON'S
PATENT
NOV 30TH
1858

bisecting a large "C." An "O" is within the "C." Another, but small, "o" lies within the opening of the "C." Above is 'MASON'S,' arched and below are three lines: 'PATENT,' 'NOV 30TH,' and '1858'

Maker unknown

See L G Co for a very similar monogram, differing only as if the "I" were not completed

IVANHOE (1)

Late modern
Lightning closure, beaded neck design
Machine-made round, in flint
Bottom: '797,' 'IVANHOE,' and '11'
Probably made by Hazel Atlas for Ivanhoe Fine Foods

IVANHOE (2)

Same except Lightning dimple neck design

J

JAR, IMPROVED

Circa 1915
Glass lid and metal screw-band top seal
Machine-made round, in flint
Side: 'Improved' above 'Jar,' in two lines of slanting script, over 'IMPERIAL,' in block letters, above "Qt"
Dominion Glass Co., Montreal, Que., 1913 to date

JAR SALT

1940 to modern
Mason beaded neck design
Machine-made round, in flint
Side: three lines: "JAR SALT" arched above 'DETROIT SALT Co.' and 'MASON'S PAT'
Maker unknown

J & B FRUIT JAR

Circa 1898
Mason shoulder seal
Handmade round, ground lip, with octagonal shoulder, in aqua
Side: an octagon enclosing 'J. & B.' Below is 'FRUIT JAR' and 'PAT'D JUNE 14TH, 1898'
Maker unknown
Patent No. 605,482 by S. P. Jaggard of Blackwood, N.J., discloses that the shoulder was octagonal so that a closed end octagonal spanner wrench at the shoulder, and a similar smaller wrench at the octagonal top of the zinc cap, could be used to tighten and loosen the seal

JEANNETTE HOME PACKER (1)

Circa 1920-30
Mason beaded neck design, sold with glass lid and metal screw-band as a top seal
Machine-made round, in flint
Side 'Jeannette,' in capital and lower case letters, arched over a "J" in a square, followed by 'MASON' in block letters, and 'Home Packer,' in capital and lower case letters

Lid: "J" in a square, above 'MASON'

Jeannette Glass Co., Jeannette, Pa., 1898 to date

Jeannette stopped making bottles and jars about 1930 to concentrate on fine tableware, which they still make

JEANNETTE HOME PACKER (2)

Circa 1900

Mason shoulder seal

Handmade round, ground lip, in flint

Side: 'JEANNETTE'

Jeannette Glass Co., Jeannette, Pa., 1898 to date

JEWEL JAR (1)

Circa 1915-20

Glass lid and metal screw-band top seal

Machine-made round, in flint

Side: two lines: 'JEWEL' and 'JAR' in a doubly outlined panel

Consumers Glass Co., Toronto, Ont., 1917 to date

JEWEL JAR (2)

Same except that the panel is omitted, and with the addition of 'MADE IN CANADA,' which indicates manufacture after 1920

J H F as a ligature

See FLICKENGER, J. H.

JOHNSON & JOHNSON (1)

Used 1887-1891

Glass lid and clamp, see COHANSEY (3) of 1876

Handmade square, ground lip, in amber and blue

Side: two lines reading vertically: 'JOHN-
SON & JOHNSON' and 'NEW BRUNS-
WICK, N.J. U.S.A.'
Cohansey Glass Manufacturing Co., Philadelphia, Pa., 1870-1900
Johnson & Johnson used this jar holding
slightly more than a quart to hold moist
dressings, which were sterilized in the
sealed container, so that moisture and
sterility would not be lost

JOHNSON & JOHNSON (2)

Same except with 'NEW YORK' replacing
'NEW BRUNSWICK, N.J.'

JOHNSON & JOHNSON (3)

Used 1891-95
Glass lid and metal screw-band top seal
Handmade square, ground lip, in cobalt
blue
Side: same as (1)
Cumberland Glass Co., Bridgeton, N.J.,
1882-1920
Cumberland was an early cobalt-blue
specialist, whose chief customer was the
Emerson Drug Co., Baltimore (makers
of Bromo Seltzer) until they built their
own Maryland Glass Co.

JOHNSON & JOHNSON (4)

Same as (3) except "NEW YORK U.S.A."
as the address

JOHNSON & JOHNSON (5)

Used 1896-99
Safety Valve seal; glass lid held by spring
and cam lever
Handmade square, ground lip, in amber
Side: Same as (1)

Cumberland Glass Manufacturing Co., Bridgeton, N.J., 1882-1920. "Manufacturing" was added to glass company name in 1896

JOHNSON & JOHNSON (6)

Same as (5) except "NEW YORK U.S.A." as address

JOHNSON & JOHNSON (7)

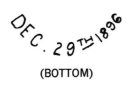

(BOTTOM)

Used 1900-13

Columbia seal; glass lid with ramps for tightening yoke

Handmade square, ground lip, in amber

Side: same as (1)

Bottom: 'PATENTED' and 'Dec. 29TH, 1896' in a circle; 'COLUMBIA' across the diameter

Cumberland Glass Manufacturing Co., Bridgeton, N.J., 1882-1920

JOHNSON & JOHNSON (8)

Same as (7) except "NEW YORK U.S.A." as address

JOHNSON & JOHNSON (9)

Used 1905-13

Glass lid and metal screw-band top seal

Handmade square, ground lip, in amber. [Amber indicates a later date than (3)]

Side: same as (1)

Cumberland Glass Manufacturing Co., Bridgeton, N.J., 1882-1920

JOHNSON & JOHNSON (10)

Same as (9) except "NEW YORK U.S.A." as an address

K

"K"

Circa 1860-80
Groove-ring wax sealer
Handmade round, pressed laid-on-ring, in
  dark green
Bottom: 'K' and 'MONROE Co, OHIO'
Maker unknown

KALAMAZOO, THE

THE KALAMAZOO

Circa 1920-29
Mason beaded neck design

JAY B. RHODES COMPANY

Machine-made round, in flint

KALAMAZOO MICHICAN

Side: three lines: 'THE KALAMAZOO,'
  'JAY B. RHODES COMPANY,' and
  'KALAMAZOO MICHIGAN'
Bottom: "I" in a diamond
Illinois Glass Co., Alton, Ill., 1873-1929

K B G Co monograms

See KILNER monogram

K C MASON

Circa 1915-30
Mason shoulder seal
Machine-made rounded square, in flint
Side: four lines: 'K C,' very large and
  doubly outlined, above 'FINEST
  QUALITY,' in a V-shaped panel,
  'MASON,' and 'SQUARE SPACE
  SAVER STYLE'
Maker unknown

KEEFFER'S No. 1

Circa 1870
Internal-screw stopper, first may have
  been in glass, but later in metal
Handmade round, pressed laid-on-ring, in
  blue-green

Side: 'KEEFFER'S arched over 'No. 1'

Lid: 'PAT DEC 20th, 1870' (Also reported preceeded by 'C.M. KEEFFER')

Maker may be Holz, Clark & Taylor, since William Taylor patented, No. 88,439, on July 18, 1871, an improvement calling for a glass facing to the metal lid

A different sealing type but with the same patent date, was lettered "KIEFFER'S No. 1," which see. The patent found for this date, by Peter John Biesenbach, agreed with the KIEFFER No. 1

KENNEY'S, MANUFACTURED FOR

This name appeared on a dealer's want-list, but has not been seen, nor verified

KENTUCKY

Circa 1855-73

Groove-ring wax sealer

Handmade round, pressed laid-on-ring, in green

Side: 'KENTUCKY' and 'L G Co.'

Louisville Glass Co., Louisville, Ky., 1855-73. See L G W and K Y G W; also McKearin, p. 606, and Knittle, p. 416. Formerly known as the Kentucky Glass Works, hence the name KENTUCKY

KERR

Kerr jars will be found to have minor differences in lettering style as well as the factory city shown on the bottom. See ECONOMY for jars made before the adoption of the KERR trade mark in 1912-16

KERR ECONOMY (1)

Circa 1912-15

Metal lid with permanently adhered, heat-softening, rubber gasket, held to jar while processing by means of a narrow, flat spring clip

Machine-made round, in flint. Will sun-color

Side: 'Kerr' and 'Economy,' in two lines of rising script, above 'TRADE MARK.' The "E" of "Economy" does not connect with the "c." Double underline does not make a point

Bottom: 'Kerr Glass Manufacturing Co., Chicago., Ill.' in a circle

Kerr Glass Manufacturing Co., Chicago, Ill. This was the sales office. From 1909 to 1912 the factory was at Altoona, Kan.; then at Sand Springs, Okla. When the sales office was moved to Sand Springs in 1915, the bottom marking was changed. In 1915 the Kerr Glass Company was set up, also at Sand Springs, as the manufacturing control

(CHICAGO)

KERR ECONOMY (2)

Same as (1) except the "E" is looped to-ward "c" and without underline

(CHICAGO)

KERR ECONOMY (3)

Same as (1) except that "Economy" appears within quotation marks and double underline makes a point

(CHICAGO)

TRADE MARK

(CHICAGO)

KERR ECONOMY (4)

Same as (1) except that "Economy" appears within quotation marks, and "E" joins "c" completely

Kerr "Economy"

TRADE MARK

(SAND SPRINGS)

KERR ECONOMY (5)

Circa 1915-19

Same as (1) except address is given as Sand Springs, Okla., and quotation marks enclose "Economy"

Kerr

GLASS TOP

KERR GLASS TOP

Circa 1941-45

Lightning closure, beaded neck style

Machine-made rounded square, in flint

Side: two lines: 'Kerr,' in script, above 'GLASS TOP'

These jars were made for Kerr by Hazel Atlas Glass Co., Wheeling, W. Va., 1902-64

Kerr

GLASS TOP

MASON

KERR GLASS TOP MASON (1)

Circa 1941-45

Mason beaded seal, sold with glass lid and metal screw-band as top seal

Machine-made round, in flint

Side: three lines: 'Kerr,' in script, 'GLASS TOP' and 'MASON'

Kerr Glass Maunfacturing Corp., Los Angeles, Cal., 1903 to date, except for name changes

KERR GLASS TOP MASON (2)

Same except in rounded square shape

KERR SELF SEALING MASON (1)

Circa 1915-19

Mason beaded neck seal, with two-piece metal lid and screw-band, heat-softening rubber gasket

Machine-made round, in flint and blue

Side: four lines: 'Kerr,' in script, above 'SELF SEALING,' with both lines in large letters, followed by 'TRADE MARK REG' in ribbon finial from the "G," and 'MASON.' The words "SELF SEALING" are in quotation marks

Bottom: 'Sand Springs'

Kerr Glass Manufacturing Co., Sand Springs, Okla., 1903 to date with several name changes

KERR SELF SEALING MASON (2)

Same as (1) except bottom bare, indicating post-1919 manufacture. "SELF SEALING" not in quotation marks and has 'PATENTED' below and to the right of the ribbon

KERR SELF SEALING MASON (3)

Same as (1) except "SELF SEALING" in much smaller letters

KERR SELF SEALING MASON (4)

Same as (3) except entire lettering panel and letters are narrower

KERR SELF SEALING MASON (5)

Same as (3) except a line: 'PAT AUG 31, 1915' added above MASON

KERR SELF SEALING WIDE MOUTH

Circa 1920-40

Mason beaded neck design

Machine-made wide-mouth round, in flint and light green

Side: four lines: 'Kerr,' in script, 'SELF SEALING,' in small letters and in quotes, 'TRADE MARK REG,' on ribbon finial, and 'WIDE MOUTH'

Kerr Glass Manufacturing Co., Los Angeles, Cal., 1903 to date

KERR SELF SEALING PATENTED WIDE MOUTH

Same as KERR SELF SEALING WIDE MOUTH except 'PATENTED' added before 'WIDE MOUTH'

Kerr " SELF SEALING " TRADE MARK REG

PATENTED

WIDE MOUTH

KERR SELF SEALING WIDE MOUTH MASON

Same as KERR SELF SEALING WIDE MOUTH except 'MASON' added after 'WIDE MOUTH'

Kerr " SELF SEALING " TRADE MARK REG

WIDE MOUTH

MASON

KEYSTONE

Circa 1900-15
Lightning closure, old-style neck design
Machine-made round, in flint
Side: three lines: 'TRADE MARK,' arched, 'KEYSTONE,' in seriffed letters, and 'REGISTERED'
Maker unknown. See more keystones (figures) under MASON

TRADE MARK

KEYSTONE

REGISTERED

K – G

Circa 1915-29
Lightning closure, beaded neck design
Machine-made round, in flint
Bottom: 'K – G' in an oval panel

Kearns-Gorsuch Glass Co., Zanesville, Ohio, 1895-1929. Hazel Atlas bought Kearns-Gorsuch in 1920; changed name in 1929

Gearge Kearns and the Kearns family of brothers were in the glass-bottle business in Pittsburgh in 1838. There is a romantic story that they loaded their glass-blowing equipment on a scow, bound for Louisville, in 1842 and were driven up a "creek" to avoid a storm— but it is a long way *up* the Muskingum River to Zanesville. Kearns bought the old Shepard glass plant and the company became Kearns-Gorsuch after a number of partnerships. For one of them, see K H & G, following

K H & G

Circa 1876

Groove-ring wax sealer

Handmade round, pressed laid-on-ring, in green

Bottom: 'K H & G' and 'Z O'

Kearns, Herderson & Gorsuch, Zanesville, Ohio, 1876-95

KIEFFER'S No. 1

Circa 1870

Glass lid, stopper seal without screw threads held by three-pronged yoke

Handmade round, pressed laid-on-ring, in light green

Side: 'KIEFFER'S' arched above 'No. 1'

Lid: 'PAT. DEC. 20TH, 1870'

Maker unknown

The patent is Design Patent No. D4,522, by Peter John Biesenbach, and describes the details of the yoke only. See also KEEFFER'S No. 1

KILNER JAR, THE (1)

Circa 1910-25

Glass lid and metal screw-band top seal

Machine-made round, in flint

Side: three lines: 'THE,' 'KILNER,' in quotes, and 'JAR'

Lid: 'ORIGINAL KILNER JAR LID' in a circle

Kilner Bros., Ltd., Conisbrough and Thornhill Lees, Yorks, Eng., 1873-1937 (Kilner Bros. Glass Co., 1863-73)

KILNER JAR, THE (2)

A Kilner jar has been reported with a ground lip, but not verified

KILNER monogram, K B G Co, with MASON'S PATENT

Circa 1870

Mason shoulder seal

Handmade round, ground lip, in green

Side: a monogram of large "K" and "G," doubly outlined, with "B" interlacing the left leg of the "K," and "C" the right leg of the "K," followed by a small "o." 'MASON'S' is arched above it, and 'PATENT' below

Kilner Bros. Glass Co., Conisbrough and Thornhill Lees, Yorks, Eng., 1863-73

KILNER monogram, K B G Co, with MASON'S PATENT NOV 30th, 1858

Circa 1870

Mason shoulder seal

Handmade round, ground lip, in green and light green

Side: a different monogram, with a large "K" interlaced by a large "G." "B" interlaces the left side of the "G"; "C" is to the right of the "K," within the "G,"

with "o" in the opening of the "G."
MASON'S is arched above, while below
are 'PATENT,''NOV 30ᵀᴴ,' and '1858'
Kilner Bros. Glass Co., Conisbrough and
Thornhill Lees, Yorks, Eng., 1863-73

KILNER monogram, K B G Co, with MASON'S PATENT and K B L^D

A variant of the KILNER MASON'S
PATENT, made after 1873, as identified
by K B L^D, for Kilner Bros. Ltd., on the
bottom

KILNER monogram, K B G Co, with MASON'S PATENT and K B L

Another variant of KILNER MASON'S
PATENT, made after 1873, as identified
by K B L, for Kilner Bros. Ltd.

KINNEY & LEVAN

See HIGH GRADE

KING (1)

Circa 1907-19
Lightning closure, adjustable design to
change spring tension
Machine-made oval, in flint
Side: 'KING' slanting across a banner, a
flag on each side, with a wreath and
crown above. Banner and crown are
stippled
Bottom: in a circle: 'SMALLEY, KIVLAN
& ONTHANK, BOSTON'
Unknown maker for Smalley, Kivlan &
Onthank, Boston jobbers of china,
pottery, and glassware

KING (2)

Same, except that the crown and wreath are replaced by the face of a bearded man and banner is plain

See IMPERIAL BRAND, TRUE'S and WEARS for very similar jar shape and decoration

KINSELLA 1874 TRUE MASON

Not 1874 but circa 1915-30

Mason beaded neck design

Machine-made round, in flint and light green

Side: four lines: 'Kinsella,' in descending script, '1874,' 'TRUE,' and 'MASON'

Maker unknown

1874 must refer to a Kinsella anniversary of some kind. It is not the date of any Mason patent, and the beaded seal dates after 1915-20

KIVLAN & ONTHANK (1)

Circa 1921 when Hazel Atlas made jars for them

Glass lid, held by twin toggles on opposite sides

Machine-made squat round, in pinkish amber

Bottom: 'KIVLAN & ONTHANK, BOSTON,' in circle; Hazel Atlas trade mark in center, with 'PAT$\underline{\mathrm{D}}$' above it, and 'June 28, 21' below

Hazel Atlas Glass Co., Wheeling, W. Va., 1902-64, for Kivlan & Onthank, Boston jobbers of china, glassware, and pottery

John Algeo of Hazel Atlas tells me that Kivlan & Onthank used many suppliers from year to year, often over-ordering their supply, and sometimes changing suppliers after a disagreement

KIVLAN & ONTHANK (2)

Circa 1922

Same as (1) except an "I' in a diamond as the trade mark of the Illinois Glass Co., Alton, Ill., 1873-1929, placed on the bottom

Patent No. 1,383,215 was issued to John Kivlan on June 28, 1921, for his improved design of his 1909 patent. The linkage was reduced to two elements, and a groove circling the top edge of the lid held the hooked end of the toggle from slipping off. It was again changed in 1929

KLINE, A. R.

Circa 1863

Glass stopper, with rubber ring seal, in tapered neck

Handmade round, pressed laid-on-ring, in blue and blue-green

Stopper: 'A. R. KLINE' and 'PAT OCT 27 1863'

Maker unknown

Patent No. 40,415 was issued to A. R. Kline, of Philadelphia, Pa., on Oct. 27, 1863, for a pure stopper design. The patent picture of the stopper showed a knob not seen on any jar

KLINE'S, MADE FOR

This jar reported but not verified

KNIGHT PACKING CO.

Circa 1925-30

Mason beaded neck design

Machine-made round, in flint

Bottom: In circle, 'KNIGHT PACKING CO.' around "P C" in a divided rectangle

Pacific Coast Glass Co., San Francisco, Cal., 1925-30

KNOWLTON VACUUM FRUIT JAR (1)

Circa 1903-10

Glass lid under metal disc spring, held by perforated metal cap

Handmade round, ground lip, in flint, green, and blue

Side: 'KNOWLTON VACUUM' in an arch over a five-pointed star, and 'FRUIT JAR' below the star

Maker unknown

Patent No. 727,808 was issued to Dallas Knowlton on May 12, 1903, for substantially this design, but he changed it as in (2)

KNOWLTON VACUUM FRUIT JAR (2)

Circa 1903-10

Glass lid with perforated full cap to give spring action

Machine-made round, in flint, green, and blue

Side: 'KNOWLTON VACUUM' arched above a star and 'FRUIT JAR' below the star

Maker unknown

This design, which does not have the spring disc, is the commonly known KNOWLTON

KNOX

K

MASON

KNOX MASON (1)

Circa 1924-51
Mason beaded neck design
Machine-made round, in flint
Side: 'KNOX' above a "K" in a keystone,
below which is 'MASON'
Knox Glass Associates, Knox, Pa., 1924-51

KNOX MASON (2)

Same, except a rounded square jar

KOENIG

KOENIG

Circa 1925
Mason beaded neck design
Machine-made rounded square, in flint
Side: 'KOENIG' above a very large '5¢'
Maker unknown. Koenig was a "dime-
store" group

KOHRS

Circa 1930-40
Lightning closure, dimple style neck
design
Machine-made round, in flint
Side: in an oval outline: 'Kohrs,' in script,
above 'DAVENPORT, IA.'
Bottom, intersecting "O," "I," and a
diamond
Owens Illinois Glass Co., Toledo, Ohio,
1929 to date
Trade mark used 1929-56

K Y G W

Circa 1855—probably continued by Louisville Glass Works

Groove-ring wax sealer

Handmade round, pressed laid-on-ring, in green

Bottom: 'K Y G W'

Kentucky Glass Works, Louisville, Ky., 1849-55

Louisville Glass Works, Louisville, Ky., 1855-85 or later

Since the Arthur groove-ring patent is dated Jan. 2, 1855, K Y G W could have made the jar only in its last year—except that there is some indication that Arthur's patent relates only to an improvement of an existing design

K Y G W Co

A variation of the bottom lettering of K Y G W

See also KENTUCKY and L G W

L

LAFAYETTE (1)

Circa 1864

Friction side seal, based on Harris patent of Feb. 9, 1864, No. 41,575

Handmade round, fired lip (occasionally also ground), in green and aqua

Side: the signature, 'Lafayette' in script

Maker unknown

LAFAYETTE (2)

Same except bottom has 'PAT. DEC. 27, 1864' in a circle

This was J. F. Griffen's patent No. 45,601, improving the Harris design

LAFAYETTE (3)

Same except signature underscored

LAFAYETTE (4)

Same as (3) except the bust of a man added above the signature

See HARRIS for patent description

LAFAYETTE (5)

Circa 1884

Glass lid with ramp, tightening wire hook to jar finish, sealing on side of finish

Handmade round, tapered finish, ground lip, in green

Side: 'Lafayette' in script as a signature

Lid: 'PATENTED SEPT. 2, 1884 & AUG. 4, 1885' in a circle

Maker unknown

The May, 1886, issue of *American Drug Trade* magazine refers to a "new clamp-on lid Lafayette"

LAMB
MASON

LAMB MASON (1)

Circa 1940-50

Mason beaded neck design

Machine-made round, in pinkish (milk bottle) flint

Side: 'LAMB' above 'MASON'

Lamb Glass Co., Mt. Vernon, Ohio, 1921-63

Now a unit of the Chattanooga Glass Co, Chattanooga, Tenn.

See "C" in a circle

LAMB MASON (2)

Same except rounded square design

LANDSBERGER

Circa 1903 only

Metal lid with heat-softening gasket top seal

Machine-made round, in flint and light green

Side: 'LANDSBERGER'

Probably made by Illinois Pacific Glass Co., San Francisco, Cal., 1902-30

This jar is exactly like the ECONOMY and adds to the ECONOMY story. Ewald Goltstein of Germany patented the heat-softening gasket in Patent No. 730,760, June 9, 1903, and assigned it to Landsberger, of Alameda, Cal. Julius A. Landsberger obtained Patent No. 731,793 on June 23, 1903, for the spring clip that held the cap in place during processing. Evidently (from this jar) he had the jar made into glass, but he sold the rights of its use to Alexander Kerr that same year. Landsberger then went on to become a one-fourth partner in the Phoenix Metals Co., of Chicago, who made the metal lid

LEADER, THE (1)

Circa 1892

Glass lid and wire lever, one part of which slipped under the finish ledge, and the other over the lid—lever operates to impose pressure on top of the lid

Handmade round, ground lip, in light green

Side: 'THE LEADER' on one line

THE LEADER

THE
LEADER

Lid: 'PAT JUNE 28, 1892'
Maker unknown
Patent No. 477,955 was issued June 28,
1892, to R. I. Patterson for this seal
exactly as found on jars

LEADER, THE (2)

Same except 'THE' and 'LEADER' in two
lines

LEE & Co., J. ELLWOOD

Circa 1880-1900
Glass lid and metal screw-band top seal
Handmade rounded square, ground lip, in
amber
Lid: 'J. ELLWOOD LEE & Co., CON-
SHOHOCKEN, Pa.' in a circle
Maker unknown

LEOTRIC (1)

Circa 1890-1910
Lightning closure, old style neck design
Handmade round, ground lip, in flint,
green, blue, and aqua
Side: 'LEOTRIC' in an oval panel
Bottom: 'REG. T. M. No. 43,288' in a circle
John Gayner, lessee from Holz, Clark &
Taylor (1860s-1879) in 1879; incorpor-
ated as Gayner Glass Works, 1898-56

LEOTRIC

LEOTRIC (2)

Same except without oval panel, and
machine-made, and therefore after 1915
installation of machines by Gayner
The ELECTRIC bears the same trade
mark number

L G Co

Circa 1855-85

Groove-ring wax sealer

Handmade round, pressed laid-on-ring, in green

Bottom: 'L G Co'

Louisville Glass Works (and Co.), Louisville, Ky., 1855-85. This jar probably made late in company years, after they had abandoned "Works" for "Company." See K Y G W and KENTUCKY

L G Co MASON'S PATENT NOV 30th 1858

Circa 1875-85

Mason shoulder seal

Handmade round, ground lip, in green

Side: 'MASON'S,' arched over a monogram of "L G Co.," followed by 'PATENT,' 'NOV 30ᵀᴴ,' and '1858'

Louisville Glass Co., Louisville, Ky., 1855-85

L G W MASON'S IMPROVED

Circa 1910-30

Glass lid and metal screw-band top seal

Machine-made round, in flint

Side: 'MASON'S,' arched above a monogram of "L G W," followed by 'IMPROVED'

Maker unknown

Machine-making, flint color, and fine workmanship place making of this jar long after the Louisville Glass Works (Co.) closing

L'IDEALE

See listing under IDEALE, since "L'" is French for "the"

(SIDE)

ADLAM'S

M

PATENT

(BOTTOM)

LICORICE LOZENGES

Circa 1900

Seal uncertain—no threads or bulges; no cap found

Handmade round, ground lip, in flint

Side: 'LICORICE' and 'LOZENGES' forming top and bottom of a circle around a monogram of "S & Y" or "Y & S." Gadrooned around entire jar at top and bottom

Bottom: "M," with 'ADLAM'S' above and 'PATENT' below

Maker unknown—thought to be British. Yarnell & Samuels, 1863, made no glass

LIGHTNING (general)

As pointed out in the section "Fruit Jar Seals" of this book, under "Toggles," the word "Lightning" started out as the name of a beverage bottle and ended up as a generic name for a style of seal. Its use as a beer-bottle seal is quite general today in Germany

LIGHTNING (1)

Circa 1882-1900

Glass lid, held by wire lever and toggle system generally referred to as the "Lightning closure." All handmade LIGHTNINGS were made with what is referred to as the "old-style design," in which the glass above the tie-wire around the neck resembled a band

Handmade round, old-style neck design, ground lip, in amber, green, and other colors

Side: 'LIGHTNING'

Bottom: 'PUTNAM'

LIGHTNING clamp
adapted to
PERFECTION lid

Maker not proved. One collector from Vermont states that all jars with "LIGHTNING" on the side and "PUTNAM" on the bottom were made by the Lyndeboro Glass Co., Lyndeboro, N.H., 1866-86 (see McKearin, pp. 207 and 612), but they closed about the time the seal was beginning to be accepted. The Hazel Glass Co. started to make LIGHTNING jars in 1886, and Atlas Glass Co., in 1896

LIGHTNING (2)

Same except 'TRADE MARK' arched over 'LIGHTNING'

LIGHTNING (3)

Same as (1) except 'REGISTERED' above 'LIGHTNING' and 'U. S. PATENT OFFICE' below

In all three versions there are variations in lettering

LINDELL GLASS CO.

Circa 1860-80

Groove-ring wax sealer

Handmade round, pressed laid-on-ring, in amber

Bottom: 'LINDELL GLASS CO.'

Maker not identified, as no record of a Lindell Glass Co. could be found

LIQUID CARBONIC Co.

Circa 1930

Lightning closure, dimple neck design

Machine-made round, in flint

Side: 'LIQUID CARBONIC Co.' above 'CHICAGO' and 'PAT JULY 14, 1908'

Bottom: side legend except patent date repeated

Maker unknown

The Liquid Carbonic Co. is a leading manufacturer of supplies and equipment for the carbonated-beverage industry and probably used this container for paste-type flavors or caramel color

LIQUID CARBONIC (2)

Same except bottom legend only

LOCKPORT MASON (1)

LOCKPORT MASON

Circa 1900-20

Mason shoulder seal

Machine-made square-shoulder round, in flint

Side: 'LOCKPORT' arched above 'MASON'

Lockport Glass Co., Lockport, N.Y., 1900-1919. Converted into milk bottle plant by Thatcher Glass Mfg. Co. in 1920

Do not confuse with the Lockport Glass Co., known as the Hitchen's Glass Works in 1862, purchased by Hero in 1879 and resold to become the Mansfield Glass Co. in 1882, closed 1908.

LOCKPORT MASON (2)

Same except with tapered shoulder

LOCKPORT MASON, IMPROVED

Circa 1915-30
Glass lid and metal screw-band top seal
Machine-made round, in aqua
Side: three lines: 'LOCKPORT' arched
above 'MASON' and 'IMPROVED'
Lockport Glass Co., Lockport, N.Y., 1900-
19

LORILLARD & Co., P. (1)

Circa 1872-90
Glass lid with spring-steel wire yoke, hav-
ing two loops which tightened when ro-
tated under two helical neck lugs
Handmade round, ground lip, in green and
amber
Side: 'P. LORILLARD & Co.'
Lid: 'G. W. HELME OF N.J.' and PAT^D
JULY 16 1872' in a circle
Cohansey Glass Mfg. Co., Philadelphia,
Pa., 1870-1900
The bottle was probably used for snuff,
which was very popular about that
time. See also RAIL ROAD MILLS,
HELME'S
Patent No. 129,235 is by Charles G. and
William M. Imlay of Camden, N.J. See
also COHANSEY for the same jar under
glass company name

LORILLARD & Co., P. (2)

Same except side is lettered: 'P. LORIL-
LARD & Co.' and 'G. W. HELME Co.,
PROP.

LORILLARD & Co., P. (3)

Circa 1876-1900
Glass lid, completely covered by, and tightened by, a full metal cap having three
indentations at the edges of the skirt,

to engage three helical lugs on jar neck. Very modern in appearance

Handmade round, ground lip, in green and amber

Side: 'P. LORILLARD & Co.'

Lid: 'PAT JULY 16, 1872' and 'PAT JAN 18, 1876' in a circle

Cohansey Glass Manufacturing Co., Philadelphia, Pa., 1870-1900

See (1) for first patent. The second is No. 172,289, by John Young of Amsterdam, N.Y., and was used on other COHANSEY jars, which see

L & S

Circa 1920-30

Lightning closure, dimple neck design

Machine-made tall round, in flint

Side: 'PAT JULY 14, 1908'

Bottom: 'L & S'

Maker unknown

LUSTRE (1)

Circa 1890-1900

Mason shoulder seal

Handmade round, ground lip, in light green

Side: a large keystone containing the word 'Lustre,' in script

Maker unknown

LUSTRE (2)

Circa 1890-1900

Mason shoulder seal

Handmade round, ground lip, in light green

Side: an oval, with 'Lustre' in script;
following are four lines: 'R. E.
TONGUE,' '& BROS CO,' 'INC,' and
'PHILA'
Maker unknown

LUSTRE (3)

Same as (2) with "INC" omitted

LUSTRE (4)

Circa 1910-45
Mason beaded neck design
Machine-made round, in flint
Side: a square design, notched at the
corners like the Hero cross. 'Lustre' in
script across the center, and with 'R.
E. TONGUE & BROS CO' arched over
'INC' above "Lustre," and PHILADEL-
PHIA Pa' below it
Maker unknown
R. E. Tongue & Bros. Co. was a dealer and
wholesaler in glassware, lamp chimneys,
and pottery from 1890 to 1945

LUSTRE (5)

Same as (4) except Lightning closure,
beaded neck design, circa 1915

L & W (1)

Circa 1851-71
Groove-ring wax sealer
Handmade round, pressed laid-on-ring, in
dark green and amber
Side: 'L & W' in very large script letters
Lorenz & Wightman, Pittsburgh, Pa., 1851-
71, except for 1860-62 when the plant
was leased to Fahnstock, Albree & Co.
See FAHNSTOCK for jars made by
Fahnstock, Albree & Co., and by Fahn-
stock, Fortune & Co.

L & W (2)

Same except that a six-pointed star was added at the bottom of the jar. See "W" for jars made by Wightman after the death of Lorenz in 1871. Some jars were made after merely peening out "L &" from the mold, leaving only "W," but the peened-out portion is still legible

LYMAN, W. W. (1)

Circa 1864

Thin metal lid, with side seal on tapered finish above a bulbous neck

Handmade round, ground lip, in aqua

Side: 'W. W. LYMAN' as the diameter of semicircle made up of 'PAT<u>D</u> AUG 5<u>TH</u> 1862.' '34' is mold serial number

Maker unknown

Lyman had many patent dates claimed, but this one could not be found. Most of his known patents are stoppers

LYMAN, W. W. (2)

Same, except with a full circle around 'W. W. LYMAN,' consisting of 'PAT<u>D</u> AUG 5<u>TH</u> 1862' above and '& FEB 9<u>TH</u> 1864' below. '12' is a mold serial number

LYMAN, W. W. (3)

Same except a half circle above the name, of 'PAT<u>D</u> FEB 9<u>TH</u> 1864.' '45' is a mold serial number

LYMAN, W. W. (4)

Same except a full circle about the name, of 'PAT⁰. FEB. 9ᵀᴴ 1864' above, and 'REIS⁰. JAN. 22⁰ 1867' below

None of these patents were found. The known Lyman patents of Jan. 2, 1866, and July 28, 1868, do not apply

LYNCHBURG STANDARD MASON

See STANDARD MASON, LYNCHBURG

LYON & BOSSARD'S JAR with moldmaker's error

Circa 1884

Glass lid, yoke and wheel operating as a cam

Handmade round, ground lip, in aqua

Side: four lines: 'LYON & BOSSARD'S' arched over 'JAR,' 'EAST STROUDS-BURG,' and 'PA'

Lid: 'PAT. APRIL 15ᵀᴴ, 1884' with the "4" cut backwards

Possibly by the East Stroudsburg Glass Co., East Stroudsburg, Pa., as in the VAN VLIET JAR

LYON JAR PATENT ALLOWED

This wording appears on the stoppers of both a plain jar and a STEERSHEAD stopper-type jar, but without some indication of a date, a patent search was useless

M

MACOMB [stoneware or pottery]

Circa 1899-1910

Mason shoulder seal

Wheel-turned pottery

Bottom: stamped and fired with maker's name, 'MACOMB POTTERY C⁰' and 'MACOMB ILL' in a circle around 'PAT JAN' and '24 1899'

Macomb Pottery Co., Macomb, Ill., dates unknown

See HERMANN and STONE MASON for other pottery jars having the same patent date. See PEORIA in section UNLETTERED JARS at end of GLOSSARY for a pottery groove-ring wax sealer

MAGIC FRUIT JAR (1)

Circa 1866

Class lid and yoke, whose hooked ends were at a slant in order to form a helix and tighten lid when rotated in contact with two neck lugs

Handmade round, ground lip, in green

Front: five lines: 'MAGIC,' 'FRUIT JAR,' 'Wᴹ MᶜCULLY & Co.,' 'PITTSBURGH, PA,' and 'SOLE PROPRIETORS.' '7' is a mold serial number

Back: four lines: 'PATENTED,' 'BY,' 'R. M. DALBEY,' and 'JUNE 6ᵀᴴ 1866'

William McCully & Co., Pittsburgh, Pa., 1832-85

See also DALBEY'S FRUIT JAR

MAGIC FRUIT JAR (2)

Circa 1910

Glass lid held by twin toggles on opposite
sides of finish

Machine-made round, in flint

Side 'THE MAGIC' and 'FRUIT JAR' in
a circle around a five-pointed star

Lid: 'KANT KRACK,' 'TRADE MARK,'
and 'PAT FEB 23, 1909'

Unknown maker for Smalley, Kivlan &
Onthank, Boston glass jobbers

The patent, by John Kivlan, and his first
of three, is No. 913,214. It was for a
pair of toggles, of three elements each,
rising from a tie-wire around the neck,
and hooking over the edge of the lid

MAINE CONDENSED MILK CO.

Circa 1880-1900

Glass lid and metal screw-band top seal

Handmade hexagonal pint, ground lip

Lid: 'BABY'

Side: 'MAINE' and 'CONDENSED' in
rough, doubly outlined letters in two
lines on one panel; 'MILK' and 'COM-
PANY' on another

Maker unknown

See also BORDEN'S CONDENSED
MILK CO. for identical jar

MALLINGER

Circa 1931-40

Mason beaded neck design

Machine-made round, in flint

Side: 'MALLINGER'

Glenshaw Glass Co., Glenshaw, Pa., 1894
to date, for another glassmaker, the
Samuel Mallinger Co., Neville Island,
Pittsburgh, Pa., who made opal liners

MANSFIELD

IMPROVED

MASON

MANSFIELD IMPROVED MASON

Circa 1900-1910

Glass lid and metal screw-band top seal

Machine-made round, in light green

Side: three lines: 'MANSFIELD' arched above 'IMPROVED' and 'MASON'

Probably the Reid Bottle Co., Mansfield, Ohio, ?-1904 when merged with Edward H. Everett Glass Co., or possibly the Mansfield Glass Works, Lockport, N.Y., 1882-1909. The latter, however, is not known to have used machines

THE MARION JAR

MASON'S

PATENT

NOV 30

1858

MARION JAR, THE, with MASON'S PATENT NOV 30th 1858 (1)

Circa 1890-1904

Mason shoulder seal

Handmade round, ground lip, in green

Side: five lines: 'THE MARION JAR' in deliberately roughened letters around the shoulder, above 'MASON'S,' arched over 'PATENT,' 'NOV 30,' and '1858'

Marion Fruit Jar & Bottle Co., Marion, Ind., 1890-1904, with branch factories at Conners and Fairmount, Ind., and Coffeeville, Kan. Purchased by Ball Bros. Co. in 1904

THE MARION JAR

MASON'S

PATENT

NOV 30

1858

MARION JAR, THE, with MASON'S PATENT NOV 30th 1858 (2)

Same except well-formed block letters for 'THE MARION JAR' instead of deliberately roughened

MARSTON'S RESTAURANT, BOSTON

Circa 1910

Lightning closure, old-style neck design

Handmade round, ground lip, in pinkish flint

disk, connected by pillar and bolted together. Rather slender and fragile

July 20, 1886, No. 345,999, by W. Somerville, of St. Louis, Mo. The fragility of
Andrew's connecting pillar was overcome by making entire device of one
piece with very short connecting pillar.
This seems to be the only patent put
into practice

See G J [Gilchrist Jar] for a later idea

MASON FRUIT JAR (1)

Circa 1890-1910

Mason shoulder seal

Handmade round, in green, blue-green,
light green, aqua, and amber

Side: 'MASON' arched above 'FRUIT JAR'

Maker unknown

MASON FRUIT JAR (2)

Circa 1913-20

Mason shoulder seal

Machine-made round, in flint

Side: 'MASON,' in large block letters,
above 'FRUIT JAR'

Bottom: "D" in a diamond

Dominion Glass Co., Montreal, Que., 1913
to date

MASON FRUIT JAR (3)

Circa 1900-10

Same lettering style as (2) but without
maker identification

Probably Diamond Glass Co., Montreal,
Que., 1891-1901, or

Diamond Flint Glass Co., Montreal, Que.,
1901-1913

MASON

FRUIT JAR

MASON
FRUIT JAR

MADE IN CANADA

MASON FRUIT JAR (4)

Circa 1920-30
Same as (2) except 'MADE IN CANADA' added

MASON
FRUIT
JAR

MASON FRUIT JAR (5)

Circa 1910-20
Mason shoulder seal
Machine-made round, in flint
Side: three lines: 'MASON' arched above 'FRUIT' and 'JAR'
Maker unknown

MASON'S FRUIT JAR

Differs from MASON FRUIT JAR (2) only by the use of the possessive 'MASON'S'

MASON FRUIT JAR PATENT NOV 30th 1858 (1)

MASON
FRUIT JAR
PATENT
NOV 30 TH
1858

Circa 1885-1900
Mason shoulder seal
Handmade round, ground lip, in blue-green
Side: in five lines below a keystone: 'MASON,' 'FRUIT JAR,' 'PATENT,' 'Nov 30TH,' and '1858'
Inside cap: 'MASON FRUIT JAR CO., PHILADELPHIA, PA.' in a circle
Liner: in opal glass, same as cap legend
Mason Fruit Jar Co., Phildelphia, Pa., 1885-1900

MASON FRUIT JAR PATENT
NOV 30th 1858 (2)

Same except maker's name repeated on bottom of jar

MASON, GENUINE

See GENUINE MASON

MASON IMPROVED with possible moldmaker's error

Circa 1880-1900
Glass lid and metal screw-band top seal
Handmade round, ground lip, in green
Side: 'MASON' arched above 'IM-PROVED.' The line "MASON" is imbalanced. There is enough room for " 'S," which may have been left out by the mold-cutter
Maker unknown

MASON
IMPROVED

MASON'S IMPROVED (1)

Circa 1885-95
Glass lid and metal screw-band top seal
Handmade round, ground lip, in green
Side: 'MASON'S' arched above 'IM-PROVED'
Bottom: 'NOV 26 67,' a HERO date
Hero Fruit Jar Co., Philadelphia, Pa., 1884-1909
Dating would be from 1882 take-over of Consolidated's assets

MASON'S
IMPROVED

MASON'S IMPROVED (2)

Same except without 'NOV 26 67' on bottom

MASON'S IMPROVED (3)

Circa 1890-1900
Lightning closure, old neck style
Handmade round, ground lip in light green
Side 'MASON'S' above 'IMPROVED'
Maker unknown—and should remain so after placing *Mason's* name on a *Lightning* closure!

"MASON'S" IMPROVED (4) [Note quotation marks]

Circa 1885-1900
Glass lid and metal screw-band top seal
Handmade round, ground lip, in light green
Side: 'MASON'S,' in quotation marks, arched above 'IMPROVED'
Mason Fruit Jar Co., Philadelphia, Pa., 1885-1900
This another of the Mason Fruit Jar Co.'s use of quotation marks around either MASON'S or MASCOT

MASON'S IMPROVED with C F J Co. monogram

See under C F J Co.

"MASON'S" IMPROVED, THE [Note quotation marks]

Circa 1885-1900
Glass lid and metal screw-band top seal
Handmade round, ground lip, in amber
Side: three lines: 'THE,' 'MASON'S,' in quotation marks, arched over 'IMPROVED'
Mason Fruit Jar Co., Philadelphia, Pa., 1885-1900

This jar is identical in lettering with MASON'S IMPROVED (4) except that "THE" has been added above "MASON'S." Note also that both use the quotation marks with MASON'S

MASON JAR (1)

Circa 1880-1900
Mason shoulder seal
Handmade round, ground lip, in pinkish flint (or sun-colored)
Side: 'MASON' arched above 'JAR'
Maker unknown

MASON JAR (2)

Modern, circa 1960
Mason beaded seal
Machine-made rounded square, in flint
Side: the outline of a star, and in heavy letters: 'MASON' above and 'JAR' below
Bottom: "O" containing an "I," the Owens Illinois trade mark since 1956, and Owens Illinois code for 1965
Owens Illinois Glass Co., Toledo, Ohio, 1929 to date

MASON JAR OF 1872, THE (1)

Circa 1890-1900
Glass lid and metal screw-band top seal
Handmade round, ground lip, in aqua and green
Side: four lines: 'THE,' 'MASON,' in large, double-outlined letters, 'JAR,' and 'OF 1872'
Bottom: 'WHITNEY GLASS WORKS, GLASSBORO, N.J.' in circle

Whitney Glass Works, Glassboro, N.J., 1887-1918

The date is that of Mason's last, and most successful, top seal patent, and *does not* date the jar

THE MASON JAR
OF 1872

MASON JAR OF 1872, THE (2)

Same except in lettering layout. 'THE MASON JAR' is arched over 'OF 1872.' The bottom does not carry the Whitney identification

"MASON"
PATENT
NOV 30 ᵀ͟ᴴ
1880

"MASON" PATENT NOV 30th 1880 [Note quotation marks around MASON and 1880 date instead of 1858—not a moldmaker's error]

Circa 1885-1900

Mason shoulder seal

Handmade round, ground lip, in flint and sun-colored purple

Side: 'MASON,' in quotation marks, arched above 'PATENT,' 'NOV 30ᵀᴴ,' and '1880'

Mason Fruit Jar Co., Philadelphia, Pa., 1885-1900

See MASON DISK PROTECTOR CAP for reason of the 1880 date, which was the fourth and last patent for the disk

MASON'S
PATENT

MASON'S PATENT (1)

Circa 1900-15

Mason shoulder seal

Machine-made rounded-shoulder round, in green and blue-green

Side: 'MASON'S' arched above 'PATENT'

Maker unknown

MASON'S PATENT (2)

Same except very square shoulder

MASON'S PATENT (3)

Same except that shoulder is tapered

MASON'S PATENT 1858 with S

See under S for two variations: one with S above "MASON'S," the other below

MASON'S PATENT NOV 30th 1858

There are many versions of this lettering, and all cannot be listed because only photographs and measured drawings would distinguish some of them. The expiration of the patents brought a flood of imitators, who neglected to identify themselves. The more important variations are listed

MASON'S PATENT NOV. 30$^{\text{TH}}_{\text{..}}$ 1858 (1)

Circa 1858

Mason shoulder seal

Handmade round, ground lip, in green

Side: four lines: 'MASON'S' arched over 'PATENT,' 'NOV 30$^{\text{TH}}_{\text{..}}$,' and '1858.' Note the dots beneath the 'TH,' a departure

Most probably by Samuel Crowley, in his Crowleytown Glass Works, Crowleytown (also called Crowleyville), N.J., who is credited with blowing the first jars for Mason. This jar was obtained by J. E. Pfeiffer, of Pitman, N.J., from silt at the site of the factory. It has sharp shoulders and a very square angle where the sidewall joins the bottom, very like Mason's patent drawings

MASON'S PATENT NOV 30th 1858 (2)
[and a real "boner"]

Circa 1880-90

Glass lid and metal screw-band top seal (*not* shoulder seal)

Handmade round, ground lip, in blue-green

Side: 'MASON'S' arched above 'PATENT,' 'NOV 30TH,' and '1858'

Maker unknown

Note that this is shoulder-seal patent wording on a top-seal jar!

MASON'S PATENT NOV 30th 1858 (2)

Circa 1885-90

Mason shoulder seal

Handmade round, ground lip, in green

Side: 'MASON'S' arched above 'PATENT,' 'NOV 30TH,' and '1858'

Bottom: 'NOV 26 67,' a HERO date

Hero Fruit Jar Co., Philadelphia, Pa., 1884-1909

MASON'S PATENT NOV 30th 1858 (3)

Circa 1880-1900

Mason shoulder seal

Handmade round, ground lip, in flint and green

Front: 'MASON'S' arched above 'PATENT,' 'NOV 30TH,' and '1858'

Back: 'N C L'

Maker unknown

MASON'S PATENT NOV 30th 1858 (4)

Same except 'N C L Co' on back

MASON'S PATENT NOV 30th 1858 (5)

Circa 1904

Mason shoulder seal

Handmade round, ground lip, in light green

Side: 'MASON'S' arched above 'PAT-
ENT,' 'NOV 30$\underline{^{TH}}$,' and '1858'
Back: 'Port' in script
Port Glass Co., Belleville, Ill., 1902-10 or
13

MASON'S PATENT NOV 30th 1858 (6)

Same as (5) except 'Port' in script on the
bottom

MASON'S PATENT NOV 30th 1858 (7) [with numbers]

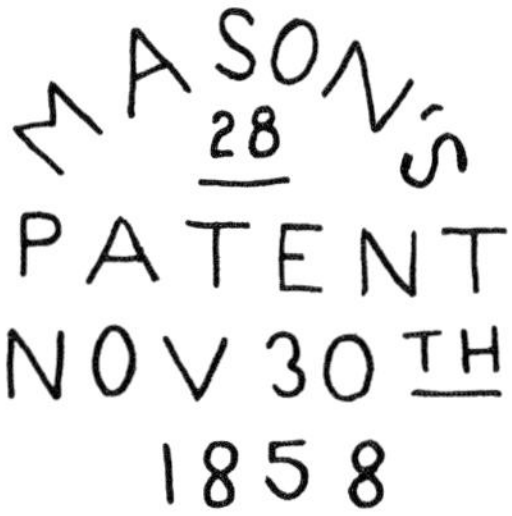

Circa 1880-1900
Mason shoulder seal
Handmade round, ground lip, in green,
aqua, and blue-green
Side: 'MASON'S' above a number, fol-
lowed by 'PATENT,' 'NOV 30$\underline{^{TH}}$,' and
'1858'
Maker unknown
Figures include 5, 7, 8, 15, 20 and 28. They
are probably mold numbers

MASON'S
28
PATENT
NOV 30 TH
1858

MASON'S PATENT NOV 30th 1858 (8) [with plain keystone]

Circa 1885-1900
Mason shoulder seal
Handmade round, ground lip, in green
and aqua
Side: 'MASON'S,' arched over a keystone,
followed by 'PATENT,' 'NOV 30$\underline{^{TH}}$,' and
'1858'
Mason Fruit Jar Co., Philadelphia, Pa.,
1885-1900
This does not apply to any keystone in a
circle

MASON'S
PATENT
NOV 30 TH
1858

MASON'S PATENT NOV 30th 1858 (9) [with circled keystone]

Circa 1890-1900

Mason shoulder seal

Handmade round, ground lip, in aqua

Side: a circled keystone at the top, followed by 'MASON'S,' 'PATENT,' 'NOV 30TH,' and '1858.' Keystone and circle are quite small

Maker unknown

MASON'S PATENT NOV 30th 1858 (10) [with circled keystone]

Circa 1870-90

Mason shoulder seal

Handmade round, very rough ground lip, quite heavy glass, in aqua

Side: 'MASON'S' above a large circled keystone, followed by 'PATENT,' 'NOV 30TH,' and '1858'

Maker unknown

Sometimes attributed to the Consolidated Fruit Jar Co., but specific proof is entirely lacking

MASON'S PATENT NOV 30th 1858 with illuminated letters

Commonly known as the "CHRISTMAS Mason." See description under that name

MASON'S PATENT NOV 30th 1858 with letters

See under the specific letter involved

MASON'S PATENT NOV 30th 1858 with the letter "N"

This appears in three places: under "N," under BALL, and under PORT

MASON'S PATENT NOV 30th 1858 with MOON, STAR, and SUNBURST (1)

Circa 1880-1900
Mason shoulder seal
Handmade round, ground lip, in aqua
Side: a sunburst surrounding a moon and star, above 'MASON'S,' arched, 'PATENT,' 'NOV 30TH,' and '1858'
Back: 'Ball' in script
Ball Bros. Co., Muncie, Ind., 1888 to date

MASON'S PATENT NOV 30th 1858 with MOON, STAR, and SUNBURST (2)

Same except without BALL identification
Alberta and Bill Kerr call this their "SUN, MOON, and STAR" Mason

MASON'S
PATENT
NOV 30TH
1858

(SUN, MOON, & STAR)

MASON'S PATENT NOV 30th 1858 with moldmaker's error (1)

Circa 1885-1900
Mason shoulder seal
Handmade round, ground lip, in green
Side: 'MASON'S' arched and off center above 'PATENT,' 'NOV 30TH,' and '1858.' Neither "A" has a crossbar
Bottom: 'Nov 26 67,' a HERO patent date, but jar dates much later
Hero Fruit Jar Co., Philadelphia, Pa., 1884-1909

MASON'S PATENT NOV 30th 1858 with moldmaker's error (2)

Same as (1) except without "NOV 26 67" on bottom. Jar (1) is definitely by Hero; (2) by uncertain company making same error

MASON'S
PATENT
NOV 30TH
1858

MASON'S
PATENT
NOV 30TH
1858

MA ON'S
PATENT
NOV 30 ᵀᴴ
1858

MASON'S PATENT NOV 30th 1858 with moldmaker's error (3)

Circa 1885-1900
Mason shoulder seal
Handmade round, ground lip, in green
Side: 'MA ON'S' (without the first "S") arched above 'PATENT,' 'NOV 30ᵀᴴ,' and '1858.' It appears as though the moldmaker cut into a blow-hole, tried to weld it full, and then forget to finish the job
Maker unknown

MASON'S
PATENT
NOV 30
1858

MASON'S PATENT NOV 30th 1858 with moldmaker's error (4)

Circa 1900-15
Mason shoulder seal
Machine-made round, in aqua
Side: 'MASON'S' arched above 'PATENT,' 'NOV 30 ,' and '1858.' The "th" was omitted after "30," even though space was left
Maker unknown

MASONS
PATENT
NOV 30ᴴᵀ
18 58

MASON'S PATENT NOV 30th 1858 with moldmaker's error (5)

Circa 1885-1900
Mason shoulder seal
Handmade round, ground lip, in aqua
Side: 'MASON'S' arched above 'PATENT,' 'NOV 30ᴴᵀ,' and '1858.' The "T" and "H" after "30" are reversed
Maker unknown

MASON'S PATENT NOV 30th 1858 with moldmaker's error (6)

Circa 1870-82
Glass lid and metal screw-band top seal [in spite of the lettering]

Handmade round, ground lip, in green
Side: 'MASON'S' arched above 'PATENT,'
'NOV 30ᵀᴴ,' and '1858.' The last two "N's"
are reversed in form
Lid: C F J Co monogram, but lid may
not be original
Maker not proved. The Consolidated lid
could have easily been a substitute and
is not maker's evidence

MASON'S PATENT NOV 30th 1858 with moldmaker's error (7)

Circa 1870-1882
Mason shoulder seal
Handmade round, ground lip, in green
Side: 'MASON'S' arched above 'PATENT,'
'NOV 30th,' and '1858.' All the "N's" are
reversed in form
Back: C F J Co monogram of Consolidated
Fruit Jar Co.
Probably Clyde Glass Works, Clyde, N.Y.,
for the Consolidated Fruit Jar Co.
Note: other reversals of a single "N" re-
ported but not verified as to which one
of the three

MASON'S PATENT NOV 30th 1858 with moldmaker's error (8)

Circa 1880-1900
Mason shoulder seal
Handmade round, ground lip, in aqua
Side: 'MASON'S' arched over 'PATENT,'
'NOA 30ᵀᴴ,' and '1858.' "A" instead of
"V" in NOV
Maker unknown

MASON'S
PATENT
NOV 30ᵀᴴ
1858
(NOTE TWO N'S)

MASON'S
PATENT
NOV 30ᵀᴴ
1858

MASON'S
PATENT
NOA 30ᵀᴴ
1858

MASON'S
1
PATENT
NOA 30 TH
1 8 5 8

MASON
PATENT
NOV 30 TH
1858

MASON'S
PATENT
NOV 30 TH
858

MASON'S PATENT NOV 30th 1858 with moldmaker's error (9)

Same as (8) except there is a figure "1" between "MASON'S" and "PATENT," and repeated on the bottom

MASON'S PATENT NOV 30th 1858 with moldmaker's error (10)

Circa 1885-1900

Mason shoulder seal

Handmade round, ground lip, in light green

Side: 'MASON' ' arched above 'PATENT,' 'NOV 30$\underline{TH}$,' and '1858.' The possessive "S" is omitted from "MASON'S" but the spacing shows that the omission was not intentional. There is a keystone between "MASON' " and "PATENT"

Mason Fruit Jar Co., Philadelphia, Pa., 1885-1900

MASON'S PATENT NOV 30th 1858 with moldmaker's errors (11)

Circa 1880-1900

Glass lid with metal screw-band top seal. [This is the first error—the legend is for a shoulder seal]

Handmade round, ground lip, in light green

Side: 'MASON'S' arched over 'PATENT,' 'NOV 30$\underline{TH}$,' and '858.' The "1" was left off the "1858"

Maker unknown

MASON PORCELAIN LINED

Circa 1870

Mason shoulder seal

Handmade round, ground lip, in light green

Side: 'MASON' in large letters, followed by 'PORCELAIN' and 'LINED' in smaller letters

Bottom: 'C'

Possibly made for Consolidated Fruit Jar Co., before the 1871 adoption of the C F J Co. trade mark monogram. If so, this jar is almost the oldest jar made under Mason's own auspices

MATHIAS & HENDERSON (1)

Circa 1899

Glass lid and heavy wire yoke, swiveled to the top of the metal lid, and shaped to the profile of the helical neck lugs

Machine-made round, in flint

Bottom: 'MATHIAS & HENDERSON' above 'LIVERPOOL' and '1899'

Maker unknown. Neither a 1934 history of glassmaking in Lancashire nor the present catalog of British punt marks contains this name

MATHIAS & HENDERSON (2)

Circa 1910-20

Lightning closure, old neck design

Machine-made round, in flint

Bottom: 'MATHIAS & HENDERSON' and 'LIVERPOOL'

Maker unknown

McCARTY VACUUM FRUIT JAR, THE

Circa 1865

Sealing means unknown as cap unavailable

Handmade round, ground lip, in amethyst

Side: nine lines [the record]: 'THE,' 'MᶜCARTY,' 'VACUUM,' 'FRUIT JAR,' 'PAT MAR 1, 1859,' 'THE,' 'FRANK GLASS CO,' 'SOLE MFG'S.,' 'WELLS-

MASON

PORCELAIN
LINED

THE
MᶜCARTY
VACUUM
FRUIT JAR
PAT MAR 1 1859
THE
FRANK GLASS Co
SOLE MFG'S
WELLSBURG, W.VA

BURG, W.VA.' The 1859 date cannot be that of the jar since there was not a *West* Virginia until about 1865

Frank Glass Co., 1859 or 1865, could not be traced

M C Co.

Circa 1860-80
Groove-ring wax sealer
Handmade round, pressed laid-on-ring, in green
Bottom: 'M C Co.'
Maker unknown

McDONALD NEW PERFECT SEAL

Circa 1925-30
Lightning closure, dimple neck design
Machine-made round, in flint
Side: 'M^cDONALD' and 'SEAL' forming a circle, containing 'NEW' and 'PER-FECT.' Below is 'PAT'D JULY 14 1908'
Maker unknown

McDONALD PERFECT SEAL

Circa 1920
Lightning closure, beaded neck design
Machine-made round, in bluish glass
Side: 'McDONALD' and 'SEAL' forming an oval, with 'PERFECT' across the center
Maker unknown

McKEE & Co., S.

Circa 1860
Groove-ring wax sealer
Handmade round, pressed laid-on-ring, in green
Bottom: 'S. McKEE & Co.'

Samuel McKee & Co., Pittsburgh, Pa., 1836-86 or later

Samuel McKee died in 1877, but glass was being made by the company in 1886 (McKearin, p. 601)

METRO

See EASI-PAK

M F A

Circa 1941-45 only

Mason beaded neck design

Machine-made rounded square, in flint

Side: a shield bearing three stars above 'M F A'

Bottom: H over A trade mark

Hazel Atlas Glass Co., Wheeling. W.Va., 1902-64

The jar was used as a coffee container by the Producer's Grocery Association, an affiliate of the Missouri Farmers Association, during World War II

M F G Co

Known only from a dealer's want-list. But see following

M F J Co.

Circa 1860-80

Groove-ring wax sealer

Handmade round, pressed laid-on-ring, in light green

Bottom: 'M F J Co.'

Maker unknown

M F J & B Co. with MASON'S PATENT NOV 30th 1858

Circa 1890-1904
Mason shoulder seal
Handmade round, ground lip, in green
Side: 'MASON'S' arched above 'PATENT,'
'NOV 30th,' and '1858'
Bottom: 'M F J & B Co.'
Marion Fruit Jar & Bottle Co., Marion, Ind., 1890-1904

M G Co.

Circa 1860-80
Groove-ring wax sealer
Handmade round, pressed laid-on-ring, in green
Bottom: 'M G Co.'
Maker unknown

MICHIGAN MASON

MICHIGAN MASON

1911-16
Mason beaded neck design
Machine-made round, in flint
Side: 'MICHIGAN' arched above 'MASON'
Michigan Glass Co., Saginaw, Mich., 1911-16

MIDDLEBY, JR., INC., JOS. (1)

JOS.MIDDLEBY JR INC
(SIDE)

M
I
D
MID(B)DLE
D
L
E
(BOTTOM)

Age uncertain, circa 1910-40
Sealing means uncertain—double beaded finish formed into a V-shaped groove on top
Machine-made round, in flint
Side: 'JOS. MIDDLEBY JR INC'
Bottom: an acrostic, consisting of a "B" in a small circle, with 'MID' above and to the left; 'DLE' below and to the right, the letters forming a vertical and a horizontal row
Maker unknown

MIDDLEBY, JR., INC., JOS. (2)

Same except with a Mason beaded neck design

MID WEST

Circa 1929-37

Glass lid and metal screw-band top seal

Machine-made round, in flint

Side: 'Mid' and 'West,' in two lines of slanting, double-outlined script, above 'CANADIAN MADE'

Midwest Glass Co., Winnepeg, Man., 1929-37

CANADIAN MADE

MILLVILLE

Circa 1861

Glass lid sealing cornerwise on rubber ring, held by wire yoke

Handmade round, pressed laid-on-ring, in light green

Side: 'MILLVILLE' above 'PAT. JUNE 18 1861'

Whitall-Tatum & Co., Millville, N.J., 1857-1938. See McKearin, p. 508; Knittle, p. 221

Patent No. 32,594 was issued to John Whitall, and when he brought out the MILLVILLE ATMOSPHERIC FRUIT JAR the following year, he used this patent date in spite of the fact that the later jar was under a totally different patent! This jar is *not* the MILLVILLE ATMOSPHERIC FRUIT JAR

MILLVILLE ATMOSPHERIC FRUIT JAR

Circa 1862 (Nov. 4, 1862 patent) in spite of the date on the jar

Glass lid held by yoke and thumbscrew

MILLVILLE

PAT. JUNE 18 1861

Handmade round, pressed laid-on-ring, in light green

Front: 'MILLVILLE' and 'FRUIT JAR' forming the top and bottom of a circle, with 'ATMOSPHERIC' across the diameter

Back: 'WHITALL'S PATENT' and 'JUNE 18TH, 1861' forming the top and bottom of a circle. This statement is untrue as to the jar

Lid: repeats back lettering in a circle

Whitall-Tatum & Co., Millville, N.J., 1857-1938

The patent to which the jar was made was No. 36,853, issued to Thomas G. Otterson, of Millville, N.J., on Nov. 4, 1862. Moore Bros. (see MOORE) had already started to make a stopper seal with a thumbscrew and yoke, and perhaps there were sales reasons for quoting a date prior to Moore

MILLVILLE IMPROVED

Circa 1880-90

Glass lid and metal screw-band top seal

Handmade round, ground lip, in light green

Side: 'MILLVILLE' and 'IMPROVED' forming the top and bottom arcs of a circle around an elaborate monogram of "W T Co"

Whitall-Tatum Co., Millville, N.J., 1857-1938

MISSION MASON JAR (1)

Circa 1925-38

Mason beaded neck design

Machine-made round, in flint and aqua

Side: a Mission bell, with 'MISSION,' in double-outlined letters, above, 'TRADE'

and 'MARK' flanking the bell, and 'MA-
SON JAR' below it
Bottom: 'W. J. LATCHFORD GLASS
CO., LOS ANGELES, CAL.' in a circle
W. J. Latchford Glass Co., Los Angeles,
Cal., 1925-38

MISSION MASON JAR (2)

Same except 'MADE IN CALIFORNIA'
added to lower side-wall

MISSION MASON JAR (3)

Same except bottom carries the circular
legend: 'LATCHFORD MARBLE
GLASS CO., LOS ANGELES, CAL.,'
which succeeded W. J. Latchford Glass
Co., 1938-56. It is now Latchford Glass
Company

M J Co.

Circa 1860-80
Groove-ring wax sealer
Handmade round, pressed laid-on-ring, in
green
Bottom: 'M J Co.'
Maker unknown

MOCKING BIRD FOOD

Modern or late-modern
Mason beaded neck design
Machine-made round, in flint
Side: 'F. F. McALLISTER'S,' 'MOCKING
BIRD FOOD' and 'NEW YORK,' in
three lines
Maker unknown

MODEL MASON

This jar has been reported as a machine-
made Mason shoulder seal, but has not
been verified
Model Glass Works, Summitville, Ind.,
1900-19

JOHN M. MOORE
MANUFACTURERS
FISLERVILLE
N. J.

J. B. WILSON'S
AIR TICHT FRUIT JAR
PATENTED
JUNE 20th
1861

(BACK)

John M Moore & Co
Manufactures
Fislerville N J

MOORE, JOHN M.

Circa 1861

Glass stopper, held by yoke and thumb-screw

Handmade round, pressed laid-on-ring, in green

Front: 'JOHN M. MOORE' arched over 'MANUFACTURERS,' 'FISLERVILLE,' and 'N.J.' The imbalance of the lettering may be due to starting "JOHN" too far to the left, leaving no room for "& Co."

Back: 'J. B. WILSON'S,' 'AIR TIGHT FRUIT JAR,' 'PATENTED,' 'JUNE 20th,' and '1861.' No patent for this date has been found, so it may be the date of application which resulted in the Dec. 3, 1861 patent, No. 33,870

John M. Moore & Co., Fislerville (now Clayton), N.J., 1859-63. There were several changes in this company's name

MOORE & CO., JOHN M.

Circa 1963 only [company name change]

Glass stopper held by yoke and thumb-screw

Handmade round, pressed laid-on-ring, in green

Side: first three lines in script: 'John M Moore & Co,' 'Manufactures' [sic], 'Fislerville, N J,' followed by 'PATENTED DEC 3ⁿ 1861.' There may be a mold-cutter's error in leaving off the final "R" in "Manufacturers"

John M. Moore & Co., Fislerville (now Clayton), N.J., 1859-63

MOORE'S PATENT (1)

From 1863 to 1867

Glass stopper held by yoke and thumb-screw

Handmade round, pressed laid-on-ring, in green and blue-green

Side: 'Moore's,' in arched script, above 'PATENT' and 'DEC 3ᴰ, 1861'

Bottom: 'Moore Bros., Fislerville, N.J.'

Moore Brothers Company, Fislerville, N.J., 1863 only, and Moore Brothers, Fislerville, N.J., 1864-80

Patent No. 33,870 was issued to J. B. Wilson of Camden, N.J., on Dec. 3, 1861, and calls for the details actually found on all three Moore jars. But note the "delicate" process of withdrawing the inventor from the limelight! The first MOORE jar used his name in full; the next made no mention of him but quoted the correct patent date; and the last called it Moore's Patent!

MOORE'S PATENT (2)

With the official change of the town name to Clayton, the jars carried this name on the bottom after 1867

MOORE BROS. MASON'S PATENT NOV. 30th 1858

Circa 1875-80

Mason shoulder seal

Handmade round, ground lip, in green

Side: four lines: 'MASON'S,' arched, 'PATENT,' 'NOV. 30ᵀᴴ,' and '1858'

Bottom: in circle: 'MOORE BROS.' and 'GLASS CO.' circled around 'CLAYTON, N.J.'

Moore's
PATENT
DEC 3ᴰ 1861

MASON'S
PATENT
NOV 30ᵀᴴ
1858
(SIDE)

MOORE BROS
CLAYTON
N.J.
GLASS CO.

(BOTTOM)

Moore Bros., Fislerville (called Clayton after 1867), N.J., 1864-80

Probably made after Mason patent expired in 1875

MOUNTAIN

MASON

MOUNTAIN MASON

Circa 1920-40

Mason beaded neck design

Machine-made rounded square, in straw-colored amber (or sun-colored selenium)

Side: in two widely separated lines, 'MOUNTAIN' and 'MASON'

Maker unknown

MUTUAL GLASS CO.

Circa 1860-80

Groove-ring wax sealer

Handmade round, pressed laid-on-ring, in emerald green

Bottom: 'MUTUAL GLASS CO., PITTS-BURGH, PA.' in a circle

No record of this company was found

MYERS

TEST JAR

MYERS TEST JAR

Circa 1880-1900

Glass lid, metal yoke, and two lugs on jar neck

Handmade round, ground lip, in green

Side: 'MYERS' and 'TEST JAR' forming the top and bottom of an oval

Maker unknown

N

"N" with MASON'S PATENT NOV 30th 1858 (1)

Circa 1902-10

Mason shoulder seal

Handmade round, ground lip, in light green

Side: 'MASON'S' arched above 'N,' followed by 'PATENT,' 'NOV 30TH,' and '1858'

Port Glass Co., Belleville, Ill., 1902-04, when bought by Ball Bros. Co. and operated until 1910

"N" with MASON'S PATENT NOV 30th 1858 (2)

Same except with 'PORT' on back

"N" with MASON'S PATENT NOV 30th 1858 (3)

Same except with 'PORT' on the bottom

NATIONAL (1)

Circa 1876

Metal cap with small diamond ramps, meshing with similar small diamonds on the neck of the jar

Handmade round, ground lip, in green

Side: three lines: 'NATIONAL' arched above 'PATENTED JUNE 27TH' and '1876'

Probably the National Glass Co., of Pittsburgh, Pa. (dates uncertain), but who purchased the Canton Glass Co. of Marion, Ind., in 1899 and closed it

Patent No. 179,231 was issued to D. E. Stevens on June 27, 1876

MASON'S
N
PATENT
NOV 30TH
1858

NATIONAL
PATENTED JUNE 27TH
1876

NATIONAL (2)

A NATIONAL has been reported with a large, bulbous neck; not verified

NATIONAL PRESERVE CAN

Circa 1864

Glass lid and clamp securing under a bulged neck, details unknown

Handmade round, ground lip, in aqua

Front: 'NATIONAL' arched above a shield, with 'PRESERVE CAN' completing the circle below

Back: 'EARLE'S PATENT' arched over a fouled anchor, with 'FEB 2$\underline{ND}$, 1864' completing the circle below

Maker unknown

This patent was not found, but Timothy Earle obtained patents for venting devices on Nov. 10 and Dec. 22, 1863

NATIONAL SUPER MASON

Circa 1915-40

Mason bead style seal

Machine-made round half-gallon, in flint

Side: three lines: 'National' in upward-slanting script, 'SUPER,' and 'MASON'

Maker unknown

N C L with MASON'S PATENT
NOV 30th 1858

Circa 1880-1900

Mason shoulder seal

Handmade round, ground lip, in light green

Front: 'MASON'S' arched over 'PATENT,' 'NOV 30th,' and '1858'

Back: 'N C L'

Maker unknown

N C L

N C L Co. with MASON'S PATENT
NOV 30th 1858

Same jar as N C L but 'N. C. L. Co.' in heavy letters on back

N.C.L.Co.

NE PLUS ULTRA AIR TIGHT
FRUIT JAR

Circa 1861

Glass stopper held by metal cage having arms set in a helix to rotate on two lugs on the neck

Handmade round, ground lip, in green

Side: in three lines, each going completely around the jar, and the most involved and longest lettering found on any fruit jar: 'NE PLUS ULTRA AIR TIGHT FRUIT JAR,' 'MADE BY BODINE & BROS. W'MSTOWN, N.J.,' and 'FOR THEIR PATENT GLASS LID'

Lid: in circle: 'LUDLOW'S PATENT' and 'AUGUST 6 1861,' with 'JUNE 28 1859' in an inside arc

Washington Glass Works, Williamstown, N.J., 1839-64. Built by Joel Bodine in 1839 and operated by his three sons after his death in 1850 or 1856, until sold to Bodine & Thomas in 1864

NE PLUS ULTRA   AIR TIGHT FRUIT JAR

MADE BY BODINE & BROS. W'MSTOWN, N.J.

FOR THEIR PATENT GLASS LID

(AROUND TWO SIDES)

LUDLOW'S PATENT   JUNE 28 1859 AUGUST 6 1861

(BOTTOM)

W. D. Ludlow's two patents were No. 24,-566 on June 28, 1859, and No. 33,002 on Aug. 6, 1861. The latter most applied to this jar

NEWARK

On a dealer's want-list. May have been confused with NEWMARK; or may have been a product of Edward H. Everett Glass Co., Newark, Ohio

NEWMARK SPECIAL EXTRA

Circa 1925-38

Mason beaded neck seal

Machine-made round, in flint

Side: 'NEWMARK,' in old English lettering, over 'Special Extra' in script

Bottom: 'MFG. FOR M. A. NEWMARK CO., LOS ANGELES' circled about an "L" in an oval, the Latchford trade mark

W. J. Latchford Glass Co., Los Angeles, Cal., 1925-38

Latchford also made MISSION and BERNARDIN

NEWMARK SPECIAL EXTRA MASON JAR

Same, except 'MASON JAR' added as third line

NIFTY, THE

Circa 1890-1910

Glass lid and spring clip

Handmade wide-mouth round, ground lip, in flint

Side: 'The Nifty,' in script, over 'PAT. APPLIED FOR'

Maker unknown

NONPAREIL

Circa 1866

Tin cap, forming an inverted cup, filled with wax, which softens when placed on hot jar

Handmade round, ground lip, in green

Side: three lines: 'NONPAREIL,' 'PATENTED JULY 17,' and '1866'

Maker unknown

Patent No. 56,390 was issued to B. F. Ells of Dayton, Ohio

NONPAREIL
PATENTED JULY 17
1866

NORGE (1)

Circa 1936-40

Screw cap with small diameter, short height

Machine-made oblong, vertically ribbed, in green

Side: letters in vertical line: 'NORGE'

Unknown maker for the 1936 model Norge refrigerator, as a cold-water bottle. The jar is part No. 482-1836; the cap No. 482-1837

NORGE (2)

Circa 1940 to date

Glass lid with some kind of clamp

Machine-made round, in light green

Side: 'Norge' in script

Bottom: a gas light with 'DRAMMEN'S' and 'GLASS' in a circle around 'D G'

Maker unknown—possibly Norwegian

NU-SEAL

Circa 1915-19

Lightning closure, old neck design

Machine-made round, in flint

Side: from the top: a crown, 'NU-SEAL,' 'TRADE MARK,' 'REGISTERED,' and 'QUART'

Bottom: 'SMALLEY FRUIT JAR CO., BOSTON, MASS' in a circle around 'PAT JAN. 5, 1904'

Unknown maker. The Smalley Fruit Jar Co. was a short-lived subsidiary of Smalley, Kivlan & Onthank, successor to A. G. Smalley and Co., and was in existence from 1915 to 1919

NU-SEAL, SMALLEY'S (1)

Circa 1904

Lightning closure, old neck design

Machine-made round, in flint and suncolored

Side: two double-outline diamonds, with a space between the pairs. In the upper annular space: 'SMALLEY'S'; in the lower, 'TRADE MARK.' Across the center is 'NU-SEAL'

Bottom: 'A. G. SMALLEY, INC., BOSTON, MASS.' in a circle around 'PAT<u>D</u> JAN 5, 1904'

Maker unknown. Smalley was a jobber of china, glass, and porcelain

The only patent found for that date did not apply

NU-SEAL, SMALLEY'S (2)

Same except bottom marked only 'SMALLEY FRUIT JAR CO., BOSTON, MASS.' in a circle

N W ELECTROGLAS

See ELECTROGLAS

O

O G (1)

Circa 1929-33
Mason beaded neck style
Machine-made round, in flint
Side: a tall, oval "O" overlaid with a wide,
  oval "G"
Olean Glass Co., Olean, N.Y., 1890-1933
The jar was probably made after Olean
  purchased ACME in 1929, and until the
  Thatcher Glass Mfg. Co. purchased
  Olean in 1933

O G (2)

Circa 1900
Lightning closure, old-style neck design
Handmade round, ground lip, in light
  green
Bottom: 'O G'
Olean Glass Co., Olean, N.Y., 1890-1933

OHIO QUALITY MASON

Circa 1924-26
Mason beaded neck design
Machine-made round, in flint
Side: 'OHIO,' with both "O's" very much
  larger than "HI," above 'QUALITY' and
  'MASON'
Ohio Glass Products Co., Massilon, Ohio,
  1924-26
First listed in *Glass Factory Directory* for
  1925, and in receivership in 1926

O K

Circa 1867
Glass lid and metal screw-band top seal
Handmade round, ground lip, in green
Side: as a circle: 'PAT^D FEBY 9TH, 1864' as
  the top, and 'REIS^D JUNE 22^D, 1867' as

the bottom; 'OK' in large letters across diameter

Pacific Glass Works, San Francisco, Cal., 1865-79

See also PACIFIC GLASS WORKS and VICTORY for identical jar

OPLER BROTHERS

Circa 1910-30

Lightning closure, dimple neck design

Machine-made rounded square, in flint

Side: 'OPLER BROTHERS, INC.' in a circle within a double outline, enclosing 'O B' as a monogram. 'COCOA AND CHOCOLATE' on ribbon below. A straight panel below is lettered 'NEW YORK USA'

Bottom: 'SMALLEY, KIVLAN & ON-THANK'

Maker unknown. Smalley, Kivlan & On-thank were jobbers

OSOTITE

Modern, age uncertain

Apparently a friction side seal

Machine-made round, in flint

Side: a diamond, enclosing 'OSOTITE'

Maker unknown

The jar had an internal ledge, or step, but it seemed to be only a following of the external contour since it was not formed or even in structure

O V G CO JAR 1881

Circa 1886

Mason shoulder seal

Handmade round, ground lip, in green

Side: a monogram of "O V G Co" above 'JAR' and '1881'

Ohio Valley Glass Co., Bridgeport, Ohio.
Dates unknown but listed in 1886 *Directory of the Glass Factories of U.S. and Canada*

P

PACIFIC GLASS WORKS (1)

Circa 1867

Glass lid and metal screw-band top seal

Handmade round, ground lip, in green and aqua

Side: 'PACIFIC,' forming the top of a circle, and 'GLASS WORKS,' the bottom, around 'S. F.'

Back: as a circle: 'PAT$^{\underline{D}}$ FEBY 9$^{\underline{TH}}$, 1864' as the top; 'REIS$^{\underline{D}}$ JUNE 22nd, 1867' as the bottom

Pacific Glass Works, San Francisco, Cal., 1865-79. This was San Francisco's first glass plant

See also OK and VICTORY for identical jars

PACIFIC GLASS WORKS (2)

Same except 'SAN FRANCISCO' instead of 'S. F.'

PACIFIC MASON

Circa 1925-30

Mason beaded neck design

Machine-made round, in flint

Side: 'Pacific,' in script, slanted upward above 'MASON'

Bottom: "P" and "C" in a divided rectangle

Pacific Coast Glass Co., San Francisco, Cal., 1925-30. Was Pacific Coast Glass Works, 1902-25

PALACE HOME JAR

PALACE HOME JAR, HANSEE'S

Circa 1900

Glass straddle-lid top seal, closed by lever
with fulcrum in wire bail

Handmade round, ground lip, in green

Side: a monogram of "PH," with 'HAN-
SEE'S' arched above and 'PALACE
HOME JAR' below

Maker unknown

Rimmon H. Hansee of Monticello, N.Y.,
received Patent No. 639,559 for a top
cam lever design used on this jar

NEW

PARAGON

PARAGON, NEW

Circa 1870-80

Glass lid, and clamp to three lugs on neck

Handmade round, ground lip, in green and
blue-green

Side: 'NEW' above 'PARAGON'

Maker unknown

PATENT

SEPT. 18.1860

PATENT SEPT. 18, 1860 with moldmaker's error

Circa 1860-80

Blown-wax sealer, with mold-formed bulge
formed into a groove by downward pressure on the blowpipe while form was
still hot from the mold, giving a horizontal circular depression

Handmade round, ground lip, in aqua

Side: 'PATENT' (note missing crossbar on
the 'A') over 'SEPT 18, 1860'

Maker unknown

Agnew & Co. made this design as late as
1880; see AGNEW

PATENT SEPT 18, 1860 with another moldmaker's error

The year is given as 1880

PATENT APPLIED FOR

Circa 1855-70

Groove-ring wax sealer

Handmade round, pressed laid-on-ring, in aqua

Side: 'PATENT' and 'FOR' as top and bottom arcs of a circle, with 'APPLIED' across the diameter

Maker unknown

PANSY, THE

Known only from a dealer's want-list—not seen. One wonders if it was a companion to THE DAISY by F. E. Ward Co.

P C

Circa 1925-30

Lightning closure, beaded neck design

Machine-made round, in flint

Bottom: "P" and "C" in a divided rectangle

Pacific Coast Glass Co., San Francisco, Cal., 1925-30. Continuation of Pacific Coast Glass Works, 1902-25

P C G Co.

Circa 1860-80

Groove-ring wax sealer

Handmade round, pressed laid-on-ring, in green

Bottom: very faint, 'P C G Co.'

Probably the Pittsburgh City Glass Works, Pittsburgh "factory" name used beginning with Cunningham & Jackson, 1849 (Wilson Cunningham and George Whitten Jackson) through several partnership names until closing in 1909 as Cunninghams & Co. See CUNNINGHAM & IHMSEN, CUNNINGHAMS & Co., and D O C (for D. O. CUNNINGHAM & Co.)

P C G W

The same as P C G Co., but definitely P C G W on the bottom of an almost identical jar

There would be confusion with P C, P C G Co., and P C G W (see P C) if it were not for the handmade vs. machine-made aspects, and the obvious better workmanship of Pacific Coast's jars

PEARL

Late 1870s

Glass lid and metal screw-band top seal

Handmade tapered-shoulder round, ground lip, in green, light green, and aqua

Side: 'PEARL'

Bottom: several HERO patent dates

Hero Glass Works, Philadelphia, Pa., 1856-84

THE PE A RL

PEARL, THE

Same except 'THE PEARL,' in a sagging arc, and of an earlier date, circa 1868

PEERLESS (1)

PEERLESS

Circa 1863-70

Glass lid held by iron yoke engaging screw-threads on jar neck. Yoke had a central hole enclosing the rising center of the lid

Handmade round, ground lip, in green

Side: 'PEERLESS'

Maker unknown

PEERLESS (2)

Same except second line: 'PAT FEB 15, 1862' which was not a patent issue date. Feb. 14 would have been an issue date

PEERLESS (3)

Same except lettered: 'PAT FEB 15, 1863' on a second line on the side. Feb. 15, 1863 was not a patent issue date, as for 1963 it would be Feb. 10; Feb. 17, etc.

PEERLESS (4)

Circa 1860
Stopper finish for WILLOUGHBY STOP-PLE, which see
Handmade round, pressed laid-on-ring, in green
Side: 'PEERLESS'
Maker unknown

PEERLESS, CLARK'S

See CLARK'S PEERLESS

PENN, THE

THE
PENN

Circa 1866-74
Groove-ring wax sealer
Handmade round, pressed laid-on-ring, in green
Side: 'THE' and 'PENN' in two lines of seriffed letters
Bottom: 'BECK, PHILLIPS & Co., PITTS., PA.' forming a circle
Beck, Phillips & Co., Pittsburgh, Pa., 1866-74, a window-glass maker. See McKearin, p. 611
It was not unusual for a window-glass house to make bottles and jars, for "the top quarter of the pot was for bottles." This was because making bottles from the top glass, which was most seedy, would use up the seedy portion before they would make window glass

A feature of this jar was the three blown "legs" on the bottom, on which the jar would rest as a tripod, and prevent heat shock in use

PERFECTION (1)

Circa 1887

Glass lid with high, serrated wing. Two wire bails, about an inch apart and fastened to the neck tie-wire, could be pushed up the serrations until tight

Handmade round, ground lip, in flint

Side: 'PERFECTION' in an arch

Lid: 'PAT MAR 29, 1887'

Maker unknown

Lewis P. R. LeCompte's Patent No. 360,165, of March 29, 1887, called for the two wire bails to be held by dimples in the neck, but hand blowing was not yet up to this technique. It was not attained until just before the machine age

PERFECTION (2)

Same except only one bail. Inspection of the jar showed that the neck tie-wire was designed for only one bail. An oddity

PERFECT SEAL (1) [Note; not **THE PERFECT SEAL**]

Circa 1920 and later

Lightning closure, adjustable neck tie-wire design

Machine-made rounded square, in flint

Side: 'MADE IN CANADA' arched above a shield, which contains: 'PERFECT' and 'SEAL' in two slanting lines. Below the shield: 'WIDE MOUTH' above 'ADJUSTABLE'

Dominion Glass Co., Montreal, Que., 1913 to date

Note: There are many variations of this design: the position and length of the slanting lines within the shield, the shape of "P" and of "S" and whether round or rounded square in shape

PERFECT SEAL (2)

Same except round shape

PERFECT SEAL (3)

Same as (1) except also a "D" in a diamond trade mark on the bottom, which confirms Dominion as the maker

PERFECT SEAL (4)

Same as (2) except "WIDE MOUTH" omitted

PERFECT SEAL (5)

Same as (2) except "ADJUSTABLE" omitted

PERFECT SEAL (6)

Same as (1) except shield stippled
Minor variations in decorating lines on the shields are found in all of the above. "MADE IN CANADA" dates from 1920

PERFECT SEAL (7) [A totally different jar than other PERFECT SEALS]

Modern, date uncertain
Wide, flaring lip, with metal cap having permanently adhered soft-rubber ring, like a balloon
Machine-made squat round, in flint
Side: a circle containing 'Perfect' and 'Seal' in two lines of script
Maker unknown

PERFECT SEAL, THE (1) [Note: "THE" indicates older jars]

Circa 1913

Lightning closure, dimple neck design

Machine-made round, in flint and aqua (or sun-colored)

Side: 'The,' on a scroll, over 'PERFECT' and 'SEAL'; all three lines slanted upward

Attributed to the Jefferson Glass Co., Toronto, Ont., 1913-25, or to the Dominion Glass Co. (Hamilton plant ?), 1913 to date

Probably the oldest PERFECT SEAL

PERFECT SEAL, THE (2)

Circa 1913

Lightning closure, adjustable neck design

Machine-made rounded square, in flint

Side: vine and leaf design on either side of lettering; 'The' in a ribbon scroll at top, followed by 'PERFECT' and 'SEAL' in two slanting lines; 'WIDE' and 'MOUTH' on opposite ends of ribbon tieing vine at bottom; 'ADJUSTABLE' on another ribbon scroll at very bottom of design

Attributed to either Jefferson or Dominion as in (1)

Note: In addition to changes in "P" and "S," many variations exist in minute differences in the vine and leaves, the knot by which they are tied, and the ribbon making the knot

PERFECT SEAL, THE (3)

Same as (2) except: "THE" not in a ribbon scroll; "Perfect" and "Seal" in script; "WIDE" and "MOUTH" not on a ribbon; and no ribbon to tie the vines

PERFECT SEAL, THE (4)

Similar to (3) except entire lettering area somewhat foreshortened and not so tall and less pointed in vines at top

PERFECT SEAL, THE (5)

Circa 1913

Lightning closure, adjustable neck design

Machine-made rounded square, in flint

Side: without vines; 'The' in small ribbon scroll at top; 'PERFECT' and 'SEAL' in two slanting lines; 'WIDE MOUTH' in an arched panel; and 'ADJUSTABLE' in a straight panel

Attributed to Jefferson or Dominion as in (1)

PERFECT SEAL, McDONALD

See McDONALD PERFECT SEAL and McDONALD NEW PERFECT SEAL

PERFECTION

Circa 1890-1900

Lightning closure, old-style neck design

Handmade round, ground lip, in flint and aqua

Side: 'PERFECTION' in an arch

Maker unknown

PERRIN & Co., D. S.

Circa 1880-1900

Heavy-threaded screw finish, for metal cap or glass lid and screw-band

Handmade round, ground lip, in flint

Side: two lines: 'D S PERRIN & Co' and 'LONDON. ONT.'

Maker unknown. Perrin was a candy-maker

PET

PET (1)

Circa 1866-74

Groove-ring wax sealer

Handmade round, pressed laid-on-ring, in green and light green

Side: 'PET'

Bottom: 'BECK, PHILLIPS & Co., PITTS., PA.' in a circle

Beck, Phillips & Co., Pittsburgh, Pa., 1866-74

See PENN for remarks about Beck, Phillips & Co.

PET (2)

Circa 1870

Glass stopper with rubber ring side seal

Handmade round, pressed laid-on-ring, in light green

Side: 'PET'

Stopper: 'PAT AUGUST 31th, 1869'

Bottom: 'T G O,' meaning unknown

Possibly Beck, Phillips & Co., Pittsburgh, Pa., 1866-74, but uncertain

PET (3)

Perhaps circa 1870-80, but uncertain

Glass lid held by wire snap or clamp

Handmade small-mouth fruit *bottle,* pressed laid-on-ring, in green

Side: 'PET'

Maker unknown; possibly Beck, Phillips & Co., Pittsburgh, Pa., 1866-74

Only the similarity in lettering style indicates Beck, Phillips as the maker of PET (2) and (3) as identified in PET (1)

PETTIT (1)

Circa 1900-10

Glass lid, yoke, spring, and cam-lever SAFETY VALVE seal

Handmade round, ground lip, in light green

Bottom: 'H. W. PETTIT' and 'WEST-VILLE . N.J.' in a circle

Salem Glass Works, Salem, N.J., 1895-1937 (now part of Anchor Hocking) for H. W. Pettit, a hardware dealer

J. E. Pfeiffer of Pitman, N.J., gave me an envelop that Salem's frugal bookkeeper had slit open to use as note paper to record orders and other matters. The envelop carried Pettit's printed name, address, and "SAFETY VALVE" in the upper left corner

PETTIT (2)

Same, except the bottom reads 'H. W. PETTIT' and 'SALEM . N.J.' Since Pettit did not do business in Salem, that name is probably due to a mold-cutter's absentmindedness

PINE DELUXE

Circa 1927-29 only

Lightning closure, beaded neck design

Machine-made round, in flint

Side: in two lines: 'PINE' above 'DELUXE'

Pine Glass Co., Okmulgee, Okla., 1927-29

PINE DELUXE JAR

Circa 1927-29, probably later than PINE DELUXE

Lightning closure, beaded neck design

Machine-made round, in flint

Side: three lines: 'PINE,' 'DELUXE,' and 'JAR'

Pine Glass Co., Okmulgee, Okla., 1927-29
Ball Bros. Co., after buying Pine in 1929,
continued this jar by substituting "BALL"
for "PINE." See BALL DELUXE JAR

PINE

P

MASON

PINE MASON

Circa 1927-29
Mason beaded neck design
Machine-made round, in flint
Side: "P" in a square, with 'PINE' above
and 'MASON' below
Pine Glass Co., Okmulgee, Okla., 1927-29

PINE MASON (2)

Same except also "P" in a square on the
bottom

Mr. R. D. Pine, a vice-president of Pine
Glass Co., tells me that it was a home-
financed company and that it took particular pride in the clarity of its glass and
the subsequent demand for it to use in
exhibiting home canning at fairs

W^M POCUE

BRIDGETON

N. J.

(SIDE)

FOR

PRESERVING

FRUIT.

(BACK)

POCUE, WM., BRIDGETON, N.J.

Circa 1850
Wax sealer with groove made by depress-
ing the shoulder while hot
Handmade squat round, fired sheared lip,
in light green, using bare pontil and leaving iron rust on bottom
Side: three lines: 'W^M POCUE,' arched
over a small sunburst, 'BRIDGETON,'
and 'N.J.'
Back: three lines: 'FOR,' 'PRESERVING,'
and 'FRUIT.'
Maker unknown. Pocue is believed to be a
Bridgeton merchant or food packer as
the name is not known as a glassmaker

The use of the bare iron pontil, as noted under RAVENNA and under Wax sealers, under Miscellaneous in the glossary, ranks this as one of the oldest known fruit jars other than early pottery jars

POMONA

Circa 1868

Seal unknown. Jar has a stopper-like recessed ledge

Handmade round, pressed laid-on-ring, in green

Side: four lines: 'POMONA,' arched, 'PATENTED,' 'MAR. 10th' and '1868'

Bottom: 'MASS. GLASS CO.' in circle widely spaced

Maker unknown. The Massachusetts Glass Company has not been identified

The patent date is the same as that of Imlay's No. 75,275, used on the VALVE JAR, but the finish does not agree with that design

PORCELAIN LINED

Circa 1873-80

Mason shoulder seal

Handmade round, ground lip, in green

Side: 'PORCELAIN' arched above 'LINED'

Bottom: in circle: 'PAT NOV 26 67 & FEB 4 73,' both HERO dates

Hero Glass Works, Philadelphia, Pa., 1856-84

One collector has a "MASON'S PATENT NOV 30th 1858" with "PORCELAIN LINED" partly obliterated by peening. Since HERO began using the Mason reference about 1882-84, that could be the "end" of the PORCELAIN LINED era for them. But see also B B G M Co

POMONA
PATENTED
MAR. 10th
1868

PORCELAIN
LINED

PORCELAIN LINED and AMERICAN PORCELAIN LINED which came out soon thereafter

Nov. 26, 1867 was Hero's most commonly used date and does not truly apply. Neither does Henry Howson's Patent No. 135,430 of Feb. 4, 1873, since it was for an all-glass lid!

MASON'S
PATENT
1858

Port

PORT MASON'S PATENT 1858 (1)

Circa 1902-10 or 13
Mason shoulder seal
Handmade round, ground lip, in light green
Front: 'MASON'S' arched above 'PATENT' and '1858'
Back: 'Port' in script
Port Glass Co., Belleville, Ill., 1902-10 or 13. Bought by Ball Bros. Co. in 1904 and operated until either 1910 or 1913.

PORT MASON'S PATENT 1858 (2)

Circa 1910
Same except machine-made in aqua

PORT MASON'S PATENT 1858 (3)

Same as (1) except "Port" on bottom instead of on the back

PORT MASON'S PATENT NOV 30th 1858, with the letter N

Circa 1902-10 or 13
Mason shoulder seal
Handmade round, ground lip, in light green
Side: 'MASON'S,' arched above 'N,' followed by 'PATENT,' 'NOV 30th,' and '1858'
Bottom: 'Port' in script
Port Glass Co., Belleville, Ill., 1902-10 or 13

See also under "N" and under "BALL."
Evidently PORT originated the use of
"N" with the MASON'S PATENT word-
ing, first without the PORT identifica-
tion, then with it, and finally adopted by
BALL under their own identification

POTTER & BODINE (1)

Circa 1858
Glass lid held by metal yoke to two helical
lugs on jar neck
Handmade round, ground lip, in blue tint
Side: 'Potter & Bodine' arched above 'Philadelphia,' both in script
Potter & Bodine, Philadelphia, Pa., 1855-
63. Became Bodine Brothers, 1863-70,
and Cohansey Glass Mfg. Co., 1870-1900.
All three maintained offices in Philadelphia, but operated the Bridgeton Glass
Works, at Bridgeton, N.J. (McKearin, p.
602; Knittle, p. 355)

POTTER & BODINE (2)

Same except with three lugs, which gave
better sealing because of three-point
contact and center of pressure

POTTER & BODINE (3)

Same as (1) with two lugs, and lettered
'PAT OCT 19, 1858' on the lid. This patent was not found

PRATIQUE, LE (THE PRACTICAL or
THE CUSTOM)

Modern French jar
Glass lid held by wire hinge, or linkage, on
one side, and sealed by a wire snap lock
on the other
Machine-made round, in flint

Le Pratique

Side: 'Le Pratique,' in script, with capacity in liters
Verreries Hemain Frères, S.A., Rive-de-Gier, France
ERMEBLOK, L'IDEALE, and TRIOMPHE use the same seal

PREMIER

Circa 1930-50
Mason beaded neck design
Machine-made round, in flint
Side: 'PREMIER'
Bottom: "O" and "I" intersecting a diamond
Owens Illinois Glass Co., Toledo, Ohio, 1929 to date
Probably made for Premier Foods

PREMIUM
COFFEYVILLE KAS

PREMIUM COFFEEVILLE

Circa 1904-15
Glass lid with spring clip pressed from side to clamp lid and top ledge of the finish together
Handmade round, ground lip, in flint
Side: 'PREMIUM' arched above 'COFFEE-VILLE'
Lid: in circle: 'PAT'D MARCH 19TH 1901'
Premium Glass Co., Coffeeville, Kan., 1904-15
Ball Bros. Co. purchased the plant in 1909 and operated it until 1915
Patent was not found

PREMIUM IMPROVED

Circa 1904-15, probably late
Mason shoulder seal
Machine-made round, in flint
Side: 'Premium' in script, above 'IMPROVED'

Premium

IMPROVED

Note that this is not the usual application of the word "IMPROVED," but, of course, in the eyes of the maker was an improvement

PRESTO

Circa 1925-46
Mason beaded neck design
Machine-made round, in flint
Side: 'Presto,' in slanting italics, capital and lower case
Illinois Glass Co., Alton, Ill., 1873-1929, and
Illinois Pacific Glass Co., San Francisco, Cal., 1902-30, and
Owens Illinois Glass Co., Toledo, Ohio, 1929 to date

PRESTO FRUIT JAR

Same except two additional lines: 'FRUIT' and 'JAR'
'Presto' similar to preceeding in shape, but doubly outlined

PRESTO GLASS TOP (1)

Circa 1925-46
Lightning closure, beaded neck style, in flint
Machine-made round, in flint
Side: 'Presto' in slanting, doubly outlined italics above 'GLASS' and 'TOP'
Illinois Glass, Illinois Pacific Glass, and Owens Illinois as for PRESTO

PRESTO GLASS TOP (2)

Same except with Owens Illinois trade mark on bottom

PRESTO GLASS TOP (3)

Same as (1) except with dimple Lightning finish

SUPREME
MASON

PRESTO SUPREME MASON (1)

Circa 1929-46
Mason beaded neck design
Machine-made round, in flint
Side: 'Presto' in slanting, doubly outlined
    italics above 'SUPREME' and 'MASON'
Bottom: "O" and "I" intersecting a diamond
Owens Illinois Glass Co., Toledo, Ohio,
    1929 to date

PRESTO SUPREME MASON (2)

Circa 1925-30
Same as (1) except with Illinois Pacific
    Glass Co., San Francisco, Cal., 1902-30,
    trade mark on bottom

WIDE MOUTH

PRESTO WIDE MOUTH

Circa 1925-46
Wide-mouth Mason, beaded neck design,
    with 'Presto,' in doubly outlined italics,
    above "WIDE MOUTH"

WIDE MOUTH
GLASS TOP

PRESTO WIDE MOUTH
GLASS TOP (1)

Circa 1925-46
Wide-mouth Lightning finish, with 'Presto,'
    in doubly outlined italics, above 'WIDE
    MOUTH' and 'GLASS TOP' in two more
    lines

PRESTO WIDE MOUTH
GLASS TOP (2)

Same except glass lid and metal screw-band

PRESTO WIDE MOUTH with Duraglas

After 1944 the name "Duraglas" was an
    additional trade mark of the Owens Illi-
    nois Glass Company. 'Duraglas' is in
    script as a fourth line on the side. It was
    also on the bottom of some jars

PRINCESS (1)

Circa 1915-25

Lightning closure, adjustable neck tie-wire design

Machine-made round, in aqua

Side: a draped shield containing the word 'PRINCESS' in an arch

Maker unknown

Workmanship, elaborateness of design, and the name itself "sounds" like Smalley and his love for "royal" names on fruit jars. His ROYAL, CROWN, KING, and QUEEN are well known and identified with him. Then there was MAGIC, and, who knows, perhaps a little PRINCESS! But it is very, very unlike Smalley not to place his name on the jar

PRINCESS (2)

The same jar has been found with the old design neck contour for the Lightning seal, which would date it circa 1900-15. Machine-made

PROTECTOR (1)

Circa 1867

Metal lid to which a wire clip was soldered. The clip fitted two helical lugs on the neck

Handmade round, ground lip, in green. The round shape is rare

Side: in an arch: 'PROTECTOR'

Maker unknown

PROTECTOR (2)

Same, except the more common six-sided style with 'PROTECTOR' lettered vertically on one panel

One jar found with a faint patent reference, undecipherable except for what appeared

to be "1867." Also, D. I. Holcomb, in the application for his Patent No. 97,920, granted Dec. 14, 1869, refers to the shortcomings of a previous patent in which the wire clip was permanently fastened to the lid—this partially confirms the date

PURITAN, THE (1)

Circa 1870-80
Closure uncertain—probably a glass lid and
    some kind of clamp
Handmade round, ground lip, in aqua
Side: 'THE' and 'PURITAN' in two lines
Back: a monogram of "L S Co"
Maker unknown
The finish was rounded on top and had no
    particular flat sealing area

PURITAN, THE (2)

Differs in having a flat external ledge to
    hold a sealing ring or clip
This PURITAN is very similar to the ELECTRIC. Alberta Kerr points out that the PURITAN, the GEO. D. BROWN, and the FRUIT KEEPER had almost identical finishes. The FRUIT KEEPER was made by the Canton Glass Co. and had a glass lid held by a clamp of cast and stamped metal, with a cam-lever action. This could be appropriate for the PURITAN neck construction, so perhaps Canton made all three

THE
PURITAN

PUTNAM

Circa 1882-90
Lightning closure, old neck design
Handmade round, ground lip, in aqua
Side: no lettering
Bottom: 'PUTNAM'

Maker only possibly the Lyndeboro Glass
Co., Lyndeboro, N.H., 1866-86
A rare variation—most have "LIGHT-
NING" on side

PUTNAM GLASS WORKS

Circa 1860-70
Groove-ring wax sealer
Handmade round, pressed laid-on-ring, in
green
Bottom: 'PUTNAM GLASS WORKS'
Putnam Flint Glass Works, Putnam, Ohio,
1852-71

Q

Q G or G Q

Circa 1900-30
Mason shoulder seal
Machine-made round, in deep amethyst
Side: a monogram of "G" enclosing a "Q,"
both very large. The order of the letters
is unknown
Maker unknown. No glass company could
be found with these initials, even con-
sidering "Q———Glass"

Q G MASON or G Q MASON

The same letters below 'MASON' in heavy
arched lettering

QUEEN (1) with moldmaker's error

Circa 1909
Lightning closure, adjustable neck tie-
wire design
Machine-made rounded square, in flint
Side: a tall shield containing 'Queen,' in
script, and 'TRAD MARK' (misspelled)
on a ribbon finial. Below the shield:

'WIDE MOUTH' in an arched panel; 'ADJUSTABLE' in a straight panel. 'S K O' arched above the shield

Bottom: in circle: 'SMALLEY, KIVLAN & ONTHANK, BOSTON'

Smalley, Kivlan & Onthank, Boston, Mass, 1907-19, were jobbers. The maker of the jar is unknown as Smalley used many sources

QUEEN (2)

Circa 1909-19

Glass lid held by three-element toggles from opposite sides, the top hooking element being flat metal

Machine-made rounded square, in flint

Side: a smaller shield than in (1), and without 'WIDE MOUTH' or 'ADJUST-ABLE.' "S," "K," and "O" in individual, small shields

Bottom: 'SMALLEY, KIVLAN & ON-THANK, PAT FEB 9, 1909,' in a circle

Maker unknown

Patent No. 913,214 was issued to John Kivlan on Feb. 9, 1909, for the first of his twin-toggle clamps. In this design, each toggle is made up from three elements. The second patent eliminated the unnecessary third toggle element, and the third converted it into a one-element snap

QUEEN (3)

Circa 1909

Lightning closure with adjustable neck tie-wire

Machine-made rounded square, in flint

Side: same shield as in (2) with 'IM-PROVED' near the neck and 'WIDE MOUTH' in an arched panel, and 'AD-JUSTABLE' in a straight panel as in (1)

Unknown maker for Smalley, Kivlan & Onthank

QUEEN (4)

Lettered as in (3) but fitted with Kivlan's twin toggle as in (2). This seems to be a factory error in assembly and easily possible since the two seals could go on the same jar design. It is very possible that Smalley, Kivlan & Onthank bought the jars and added the sealing mechanisms themselves

QUEEN (5)

Same as (3) except "TIGHT" replaces "IMPROVED"

QUEEN (6)

Same as (5) except stippled shield

QUEEN (7)

Same as (1) except "WIDE MOUTH" omitted

QUEEN (8)

Same as (2) except "KIVLAN & ON-THANK" on bottom, which dates the jar to after the 1919 formation of this successor to Smalley, Kivlan & Onthank

QUEEN (9)

Same as (2) except without bottom identification, which is very unlike the Smalley practice. Possibly made by Consumers Glass Co., Toronto, Ont., but the jar lacks their "C" in a triangle trade mark

QUEEN (10)

Similar to (9) except also lettered 'MADE IN CANADA,' which would date the jar to 1920 or later. Possibly Smalley had a working agreement with Consumers, since the latter used several Smalley designs and names

QUEEN, THE (1)

Circa 1868

Glass lid and metal screw-band top seal

Handmade round, ground lip, in aqua

Side: 'THE' and 'QUEEN' in two lines in the center of a circle made up of 'PAT'ᴰ DEC 28ᵀᴴ 1858' as its top and 'PATᴰ JUNE 16ᵀᴴ 1868' as its bottom

Maker unknown

The only Dec. 28, 1858, patent found was for a sealing-wax composition which may indicate that the first QUEEN was a wax sealer. Patent No. 78,976 of June 16, 1868, does not apply and no other of that date was found. The glass lid has a high arch and protrudes more than the usual glass lid used with a metal screw-band

THE QUEEN

QUEEN, THE (2)

Circa 1869

Glass lid and metal screw-band top seal as in (1)

Handmade round, ground lip, in aqua

Side: 'THE' and 'QUEEN' in two lines

Bottom: in circle: 'PAT NOV 2, 1869'

Maker uncertain

Collectors have called this a HERO jar. Patent No. 96,490 was issued on Nov. 2, 1869, to H. E. Shaffer of Rochester, N.Y. The jar may have been made by the Rochester Glass Works, Rochester, N.Y., 1865-87, or by the nearby Hitchens Glass Works of Lockport, N.Y., 1840-69, which HERO bought in 1869 and sold in 1872, to become the Mansfield Glass Works, 1872-1909. No HERO jars have been found with the Nov. 2, 1869, date, and it was HERO's custom to show every date possible, whether it applied or not. Further, the name does not appear on HERO's 1878 letterhead, nor is it mentioned in the Lockport Journal of July 13, 1870, which carried a story about HERO and its reopening of the Lockport plant. I believe that both QUEEN (1) and (2) are Rochester jars

QUEEN, THE (3)

Same as (2) except patent date is shown below "THE" and "QUEEN" on the side, while the lid reads: 'THE QUEEN JAR PAT NOV 2 1869' in a circle

QUICK SEAL (1)

Circa 1930-40
Lightning closure, dimple neck design
Machine-made round, in blue tint
Side: 'Quick' and 'Seal,' in two lines of
  slanting script
Ball Bros. Co., Muncie, Ind., 1888 to date,
  for Woolworth's

QUICK SEAL (2)

Same except 'PAT'D JULY 14, 1908' below
  name

QUICK SEAL (3)

Same as (1) except with an oval outline
  around name

QUICK SEAL (4)

Same as (1) except without dimple, and
  with old-style Lightning finish, circa
  1910-30

QUONG HOP & Co. (1)

Circa 1925-30
Lightning closure, dimple neck design
Machine-made round, in flint
Side: 'QUONG HOP & Co.,' '133 WAV-
  ERLY PLACE,' and 'S. F. CAL.' in three
  lines with many Chinese characters
Bottom: "P" and "C" in a divided rectangle
Pacific Coast Glass Co., San Francisco,
  Cal., 1925-30

QUONG HOP & Co. (2)

Same except without the "P" and "C"
  identification

R

RADER BROS. & LAMPKIN
See SEALFAST

R A G monogram
See GJ [Gilchrist Jar] for "Ruth A. Gilchrist" monogram

HELME'S

RAIL ROAD

MILLS

RAIL ROAD MILLS, HELME'S
Circa 1870-1900

Glass lid and metal screw-band top seal

Handmade round, ground lip, in amber

Side: three lines: 'HELME'S' arched above 'RAIL ROAD' and 'MILLS'

Maker unknown

The jar has a distinct "waist" in the neck, probably functional in preventing loss of contents, for the jar is probably a snuff container used by P. Lorillard & Co., then owned by the G. W. Helme Co. of New Jersey. The opening was as large as the body of the jar

R A M S A Y

J A R

RAMSAY JAR
Circa 1867

Glass lid, oval below a deep circular groove, and which passed through an oval neck opening, turning to seal as on an internal lug

Handmade twelve-sided jar, ground lip, in dark green. A pressing operation was used to maintain uniformity in opening; laid-on-ring

Side: 'RAMSAY,' one letter to a panel, above 'JAR,' in three panels beginning under the "M" of RAMSAY

Maker unknown

RATH'S (1)

From 1921 to date
Mason beaded neck design
Machine-made round, in flint
Side: four lines: 'RATH'S,' 'FOOD PRO-
DUCTS,' 'WATERLOO,' and 'IOWA'
Variously made by Ball Bros. Co., Owens
Bottle Co., Owens Illinois, Hazel Atlas,
and Anchor Hocking, from information
furnished by Rath's
Used by Rath Packing Co., Waterloo,
Iowa

RATH'S (2)

From 1921 to date
Lightning closure, beaded neck design
Machine-made round, in light blue-green
Side: 'RATH'S,' as the top of a circle,
'WATERLOO, IOWA,' as the bottom,
with 'PACKING CO.' across the
diameter
Variously made as in RATH'S (1)

RAU'S IMPROVED GROOVE RING JAR

See GROOVE RING JAR, RAU'S IM-
PROVED

RAVENNA GLASSWORKS

Circa 1850
Tooled groove-ring wax sealer
Handmade round barrel, showing hoops
but not staves, with tooled rather than
pressed laid-on-ring, with red-black
bottom discoloration showing the use
of a bare iron pontil, in dark blue-green
Front: three lines: 'RAVENNA,' 'GLASS-
WORKS,' and 'OHIO'
Back: 'AIR TIGHT' above 'FRUIT JAR'
Ravenna Glassworks, Ravenna, Ohio, pos-
sibly circa 1850-57 or 64.

RAVENNA

GLASSWORKS

OHIO

McKearin, p. 232, and Knittle, p. 383, discuss this company as the Ravenna Glass *Company,* as well as the question of an earlier operation than the known dates of 1850-57. This might have been as the Ravenna Glass *Works*

This might be the oldest *identified* fruit jar herein listed, although other unlettered and unidentified cork-and-wax sealers may be older

RED KEY MASON

Circa 1892-98

Mason shoulder seal

Handmade round, ground lip, in aqua and green

Side: 'RED,' in doubly outlined letters superimposed on a key, above 'MASON'

Safe Glass Co., Redkey, Ind., 1892-98; Bowling Green, Ohio, until natural gas exhausted in 1892; moved to Marion, Ind., 1898-1905 when gas exhausted at Redkey

RED KEY with MASON'S PATENT NOV 30th 1858

Circa 1892-98

Mason shoulder seal

Handmade round, ground lip, in green and aqua

Side: five lines: 'RED,' superimposed on a key, 'MASON'S,' arched, 'PATENT,' NOV 30$\underline{\text{TH}}$,' and '1858'

Safe Glass Co., Redkey, Ind., 1892-98. See RED KEY MASON for other dates

On some jars the RED KEY design is cut so strongly in an otherwise faintly lettered mold that it indicates a recutting of an old mold, possibly brought from Ohio

REID, MURDOCH & CO.

Circa 1915-30
Mason beaded neck design
Machine-made round, in flint
Side: 'REID, MURDOCH & CO' arched
above 'CHICAGO'
Maker unknown

REISS & BRADY

Circa 1903
Glass lid held by ECONOMY style metal
band spring clip
Machine-made oval, in flint
Side: a double circle outline, with 'MORE
THAN A LITTLE BETTER' in the
upper annular space and 'REISS &
BRADY NEW YORK' in the lower.
Within the circles is the drawing of a
ship, and 'CRESCA' with an "R & B"
monogram
Bottom: 'PAT JUNE 9, 1903' which is the
date of the Goltstein patent used on
ECONOMY jars
Probably by the Hazel Atlas Glass Co.,
Wheeling, W. Va., 1902-64, which
bought the commercial rights to the seal
used on the ECONOMY jar, and which
was an early partner in the Phoenix
Metals Co., which made the metal
ECONOMY lid

RELIABLE HOME CANNING MASON

Circa 1940-50
Mason beaded neck design
Machine-made round, in flint
Side: 'Reliable' in script, above 'HOME
CANNING' and 'MASON'
Bottom: "F" in a hexagon
Fairmount Glass Co., Indianapolis, Ind.,
1888 to date

RELIANCE BRAND

Circa 1935-45
Mason beaded neck design
Machine-made wide-mouth rounded square, in flint
Side: 'RELIANCE' above 'BRAND'
Bottom: "O" and "I" intersecting a diamond, with date code for either 1934 or 1944
Owens Illinois Glass Co., Toledo, Ohio, 1929 to date

RELIANCE BRAND WIDE MOUTH MASON

Same jar as RELIANCE BRAND and similarly lettered on front, but with 'RE-LIANCE,' 'BRAND,' 'WIDE MOUTH,' and 'MASON' on the back

RETENTIVE

Circa 1890-1910
Bulbous neck, for clamp and either glass or metal lid
Handmade round, ground lip, in light green
Side: 'RETENTIVE' reading vertically
Maker unknown

RICE & BURNETT

Circa 1860-70
Stopper finish, for WILLOUGHBY STOPPLE, which see
Handmade round, pressed laid-on-ring, in light green
Side: three lines: 'MANUFACTURED FOR,' 'RICE & BURNETT,' arched above 'CLEVELAND OHIO'
Bottom: 'L & W'

Lorenz & Wightman, Pittsburgh, Pa., 1851-71

The WILLOUGHBY STOPPLE was invented in 1859

RIVERS, 3 or 3 RIVERS

See THREE RIVERS, although the 3 Rivers Glass Co., Three Rivers, Texas, 1925-37, seldom spelled out the number

ROOT (1)

Circa 1902-09

Mason shoulder seal

Handmade round, ground lip, in light green, yellow-green, and aqua

Side: 'Root,' in script, with a long, curved finial

Root Glass Co., Terre Haute, Ind., 1902-09

Do not confuse with Root's separate beverage-bottle factory, also located in Terre Haute, which designed the first trade-marked bottle used by Coca-Cola. The fruit-jar factory was sold to Ball Bros. Co. in 1909 and closed. The beverage-bottle factory was sold to Owens Illinois in 1932 and was operated as their Terre Haute factory unit

ROOT (2)

Circa 1908-09

Same design as (1) except very crudely machine-made. Root had developed a semi-automatic bottle-blowing machine in 1908, just before he sold the fruit-jar factory to Ball Bros Co.

ROOT MASON

Similar to ROOT (1), except the word 'MASON' added below the script 'Root'

RORDEN & Co., L.

See SEALFAST

ROSE, THE (1)

Circa 1915-30
Mason beaded neck design
Machine-made round, in flint
Side: 'The Rose' in script, ending as a long finial
Bottom 'IMP'
Maker unknown, but probably Canadian

ROSE, THE (2)

Same, without "IMP" on the bottom

ROYAL (1)

Circa 1896-1907
Lightning closure, old-style neck design
Handmade rounded square, ground lip, in flint and green
Side: a crown, followed by 'ROYAL' and 'TRADE MARK'
Bottom: 'A. G. SMALLEY & Co., BOSTON' in a circle around 'PAT. APRIL 7, 1896'
Maker unknown, for Smalley, a jobber, changed supply source from year to year
Patent No. 572,281 was issued to Albert G. Smalley on Dec. 1, 1896, for the rounded-square shape and for a tabbed, rubber sealing ring, but no patent was found for the April 7, 1896, date. He, as many patentees do, could have used the application date

ROYAL (2)

Circa 1896-1907

Lightning closure, old-style neck design

Handmade rounded square, ground lip, in green

Side: a crown at the top, followed by: 'ROYAL,' 'TRADE MARK,' 'FULL MEASURE,' in an arched panel, 'REGISTERED,' and 'QUART'

Bottom: 'A. G, SMALLEY & Co.' 'PATENTED APRIL 7, 1896' and 'BOSTON & NEW YORK'

Maker unknown, since Smalley was a jobber

ROYAL (3)

Same as (2) except "ROYAL," repeated, superimposed on the crown

ROYAL (4)

Same as (2) except "ROYAL" lettered above the crown

ROYAL (5)

Circa 1877
Glass lid and metal screw-band top seal
Handmade round, ground lip, in amber and cobalt blue
Side: 'ROYAL'
Lid: 'PAT FEB 27, 1877'
Maker unknown

ROYAL (6)

Circa 1913
Lightning closure, old-style neck design
Machine-made rounded square, in flint
Side: same lettering as in ROYAL (2)
Bottom: "C" in a triangle
Consumers Glass Co., Toronto, Ont., 1913 to date

ROYAL OF 1876

Circa 1880-1900
Glass lid and metal screw-band top seal
Handmade round, ground lip, in aqua
Side: three lines: 'ROYAL' arched over 'OF' and '1876'
Maker unknown
Compare with MASON JAR OF 1872

S

"S" with MASON'S PATENT 1858 (1)

Circa 1882
Mason shoulder seal
Handmade round, ground lip, in green
Side: an unlettered HERO CROSS above an arched 'MASON'S,' followed by 'S,' 'PATENT,' and '1858'
Hero Glass Works, Philadelphia, Pa., 1856-1884

"S" with MASON'S PATENT 1858 (2)

Same except without the HERO CROSS. The form is nearly identical in other respects to (1) above, and indicates a strong probability that HERO used the "S" design

"S" with MASON'S PATENT 1858 (3)

Similar to (2) above, except that the "S" is above "MASON'S." The "S" is very crudely formed and cut

"S" with MASON'S PATENT 1858 (4)

Same arrangement as (3) except that the "S" is well formed and all lettering is doubly outlined

The use of "S" has also been attributed to the Salem Glass Works, Salem, N.J., 1895-1938, but I do not agree. The workmanship is earlier in execution, and one jar has definite identification with HERO. Perhaps all four listed are by HERO

SAFE SEAL (1)

Circa 1920-40
Mason beaded neck design
Machine-made round, in flint
Side: 'SAFE' and 'SEAL' in two slightly
    slanted lines
Ball Bros. Co., Muncie, Ind., 1888 to date
Made for the S. S. KRESGE STORES

SAFE
SEAL

PAT'D JULY 14,1908

SAFETY

SAFE SEAL (2)

Circa 1920-40
Lightning closure, dimple neck style
Machine-made round, in flint
Side: 'SAFE' and 'SEAL' in two slightly slanted lines, above 'PAT'D JULY 14, 1908'
Ball Bros. Co., Muncie, Ind., 1888 to date

SAFETY (1)

Circa 1895-1910
Glass lid held by a wire clip locking in slanting neck indentations like the ALL RIGHT, but with the indented neck slots ending in a horizontal "holding" position, not serrated as in the ALL RIGHT
Handmade round, ground lip, in flint and amber
Side: 'SAFETY'
Salem Glass Works, Salem, N.J., 1895-1938; now a unit of Anchor Hocking

SAFETY (2)

Circa 1910-25
Mason shoulder seal
Machine-made round, in aqua and light green
Side: same as (1)
Salem Glass Works, Salem, N.J., 1895-1938; now a unit of Anchor Hocking

SAFETY NOTCH COVER

Age unknown—any time since 1890 to date
Maker unknown

A replacement for the usual Lightning closure lid. The glass lid had a diagonal rib rising across the center, with two notches to catch the locking wire of the Lightning closure. A notch in the center top was marked 'SEAL' and one halfway down the rib was marked 'BOIL,' as a position of less tension that would allow air to escape. Also lettered: 'SAFETY NOTCH COVER' and 'PATENT PENDING' as the top and bottom arcs of a circle

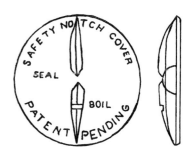

SAFETY SEAL (1)

Circa 1917-20
Lightning closure, old-style neck design
Machine-made round, in flint
Side: two lines: 'SAFETY' above 'SEAL'
Bottom: "C" in a triangle
Consumers Glass Co., Toronto, Ont., 1917
to date

SAFETY SEAL (2)

After 1920
Lightning closure, dimple neck design
Machine-made round, in flint
Side: three lines: 'SAFETY,' 'SEAL,' and
'MADE IN CANADA'
Bottom: "C" in a triangle
Consumers Glass Co., Toronto, Ont., 1917
to date

SAFETY SEAL (3)

Circa 1930
Lightning closure, adjustable neck tie-wire
style
Rest of details as in SAFETY SEAL(2)

SAFETY
SEAL

SAFETY
SEAL

MADE IN CANADA

SAFETY VALVE (1)

Circa 1895 until about 1930

Glass lid held by metal strip yoke hooking under finish ledge, with a spring to hold in venting tension during the boiling, and a cam lever to seal tightly after boiling

Handmade round, pressed laid-on-ring, in green

Side: a Greek Key design circles the entire jar at shoulder and heel

Bottom: 'SAFETY VALVE' and 'PAT^D MAY 21 1895' in a circle. A large intersecting "H" and "G" superimposed on a triangle in the center

Hamilton plant of the Diamond Glass Co., Montreal, Que., 1891-1901, Diamond Flint Glass Co., 1901-13, and Dominion Glass Co., 1913 to date

SAFETY VALVE (2)

Same except with "H" and "G" in a diamond on the bottom

SAFETY VALVE (3)

Same as (1) except without the Greek Key design

SAFETY VALVE (4)

Not identifiable as to maker; lettered 'SAFETY VALVE' on the bottom. See PETTIT for SAFETY VALVE made by the Salem Glass Co., Salem, N.J., 1895-1938, and JOHNSON & JOHNSON for one made by the Cumberland Glass Mfg. Co., Bridgeton, N.J., 1896-1920 (Cumberland Glass Co., 1882-96)

Patent No. 539,674 was issued to Henry C. Dilworth of East Orange, N.J., on

May 21, 1895, for this seal. John Algeo, former Sales Manager of Hazel Atlas tells me that it was considered a good seal, but expensive. It was used commercially, as by J. Hungerford Smith & Co. for glassed fruits for the hotel trade, as well as for fruit jars, and was not discarded until about 1930

SAFETY WIDE MOUTH MASON (1)

Circa 1910-25
Glass lid and metal screw-band top seal
Machine-made round, in aqua
Side: five lines: 'SAFETY,' 'WIDE MOUTH,' 'MASON,' 'SALEM GLASS WORKS,' and 'SALEM, N.J.'
Salem Glass Works, Salem, N.J., 1895-1938; now a unit of Anchor Hocking

SAFETY
WIDE MOUTH
MASON
SALEM GLASS WORKS
SALEM, N.J.

SALEM JAR, THE

See HOLZ CLARK & TAYLOR

SAMCO GENUINE MASON

Circa 1920-40
Mason beaded neck design
Machine-made rounded square, in flint
Side: 'Samco,' in script inside a small circle, written in a slant above 'Genuine,' in capital initial letter followed by lower case letters, double-outlined, and 'MASON,' in block print
Maker unknown, but possibly Illinois Glass Co., Alton, Ill., 1873-1929, Illinois Pacific Glass Co., San Francisco, Cal., 1902-30, and Owens Illinois Glass Co., Toledo, Ohio, 1929 to date. Bottle, however, carries none of the identifications normally used by these companies. They used "GENUINE" as a designation, however

SAMCO SUPER MASON

Circa 1920-40
Mason beaded neck design
Machine-made round, in flint
Side: 'Samco' in large script without the
circle, above 'SUPER' and 'MASON'
Maker unknown, unless also as in SAMCO
GENUINE MASON

SAMPSON IMPROVED BATTERY

Circa 1880
Mason threads, shoulder seal, but probably
used with a special fitting
Handmade square, ground lip, in aqua.
(Very square cornered)
Side: three lines: 'IMPROVED,' 'SAMP-
SON,' and 'BATTERY'
Maker unknown
From the name, it appears to be an old
style "wet" battery cell. The Bell Tele-
phone Museum tells me that it appears
to be similar to the jar used in the La-
Clanche battery made for the Bell
Company by Charles Williams, Jr., of
Boston, in 1879, and pictures from the
Museum bear it out. But Bill Hart, of
Sarnia, Ont., tells this interesting story:
"The old codger we got this from told us
a traveling salesman swayed their
mother into buying some sort of con-
traption for healing purposes, along the
lines of a vibrator."

SAMUELS, A. R. from initials A. R. S.

Circa 1859
Stopper finish as for WILLOUGHBY
STOPPLE, which see, 1859 patent
Handmade round, pressed laid-on-ring, in
aqua

Side: 'A R S' in flowing script
Attributed to the A. R. Samuels Glass Co.,
Philadelphia, Pa., but dates and exact
company name uncertain. Through
these initials, A. R. Samuels is identified
with at least four historical flasks. When,
how, and under what name he operated
is uncertain, also. McKearin, pp. 603-
604, records that Yarnall & Samuels
bought a glass house at Medford, N.J.,
in 1863 and failed before they could
finish the improvements they undertook

SANETY WIDE MOUTH MASON (1) [Note misspelling of SAFETY or SANITY]

Circa 1915-38
Mason beaded neck design
Machine-made wide-mouth round, in flint
Side: five lines: 'SANETY' [sic], 'WIDE
MOUTH,' 'MASON,' 'SALEM GLASS
WORKS,' and SALEM. N.J.'
Salem Glass Works, Salem, N.J., 1895-
1938; now a unit of Anchor Hocking
It is difficult to decide whether SANETY
is a misspelling of SAFETY, which
Salem also made, or of SANITY

SANETY WIDE MOUTH MASON (2)

Circa 1910
Same except Mason shoulder seal, which
would be earlier than (1)

SANFORD

Circa 1920-40
Glass lid and metal screw-band top seal
Machine-made round, beaded side, in flint
Bottom: 'SANFORD' arched over H - A
trade mark, with '451' completing the

SANETY
WIDE MOUTH
MASON
SALEM GLASS WORKS
SALEM. N.J.

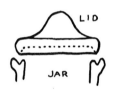

SAN FRANCISCO
GLASS WORKS

circle. So large a number as 451 is probably a "design number"

Lid: 'SANFORD MFG. CO., CHICAGO' and 'PAT JULY 10, 1900'

Hazel Atlas Glass Co., Wheeling W. Va., 1902-64, for Sanford's inks or paste

In spite of the patent date, for which a patent was not found, the jar in question could not have been made before Hazel Atlas adopted its trade mark about 1921

SAN FRANCISCO GLASS WORKS

Circa 1869-76

Groove-ring wax sealer, fitted with glass lid with ring "V" bead that fitted the groove

Handmade round, pressed laid-on-ring, in green and dark green

Side: two lines: 'SAN FRANCISCO' and 'GLASS WORKS'

San Francisco Glass Works, San Francisco, Cal., 1869-76. This plant was built immediately after the Pacific Glass Works, in the same year of 1865, as the San Francisco Flint Glass Works. Burned in 1869, it was rebuilt and renamed without "Flint." The two companies merged as the San Francisco & Pacific Glass Works in 1876 and continued to make each other's former jars

SANI-JAR

This name has been reported without description, but not verified

SANITARY

Circa 1900-10

Lightning closure, old style neck design

Handmade round, ground lip, in aqua

Side: 'SANITARY'

Bottom: 'H. W. PETTIT' and 'SALEM, N.J.' in a circle

Salem Glass Works, Salem, N.J., 1895-1938

Pettit was a Westville, N.J. hardware dealer, and the use of "SALEM" as his address repeats an error in mold-cutting that was also made on one of Pettit's SAFETY VALVE jars. See also PETTIT and SAFETY VALVE (4)

"SANITARY" FREEZER, THE

Circa 1899

Glass lid top seal, held by wire passing completely around jar

Handmade tall round, ribbed, ground lip, with cork opening in bottom

Side: three lines: 'MFG'R'D BY,' 'CONSOLIDATED MFG. CO.,' and 'HARTFORD, CONN.'

Lid: 'THE "SANITARY" FREEZER'

Bottom: 'PATENTED FEB. 14, 1899, JULY 15, 1902. G. H. FOX' in a circle

Maker unknown

The device was an ice-cream mold. The ice-cream was removed by pushing through the bottom hole onto a round plate in the bottom of the jar. It has been mistaken for a fruit jar, hence recorded here

Fox received Patent No. 619,554 on Feb. 14, 1899 and Patent No. 704,873 on July 15, 1902

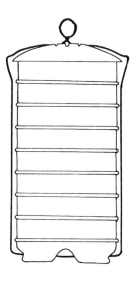

SANITARY

H.W. PETTIT SALEM, N.J.

SANITARY SURE SEAL

See BALL SANITARY SURE SEAL

SAN YUEN Co.

Circa 1920-30

Lightning closure, beaded neck design

Machine-made rounded square, 12-oz. capacity, in flint

Side: 'SAN YUEN Co.,' '822 WASHING-TON ST.,' and 'San Francisco' in three lines, together with Chinese characters

Bottom: "I" in a diamond

Illinois Glass Co., Alton, Ill., 1873-1929

SCHAFFER JAR, THE

THE
SCHAFFER
JAR
ROCHESTER
N.Y.
(FRONT)

(BACK)

Circa 1880-1900

Glass lid and looped spring bail for tension

Handmade tall round, ground lip, in light green

Side: five lines: 'THE,' 'SCHAFFER,' arched, 'JAR,' 'ROCHESTER,' in a drooped arc, and 'N.Y.'

Back: a monogram of "J," "S," and "C," said variously to mean either the SCHAFFER JAR CO. or J. C. SCHAFFER

Possibly the Rochester Glass Co, Rochester, N.Y., 1865-87 or its successor, Kelly, Reed & Co., 1887-98

SCHRAM AUTOMATIC SEALER (1)

Circa 1920-25

Metal cap fitted with permanently fastened soft-rubber side seal, probably the first of its kind. The cap was held in place by a spring clip at first, hooking below a finish ledge

Machine-made round, beaded neck, in flint
Side: three lines of script: 'Schram,' 'Automatic,' and 'Sealer'
Schram Glass Manufacturing Co., St. Louis, Mo., 1905-25
The SCHRAM was also licensed in Canada

SCHRAM AUTOMATIC SEALER (2)

Same, except after "Schram" in rising script, there is a ribbon finial from the "m" containing 'AUTOMATIC SEAL-ER' in block letters

SCHRAM AUTOMATIC SEALER B (1)

Circa 1920-25
The "B" series introduces a finish design without a ledge to hold a spring clip
Same general jar as SCHRAM AUTO-MATIC SEALER except without a ledge under the finish. Lettering as in SCHRAM AUTOMATIC SEALER (2) with "B" added

SCHRAM AUTOMATIC SEALER B (2)

Same as (1) except a third line: 'TRADE MARK REG'D'

SCHRAM AUTOMATIC SEALER B (3)

This lettering appears on a jar having the original SCHRAM AUTOMATIC SEALER design, including the finish ledge. Perhaps Schram was taking no chances with the "B" finish, even though labeled as such

SCHRAM AUTO SEALER

Similar to SCHRAM AUTOMATIC SEAL-
ER (2) in jar make-up, except "AUTO-
MATIC" abbreviated to "AUTO" on the
ribbon finial

SCHRAM FRUIT JAR

Similar to SCHRAM AUTOMATIC
SEALER (2) except "FRUIT JAR" on
the ribbon instead of "AUTOMATIC
SEALER"

SCRANTON JAR, THE

Circa 1870

Glass stopper sealing on a slanting surface,
with rubber ring seal. A spring wire held
the stopper in place, bent over a wood
roller and hooking under a strap. The
yoke assembly was held by a wire passing vertically around the jar as in the
VAN VLIET and the GILBERDS, and
antedated both

Handmade round, ground lip, in light
green

Side: three lines: 'THE,' 'SCRANTON,'
arched, and 'JAR'

Lid: 'GRIFFEN'S PAT. OCT. 7, 1869'

Maker unknown

There was a Scranton Glass Co. at Scranton, Pa., advertizing beverage bottles

in 1889, but no record of its earlier
operations

The Griffen patent was not found; it
would be one of several that he patented, as a New York jobber of bottles

SEALFAST

Circa 1912-24

Lightning wide-mouth closure, old-style
neck design

Machine-made round, in flint

Side: 'SEALFAST'

Bottom: 'FOSTER'

Made by Ball Bros. Co. and Hazel Atlas
for the Upland Glass Co., Upland, Ind.,
1911-22; Marion, Ind., 1922-29. Now
Foster Forbes Glass Co., 1929 to date

SEALFAST, FOSTER (1)

Similar to SEALFAST, except 'FOSTER'
and 'SEALFAST' in two lines on the
side; nothing on the bottom

SEALFAST, FOSTER (2)

Same as (1) except with "FOSTER" repeated on the bottom

SEALFAST SOLD BY BOLSTER & BARNES

Circa 1912-24

Lightning closure, old-style neck design

Machine-made round plated mold, in
flint. A "plated mold" has an opening in
the side, usually round but appearing
oval because of jar curvature, into which
a replaceable mold part may be inserted.
The replaceable part can be lettered for a
specific user who wishes less than the
normal quantity order of bottles. After
filling his order, another replaceable
part may be inserted with another short-

SEALFAST

FOSTER
SEALFAST

SEALFAST SOLD BY
BOLSTER & BARNES
GROCERIES
OLYMPIA, WASH.

run customer's name. This enables a stock mold to be used for many customers. This series of jars is the only known use of plated fruit-jar molds

Side: 'SEALFAST' arched above 'SOLD BY' lettered in the permanent portion of the mold. In the oval-appearing "plate": 'BOLSTER & BARNES' along the upper curve, 'OLYMPIA, WASH.' along the lower curve, and 'GROCERIES' across the center

Made for Upland Glass Co., Upland, Ind., as in SEALFAST

SEALFAST SOLD BY C. B. HOBBS

A plated mold with 'C. B. HOBBS' along the upper curve, 'GROCER,' 'PHONE,' and '581' across the center, and 'TIPTON, IND.' along the lower curve

SEALFAST SOLD BY MONARCH HARDWARE CO.

A plated mold with 'MONARCH HARDWARE CO.' along the upper curve, 'SALT' and 'LAKE' in two lines across the center, and 'UTAH' along the lower curve

SEALFAST SOLD BY P. A. NIELSEN & SON

A plated mold with: 'P. A. NIELSEN & SON' along the upper curve, 'LOGAN, UTAH' along the lower curve, and 'GROCERIES' across the center

SEALFAST SOLD BY RADER BROS. & LAMPKIN CO.

A plated mold with 'RADER BROS & LAMPKIN CO.' along the upper curve, 'ONTARIO' and 'ORE' in two lines across the center

SEALFAST SOLD BY L. RORDEN & CO.

A plated mold with 'L. RORDEN & CO' along the upper curve, 'THE DALLES' across the center, and 'OREGON' along the lower curve

SEALTITE

Circa 1920-30
Lightning closure, old-style neck design
Machine-made round, in flint
Side: 'SEALTITE' above 'TRADE MARK'
Maker unknown

SEASONS MASON, 4

Circa 1900-20
Glass lid and metal screw-band top seal
Machine-made round, in flint
Side: three lines all in double-outlined lower case letters: '4,' 'seasons,' and 'mason'
Maker unknown

SECURITY (1)

Circa 1890

Lightning closure, old-style neck design

Handmade round, ground lip, in flint and purple (or sun-colored)

Side: 'Security' in heavy slanting script with a finial from the "S" as an overline, and another from the "y" as an underline

Maker unknown

SECURITY (2)

Same except the glass lid is lettered in a circle, 'J. HUNGERFORD SMITH Co.,' and 'ROCHESTER, N.Y.' Smith, who also did business at Albany, N.Y., packed fine fruits for the hotel trade. "Security" is similar to that in (1) but lighter in cut

SECURITY SEAL (1)

Circa 1900

Lightning closure, old-style neck design

Handmade round, ground lip, in flint

Side: a large triangle, with 'SECU' and 'RITY' along the inner edges of the peak, and 'SEAL' along the bottom inside. Within a bowed inner triangle is a monogram of "F G Co"

Possibly the Fairmount Glass Co., Indianapolis, Ind., 1888 to date

SECURITY SEAL (2)

The same except machine-made

SELCO SURETY SEAL (1)

Circa 1930
Lightning closure, dimple neck design
Machine-made round, in flint and aqua
Side: in oval outline: 'SELCO' along the top, and 'SURETY SEAL' along the bottom
Maker unknown

SELCO SURETY SEAL (2)

Same except 'PAT'D JULY 14, 1908' added below the oval

SELLER & CO., M.

Circa 1870-1900
Groove-ring wax sealer
Handmade round, in green. The pressed laid-on-ring is very smoothly made, indicating late manufacture
Side: 'M. SELLER & CO.' and 'PORT-LAND, O.'
Maker unknown

S G CO

Circa 1880-1900
Mason shoulder seal
Handmade round, ground lip, in yellow-green and aqua
Side: a monogram of "S G Co"
Safe Glass Co., Bowling Green, Ohio, 1880-92; Redkey, Ind., 1892-98: and Upland, Ind., 1898-1905
See also RED KEY

S G CO with MASON PATENT NOV. 30th 1858 [has a mold-cutting error]

Circa 1880-1900
Mason shoulder seal
Handmade round, ground lip, in green
Side: 'MASON' with room for, but with-

out, "'S." It is arched above the same
monogram as in S G Co, followed by
'PATENT,' 'NOV 30ᵀᴴ,' and '1858'

Safe Glass Co., Bowling Green, Ohio, Redkey, Ind., and Upland, Ind., as for S G
Co., above

S G CO with MASON'S PATENT NOV 30th 1858

Same as the preceeding except lettered
correctly

S G W MASON (1)

Circa 1895-1910
Mason shoulder seal
Handmade round, ground lip, in light green
and pink (sun-colored)
Side: 'MASON' arched over a monogram of
a large "G" containing "S" overlaid with
"W"
Salem Glass Works, Salem, N.J., 1895-1938;
now a unit of Anchor Hocking

S G W MASON (2)

Circa 1915-38
The same except machine-made

SIERRA MASON

This jar has been reported, but not verified,
as a machine-made Mason with shoulder
seal

SILICON (1)

Circa 1930
Lightning closure, beaded neck design
Machine-made round, in flint
Side: 'SILICON' in an oval outline
Maker unknown

SILICON (2)

Circa 1925-30

Lightning closure, beaded neck design

Machine-made round, in flint

Side: four lines: 'SILICON,' arched, 'GLASS COMPANY,' 'PITTSBURGH,' and 'PENNA.' completing the circle below

Bottom: "B" in a circle

Brockway Glass Co., Brockway, Pa., 1907 to date

The trade mark, "B" in a circle dates from 1925. The Silicon Glass Co. was not a glass maker, since it was not listed in any annual issue of the *Glass Factory Directory* during the period concerned

SIMPLEX (1) [the cap]

An all-glass cap, threaded for Mason jars, Patent No. 806,602, issued to Russel Uhl of Wilkes Barre, Pa., Dec. 5, 1905. It was used as a shoulder seal. A claimed feature in the patent was the shape, or cross-section, of the thread, being sloped so as to give better contact on the pressure side of the thread, and freedom from contact on the non-pressure side, thus reducing friction drag of glass-on-glass. It was also claimed that the slope of the thread contour allowed it to fit uneven threads on the jar

The SIMPLEX was the last, and almost the most successful, of all-glass caps developed over a thirty-year period

Top: 'SIMPLEX' in a diamond outline

SIMPLEX (2) [the cap]

An alternate lettering has 'SIMPLEX GLASS CAP' above, and 'FOR MASON JARS' below, forming a circle, and 'PAT^D' and 'DE · · · DE' in the center

SIMPLEX (2) [the jar]

Circa 1905

Mason shoulder seal

Machine-made round, in flint

Side: 'SIMPLEX' in a diamond, matching the all-glass cap

Maker unknown

SINCLAIR & Co., LTD., T. M. (1)

Circa 1910-25

Glass lid, held by a spring band clip like the ECONOMY jar

Machine-made round, in flint and sun-colored

Side: five lines: 'T. M. SINCLAIR & Co. LTD,' 'CEDAR RAPIDS,' 'IOWA,' 'PORK AND BEEF,' and 'PACKERS'

Probably made by Hazel Atlas Glass Co., Wheeling, W. Va., who purchased the commercial rights to the ECONOMY patent when Kerr purchased the fruit-jar rights

SINCLAIR & Co., LTD., T. M. (2)

Same except with ECONOMY metal lid

SMALLEY (1)

Circa 1896-1907

Mason shoulder seal

Handmade rounded square, ground lip, in flint, aqua, and amber

Side: three lines: 'SMALLEY' and 'FULL MEASURE,' in an arched panel, over a monogram of "A," "G," and "S," followed by 'QUART'

Bottom: 'APRIL 7, 1896; Dec. 13, 1897' in a circle

Maker unknown. Smalley was a jobber

Neither of these patents was found, but Albert G. Smalley did receive Patent No. 572,281 on Dec. 1, 1896, for the rounded-square shape, and for a pull-tab sealing rubber ring for the shoulder seal

SMALLEY (2)

Same except 'APRIL 21 1896' added to the patent dates as the bottom part of an inner circle on the bottom

SMALLEY'S NU-SEAL

See NU-SEAL, SMALLEY'S

SMALLEY'S ROYAL (1)

Circa 1915-19

Lightning closure, old-style neck design

Machine-made rounded square, in flint and sun-colored

Side: 'SMALLEY'S' above a crown with a cross on top and 'ROYAL' superimposed across the crown. 'ROYAL' is repeated below the crown, followed by 'TRADE MARK' and 'NU-SEAL'

Maker unknown

SMALLEY'S ROYAL (2)

Same except an orb instead of a cross on top of the crown

SMALLEY SELF SEALER, THE (1)

Circa 1900-09

Lightning closure, old-style neck design

Machine-made round, in flint and sun-colored

Side: three lines: 'TRADE MARK' in an arch above 'THE SMALLEY' and 'SELF SEALER'

Bottom: 'A. G. SMALLEY & Co., BOSTON, MASS.'

Maker unknown

SMALLEY SELF SEALER, THE (2)

Circa 1915-19

Same as (1) except 'SMALLEY FRUIT JAR Co., Boston, Mass.' on bottom

SMALLEY SELF SEALER, THE (3)

Circa 1905-11

Same as (1)' except 'SMALLEY JAR Co., BOSTON, MASS.' on bottom

SMITH SON & Co., J. P. (1)

Circa 1860-70

Groove-ring wax sealer

Handmade round, pressed laid-on-ring, in dark green

Side: 'J. P. SMITH SON & Co.' in a drooped arc above 'PITTSBURGH'

Maker uncertain, since there is no data on Smith as a glass-maker or as a dealer

SMITH SON & Co., J. P. (2)

Same except "PITTSBURGH" is on the back instead of on the front

SMITH, HARLAN C.

A patent, No. 43,232, was issued to Harlow C. Smith on June 21, 1864, for a fruit jar with a stopper, rubber cushioned, and employing a hand pump to exhaust the inner air. Such a jar was reported but not verified

SOCIÉTÉ (1)

Circa 1925-35

Lightning closure, beaded neck design

Machine-made round, in flint

Side: 'Société' in capital and lower case letters, over 'SEATTLE'

Bottom: 'SOCIÉTÉ, SEATTLE,' in a circle with trade mark, H - A

Hazel Atlas Glass Co., Wheeling W. Va., 1902-64

Note: There are many variations of the lettering and many sizes of small jars. Some do not have letters blown in the side but paper labels which show that SOCIÉTÉ was a candy maker. Note the accented E's; pronounced So-See-Ay-Tay

SOCIÉTÉ (2)

Same as (1) except dimple neck design

SOCIÉTÉ (3)

Same as (1) except rounded square

SOUTHERN DOUBLE SEAL MASON

Circa 1918-30

Mason beaded neck design

Machine-made very heavy round, in flint

Side: 'Southern' in slanting script, above 'DOUBLE SEAL' and 'MASON'

Probably the Southern Glass Co., Los Angeles, Cal., 1918-30

SOUTHERN METHODIST ORPHANS HOME

See BALL IDEAL (6)

SPENCER (1)

Circa 1865

Stopper finish, for rubber-sealed metal lid with a ring projection to grasp for removing

C.F. SPENCER'S
PATENT
ROCHESTER
N.Y.

Handmade round, pressed laid-on-ring, in blue-green

Side: four lines: 'C. F. SPENCER'S' in an arch above 'PATENT,' 'ROCHESTER,' and 'N.Y.'

Probably made by Rochester Glass Works, Rochester, N.Y., 1865-87

This jar was made to Spencer's Patent No. 37,647 of Feb. 10, 1863. The reason for the ring projection in the finish is not clear since the metal lid was held only by the vacuum in the jar

SPENCER (2)

Circa 1868

Metal lid seating on a flat jar-top, and incorporating two hinged wire loops which hooked into notched ears on either side of the jar neck

Handmade round, ground lip, in green

Side: five lines: 'C. F. SPENCER'S' in an arch above 'PATENT,' 'ROCHESTER,' 'N.Y.,' and 'PAT JAN. 28, 1868'

Probably the Rochester Glass Works, Rochester, N.Y., 1865-87

Charles F. Spencer of Rochester, N.Y., received Patent No. 73,846 on Jan. 28, 1868. The notched ears which were to hold the hinged loops would be difficult to make, and none have been found that would have been really effective

SPENCER

SPENCER (3)

Circa 1865-80

Glass lid held by iron yoke and central thumbscrew

Handmade round, ground lip, in green

Side: 'SPENCER' in an arch

Probably the Rochester Glass Works, Rochester, N.Y., 1865-87

This jar seems to be a direct copy of the MILLVILLE ATMOSPHERIC, which was patented three years before the Rochester Glass Works was founded

STANDARD (1)

Circa 1860

Groove-ring wax sealer

Handmade, pressed laid-on-ring, in green and light green

Side: 'STANDARD' arched above 'W. M^{C}C & Co'

William McCully & Co., Pittsburgh, Pa., 1832-85 or later

See McKearin, p. 600; Knittle, p. 320

STANDARD (2)

Same as (1) except 'STANDARD' on front, and 'W. M^{C}C & Co' on back

STANDARD (3)

Same as (2) except four additional lines on front below 'STANDARD': 'FROM,' 'FOOTE, BAER & Co.,' 'CLEVELAND,' and 'O'

STANDARD (4)

Circa 1890-1910

Groove-ring wax sealer

Handmade round, pressed laid-on-ring, in aqua

Side: 'STANDARD,' in a descending line, over a squared shepherd's-crook design

Probably the Standard Co-operative Glass Co., Marion, Ind., 1890-1932

STANDARD (5)

Circa 1890-1910

Mason shoulder seal

Handmade round, ground lip, in aqua and green

Side: 'STANDARD,' in a descending line,
above a squared shepherd's-crook design
Probably the Standard Co-operative Glass
Co,. Marion, Ind., 1890-1932

STANDARD (6)

Circa 1910-30
Mason shoulder seal
Machine-made round, in aqua and green
Side: 'STANDARD,' in a descending line,
above a squared shepherd's-crook design
Probably the Standard Co-operative Glass
Co., Marion, Ind., 1890-1932

STANDARD MASON (1)

Circa 1890-1900
Mason shoulder seal
Handmade round, ground lip, in green
Side: 'Standard,' in rising script, with
'MASON' on a ribbon finial from the final
"d"
Possibly the Standard Co-operative Glass
Co., Marion, Ind., 1890-1932

STANDARD MASON (2)

Circa 1910-30
Same as (1) except machine-made

STANDARD MASON, LYNCHBURG

Circa 1920-25
Mason shoulder seal
Machine-made round, in green
Side: three lines: 'LYNCHBURG,'
'STANDARD,' slanting, and 'MASON'
Lynchburg Glass Corp., Lynchburg, Va.,
1920-27

STAR, word and figure (1)

Circa 1890-1900

Glass lid and metal screw-band top seal

Handmade round, ground lip, in flint and blue-tint

Side: a large, heavy, raised figure of a star, ribbed, above the word 'STAR' in an arch

Probably the Star Glass Co., New Albany, Ind., 1860s to circa 1900

STAR, word and figure (2)

Circa 1880-1900

Glass or metal tapered seal lid, with screw threads on jar for cap or screw-band

Handmade round, ground lip, in light green

Front: 'STAR' in seriffed letters, above the outline of a star

Back: 'A. LIEBERSTEIN & C⁰' arched above a circle made up of 'DEALERS IN CROCKERY' at the top, and '& GLASSWARE' at the bottom. In the center, four lines: '177,' 'RANDOLPH ST.,' 'CHICAGO,' and 'ILL.'

Probably the Star Glass Co., New Albany, Ind., 1860s to circa 1900

The sealing surface of this jar seems special, with the surface at an angle instead of the usual flat top used with screw caps

STAR, figure only

Circa 1860-70

Groove-ring wax sealer

Handmade round, pressed laid-on-ring, in dark green

Side: a large ribbed, heavy, raised figure of a star as in STAR (1) but without the word "STAR"

Probably the Star Glass Co., New Albany, Ind., 1860s to circa 1900

STAR figure, with N

Age uncertain, as well-formed in the old
   sealing method used circa 1860-1900
Groove-ring wax sealer
Handmade round, pressed laid-on-ring, in
   amber
Side: the outline of a star, enclosing "N"
Maker unknown

STAR AND CRESCENT, MRS. S. T. RORER'S

MRS. S. T. RORER'S

STAR & CRESCENT

SELF SEALING JAR

Circa 1910
Mason shoulder seal
Machine-made round, in light green
Side: 'MRS. S. T. RORER'S' and 'STAR
   & CRESCENT' above a star within a
   crescent; below, 'SELF SEALING JAR'
Maker unknown

STAR GLASS Co.

STAR GLASS Co

NEW ALBANY IND

Circa 1860-75
Groove-ring wax sealer
Very crudely handmade round, pressed
   laid-on-ring, in intense green
Side: 'STAR GLASS Co.' arched above
   'NEW ALBANY IND'
Star Glass Co., New Albany, Ind., 1860s to
   circa 1900. Little history for this company is developed. They may have
   started as early as 1855, before the nearby Kentucky Glass Works, as the Louisville area was an early glass center. They
   are identified with WEIR jars in the
   1890s. See WEIR

STEERSHEAD (1)

Circa 1890-98

Glass lid and metal screw-band top seal

Handmade round, ground lip, in green

Side: a decoration of flowers, leaves, and vines enclosing a steer's head in a small circle; above the head: 'FLACCUS BROS'; flanking the head: 'STEERS' and 'HEAD'; below the head: 'FRUIT JAR'

Probably made by Hazel Glass Co., Washington, Pa., 1886-1901, and Atlas Glass Co., Washington, Pa., 1896-1901

The Wheeling Chamber of Commerce (where the Flaccus Brothers were located) describes them as food packers, using these glass jars and bottles for catsup, preserves, and the like. See also FLACCUS for earlier similar jars under the name of E. C. FLACCUS, but in some instances with an elk's head instead of a steer's head

There is some confusion with others of the name Flaccus in the glass business. The Charles L. Flaccus Glass Co. was operating at Tatentum and other places in Pennsylvania. Two men by the name of Flaccus patented glass designs for pressed ware. One was from Pittsburgh, and may have been with Charles L. Flaccus; the other was from Wheeling, W. Va., and may have been with the Central Glass Co., makers of fine table and art glass in Wheeling

No attempt will be made to list separately the many slightly changed versions of the decoration forms of each jar listed

STEERSHEAD (2)

Same as (1) except fitted with a glass stopper marked 'LYON JAR PATENT ALLOWED'

STEERSHEAD (3)

Same as (1) except fitted with an all-glass screw cap

STEERSHEAD (4)

Similar to (1) except lettered "FINE TABLE DELICACIES" instead of "FRUIT JAR"

STEERSHEAD (5)

Circa 1890-98

Mason shoulder seal

Handmade squat round, ground lip, in flint

Side: 'FLACCUS BROS.' in a panel arched over a steer's head and *back.* 'STEERS' and 'HEAD' on either side of the figure. Below the figure: 'TABLE DELICACIES,' on a scroll, over 'WHEELING, W. VA.' Without the leaves, flowers, and vines featured on other STEERSHEAD jars

Probably Hazel Glass Co., Washington, Pa., 1886-1901, or Atlas Glass Co., Washington, Pa., 1896-1901

This is the only STEERSHEAD to show the back as well as the face of the steer, and may be an early transition form between the elk's head and the steer's head

STERLING MASON

Circa 1920-45

Mason beaded neck seal

Machine-made round, in flint

Side: 'Sterling,' in script, slanting upward above 'MASON.' Rest of the side has vertical ribs like the BROCKWAY SUR-GRIP and the BALL PERFECT MASON

Sterling Glass Co., 1890s-1949 when sold to Brockway by its owners, The War-field Co., Chicago food packers and brokers

STEVENS TIN TOP (1)

Circa 1876

A special form of groove-ring wax sealer, in which two small tabs were formed in the edge of the groove to engage raised portions of the metal lid, which was then rotated until the lid-lugs caught under the groove-tabs and secured the lid. The groove could then be luted with wax in the usual fashion. Stevens' patent application also mentions the use of a rubber ring as a seal instead of wax

Handmade round, pressed and tooled laid-on-ring, in green

Side: 'STEVENS' arched above 'TIN TOP' and 'PAT⁰ JULY 27 1875'

Bottom: "H" surrounded by five triangles positioned as a star

Maker unknown

Patent No. 165,962 was issued to David E. Stevens and Richard F. Lumley, of New-ark, Ohio, on July 27, 1875. Statements in the patent describe the functions as mentioned above

STEVENS TIN TOP (2)

An alternate design has a full star on the bottom, without "H"

STONE & Co., A. (1)

Age uncertain, possibly circa 1866 or 1873

Internal lugs within jar-neck and on glass stopper, which had integral bosses on top in order to apply a lever for rotation

Handmade round, pressed laid-on-ring, in green

Lid: 'A. STONE & Co., PHILADELPHIA' in a circle

Maker unknown

There is no further clue on the jar, but one of the two following patents might apply:

In Patent No. 52,379, issued Feb. 6, 1866, Edwin Bennett shows a stopper construction with threads on the stopper but not on the jar, and no lugs. The stopper "screwed" into the rubber ring between it and the inner side of the neck of the jar

In Patent No. 136,240, issued Feb. 23, 1873, to Ella G. Haller of Carlisle, Pa., she used a knobbed stopper with lug-like threads on both jar and stopper, with sealing on a rubber ring above the lugs. Her hollow stopper dispensed syrup into the jar as a vacuum formed

STONE & Co., A. (2)

Circa 1860-70

Groove-ring wax sealer

Handmade round, pressed laid-on-ring, in green

Side: two lines: 'A. STONE & Co.' above PHILAD<u>A</u>'

Maker unknown

STONE MASON

Circa 1899-1910

Mason shoulder seal, in pottery

Turn lines indicate wheel turned pottery forming

Side: stamped in black, and fired: in a rectangle: 'STONE' across the top; 'MASON FRUIT JAR' slanting from lower left to upper right; and, in three lines at lower right: 'UNION,' 'STONEWARE Co,' and 'RED WING, MINN.'

Bottom: die stamped: 'PAT'D JAN 24,1899'

Union Stoneware is now the Red Wing Potteries, who tell me that the jar was discontinued about 1910

See also MACOMB, HERMANN, and WAX SEALER, POTTERY, PEORIA STYLE in section UNLETTERED JARS

SUEY FUNG YUEN Co.

Circa 1925-30

Lightning closure, beaded neck design

Machine-made round, in flint

Side: 'SUEY FUNG YUEN Co.' and Chinese characters

Bottom: "P" and "C" in a divided rectangle

Pacific Coast Glass Company, San Francisco, Cal., 1925-30. Continuation of Pacific Coast Glass Works, 1902-25

SUN (1)

Circa 1890

Glass lid and cast-metal yoke over a bulbous finish. A cam lever below the center of the yoke exerted pressure on the glass lid

Handmade round, ground lip, in light green

Side: 'SUN' in a surrounding of radiating rays

Yoke: 'MONIERS' PATENT' and 'APR 1, 1890'

Maker unknown

The first Moniers' patent, by Fredrick and Elizabeth Monier, of New Britain, Conn., was No. 424,720, of Apr. 1, 1890. It did not provide the centering cross-piece in the yoke corrected later

SUN (2)

Circa 1895

Same jar as (1), but with a changed yoke, which includes 'MONIERS' PATENT' and 'MAR 12, 1895' instead of the previous date. The change is a centering cross member attached to the yoke. Patent No. 535,549, Mar. 12, 1895, was by Fredrick Monier alone

SUN (3)

Circa 1895

Yokes have been found with *both* patent dates: 'MONIERS' PATENT' and 'APR 1 1890 MAR 12 1895'

SUN (4)

Same as (3) but with 'TRADE MARK' on the side below the sunburst and 'SUN,' and with 'J. P. BARSTOW,' for the Barstow Fruit Jar Co., of New Jersey, on the bottom

SUN (5)

A SUN jar has been shown me with a SAFETY VALVE closure. It is probably an assembly from the two jars—not from the factory

SUNSHINE JAR (1)

Circa 1905-10

Shoulder seal using an all-glass cap, with a non-slip gripping edge as a decoration

Machine-made round, in flint and sun-colored

Lid: 'SUNSHINE' in a stippled diamond on top and "I G Co" in a diamond inside lid

Side: 'SUNSHINE JAR' on some jars, but not on others

Bottom: sometimes marked "I G Co" in a diamond

Illinois Glass Co., Alton, Ill., 1873-1929

(OUTSIDE LID)

SUNSHINE JAR (2)

Same, except cap has 'PAT OCT 24 1905' instead of 'SUNSHINE'

Patent No. 802,381 was the first of three granted to William B. Fenn on the same day, Oct. 24, 1905 (with Nos. 802,-382 and 802,383). Instead of threads on the all-glass cap, he employed ribs and other methods of securing an irregular inner surface around the rim of the cap, and into these pressed a fibrous packing that was both an air and liquid seal, and had on its inner facing a screw thread to fit the jar. This eliminated the high friction between cap and jar in the all-glass caps

See also SIMPLEX for another all-glass cap and photograph contrasting full size SIMPLEX with smaller SUNSHINE

(INSIDE LID)

SUPREME MASON

Circa 1920-25
Mason beaded neck design
Machine-made round, in flint
Side: 'SUPREME' above 'MASON'
Bottom: "I" in a diamond as a trade mark
Illinois Glass Co., Alton, Ill., 1873-1929
See also PRESTO SUPREME MASON. As in their GENUINE MASON to which "BOYD" was later added, it appears that Illinois Glass first made their own SUPREME MASON, and then, in 1925, used it as part of the name of their PRESTO line, in the PRESTO SUPREME MASON

SURE SEAL (1)

Circa 1900-05
Lightning closure, old-style neck design
Machine-made round, in light green
Side: in oval depression: 'Sure' and 'Seal,' in two lines of script
Maker unknown

SURE SEAL (2)

Circa 1910-20
Same except with Lightning closure, beaded neck design
See BALL SURE SEAL and CANADIAN SURE SEAL

SWAYZEE MASON

Circa 1894-1906

Mason shoulder seal

Handmade square-shouldered round, ground lip, in blue

Side: 'SWAYZEE' arched over 'MASON' in two lines

Swayzee Glass Co., Swayzee, Ind., 1894-1906

This one jar does *not* use the possessive "SWAYZEE'S"

SWAYZEE'S FRUIT JAR (1)

Circa 1894-1906

Mason shoulder seal

Handmade square-shouldered round, ground lip, in blue and blue-green

Side: two lines: 'SWAYZEE'S' arched above 'FRUIT JAR'

Swayzee Glass Co., Swayzee, Ind., 1894-1906

SWAYZEE'S FRUIT JAR (2)

Same as (1) except 'FRUIT' and 'JAR' on separate lines

SWAYZEE'S IMPROVED MASON

Circa 1894-1906

Mason shoulder seal (not the top seal as the name usually implies)

Machine-made rounded-shoulder round, ground lip, in blue-green

Side: three lines: 'SWAYZEE'S' arched over 'IMPROVED' and 'MASON'

Swayzee Glass Co., Swayzee, Ind., 1894-1906

The "improvement" was the elimination of the weak, square-cornered shoulder in favor of the stronger rounded contour— a real improvement

SWAYZEE
MASON

SWAYZEE'S
FRUIT JAR

SWAYZEE'S
FRUIT
JAR

SWAYZEE'S
IMPROVED
MASON

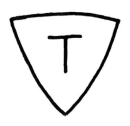

SWAYZEE'S MASON

Similar to SWAYZEE MASON except change to the possessive case

An amusing story is told by SWAYZEE'S historian, present postmaster, and one-time boy worker at the glass house: Swayzee once encountered financial trouble when they purchased some Canadian-made molds and made a considerable quantity of fruit jars before they found that the molds were for the 40-ounce Canadian quart instead of the U.S. 32-ounce quart

T

"T" in a triangular shield

Circa 1921-30

Lightning closure, beaded neck design

Machine-made round, in flint

Side: "T" in a triangular shield with slightly bowed sides

Turner Glass Co., Terre Haute and Winchester, Ind., 1921-30

TAYLOR & Co. PURE FOOD, J. E.

Circa 1915-20

Lightning closure, old-style neck design

Machine-made round, in green

Side: 'J. E. TAYLOR & Co' forming the top of a circle and 'SANTA ANA CAL' the bottom; 'PURE FOOD' across the center

Maker unknown

TELEPHONE JAR, THE

Circa 1905-10

Lightning closure, old-style neck design

Handmade round, ground lip, in green

Side: six lines: 'THE,' 'TELEPHONE,' in

an arch, 'JAR,' 'TRADE MARK,' 'REG,' and 'WHITNEY GLASS WORKS,' the latter as a drooping half-circle

Whitney Glass Works, Glassboro, N.J., 1887-1918, succeeding Whitney Brothers, 1842-87. The site dates as a glass factory from about 1775 and is now a part of Owens Illinois

TELEPHONE JAR, WIDEMOUTH, THE (1)

Circa 1905-18

Lightning closure, old-style neck design

Handmade round, ground lip, in green

Side: six lines: 'THE,' 'WIDEMOUTH,' in an arch, 'TELEPHONE,' 'JAR,' 'TRADE MARK,' and 'REG'

Whitney Glass Works, Glassboro, N.J., 1887-1918

TELEPHONE JAR, WIDEMOUTH, THE (2)

Same except machine-made

TEXAS MASON

1949-50 only

Mason beaded neck design

Machine-made round, in flint

Side: a stippled outline map of Texas, with 'TEXAS' above and 'MASON' below, both in stippled double-outlined letters

Knox Glass Co. of Mississippi, at their Palestine, Tex., plant

The bottom is also marked 'MADE IN TEXAS BY TEXANS.' The jar was discontinued because of conflict with the regular KNOX MASON

Ŧ [a ligatured combining of T with F] (1)

Circa 1910-30

Lightning closure, beaded neck design

Machine-made round, in amber and flint

Side: "T" and "F" combined as one letter, usually with a number

Bottom: ligature repeated

Hazel Atlas Glass Co., Wheeling, W. Va., 1902-64

Ŧ (2)

Circa 1920-30

Same except with trade mark H – A on bottom for Hazel Atlas

THREE RIVERS, or 3 RIVERS

Circa 1925-37

Mason beaded neck design

Machine-made round, in flint

Bottom: "3 RIVERS" in a half circle with a number, 107, indicating a design specification

Three Rivers Glass Co., Three Rivers, Tex., 1925-37. Bought by Ball Bros. Co. in 1937 and operated as their southern plant until 1947

THRIFT (1)

Since 1913

Seal unknown

Machine-made round, in flint

Side: three lines: 'THRIFT,' 'THRIFT JAR CO.,' and 'BALTIMORE, MD.,' all in rough double-outlined letters

Bottom: in circle: 'Licensed by P. F. P. Co. Balto., Md.' around 'PAT.' and 'OCT. 7, 1913' forming a smaller circle

Buck Glass Co., Baltimore, Md., 1907-1962. The Thrift Jar Co. was probably a sales company

THRIFT (2)

Same as THRIFT (1) except lettered on side 'BUCK GLASS CO.' instead of 'THRIFT JAR CO.'

TIGNER G CO. [or TIGNER & Co.] (1)

Circa 1890-1900

Mason shoulder seal

Handmade round, ground lip, in light green

Side: 'MASON'S' arched above 'PATENT,' 'NOV 30th,' and '1858'

Bottom: 'TIGNER G CO' (or 'TIGNER & CO') and 'XENIA IND' in a circle

Tigner (?) Co., Xenia, Ind., circa 1890-1900. On this jar the uncertain letter appears to be a "G." Letters to Xenia, Ind., were returned because the town no longer exists, so that further tracing was almost impossible. A double-check at Xenia, Ohio, found no trace of such a company, and therefore not an instance of confusion in State names

TIGNER G Co. [or TIGNER & Co.] (2)

On another jar the uncertain letter appears to be as much an ampersand, "&," as it does a "G" on the first jar

TIGHT SEAL (1)

Circa 1908-20

Lightning closure, dimple neck design

Machine-made round, in blue tint

Side: in an oval: 'TIGHT' and 'SEAL,' the top and bottom arcs of the oval, and 'PAT'D JULY 14 1908' below it

Maker unknown

This jar is very like the BALL IDEAL and may have been made by Ball Bros. Co.

as a private mold for a customer. It carries no BALL identification

TIGHT SEAL (2)

Same except without the patent designation

TIN TOP

See STEVENS TIN TOP

TONGUE

See LUSTRE

TRADE MILLS

Pre-1880 workmanship

Bell-mouthed stopper finish, as used with cork and wax hermetic seal in fruit jars

Handmade squat-shaped round, very crude laid-on-ring, in aqua

Side: 'COFFEE & SPICES' in a straight panel, with 'TRADE MILLS' arched above in a panel, and 'MONTREAL' in a panel completing the circle below. A zig-zag line, going from top to bottom and back again like the tightening cords of a drum, give it a drum-like appearance, in its all-around design

Maker unknown

TRIOMPHE

Modern French jar

Glass lid held on one side by a wire hinge, and on the other by a wire snap lock or toggle

Machine-made round, in flint

Lid: 'TRIOMPHE' arched above a full-drawn bow and long arrow

Verrerie Cristalleria d'Arques, C. Durand et Cie., Arques, France

See also L'IDEALE, LE PRATIQUE, and ERMEBLOK using the same seal

TROPICAL CANNERS

Circa 1929-48
Mason beaded neck design
Machine-made round, in flint
Side: 'Tropical,' in rising script, above a
diamond containing "T" above "F"; below the diamond: 'CANNERS'
Bottom: 'F G'
Florida Glass Co., Jacksonville, Fla., 1929-
47. This company became a division of
the Chattanooga Glass Co., 1947-50, but
resumed its independent status as the
Tropical Glass Co., 1950-54, and since
then a unit of Anchor Hocking

TRUE'S

See IMPERIAL

TRUE FRUIT (1)

Circa 1910
SAFETY VALVE seal: glass lid, yoke,
spring, and cam lever
Machine-made round, in flint
Side: 'TRUE FRUIT' as the top half of a
circle, with 'TRADE MARK' and 'REG-
ISTERED' in two lines forming the bot-
tom half. Within the circle: a monogram
of "J H S Co"
Lid: in circle: 'J. Hungerford Smith & Co.'
Maker unknown
The monogram has been identified as that
of J. Hungerford Smith & Co., suppliers
of fine fruits to the restaurant and hotel
trade, with offices variously at Rochester,
N.Y. and Albany, N.Y.

TRUE FRUIT (2)

The same but without the monogram. 'J I C Co.' is in a sraight line across the bottom

TRUE FRUIT (3)

Same except without either the monogram or the bottom marking

TRUE SEAL, CARROLL'S

Circa 1915-25
Lightning closure, beaded neck design
Machine-made round, in flint
Side: in a doubly outlined, arched top, oblong: 'CARROLL'S' on a slant with a six-pointed star, with 'TRUE' and 'SEAL' in two lines below
Probably by Dominion Glass Co., Montreal, Que., 1913 to date
Carroll's was a five-and-ten-cent chain store at Hamilton, Ont., and nearby towns

U

U. G. CO.

Circa 1860-80
Groove-ring wax sealer
Handmade round, pressed laid-on-ring, in aqua
Bottom: 'U. G. CO.'
Maker unknown
Several glass companies *might* have used the initials U. G. Co., but none has been

proven by any documentation. This illustrates a point in searching out the makers of fruit jars. Consider the following companies:

Union Glass Co., of Philadelphia, Pa., from 1826, owned after 1848 by Hartell & Lancaster, and still operating in 1874. Hartell was the inventor of HARTELL'S ALL-GLASS CAP and his company could have easily been the maker of the U. G. Co. fruit jar

Union Glass Co., of Somerville, Mass., built by Amory and Francis Houghton in 1854, reorganized after failure, and then went on until 1924. But this plant made pressed and blown tableware

Union Glass Co., Cleveland, N.Y., started operations in 1852, and continued until purchased in 1877 by the Cleveland Glass Co. of the same city. They were a window-glass house, but many such plants also made bottles and jars

Although the first- and last-named are possibilities, there is no documentation of their use of this trade mark

UNDERWOOD, Wm.

Shown on a dealer's want-list, but not seen. A William Underwood did business in inks and pastes and could have used the jar

UNION (1)

Circa 1860-70

Groove-ring wax sealer

Handmade round, pressed laid-on-ring, in green

Side: 'UNION,' usually with a figure, as "1," "2," or "5"; sometimes with 'N⁰' with the figure

UNION
N⁰ 1

UNION
5

Maker unknown

One tin lid found with a UNION jar was marked "1871," but whether or not this dates the jar cannot be proved. There is no certainty that the jar and the lid were always together for lids were expendable and rusted

UNION (2)

Same as (1) except in larger letters and without numbers

UNION (3)

Same as (1) except "UNION" is arched

UNION FRUIT JAR

Circa 1860-70; probably latter, as better workmanship

Groove-ring wax sealer

Handmade round, pressed laid-on-ring, in green

Bottom: 'A & D H CHAMBERS' and 'PITTSBURGH PA' in a circle around 'UNION' and 'FRUIT JAR' forming an inner circle. A figure for mold identification appears in center bottom

Alexander & David H. Chambers, Pittsburgh, Pa., 1843-75 or later. Chambers is more famous among collectors of historical flasks, including a "Union and clasped hands" in the 1860s

UNION, MASON'S

Circa 1865-70

Mason shoulder seal

Handmade round, ground lip, in aqua

Side: a shield, with 'MASON'S' arched above, and 'UNION' in a drooped arc below

Maker unknown

The workmanship is rather crude and would be an early MASON. Moreover, the UNION motif bespeaks the war years of 1861-65. I believe that this is an early Mason jar, produced before the formation of the Consolidated Fruit Jar Co. in the late 1860s

UNIVERSAL

Circa 1910-20

Mason shoulder seal

Machine-made round, in blue and aqua

Side: 'UNIVERSAL' in a panel, above 'L. F. & C.' The lettering is upside down, leading to the belief that this jar was used as a dispenser, such as a poultry waterer, fitting a drinking fountain

V

VACU-TOP

This jar was described to me, but not seen, as having a glass lid and spring clip resembling the ECONOMY, but with a patent date of Mar. 10, 1866. The jar seems too sophisticated to be of that age, and the date given is not a true patent-issue date. But see note in connection with the VALVE JAR and the patent date

VACUUM JAR

Circa 1893

Tapered slanting top and side seal, held by three loops of a wire that hooked under a finish ledge. A round rubber ring, fitting a hemispherical groove around the

TRADE MARK

VACUUM

JAR

slanting finish was compressed by the glass lid

Handmade round, pressed laid-on-ring of good workmanship, in flint

Side: "J" and "G" superimposed on the left and right legs of a large "V," with "CO" above; 'TRADE' and 'MARK' flanking opposite sides; below the monogram: 'VACUUM' and 'JAR'

Maker unknown, for Vacuum Jar Glass Co., San Francisco, Cal., a jobber

Bottom has patent date 'PAT JULY 11, 1893'

Patent No. 501,418 was issued to Franz Guilleaume and Ewald Goltstein of Germany. The latter was the patentee of the heat-softening seal used on the ECONOMY jar

See also EASY VACUUM JAR

VACUUM TITE Co.

Circa 1930

Glass lid with perforated center, over which is a small rubber dome

Pressed flint glass

Lid: 'VACUUM TITE Co.' and 'RAPID CITY, N.D.' in upper half of circle; 'PATENTED AUGUST 19, 1930' in lower half

Maker unknown

This is apparently a patented venting lid for use with some kind of clip, yoke, or screw-band on a fruit jar. The perforated lid would vent during the boil, after which the rubber dome would seal

Patent No. 1,773,311 was issued to Dan Killen of Milwaukee, Wis., for this seal

VALVE JAR (1)

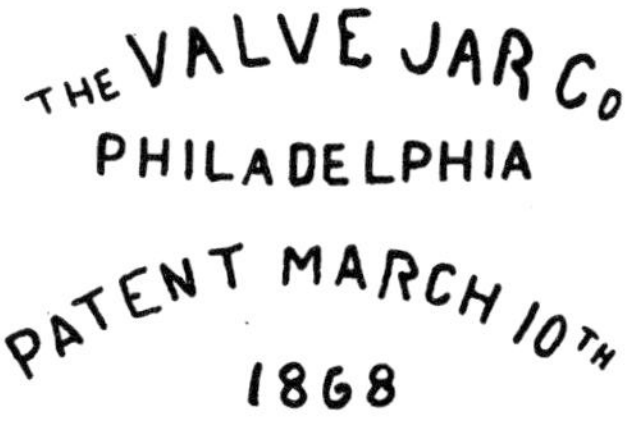

Circa 1868

Heavy wire coiled to fit jar threads, with one end extending upward to curve downward onto the top of the glass lid

Handmade slightly tapered round, ground lip, in green

Side: 'THE VALVE JAR CO.' arched over 'PHILADELPHIA' and 'PATENT MARCH 10TH,' arched over '1868'

Maker unknown

Since this finish was patented by William Imlay, of Philadelphia, as Patent No. 75,275 of Mar. 10, 1868, and made by Potter & Bodine, it is possible that the Valve Jar Co. was a merchandising subsidiary of Potter & Bodine

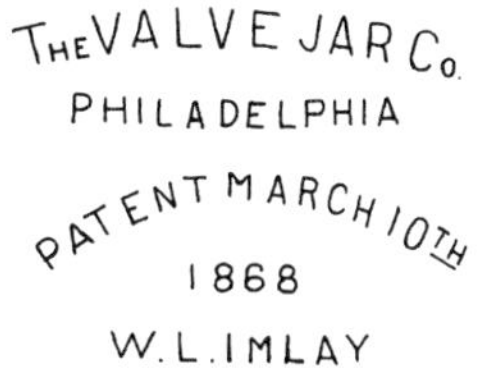

It is also possible that this jar was also known as the VACU-TOP, and that the patent date quoted for that jar should have read Mar. 10, 1868

VALVE JAR (2)

Same except 'PATENT MARCH 10TH' and '1868' on separate lines

VALVE JAR (3)

Same except 'THE VALVE JAR CO.' arched over 'PHILADELPHIA' on the side, and 'PAT^D MAR 10TH' and '1868' forming a circle on the bottom

THE
VAN VLIET
JAR
OF 1881

VAN VLIET JAR, THE

Circa 1881

Glass lid and thumbscrew, with the yoke for the thumbscrew anchored by a wire passing completely around the jar vertically, held by a groove in the bottom

Handmade round, ground lip, in green

Side: four lines: 'THE,' 'VAN VLIET,' 'JAR,' and 'OF 1881'

Maker unknown but could be the East Stroudsburg Glass Co., East Stroudsburg, Pa., 1877-1920, since Warren Van Vliet was a native of that city. This glass company advertized extensively until 1920 in the *National Bottlers Gazette*

Patent No. 241,095 was issued to Warren Van Vliet on May 3, 1881. The bottoms and lids of some jars bear this date

VICTOR (1)

Circa 1860-70

A. R. Samuels, circa 1860-70, advertized a VICTOR jar, along with the WILLOUGHBY STOPPLE, and the KLINE and his own A R S jar, both of which took the WILLOUGHBY STOPPLE. It would therefore be probable that the VICTOR was made, also, for the WILLOUGHBY STOPPLE, and, if so, it would be a handmade round, pressed laid-on-ring jar, with a stopper opening

VICTOR (2)

Circa 1900

Glass lid, held by a compression band circling finish

Handmade round, pressed laid-on-ring, in aqua

Side: 'THE VICTOR' and 'PATENTED 1899' in a circle around an elaborate "M" or decoration resembling an "M"

Maker unknown

VICTOR (3)

Same as (2) except machine-made

VICTOR (4)

Same as (2) but lettering changed to 'PAT. FEB. 20- 1900' and "M" placed within a diamond within a circle. Probably production started before the patent was granted, and the maker believed that the patent would be issued by 1899

Patent No. 643,908 was issued to Ernst R. Meyer. It introduced a new concept in sealing, in which fingers along the upper and lower edges of a horizontal band pulled lid and jar together when the band was clamped into place

VICTORY (1)

Circa 1869-76

Glass lid and metal screw-band top seal

Handmade round, ground lip, in green

Front: 'PAT'ᴰ FEB'ʸ 9ᵀᴴ 1864' as top of circle; 'REIS'ᴰ JUNE 22'ᴰ 1867' as bottom of circle; 'VICTORY' across the diameter

Back: 'SAN FRANCISCO GLASS WORKS'

San Francisco Glass Works, San Francisco, Cal., 1869-76. Note that earliest date for jar would not be patent date, but initial date of company. It had been the San Francisco Flint Glass Works, 1865 until burned in 1869, and rebuilt under new name

VICTORY (2)

Same except back lettering is for the PACIFIC GLASS WORKS, 1865-76, and rival of SAN FRANCISCO GLASS WORKS until their merger in 1876. See PACIFIC GLASS WORKS, also, for the identical jar without the name VICTORY

VICTORY (3)

Circa 1909

Glass lid held by Kivlan's three-element toggle

Machine-made tapered round, in flint

Lid: 'VICTORY' across a shield bearing a star in its upper left corner, with 'THE VICTORY JAR' on a ribbon below. What appears to be a tied ribbon and several dots is above the shield

Bottom: in a circle: 'SMALLEY, KIVLAN & ONTHANK, BOSTON'; in center: 'PAT⁻ Feb 23, 1909'

Unknown maker for Smalley, Kivlan & Onthank, bottle jobbers

VICTORY (4)

Circa 1921

Glass lid held by Kivlan's two-element toggle, his second patent

Machine-made tapered round, in flint

Lid: same as (3) except ribbon reads 'THE,' 'VICTORY,' and 'JAR'

Bottom: 'KIVLAN & ONTHANK' in a
circle around 'PAT^D JUNE 28, 1921' and
H - A trade mark
Hazel Atlas Glass Co., Wheeling, W. Va.,
1902-64
Kivlan & Onthank had succeeded Smalley,
Kivlan & Onthank in 1919

VICTORY (5)

Same as (3) except with the "I" in a diamond trade mark of the Illinois Glass
Co., Alton, Ill., 1873-1929. Ribbon not
lettered. Shield is stippled and does not
bear the star

VICTORY (6)

Circa 1929
Glass lid held by twin snap elements,
Kivlan's third patent
Machine-made tapered round, in flint
Lid: same as (3)
Bottom: 'CROWN CORK & SEAL CO.,
BALTO.' in circle around 'PAT^D APRIL
2, 1929.' Kivlan & Onthank had ceased
business about 1925
Maker not identified

VICTORY (7)

Circa 1920; discontinued before 1930
Glass lid held by Kivlan's two-element
toggle
Machine-made tapered round, in flint
Lid: same as in (3)
Bottom: "C" in a triangle
Consumers Glass Co., Toronto, Ont., 1917
to date

PAT.º FEB 9TH 1864
VICTORY
RE.IS.º JUNE 5.º 1867

VICTORY with moldmaker's error

Same as VICTORY (2) except the "22" in
the patent date is cut backward

VICTORY [Kivlan patents in general]

Jars made to the Feb. 23, 1909, patent by
John H. Kivlan may be distinguished by
the fact that the lid does not have a circular groove around the top edge, and that
each of the twin toggles is composed of
three elements. The lower element is a
metal plate hinged to the tie-wire around
the neck and to the middle wire-loop element. The long top element hooks over
the edge of the glass lid. The patent was
No. 913,214

The June 28, 1921, patent of John Kivlan
was No. 1,383,215. It can be distinguished
by the fact that the toggle has only two
elements, a metal plate hinged to the
neck tie-wire, and a wire loop that hooks
over the edge of the glass lid. The lid has
a circular groove around the outer edge,
into which the wire catches, so that it
does not slip off the edge as was possible
under the first design

Kivlan's third patent, No. 1,707,439, of
Apr. 2, 1929, was issued after his company had ceased business. It was not a
toggle, but a one-element snap lock,
hinged to the tie-wire around the neck as
with the two others, but exerting pressure on the glass lid only by means of a
hook-shaped design that gave spring action at the part over the lid

Throughout his three patents the glass contour of the jar in contact with the lid did
not change, nor did the lid change in
dimension—only in certain details at the

top edge. Consequently the lids are inter-changeable, and any mixture of lid and toggle or snap may be found together. Moreover, since apparently the company assembled its own product, they placed one fastening device on a jar lettered for another device, even to the extent of placing a Kivlan toggle on a Lightning finish, which it also fitted

In the nearly thirty years over which VIC-TORY jars were produced, under three patents, many slight changes in design of the letters evolved. The decoration above the shield took on at least three forms, one without dots below it. The shield be-came narrower, the star was removed, and the shield became stippled. The ribbon below the shield started out with 'FRUIT,' 'VICTORY,' 'JAR,' then became 'THE,' 'VICTORY,' 'JAR,' and in the last was not lettered

(VARIATIONS ABOVE SHIELD)

W

"W" (1)

Circa 1871-80

Groove-ring wax sealer

Handmade round, pressed laid-on-ring, in green and dark green

Side: a large, script, "W"

Thomas Wightman & Co., Pittsburgh, Pa., 1871-83

"W" (2)

Circa 1871

Same as (1) except the jar shows evidence that the original lettering had been "L & W," and that after the death of Moses Lorenz in 1871, thus ending the firm of Lorenz & Wightman, the molds had been converted to the use of the new Thomas Wightman & Company simply by peening out "L &." Such jars would be circa 1871—jars showing no evidence of such peening would be later (Knittle, p. 318)

W & Co.

Circa 1871-83

Groove-ring wax sealer

Handmade round, pressed laid-on-ring, in green

Bottom: 'W & Co.'

Thomas Wightman & Co., Pittsburgh, Pa., 1871-83

WALES, GEO. E.

Circa 1893

Glass lid and sloping side seal, held by metal clip to notches in finish on jar

Handmade round, pressed lip, in flint and sun-colored

Bottom: 'GEO. E. WALES' and 'NEWTON CENTRE MASS' forming a circle around 'PAT. JULY 11' arched above and '1893' in straight line below the same "V J G Co." trade mark monogram seen on the EASY VACUUM JAR and the VACUUM JAR

Maker unknown

The patent is that of Guilleaume and Goltstein discussed under VACUUM JAR,
but the jar design differs in that there are
two indentations on the side of the finish
to accommodate the metal clip ends

WAN-ETA COCOA

Circa 1920-40

Mason beaded neck design

Machine-made round, in flint, amber, and
blue-green

Side: three lines: 'WAN-ETA,' slightly
arched over 'COCOA' and 'BOSTON'

Maker unknown

WAUWIL

Modern Swiss jar

Glass lid, held by a heavy wire formed
into a spring clip over the top of the lid
where it is held in a groove

Machine-made tall round, in flint

Lid: 'WAUWIL' and a trade mark of three
bottle shapes and a cross-section of a
mold, all in silhouette

Glashutte Wauwil, St. Prex, Switzerland

WAX SEALERS, UNMARKED

See UNLETTERED JARS at end of
GLOSSARY

WEARS (1)

Circa 1910-20

Lightning closure, old-style neck design

Machine-made oval, similar to the KING,
in flint

Side: three lines: 'THE,' 'WEARS,' and
'JAR' within a doubly outlined oval; dec-
orative diamonds above and below
"WEARS"

Unknown maker

Distributed by Smalley, Kivlan & Onthank, who did not identify themselves on this particular jar

WEARS (2)

Same except sealed by the first of the Kivlan twin toggles, and marked on the bottom: 'PATENTED FEB 23, 1909,' for Kivlan's first patent

WEARS (3)

Same except bottom markings: 'PATENTED JUNE 23, 1921.' This is in error —the true date is June 28, 1921, and is the date of Kivlan's second, or revised, toggle

WEARS (4)

Same as (2) except the word "WEARS" only, and on a draped banner as on the KING jar

WEARS (5)

Same design as (4) except with Lightning closure, old-style neck design

WEIDEMAN

Circa 1920-40

Lightning closure, beaded neck design

Machine-made rounded square, in flint

Side: a large shield, bearing 'WEIDEMAN,' 'BOY BRAND,' a drawing of a boy (not shown in drawing), and 'CLEVELAND'

Maker unknown

WEIR (1)

Circa 1892

Glass lid, and wire bail holding a pointed, right-angled lever centering in a depression in the middle of the lid

Handmade round, ground lip, in green

Lid: 'THE WEIR PATENT, MARCH 1, 1892' in a circle

Bottom: 'STAR GLASS Co., NEW ALBANY, IND.' in a circle

Star Glass Co., New Albany, Ind., circa 1860-1900, exact dates unknown but the glass company made an early STAR wax sealer as well as the Weir. Made for William S. Weir, a Monmouth, Ill., potter

Patent No. 469,985 was issued posthumously to William Teamer of Evansville, Ind., and was the first of several patents, the others by Weir

WEIR (2)

Same design but in pottery. The glass lids were interchangeable

WEIR (3)

Same as (1) except a different lever and a patent date of Apr. 6, 1901. The lever had a short cross-member at the end, fitting a groove in the top of the lid, with the purpose of adding stability to the otherwise "wobbly" lever end. The patent was No. 672,049 and issued to William S. Weir, of Monmouth, Ill.

WEIR (4)

Differs from (3) in having the sealing surfaces of both the lid and the jar grooved concentrically in order to compress the rubber in ringed areas and improve the tightness of the seal. It was Weir's Patent No. 730,500, of June 9, 1903

WESTERN

PRIDE

PATENTED JUNE 2 2 1875

WESTERN PRIDE

Circa 1875

Glass lid with ramps on top, held by wire clip to a plain beaded neck

Handmade round, pressed laid-on-ring, in flint

Side: 'WESTERN' arched above 'PRIDE.' Below, 'PATENTED JUNE 22 1875'

Maker unknown

The jar closely follows the HAINES jar patent of 1870, but without the concentrically ribbed sealing surface. It was Patent No. 164,663 by D. E. Stevens and R. F. Lumley of Newark, Ohio

WHEELER

Circa 1885

Glass lid with double wire levers, hooking under each other on top of the lid, and hinged to a tie-wire at the neck

Handmade round, ground lip, in light green

Side: 'WHEELER'

Campbell Glass Mfg. Co., West Berkeley, Cal., 1884-85 only

William F. Hannes received Patent No. 314,322 on Mar. 24, 1885, for this design. The glass company was ill fated, lasting only parts of two years' production "campaigns," as the glass companies termed that part of the year left after each year's three-month summer closing

WHITALL-TATUM

Circa 1895

Glass lid and flat jar top, both ground for tight fit and held by yoke and thumb-wheel

Handmade round, pressed and ground laid-on-ring, in flint

Lid: 'WHITALL-TATUM' and 'PAT'D JUNE 11, 1895'

Whitall-Tatum Glass Co., Millville, N.J., 1857-1938; now a unit of the Armstrong Cork Company

Patent No. 540,890 was by Joseph Amia, June 11, 1895, and was for a sealing surface ground to a close fit on both lid and jar. It was actually a museum jar, but has been found in several collections

WHITE BEAR

Circa 1915-30

Lightning closure, adjustable neck design

Machine-made round, in amethyst, or sun-colored flint

Side: a polar bear on a shield (not shown in drawing). Below, in three lines: 'WHITE BEAR,' 'DURAND & CASPER Co,' and 'CHICAGO ILL'

Maker unknown

WHITE BEAR
DURAND & CASPER Co
CHICAGO ILL

WHITE CROWN CAP

Circa 1910

Opal lid and metal screw-band for machine-made, smooth-lipped Mason finish. Pressed opal glass to be used as an insert

Lid: 'WHITE CROWN' above 'CAP' with 'PAT - 11 - 22 - 10' following the curve of the edge below, on top of the lid

Maker unknown

Patent No. 976,659, of Nov. 22, 1910, was by Charles R. Keeran, of Bloomington,

WHITE CROWN
CAP
PAT - 11 - 22 - 10

Ill., who had other patents for fruit-jar seals, and who dealt in canning supplies. The patent was actually for metal and for impregnated waxed-paper disks. Either it, or the Hazel-Atlas E D G SEAL was the first attempt to seal on top of the newly possible machine-made top of the screw-cap finish. Kerr had already successfully sealed with a metal disk and heat-softening compound in the ECONOMY jar (not a screw thread) and was later to adapt the heat-softening method to the Mason finish in his SELF SEALING jars

WHITE CROWN MASON (1)

Circa 1910

Mason shoulder seal

Machine-made round, in aqua and light blue

Side: 'WHITE CROWN,' in oval outline, with 'MASON' in an attached rectangle

Maker unknown

It is my understanding that the makers of the WHITE CROWN CAP started to make the WHITE CROWN MASON in order to have better control of the smoothness of the sealing surface, vital to their cap, but of no particular moment to the makers of competing shoulder-seal Masons

WHITE CROWN MASON (2)

Circa 1915

Same but converted to the Mason beaded neck design

WHITMORE'S PATENT

Circa 1868

Notched glass lid and spring wire bail

Handmade round, ground lip, in aqua

Side: 'WHITMORE'S' arched above 'PAT-ENT' (with a reversed "N"), above 'ROCHESTER' arched above 'N.Y.'

Probably the Rochester Glass Works, Rochester, N.Y., 1865-87

The lid was lettered 'PATENTED JAN'Y 14th, 68' but the patent was not found. The lid has two rising vanes, one as a brace and the other notched in the center. The spring bail rises high, with a reverse curve downward to give spring action while resting in the notch

WHITNEY (1)

Between 1887 and 1918

Mason shoulder seal

Handmade round, ground lip, in aqua

Side: 'WHITNEY' and 'PAT'D 1858' forming a circle around 'MASON'

Whitney Glass Works, Glassboro, N.J., 1887-1918

See also GLASSBORO, TELEPHONE JAR, and MASON JAR OF 1872

WHITNEY (2)

Circa 1910-18

Same except machine-made

WHITNEY (3)

Same as (1) except machine-made and lettered only 'WHITNEY' and 'PAT'D 1858' in a circle

WHOLEFRUIT

See ATLAS WHOLEFRUIT

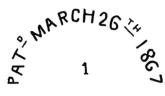

WILCOX, B. B.

Circa 1867

Glass lid held by spring-wire bail, hinged in a narrow band at the neck

Handmade round, ground lip, in green

Side: 'PAT^D MARCH 26TH, 1867' arched above 'B B WILCOX.' "1" is a mold number

Maker unknown

Patent No. 63,193, by B. B. Wilcox of New Haven, Conn., is quite different from the actual jar. The patent calls for a split-ring trunnion, instead of the one-piece band used. It also calls for a stamped metal yoke instead of the wire bail, and the yoke had an additional function in closing, with an intervening gasket, a small orifice in the center of the glass lid which would allow venting during the boiling operation

HERO did use the split-ring trunnion on its Lightning jar

WILLOUGHBY STOPPLE

This sealing device was used on many jars during the 1860-70 period. It was an assembly of two flat plates, with a rubber disk between, which would be squeezed outwardly when the two plates were tightened together by means of a thumbscrew. The jars were made with a cupped stopper-well. The STOPPLE would be inserted into the well (it was made in several diameters to fit various jars), and tightened against the side walls of the well by operating the thumbscrew. It would be removed after loosening the thumbscrew, and was completely re-

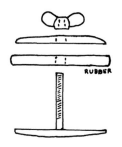

J. O. WILLOUGHBY STOPPLE
PAT. JAN. 4, 1859

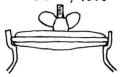

usable—no mean feature in those days
The device was stamped 'J. D. WIL-
LOUGHBY STOPPLE' and 'PAT. JAN.
4, 1859.' A common size was stamped
"2 3/8"

WILLS & Co., ALEX.

Circa 1880
Stopper-like glass lid, held by clamp or clip
Handmade round, pressed laid-on-ring, in
green and blue-green
Side: 'ALEX WILLS & CO' forming the
upper half of an oval; 'MONTREAL'
the lower half; and 'GLOBE MILLS'
across the center
Maker unknown

WILSON

See JOHN M. MOORE and MOORE'S
PATENT

WING WAH SING

Circa 1920
Lightning closure, beaded neck design
Machine-made round, in flint
Side: 'WING WAH SING' and Chinese
characters
Maker unknown

WINSLOW JAR (1)

Circa 1870
Glass lid, wire clip and twin helical neck
lugs
Handmade round, ground lip, in green
Side: 'WINSLOW JAR' on one line
Lid: 'PATENTED NOV 29th, 1870'
Winslow Glass Co., Winslow, N.J., 1831 to
after 1884

Patent No. 109,703 was issued to Theodore F. Woodward of Winslow, N.J., and assigned to Hay & Co. of Philadelphia, Pa., 1866-84, who owned the Winslow Glass Co., leasing it to others in 1884

WINSLOW JAR (2)

Circa 1873

Same except the lid now carried the added patent date of Feb. 25, 1873. This was Patent No. 136,148 by Henry Gaskill of Mount Holly, N.J., who also assigned his patent to Hay & Co. It corrected the fact that Woodward had made the seal on the ground lip

WO HOP Co.

Circa 1930
Lighning closure, beaded neck design
Machine-made round, in flint
Side: 'WO HOP Co.' and Chinese characters
Maker unknown

WOOD & SELICK

Circa 1890-1900
Lightning closure, old-style neck design
Handmade round, ground lip, in light green
Front: four lines: 'WOOD & SELICK,' arched over 'MANUFACTURING,' 'CHEMISTS,' and 'NEW YORK'
Back: '1/2 GALLON' above 'IMPERIAL BRAND'
Maker unknown

WOOD&SELICK

MANUFACTURING

CHEMISTS

NEW YORK

½ GALLON

IMPERIALBRAND

WOODBURY (1)

Circa 1884-85 only

Glass lid with a central threaded stud for a cap whose sole function was to hold the iron yoke, which passed over the stud by having a hole for that purpose. The stud was not vented, as later, nor did the cap have a gasket. The yoke engaged helical lugs on the neck of the jar

Handmade round, ground lip, in green

Side: 'WOODBURY' above an elaborate monogram of "W G W"

Woodbury Glass Works, Woodbury, N.J., 1882-90

Patent No. 308,571 was issued on Nov. 25, 1884, to J. H. and T. G. Otterson. The latter was the inventor of the MILL-VILLE ATMOSPHERIC jar in 1862

WOODBURY (2)

Circa 1885-86 only

The same jar, but with the central stud or post of the lid perforated for venting

during the boiling operation of canning. For this purpose the cap was given a gasket. This is the WOODBURY most commonly seen, and is the patent, No. 313,229, issued to T. G. Otterson and C. C. Voorhies on Mar. 3, 1885

WOODBURY

WOODBURY (3)

Circa 1886-92

Essentially the same function as to the stud and its venting, but with the glass lid held by a metal screw-band as a top seal

Patent dates of Mar. 16 and June 29, 1886, are shown on the glass lid, but only the first (Patent No. 338,185, issued to T. G. and J. H. Otterson) was found

WOODBURY

IMPROVED

WOODBURY IMPROVED

The jar is essentially the same as WOODBURY (3), but with the word, 'IMPROVED' added below 'WOODBURY,' and a slightly smaller monogram than on earlier jars

WORCESTER (1)

Circa 1860-70

Stopper well for WILLOUGHBY STOPPLE, 1859 patent, which see

Handmade tall round, pressed laid-on-ring, in flint

Side: 'WORCESTER'

Maker unknown

WORCESTER

WORCESTER (2)

Circa 1862
Glass lid and clip
Handmade round, ground lip, in green
Side: 'WORCESTER'
Lid: 'Pat. June 10, 1862' in a circle
Maker unknown

X

"X" with MASON'S PATENT NOV. 30th, 1858

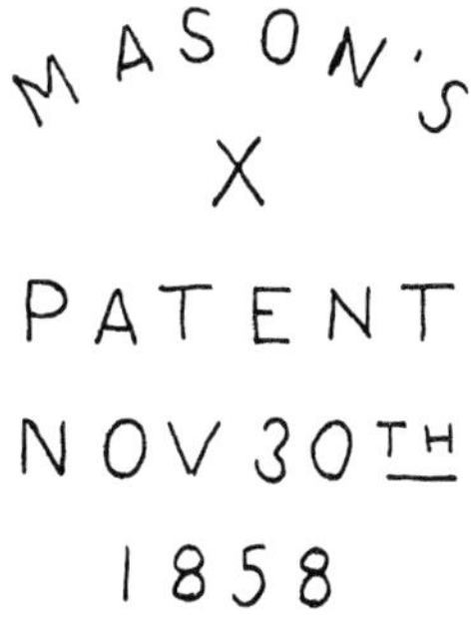

Circa 1885-1900
Mason shoulder seal
Handmade round, ground lip, in light green
Side: 'MASON'S' in an arch above an 'X', followed by 'PATENT,' 'NOV 30$^{\underline{TH}}$' and '1858'
Maker unknown

MASON'S
X
PATENT
NOV 30$^{\underline{TH}}$
1858

Y

YEOMAN'S FRUIT BOTTLE

Circa 1850-60
Bell finished for cork stopper
Handmade small-mouth round, ground lip, in aqua
Side: 'YEOMAN'S' above 'FRUIT BOT-TLE,' both crudely cut and in sagging arcs
Maker unknown
A handbill owned by collector Don Mericle describes it as a wax-sealed cork-stop-pered bottle, and states that it is made by T. G. Yeoman of Walworth, N.Y. This statement about bottle-making is not un-common by jobbers who might own the patent but have the jars made for them for their resale

YEOMAN'S
FRUIT BOTTLE

Unlettered Jars

SCREW THREAD JARS, ORNAMENTED (1)

Circa 1890-1900

Bluish opal lid and metal screw-band top seal

Handmade round, crudely ground lip, in bluish opal glass

Side: a small stylized design of little resemblance to natural objects, and quite nonsymetrical, enclosing an open area that could be used for a label

Bottom: "H"

Maker unknown — contemporary with FLACCUS and STEERSHEAD opal jars

SCREW THREAD JARS, ORNAMENTED (2)

Circa 1890-1900

Bluish opal lid and metal screw-band top seal

Handmade round, crudely ground lip, in bluish opal glass

Side: vine and leaf design, quite large and enclosing a separate oval area, of the same design, for labels

Maker unknown. Contemporary with FLACCUS and STEERSHEAD

The maker of both (1) and (2) could be the Hazel Glass Co, Washington, W. Va., 1886-1901, who had almost the only facility for blowing and pressing the same glass, and who were also known as opal specialists. The "H" on (1) *may* be for HAZEL, but has not been known to have been used for that purpose

SCREW THREAD JARS, UNORNA- MENTED

No attempt will be made to list the many, many unidentifiable plain jars that would qualify under this heading. Most were commercially used jars, excellent for re- use as home canners and fruit jars.

WAX SEALERS, BLOWN-GROOVE TYPE, UNLETTERED

In addition to the AGNEW type shown in the drawing, and the AIR TIGHT type of Potter & Bodine, both of which are lettered, there are also examples of each, unlettered and unidentifiable

BLOWN WAX SEALER

PUSHED DOWN WHILE HOT AFTER REMOVAL FROM MOLD

WAX SEALERS, GROOVE-RING TYPE

In addition to the many lettered, and there- for identifiable, wax sealers of the Arthur pressed groove-ring type, many such are not lettered

WAX SEALER

WAX SEALERS, UNLETTERED (1)

Circa 1850

Glass jar, bell-shaped for cork stopper or glass lid, to be luted with wax

Handmade, tooled lip, laid-on-ring, and bare pontil discoloration on bottom

Maker unknown

WAX SEALERS
TYPICAL FINISH AND STOPPER

WAX SEALERS, UNLETTERED (2)

The same except with glass-tipped pontil scar

WAX SEALERS, UNLETTERED (3)

The same as (1) except with paneled shoulder, scalloped around lower edges of panels

WAX SEALERS, UNLETTERED (4)

Same as (1) but without either iron or glass-tipped pontil scars

WAX SEALERS, POTTERY (1)

Age uncertain

Bell-shaped top for cork stopper or ceramic lid, to be luted with wax

Wheel-formed, with obvious turn-lines and no seams

Glazes usually brown inside; cream, tan, or varicolored in tan and brown outside, or salt glazed, and rough

Makers unknown

WAX SEALERS, POTTERY (2)

Same as (1) in general appearance except slip cast, with side seams

WAX SEALER, POTTERY (3)

Same as (2) in general appearance, but slip cast with as many as 12 panels, with side seams sometimes showing a three-part construction of the mold

WAX SEALER, POTTERY, PEORIA TYPE (1)

Circa 1855 and later

Groove-ring wax sealer

Slip cast pottery with 16 panels. Brown glaze inside and out. No evidence of vertical side seams, but since jar is wide at the shoulder and narrow at the top and the bottom, and because it shows evidence of a joining at the shoulder, it was probably cast in separate shoulder and body sections and luted together before firing

Bottom: die stamped 'PEORIA' or 'PEORIA POTTERY'

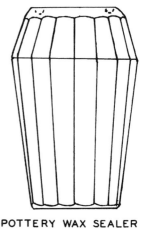

POTTERY WAX SEALER

PEORIA TYPE   GROOVE RING

WAX SEALER, POTTERY, PEORIA TYPE (2)

Similarly shaped and made, but without maker identification

Men Who Made Fruit-Jar History

While nearly two hundred glass factories have made fruit jars, and an even greater number of men and women have secured patents for them, only a few men have made lasting impressions. Mason is well known, or perhaps well *mis*-known, because of the apocryphal tales about him—his name became generic before the patents ran out. We should know something about other men, before and after Mason, who created some turning point in the industry, in addition to today's jar-makers whom we know because of their nearness to our time.

For this reason I have selected ten men whose work should be better known to all collectors of fruit jars. They are: *Nicolas (François) Appert*, chef, brewer, confectioner, vintner, and general man-about-foods whose story is told in the chapter, "Using the Jars"; *Robert Arthur*, whose early patent for the groove-ring wax sealer turned men's eyes toward mechanically made closures; *John Landis Mason*, who stumbled upon the cheapest and easiest made jar and seal, but who did not profit by its full and later success; *Salmon P. Rowley*, the glass-lid specialist who was Mason's rival, and who eventually took over Mason's business; *Lewis* (or *Louis*—he obtained patents under both spellings) *R. Boyd*, whose glass liner improved the Mason jar cap too late to save Mason or his company; *Henry W. Putnam*, whose Lightnings flashed over all east of the Hudson and north of the Poconos; *Albert G. Smalley*, who supplied New England with glass-lidded jars second only to Putnam; *Frank C. Ball*, with his brothers, who started with wood-jacketed kerosene jugs and built a name that has become almost synonymous with today's fruit-jar industry; *C. N. Brady*, the bookkeeper who built Hazel, then Atlas, and then joined them together with the first glass-blowing machine in the industry; and *Alexander Hewitt Kerr*, the tithing food-merchant who literally "put a lid" on the fruit-jar business.

ROBERT ARTHUR

Where Robert Arthur came from and lived, except at Washington, D.C., at the time he received his patent, what happened to him afterward, and whether he received any profit from his invention from the glass industry (many glass companies made it simultaneously but not in complete conformation with the patent) is not known. Little did he know, when he illustrated his Patent No. 12,153 of January 2, 1855, with drawings of a tin can and a pottery jar, that some fifteen or twenty glass companies would be the chief users of the idea.

His grooved-ring can was intended for home use as a food container, however, and he definitely was thinking of an easier way to seal the can than by soldering. His patent reference to "vessels formed in a plastic state" would include glass. While he was one of the earliest inventors in this field, he was not the first, since he mentions one Spratt, who used a rubber ring as a temporary seal, and he also refers to grooves in previous devices and their imperfectly fitting covers.

One, and the important, feature of his patent was the vertical inner wall of the groove, and the close-fitting right-angle rim around the metal lid. Its object was to prevent the differences in cooling of the wax and jar contents either from sucking wax into the jar contents or from blowing air through the partly congealed seal.

Even Arthur recognized the difference between the patent office drawing and the possibilities of actual production. He almost negates his chief patent premise by suggesting that as an adjunct to the wax, "any elastic substance . . . packed into the bottom of the groove—such as a piece of raw cotton, a strip of cotton fabric of any kind, a piece of leather, or even a piece of newspaper." In time, companies such as the Dicks-Pontius Company, of Dayton, Ohio, and the Princeton Wax Company, of Princeton, Ill., were making ready-to-use, waxed-dipped soft string to lay in the groove of the jar seal which would be softened by the heat of canning. The more frugal housewife, like the grandmother of one collector, would prepare her own, and also use the string as a ready means of opening the jar.

The glass jar used a slanting wall in the groove, and slanted the edges of the metal disk to fit. It is easily possible that the groove was in use before the Arthur patent and that he was referring to this use when he mentioned "imperfectly fitting covers." Arthur did not make reference to any tool for making the groove in "plastic" materials, so it remained to some unknown glassmaker to devise the pressing tool that would form the laid-on-ring into a standardized shape and diameter that would take the standardized lid. The dates for glass use of the groove must have been about the time of Arthur's patent, since Hero obtained its patent for the Gem glass lid in 1856, fitting the grooved-ring. The San Francisco Glass Company also made a glass lid, and still others formed the groove by tooling instead of pressing.

Dr. Harry H. Holscher has shown in "Hollow and Specialty Glass" (*The Glass Industry,* June through November, 1965), p. 29, that groove-ring sealing means was provided in stoneware jars definitely in 1840-45, and possibly as early as 1811-1835. We have no indication through patents and the like just how soon after this that tools were developed for pressing or otherwise tooling the finish in glass jars.

JOHN LANDIS MASON

Mason, a former farm boy from near Vineland, N.J., established a tinsmithing and metal-working shop on Canal Street in New York City about 1855, when he was 23 years old. In 1858 or 1859, after the demand for zinc caps for his shoulder-seal jar started, he moved his shop to 257 Pearl Street and took on T. W. Frazier, Henry Mitchell, and B. W. Payne as partners, according to the *Mason Jar Centennial* published by the Glass Container Manufacturers Institute. It seems that he licensed others to make the jars, and held to himself the business of making caps, although there is evidence that he must have licensed cap-making also. This established a precedent of selling jars and caps separately that was not broken until both Ball and Hazel Glass Company began to sell a roll of twelve caps with every case of a dozen jars, about 1890 according to John Algeo, long a sales manager for Hazel Atlas.

McKearin, *American Glass,* p. 605, lists Mason as having leased the Tansboro Glass House, near Salem, N.J., in 1856 for the purpose of making fruit jars. It is more likely that it was a contract for experimental jar-making, for this was two years before the patent was allowed, and in those days there was less time between patent application and granting than now. Perhaps he leased the factory later as the Mason Manufacturing Company, when he resumed business after the end of the Civil War. He was only 26 in 1858, and had neither glass-making experience nor the money to lease a factory.

The Glass Container Manufacturers Institute booklet gives credit for the first blowing of a Mason jar to Clayton Parker, a glass blower in the shop of Samuel Crowley. If so, Crowley also fell victim to the Mason nemesis. He had started a shop at Crowleytown, N.J., in 1851, lost it in 1852, started up again at Bulltown, now called Waldo, N.J., in 1858, the year Mason's patent was allowed, and closed in 1870.

Mason is reported by Dr. H. H. Holscher, in "Hollow and Specialty Glass—Background and Challenge," serialized in *The Glass Industry,* June–November, 1965, to have licensed J. K. Chase, himself a prior inventor of a screw-capped jar, but record of others is uncertain. Clyde Glass Works was not yet in operation. Chase later turns up as Williams & Chase, makers of canning supplies, and doing business at least in 1867 and 1869 according to the patents for a jar steamer and exhauster they marketed.

Mason's evil star began to shine when he seems to have disappeared from New York during the Civil War while his business languished, but he re-established his business, as the Mason Manufacturing Company on Spring Street in 1865. He may have lost Payne as a partner during the war, for Payne & Company appears later.

How much of the shoulder-seal jar was Mason's has been questioned. It involves William Brooke, famed in the glass industry as an early moldmaker, and father of Aries Brooke who had a moldmaking business on Fulton Street in New York from 1865 to sometime after 1899, and of Homer Brooke, later proprietor of the Brooke Glass Co. of Mt. Vernon, N.Y., and still later the designer of one of the first mechanical glass feeders for automatic machine operation.

Homer Brooke claims that his father had developed the "blowover" principle of hand glass blowing, in which a small chamber above the line of the finish would be blown thin to make the cracking-off at that point easily accomplished without involving the finish area and ruining the jar. He also claims that his father had developed the "vanishing-thread" idea, in which the threads end below the top line of the jar, and before the shoulder, and had used it in making screw-threaded insulators and salt shakers. Mason covered both of these ideas in his November 23, 1858, patent for a mold, and the November 30, 1858, patent for the Mason jar.

Homer Brooke further states that Mason and another man came to his father's shop about 1855 or 1856 to ask about making a mold for a glass jar with a three-inch opening to make a water-tight container for shipping oysters inland. Brooke advised against the small threads Mason desired, and described the vanishing-thread and blow-over ideas. He sent his son, Homer, to the machine shop to make an example of the idea.

Homer Brooke denies that Mason invented any of these principles or the fruit jar. Another writer quotes someone's description of Mason as "a man under medium size, dark complexioned, very nervous, a heavy drinker and perhaps . . . of a disagreeable disposition; a sort of a crank and very hard to get along with." He further quotes, "At the time of the liquidation of the Mason Company, two of his partners paid off all their debts. Mason, however, was reported to have refused to satisfy his creditors, although he got over $100,000 in stock. [That must have been at the formation of the Consolidated Fruit Jar Company.] It is reported further that he was once jailed for attempting to encroach on the Consolidated Fruit Jar Company after he sold his rights to them."

Mason's six top-seal patents, following the successful top seals of Imlay and others, from 1869 to 1872, came near the end of the life of his shoulder-seal patents, and after they had accumulated thirteen years of dislike for the metallic taste and zinc contamination of foods packed under the unprotected zinc of the cap. In the same year that Boyd patented his glass liner for the zinc cap, Mason started his top-seal series, showing somewhat a desperation and a singular ineptness in glassmaking design for a man whose first patents were, in patent office terminology, a "flash of genius." If Homer Brooke's story is true, then Mason needed Brooke in his later efforts.

The formation of the Consolidated Fruit Jar Company at New Brunswick, N.J., was a combination of Mason's own Mason

Manufacturing Company, Boyd's New York Metals Company, Payne & Company (Payne was his first partner), The Jersey City Glass Works, and probably others in the late 1860s. Their first identifying mark seems to be a large "C" on the bottom of the jar, with the C F J Co. monogram adopted in 1871. Mason did not move to New Brunswick until 1873, when he sold them the rights to his first two patents just before they expired. Three years later, on Feb. 8, 1876, he sold Consolidated all his jar patents, of which the only successful one, from 1872, would expire in 1889.

Consolidated's, and Mason's, stars dimmed by the beginning of the 1880s. Mason had lost much ground by the time Boyd patented his inner glass lining for the zinc cap. The glass-lid top-seal constructions of Hero, Cohansey, and others, which gave no metallic contact, were strong competitors. Boyd did not give Mason an exclusive license. In particular, the glass-lid designs became fully entrenched in New England, up-state New York, and Canada, from which they were not ousted until World War II and after the advent of the Kerr two-piece metal lid and screw-band seal, together with the virtual disappearance of the zinc cap.

It seems too bad that Mason exhibited little knowledge of the art of canning, for an early correction of the zinc contact with the jar contents might have changed the picture. Not one of his patents indicates any manner in which the jar should be used, whereas many other patents show considerable concern in the quality of their use.

The appearance of both the Hero cross and the C F J Co. monogram on the same jar about 1882 announced the end of Consolidated, for the placing of the cross *above* the word "MASON'S" and the monogram in the usual place between it and "PATENT" would indicate that the cross had been placed on an old Consolidated mold. The changing of Hero's name to "Hero Fruit Jar Company" two years later—an exact following of Consolidated's name except for the first word, seems to indicate that Hero had taken over Consolidated's business. Hero soon dropped the C F J Co. monogram and used only the Hero cross, now with the initials "H," "F," "J," and "Co" placed in the four wings. Consolidated suffered a disastrous fire in 1885, but remained in business, either as a jobber or maker of caps, for many years. Failing, and reorganizing under the same name, it is still active in a general metal-forming business.

What happened after the Mason patents expired was one of the most flagrant, widespread, and unabashed piracy of a man's name and reputation in the history of glassmaking. The patents were in the public domain and the making of the jar was legally permissible, but Mason could not fight the use of his own name as though it were generic and available to any user. Even a "Mason Fruit Jar Company," no relation, was organized in Philadelphia. The more honest glassmakers had to follow suit to defend their "Mason" jars. The name was even applied to a jar bearing a Lightning closure!

The shoulder-seal Mason was not the best seal in many ways. Its many disadvantages included: the impairment of the flavor of contents, even with the Boyd liner, and especially when users might employ two rubber rings "for sure sealing" and thus increase the distance between top of jar and under side of the glass liner; the insecurity of sealing when the skirt of the zinc cap was deformed, as by inserting a knife between it and the sealing rubber in an effort to "break" the vacuum for opening, followed by reuse of the cap; the uncertainty of venting depending upon the skill of the user; and the very effort of opening and closing, which led to the development of wrenches.

Its great advantage was that it was the easiest of all fruit jars to make, and therefore the cheapest. The zinc cap was not expensive, and could be used over and over again. A glass company could get into the business of making Mason jars with a mold and a grinding wheel, and did not have to concern itself with supplying zinc caps; it could undersell any fruit jar on the market because of its simplicity; its lids were reusable and replacements were readily available. Glass company after glass company mushroomed into the Mason-jar business, and in some cases came into being just for that purpose, especially with the new and opportune availability of natural gas in the north-central states.

Soon forty or fifty factories were making "Mason" jars, which they continued to do until the advent of glassmaking machines greatly reduced the cost to those companies using machines, such as Ball Brothers and Hazel Atlas. Other companies gradually disappeared or sold their interests to the companies using machines.

With machine-making, the lower costs, improved quality, and the bead-neck design that made either top seal or bead seal possible on the same jar brought the Mason jar into its own. Its shape had changed, the ground lip had given way to a pressed finish made by machine, the shoulder seal had moved into a bead, and the new design could take two kinds of sealing. Only one thing has remained unchanged and will probably remain so as long as the zinc cap is used—the thumb-tabbed rubber ring patented by John F. Griffen a century ago.

When the end came to Mason's brief venture with Consolidated, he was 50 years old, and without means of support at a time when the fruit-jar business was just picking up. Soon he returned to Brooklyn, N.Y. His eight daughters married; his wife died in 1898; and on February 26, 1902, aged 70, he died as a charity patient at the House of Relief on Hudson Street, in New York City, as stated by the Glass Container Manufacturers Institute.

It should be noted that several jar closures started out as some other type of sealing device and lid-holding method, and later changed to screw-band types of holding the lid, either similar to the Mason Improved or the 1858 type of Mason thread diameter. Usually they then termed their closure "Improved" but they should not be confused with Mason's use of the word "improved." This was notable with the Woodbury Jar, the Millville, the Premium, and, finally, the Kerr. Only the latter changed its trademarked name—from Kerr Economy to Kerr Self Sealing—even though the principles of sealing remained the same.

SALMON B. ROWLEY

During Hero's outstanding years, Hero was Rowley and Rowley was Hero. No certain record has been traced concerning the start of the Hero factory—only the fact that its Gem wax sealer carried three patent dates for 1856, one of which was February 12. These patents have not been found, but they are supposed to be for glass lids for use with the groove-ring wax-sealer design of Robert Arthur.

Rowley was a specialist on lid design and he listed every date possible on his lids, as well as jars. It seemed to matter little that the patent might not have reference to the jar or lid on which it was placed. This may have been to over-awe the user, but it is now of great use to the collector, who can establish a jar's Hero origin by them, even if he does have to be content to use the last date found, as the earliest date for his jar. Here are some of the dates on Hero, Gem, Pearl, Crystal, Porcelain Lined, and other Hero-made jars:

January, 1856	May 23, 1865	Jan. 19, 1869
Feb. 12, 1856	Nov. 26, 1867	Aug. 23, 1870
November, 1856	Dec. 10, 1867	Feb. 7, 1871
Dec. 17, 1861	Feb. 11, 1868	Sept. 3, 1872
Nov. 3, 1862	June 9, 1868	Dec. 31, 1872
Nov. 4, 1862	Sept. 1, 1868	Feb. 4, 1873
Dec. 17, 1862	Sept. 8, 1868	Feb. 27, 1894
Dec. 6, 1864	Dec. 22, 1868	Jan. 29, 1895

Some of these, as Nov. 3, 1862, may be mold-cutting errors, and others are in greater error, as not being a patent-issue date. But their presence on jars is an indication of Hero origin.

Hero, when it was the Hero Glass Works, used an elaborate monogram of the letters "H," "G," and "W" from an unknown date until 1882, when it adopted the Hero cross. It did not place the letters "H," "F," "J," and "Co" in the wings of the cross until the name was changed to the Hero Fruit Jar Company in 1884. Thus the H G W monogram, the unlettered cross, and the lettered cross are dating points.

Many people have called the Hero cross a Maltese cross. It is not, as reference to *Webster's Collegiate Dictionary* or the *Random House Dictionary* will show. Neither is it a cross formée or a cross pattée, by the same reference. I have not been able to find it in books on heraldry, so it must be a cross unique in itself, and therefor should be called only "the Hero cross."

As the number of patents, and the number of jar names, show, Rowley seems to have been as much an innovator as Mason was a conservative. If Mason's long holding to one jar design, one jar name, and one unlined zinc lid cost him dear, Rowley may have lost his chance to dominate the market through his seven or eight jar names, several types of closures, and vacillation between metal lids, glass lids, and an all-glass closure.

Hero's most used patent date, so often cited whether the jar was made to that design or not, was Design Patent No. D2,840, issued Nov. 26, 1867, and shown usually, when used alone, by the simple lettering, "NOV 26 67," without reference to "PAT" or use of punctuation. It covered the rounding in of the jar shape at the shoulder, to obtain strength that was being sacrificed in the Mason shape. Rowley's basic idea about sealing (largely after Mason's shoulder seal was patented and until Mason's ideas on the "top seal" began to be known, around 1869) was the top seal with a metal or glass lid straddling the ground lip, and resting on a flattened area just above the line of threads. This gave an all-glass food contact which was so much desired for taste-conscious users in New England and upstate New York. Users in these areas never forgot the zinc taste in food packed in jars with pre-Boyd zinc caps. The major fault of the top seal was the constricted opening, if the Mason thread diameter was kept. The fault had to be remedied by going to a cap with a larger diameter, with a subsequent increase in material cost, since the area of metal required changes with the square of the diameter. In general, top-seal thread diameters run from one-fourth inch to three-fourths inch larger than shoulder-seal thread diameters.

Hero licensed others to make their jars in the other's names. Cunningham & Ihmsen's Heroine was one licensee, since they showed the Nov. 26, 1867, date on the bottom. San Francisco & Pacific Glass Works made fruit jars under a Hero license until 1886 when they started to make their own. During that year Hero flooded San Francisco with cut-price jars from the east but San Francisco & Pacific weathered the storm and had the field to themselves from the following year.

The outstanding part of the Hero story is the long competition with Mason. As noted, Rowley was the champion of the glass lid and all-glass contact. He matched Mason patent for patent and more, throughout the late 1860s and early 1870s. The years before Boyd's 1869 glass-liner patent were of great benefit to Rowley's glass-lidded jars, and it was then that the great preference for them developed in the Northeast, aided by Smalley of Boston (1872), Putnam of Vermont (1882) and Hamilton of Ontario (1865).

There was no announcement that can be cited as proof that Hero finally acquired the assets of Mason's Consolidated Fruit Jar Company. There is proof, however, in that at least two jars, made about 1882-84, had both the Hero cross, unlettered, and the C F J Co monogram. Then Hero adopted the full Mason patent lettering, with the lettered Hero cross. Hero's well-known Gem jar is found with the Consolidated trade mark, also.

More confirmation is in the fact that the Clyde Glass Works, until then a principal supplier of Consolidated's jars (or at least the only one known to have identified themselves on Consolidated jars) tried to make its own jars for a few years, but then faded away and drew its fires about 1885-86. The company was reorganized in 1895 by Hoyt's Sons, and continued to about 1919. A General Electric Company factory occupied the site at the time of this writing.

At Hero's zenith, in 1878, it could list six jars on its letterhead: Hero, Hero Improved, Gem, Pearl, Crystal, and Porcelain Lined. It had made the All Right but had dropped it. It was later to make a Hero Lightning, and a Hero with Mason's Patent, Nov. 30th, 1858, on the jar. It listed factories at Philadelphia, Pa., and Lockport, N.Y., on its letterhead. This was more than a slight exaggeration, since Rowley had become the proprietor of the old Hitchen's Glass Works at Lockport in 1869 and had sold it to Alonzo J. Mansfield in 1872. (McKearin, p. 603)

In patents dated Feb. 27, 1894, and Jan. 29, 1895, Hero covered details of its Lightning-type closure. By 1909 it was ready to drop the fruit-jar business, to become the Hero Metal Products Company. It closed its doors in 1918.

LEWIS R. BOYD

The first real improvement in the Mason shoulder-seal jar was not in the jar but in the zinc cap. It was Patent No. 88,439, March 30, 1869, by Lewis R. Boyd, of New York City, followed by his No. 89,845 of May 11, 1869 (in which he spelled his name Louis). Mason's jar must have been losing ground because of the contact between the contents and the inside of the zinc cap, unprotected over the entire area of the inside top, which imparted a metallic taste to the contents. Several types of glass liners, including the first top-seal Mason had already been invented. The Hero Glass Works and the Cohansey Glass Manufacturing Co., in particular, were doing a good business in glass lids.

"To remedy this defect in metallic caps," states Boyd in his first patent application, ". . . a glass plate or partial lining, so arranged that the said glass shall be the only portion of the cap which at any time comes into contact with the jar." Well, almost the only portion because through the necessary space between the glass lining and the top of the jar there was some contact with the contents, and sometimes enough corrosion to make cap removal difficult as well as to give a slight metallic taste. Several wrenches and other tools were developed to make tightening and removal of the cap easier, and tools were also designed to straighten the edges of the zinc cap if it had been deformed by use. Boyd's invention, however, did much to save the Mason jar.

Boyd seems to have licensed Mason, Hero, and perhaps others before he took part in the formation of Consolidated Fruit Jar Company. Hero came out with its Porcelain Lined, and many jar lid liners have the C F J Co monogram of Consolidated. The North American Glass Co., of Montreal, also made a Porcelain Lined jar, as well as did Ball Brothers at their Buffalo factory circa 1885-86.

Boyd is next heard from when William Taylor and Charles Hodgetts assigned their July 18, 1871, Patent No. 117,236 to Louis R. Boyd of New York City. The closure was for their own Holz, Clark & Taylor jar, using a threaded stopper, and having "a thin sheet, plate, disk, lining, or shield of glass, porcelain, or other vitreous or equivalent in-corrodable substance . . . interposed between the contents of the vessel and that portion of the cap or cover upon which the acids would otherwise act, and thereby prevent the injurious consequences which have been mentioned." Thereupon Boyd seems to have faded from view, leaving behind this one great contribution to the fruit-jar industry—and to Mason.

Boyd never referred to the liner substance as porcelain. It must have taken the imagination of Rowley to coin the "porcelain" name for the opal glass that was used as the actual material. "Porcelain" would have sounded better than "opal," and perhaps the opaque material was needed both to convey the idea of purity and to hide the zinc that was responsible for the off-tastes. John Algeo tells me that the first business of the Hazel Glass Company, when they were formed in 1886 and had only one glass tank, was to press the opal inserts for the Mason zinc cap. Perhaps the need for getting other business to keep the tank running that first year is why Hazel became a specialist in opal ware. It is said that the only glassmaking ever undertaken by Consolidated was a small tank for making their own opal liners. After a while, Hazel refused to use the word "porcelain" as untrue, but the name still persists.

The name "Boyd" was finally placed on a fruit jar, even though he never seems to have had that honor while living, by the Illinois Glass Company of Alton, Ill., and its Pacific Coast subsidiary. It is to this effort that the liners bearing the name "Genuine Boyd Mason Cap" were made, not during the earlier years, which dates them about 1900. So far as I am aware, Boyd had no part in naming the jar, but it is a fitting idea that he be so remembered.

HENRY W. PUTNAM

Henry W. Putnam, whose name is firmly linked with the Lightning fruit-jar seal, was not its inventor. The true inventor was Charles de Quillfeldt of New York City, who secured Patent No. 158,406 on January 5, 1875, for a toggle-type seal for beverage bottles. The bail wire passed through a hole in the stopper. His patent had a checkered career.

The device may be the first of the toggle-, or linkage-type of lever-operating seals for jars and bottles. A neck tie-wire, securing the device to the bottle, had two complete loops, on opposite sides, and these served as fulcrums for the lever wire, which was hooked to fit the loops. The lever wire also had two complete loops, and these took the ends of the bail wire, which centered over the glass lid, metal stopper, or other closing system. When the lever was raised, the stopper could be moved free from the mouth of the bottle—when the lever was lowered with the stopper in place, it would be pulled down into the mouth of the bottle. The linkage operated by passing a "line of centers" at maximum tension, and then being arrested against the side of the neck to hold it in place, and lock the seal.

After de Quillfeldt applied for his patent in the fall of 1874, but before the patent was issued, he sold the rights of the patent to Emil Hollender for $1,000 cash and a royalty of 5 per cent. But Hollender did not pay the $1,000, according to a history in the *National Bottler's Gazette* on March 5, 1898, and in the spring of

1875 de Quillfeldt again sold the patent rights to Karl Hutter, a patent entrepreneur, and himself an inventor. De Quillfeldt first retained an interest in the invention, but in the following year traded his interest for the European rights. In the meantime, Hutter sold the possible fruit-jar rights to Henry W. Putnam, another inventor of sealing devices.

During 1878 and 1879 Hutter and Putnam were jointly sued by F. Hollender, Emil's brother, with the claim that Emil Hollender had invented the seal, and that de Quillfeldt merely worked under Hollender's instructions. Seven witnesses supported Hollender. De Quillfeldt spent nearly a year gathering proof that he was the true inventor, and in the end his claim was admitted.

De Quillfeldt received a patent for a wide-mouth Lightning stopper on June 5, 1877, which he sold or assigned to Putnam. This may be the reason for the earliest of all Lightning jars still having the loops in the neck tie-wire. On April 25, 1882, Putnam received Patent No. 256,857 in his own name for a modification of the seal, in which two small metal "eyes" replaced the loops on the tie-wire as fulcrums for the lever wire. De Quillfeldt received another patent, No. 260,850, on July 11, 1882, which he assigned to Putnam. While the name Lightning had been given only to the sealing method by Hutter and de Quillfeldt, its use on the fruit jar also seems to have given that name to the jar as well as the seal. Putnam's name appearing with it firmly identified him with the jar.

The wide glass lid made it difficult, if not impossible, to use the method of inserting the wire through a hole in the glass lid, because of breakage. In the beverage bottle the lid was metal rather than glass or ceramic. Hence the bail was held in position on top of the glass lid by centering it in a groove or between two raised dots. The shape and design of the raised dots has changed from year to year and from manufacturer to manufacturer without changing the function. For this reason little significance can be placed on changes in design without some additional knowledge concerning the maker. Only one design appears to have any real difference: the Safety Notch glass lid, in which there were no dots, but two notches at different levels of a wing-like ridge across the center—a lower one for the "boil" and an upper one for the final seal.

Another glass lid had six raised dots in a circle, so that the lid did not have to be rotated to get the best positioning of the bail wire.

The Lightning closure was very successful in the beverage-bottle field as well as on the fruit jar, and the name also was applied to a siphon bottle also invented by de Quillfeldt. It is still the favorite beer closure in Germany, where I saw it (and used the contents) when my wife and I had our Airstream trailer in Europe for 21 months. The Lightning fruit jar was most successful in New England, Canada, and upstate New York, where people never seemed to forget the zinc taste imparted by the early Mason lids.

Thus, any Lightning with twisted loops of wire holding the lever wire would date from 1877. Any Lightning seal with the metal eyes as the lever fulcrums would date from 1882. Putnam's name was placed on the bottom from the beginning, until at least 1886, with "Lightning" on the side, with and without the words "Trade Mark" or "Patented." The neck contour was slightly bulged above the tie-wire, but was flattened on top, almost resembling a band, until circa 1905-10 when a bead was substituted for it, after machine glassmaking had started.

Putnam was a resident of Bennington, Vt., until the success of the Lightning and other seals caused him to open his own shop in New York City. It has been claimed, but I have been unable to find confirmation, that all Lightning jars having the word "Lightning" on the side, and "Putnam" on the bottom, were made by the Lyndeboro Glass Co., of Lyndeboro, N.H. McKearin, *American Glass*, pages 207 and 612, records that this glass company was founded in 1866, burned in 1868, rebuilt, and finally closed in 1886. If so, its later years were the period after the invention of the Lightning closure, and all Putnam-Lightning lettered jars would have to date before 1886. The source of the Lyndeboro claim is still open for proof. We do know that the Hazel Glass Company, opening in 1886 with an opal tank in Wellsburg, W. Va., in 1886, moved to Washington, Pa., in 1887 and built an additional glass tank, and that one of its first productions in Washington was the Lightning jar. Perhaps it picked up the standard directly from the faltered Lyndeboro. We do know that Lightning jars continued to be made, and perhaps with better workmanship. Since the patent would not have been in the public domain until 1899, Putnam must surely have continued to license its manufacture.

When the Atlas Glass Company was established by C. N. Brady, of Hazel, in 1896, as a semi-automatic glass-machine factory, its first production is known to have been the Lightning jar, under its own trade mark of "E - Z Seal."

Other matters of the Lightning closure—the Hero design of 1894 and 1895; the Canton Glass Company version; the "dimple," or small socket, of 1914, to hold the lever wire and replace the neck tie-wire; the Drey "button" for the same purpose; the development of the bead to hold down the tie-wire about 1905; and the "adjustable" Lightning—were all matters of continued changes in the basic structure, and will be more fully discussed under "Toggles" in the chapter on patents, called "Fruit Jar Seals."

Putnam began advertising his shop at 108 Chambers Street, in New York City, in the *National Bottler's Gazette* in 1888, and continued until his last advertisement in its May, 1906, issue.

ALBERT G. SMALLEY

If Smalley had any leaning, it was for the use of names denoting royalty: Royal, Royal Crown, Royal Nu-Seal, King, Queen, and possibly Princess. He also sold the Wears, Victory, and Magic. Little else, except for his ability as an inventor and his patents, is known of the man. His company dominated fruit-jar sales in New England.

Corporation record in the Massachusetts State Historical Library show that the A. G. Smalley & Company group was founded in Boston in 1872, and remained under that name until 1907. In 1906 John Kivlan was listed as secretary of the firm. In 1907 the company became Smalley, Kivlan & Onthank. A subsidiary, the Smalley Jar Company, was set up in 1905 and closed out in 1911. Another subsidiary, The Smalley Fruit Jar Company, was established in 1915 and closed in 1919, when the parent company was dissolved. Then Kivlan & Onthank took over the business, Smalley either having retired or having died. Kivlan & Onthank closed about 1925 or 1929.

Library references term Smalley as a jobber of glass, china, pottery, and tableware. The *National Bottler's Gazette*, in a cartoon of the 1880s about bottlemakers and jobbers, includes Smalley, indicating that the company had some prominence. A bill-head dated 1882 shows the "factory" to be a multi-story, warehouse-type building, totally unlike a glass factory (and a firetrap if it were), in spite of the smoke belching out of chimneys at either end of the building.

Smalley called himself, in the bill-head mentioned, a "Manufacturer of Genuine Mason Fruit Jars." So far as is known, he was not a manufacturer nor could he, in good faith, have called his jars "genuine" unless in the early days he obtained them from the Consolidated Fruit Jar Company. The bill-head is illustrated by drawings of the Mason's Patent Nov. 30th, 1858 and the Mason's Improved in their true form, but without other identifying marks.

The use of these names would indicate that Smalley's earliest supplier was indeed Consolidated. Smalley is known to have changed his source of supply frequently; he had the bad habit of asking the glassmaker to blow many more jars than he could sell and, by failing to give shipping orders, then leaving the glassmaker with the unsold supply at the end of the contract. For this reason several glass companies, each of which has been termed *the* Smalley supplier, were just the suppliers of the moment. Among those mentioned have been Glenshaw, Whitall-Tatum, Illinois Glass Co. (with the trade mark used circa 1890-1910) and Hazel Atlas. John Algeo, of Hazel Atlas, has told me of the circumstances of Hazel's 1921 contract with Kivlan & Onthank.

Smalley, however, knew glassmaking quality and design—I cannot recall having seen a poorly made Smalley jar, and the lettering and decoration is usually of top quality. Smalley's several patents include one for a rounded square design in 1896, showing and describing the minimum radii that would be allowable for strength, and with arguments that are still valid in today's more advanced technical knowledge.

Smalley also knew how to choose men. When he advanced John Kivlan to secretary of the firm in 1900, and to full partner in 1907, he picked another man with a bent for invention. Kivlan patented a very good toggle design in 1909, being a twin toggle with a hold-down on either side of the lid. He improved it in 1921 after the firm became Kivlan & Onthank, and converted it into a clip-type holding device in 1929, after the firm had closed. Crown Cork and Seal must have taken over the latter patent, since jars bearing their name, with the Hazel Atlas mark as maker, are known.

Collectors will find jars with these seals mixed, since all lids were interchangeable. The lid diameter was the same as the Lightning jars that Smalley also used, and Smalley Lightning jars are known with factory-applied toggle clamps. It is not unusual to see a Smalley jar of 1915 vintage, with a lid bearing the 1909 patent date, held by the 1921 patent clamps. It is possible that Smalley assembled the fittings and jars at Boston, sometimes out of old warehouse stock.

FRANK C. BALL

Only because he was the president of the several companies, and because he was the leader in the successive enterprises which the brothers undertook together, do I single out the name of Frank C. Ball from Edmund B., William C., Lucius L., and George A. Ball.

The brothers, at first Edmund and Frank alone, themselves not overburdened in years and with the younger brothers still at home, tried a number of endeavors: carpet cleaning, making fish kits, and making egg crates. In 1880 they started the manufacture of metal cans, from one to ten gallons in size, covering them with a wood jacket as a protection during the shipping of oils, varnishes, and paints. The company name was "The Wood Jacketed Can Company," of Buffalo, N.Y. After a fire burned out the building in the loft of which they had rented space, they set up anew in another loft, this time joined by the other three brothers, and with the new company name of "Ball Brothers."

After a couple of years they added a wood-jacketed gallon glass jug to the list. Its purpose was to hold kerosene for kerosene lamps, or "coal-oil" lamps, as they were formerly called. (And how I remember my own daily chore, as the oldest in the family, of cleaning the lamp chimneys and refilling the oil font to which a bit of turkey-red cloth was added for color.) They had to buy the handmade glass jars—and perhaps they did not relish the idea of buying, particularly since they had been making their own cans and thus getting all the manufacturing profit.

Chance brought some itinerant glass blowers to Buffalo. Ball hired them, built a small furnace in 1885, and went into the glass business. A fire burned out the factory in 1886, and they were temporarily out of the glass business. But this was not before the several so-called "Buffalo" jars were produced under the name of Ball Brothers Glass Manufacturing Company, with this name and "Buffalo, N.Y." pressed into the glass lids or in the glass liner of the zinc cap. These "Buffalo" jars were: the Improved, the Mason's Patent, and the Porcelain Lined, all with at least two versions of a rather crude monogram of B B G M Co on the sides. As Edmund F. Ball, a son of one of the original brothers puts it in a speech before the Newcombe Society, "From Fruit Jars to Satellites," they had selected fruit jars to use their glassmaking capacity because it was a growing market, and because the original patents had expired and were in the public domain.

After a long search for a more centrally located factory site the brothers accepted an offer from Muncie, Ind. It included a small site for the factory and a gift of money toward the cost of moving to Muncie, as well as the inducement that natural gas was available. They began to build a factory in 1887, and started glass production in 1888 under the name of Ball Brothers Glass Company. Operations still continue at this site, greatly enlarged in scope as the years went by. As their manufacturing became more diversified, the name became Ball Brothers Company.

Ball Brothers contributed at least three major innovations to the fruit-jar industry: salesmanship, mechanical operation, and research into canning methods.

Perhaps the brothers developed salesmanship and marketing while at Buffalo and before they made any glass. As buyers of glass jugs they became customers of the glass industry. They made these jugs into an article of commerce that they had to get out and sell. The sales path was through jobbers, wholesalers, and commission houses, on the way to the retailer and the housewife. They learned the proper sales routes.

Soon the brothers were selling not only their own product out of Muncie, but that of other glass houses which sprang up around them during the Ohio-Indiana gas boom. (I know of one glass house that forgot to hire a salesman until glass began to pile up in the glass-house yard.) Many glass companies had begun business with a few Mason jar molds and a grinding wheel, and had no idea of sales distribution. Ball Brothers was a whole family of salesmen and could more profitably cover a wide area. Since the other companies had to pay a selling profit to Ball, and could keep only their manufacturing profit, they gradually fell in sales and many of them sold their factories to Ball Brothers. With others, competition with a larger sales force forced them to close.

Ball was not, as stated by Edmund F. Ball, the first glass company to place its name on a fruit jar—dozens had preceeded them, beginning with McCully in the 1860s, and including Hero, Rutherford, Excelsior, Empire, Clyde, and Cohansey, to name only a few. But Ball made the name so synonymous with fruit jars that this is often the general impression.

Ball's second contribution to the fruit-jar industry was the first power-driven semi-automatic glass-blowing machine, coming shortly after the first hand-powered machines. The first semi-automatic machine in the industry was the Blue machine, developed by Charles E. Blue, of the Wheeling Mould & Foundry Company under the sponsorship of C. N. Brady of the Hazel Glass Company, who built the Atlas Glass Company just for machine operation. The machine was operational in 1894; the factory was built in 1896. It is reported that Ball bought some of these machines. By 1898 Ball had developed the F. C. Ball machine, still hand-powered, but between 1900 and 1906 developed and patented the Ball-Bingham power machine, which lacked only the delivery of glass to the machine and the hand carrying of the completed bottles to the lehr.

The Blue machine and the F. C. Ball machine were hand indexed—that is to say, the rotating table was pushed around into successive positions by hand to locate the blank molds and the finishing molds for the next operation. Molds were opened and closed by hand, and during the blowing operation they were held shut by hand. The parison was picked out of the blank by hand and placed in the blow-mold. Air valves were opened and closed by hand. The plunger was activated by a hand valve, and the all-important "feeding" of glass to the machine was by hand.

The Bell-Bingham, except for bringing glass to the machine

and carrying the finished bottle away, was completely power operated, and the first of its kind. When the glass blower brought his gather of glass from the furnace to the machine, he placed his pontil in a set position and triggered a lever. First shears cut off a gob from the gather, the gob dropped into the blank mold, and the mold moved under the plunger. The plunger descended, then retracted, and the mold moved into position for transfer of the pressed parison to the finishing mold.

As this sequence started, another sequence began at the finishing mold which held that stage of the preceeding jar in line. A blow head came down on the mold now containing a parison, air was turned on, then turned off, the blow head retracted, and the finished jar could be removed to the lehr by hand. One man, a transfer boy, and a "taker-in" could operate the machine, and none need be highly skilled in the sense of the hand glass-blowing manipulations.

The effect of the machine was enormous. The speed of jarmaking in terms of time and jars-per-man increased several fold. Manpower costs dwindled; quality improved. This did not mean that the machine replaced hand blowing of fruit jars and stone grinding of the finishes overnight. Hand and machine blowing went on side by side for many years. One of my own men retired in 1960 after 52 years in the glass industry, having started as a grind-shop boy at Ball Brothers in 1908.

The third contribution by Ball Brothers was in research into canning methods. They established research and teaching fellowships at several agricultural and home economics colleges (there was one at Iowa State University when I attended there in 1926) where canning methods were perfected and many young women future teachers and canners were taught the art.

Ball Brothers jars are difficult to date and catalog in any logical manner because of the many slight changes that have been made in the lettering from time to time. Those with a ground lip speak for themselves as to date. Early jars had the name "BALL" in gothic lettering, and even in italics. When the script name was adopted the style and position varied greatly—on the back, on the front, underlined, not underlined, underlined with a straight line, underlined with a loop, underlined with a loop so positioned that it looks like a third "l," loops open at the top, loops closed, and in other ways changed. I have made no attempt to classify these variations except where outstanding. Dating is a real problem, and approximate dates are shown in the glossary wherever it can be done.

C. N. BRADY

C. N. Brady started out in the glass business as a bookkeeper for Hobbs, Brockunier & Company, makers of fine glassware at Wheeling, W. Va. The senior Hobbs had been with the New England Glass Company, and he was to develop a lime glass formula that rivaled the lead glass of former years. In 1886 Brady moved twenty-three miles up the Ohio to Wellsburg, W. Va., and founded his own Hazel Glass Company—with a capital of $600 from his own savings. He was later to move in a small circle, twenty miles to Washington, Pa., and sixteen miles back to Wheeling where he had started.

The Wellsburg factory had only one small day tank, which was generally used for opal glass. Brady's first product was the opal inner lining for the Mason zinc cap, with a pressing operation similar to that used by Hobbs, Brockunier & Co. for finer pressed ware. He probably made the E. C. Flaccus opal Steershead, since Hazel was about the only company in the area that made opal. Brady also claimed that he was the first bottlemaker to use natural gas, but the honor is also claimed by the C. L. Flaccus Glass Company, and the glass plants in the Ohio gas-boom areas of the 1880s also used gas.

Brady did not stay long in Wellsburg, nor with one furnace. After only one year there, he moved his operations to Washington, Pa., re-erecting the opal day tank, and building a pot furnace for green glass, the type used for fruit jars. About this time he must have started to make the Lightning jar. He added a second day tank in 1893, a continuous tank in 1895 (probably for the Blue semi-automatic machine), and three more continuous tanks before 1902 and the Atlas merger.

In the early 1890s he financed the work of Charles E. Blue, of the Wheeling Mould & Foundry Company, which resulted in the Blue machine, the first multiple-mold wide-mouth glass-blowing machine. It was operational, according to John Algeo, sales manager of Hazel Atlas Glass Company, in 1894. By 1896 Brady had built and opened, with J. W. Paxton, R. J. Beatty, and George Beatty as partners, the Atlas Glass Company at Washington, Pa. It is reported to be the first glass-container factory to be specifically built for machine operation. In 1898, Brady founded the Republic Glass Company at Wheeling, W. Va., to make pressed jelly glasses and tumblers, soon expanding into other tableware, and in 1900 he built a second Hazel factory at Washington.

When the Beattys withdrew from Atlas in 1900 (to found the Federal Glass Company, to make fine tableware at Columbus, Ohio), Brady was the executive of four glass factories, and he began to bring them together under one name. First, in 1901, he combined Atlas and Republic. Then that combination bought the Wheeling Metal Company, a maker of zinc caps for Mason jars, and its subsidiary, the Wheeling Hinge Company, which they converted in part into an additional cap-making facility. The new group took the name Atlas Glass & Metal Company. In 1902 he combined this company with the Hazel Glass Company, his first venture, to form the Hazel Atlas Glass Company. He added furnaces at the Hazel and the Atlas plants, giving him, after only sixteen years of operation, started on $600, three glass factories for fruit jars and other jars and bottles, with fourteen furnaces, two factories making closures, including Mason and other screw-thread caps, and metal closures for other jars and bottles, and one factory making tumblers, jelly glasses, and other tableware. In all, he was firmly entrenched in the fruit-jar business, general glassware, closures, and tableware.

Hazel was an opal specialist from the start. In addition to the zinc cap liner, I have no doubt, but also no proof, that it made the Flaccus opal fruit jar, since Flaccus was a Wheeling food broker and manufacturer. It also made commercial food jars, making jars for Kerr during 1906 and 1909, for Smalley in 1921, and for many food packers. It had the commercial food-jar rights for the heat-softening seal. Since Hazel Atlas did not use the familiar H-A trade mark until about 1920, although its use earlier on tableware is known, Hazel Atlas jars before that date are difficult to pin down.

Atlas made the E - Z Seal Lightning jar from the start in 1896.

Perhaps Hazel made the Lightning jar earlier, as from 1887 when it built the Washington, Pa., pot furnace, for, if the story about Putnam and the Lyndeboro Glass Company is true, Putnam would have been looking for a glassmaker after the 1886 Lynde boro fire. In any event, Hazel and Atlas had become Lightning specialists before their merger, and Hazel had the pressing facilities from their 1886 beginning with the pressing of the opal Mason cap liner. Of course, even if Putnam had given the Hazel and the Atlas glass companies a license, the patent would have been in the public domain after the expiration date of 1899.

Hazel is credited, along with the White Crown Mason and cap, with making the first top seal for the new machine-made Masons, about 1910, with their E D J Seal glass lid. About 1915 Hazel-Atlas developed the bead-seal Mason, as a departure from the old shoulder seal. Not only did this eliminate the abrupt angles in the glass contour at the shoulder, which Hazel Atlas capitalized upon with the new name, "Strong Shoulder," but it also provided a place to grip the bottle for hand or machine "take-out" and thus prevent distortion of the finish, hitherto one of the drawbacks for top sealing. In general, stemming from the early Atlas specializing on fruit jars, most Hazel Atlas jars bear the name"Atlas" only, with just one or two called "Hazel" and a few named "Hazel Atlas."

For many years Hazel Atlas was primarily a maker of wide-mouth food containers of all kinds. As a consequence they suffered less when Prohibition took away a great deal of the narrow-mouth market. As leaders in the field, Hazel Atlas rose to a high point, in 1951, of thirteen factories, and thirty-three furnaces. In 1958 they were taken over by the Continental Can Company, which sold most of the factories in Brockway in 1964, seventy-eight years after Brady had risked his $600 and a secure job to found the Hazel Glass Company.

ALEXANDER HEWITT KERR

When Alexander H. Kerr decided to embark on the fruit-jar business he was a junior partner in Wadhams & Kerr Brothers, a wholesale grocery firm in Portland, Ore. William Wadhams had financed the venture and Alexander and his older brother, Samuel Charles Kerr and a younger half-brother Francis Robert Kerr managed the company. Since his father, Thomas McMurtrie Kerr, had been a coffee merchant in Philadelphia, young Alex was no stranger to food merchandising.

Kerr dates the beginning of all his successes to a decision to begin tithing for the church reached on June 1, 1902. Three months later he met either Julius Landsberger, who had designed a new clip for holding jar caps, or Ewald Goltstein, of Germany, who had invented a new method of sealing fruit jars by the use of a heat-softening gasket and who had assigned his invention to Landsberger. Goltstein was granted Patent No. 730,760 (which he assigned to Landsberger) on June 9, 1903, and Landsberger Patent No. 731,795 on June 23, 1903. Both had been applied for on October 15, 1902, and were to be combined to form what became first the Landsberger and then the Economy fruit jar. In general, Kerr would show the June 9, 1903, date, sometimes the June 23 date, and sometimes both.

In any event Kerr must have had an understanding with the inventors before the patent was issued, for on February 19, 1903, he formed the Hermetic Fruit Jar Company in Portland, Ore. John S. Giles, then owner of the Safe Glass Company of Marion, Ind., and himself a fruit-jar manufacturer founded the Hermetic Closure Company, in Chicago, Ill., to make the metal lids and spring clips. On March 5, 1904, Kerr changed his company name to the Kerr Glass Manufacturing Company. The Hazel Atlas Glass Company, and Julius Landsberger, joined in with Giles' Hermetic Closure Company. Hazel Atlas had secured the commercial food-jar rights to both inventions.

It was the rubber composition of the seal that made the new closure possible. It would flow slightly when heated, adjust itself to any jar-top irregularities, and flow down the side under the skirt of the cap, to give a slight additional gripping. It was held in place during the boil by Landsberger's spring clip, but the clip could be removed after the jar cooled. At first the compound was cut into rings and permanently adhered to the metal lid by application of low heat. Later a solvent was used, and the compound flowed into a circular depression that formed the edge of the lid after which the solvent was evaporated. This was followed by two patents to Kerr himself for a sealing compound, one composed of balata with a gum plasticizer, the other without the gum, and both mixed with inert compounding materials. Phoenix-Hermatic (its later name) improved the making of the lids and the applica tion of the solvent-thinned compound, in a patent obtained January 27, 1925, including the evaporation of the solvent.

So much for the Economy seal, which Kerr was to make until 1957 in jars, and until 1961 in caps.

From the beginning, in 1903, and until 1909, the Western supplier of Kerr's Economy jars was the Illinois Pacific Glass Company, of San Francisco, Cal. Kerr's luck, and that of the glass company, held when during the great earthquake of April 18, 1906, the glass company received little earthquake damage, while the great fire that followed came up to the glass plant, split at its borders, and passed down either side without involving the structure. This was probably due to the fact that the glass plant was surrounded by an open area of piled glassware, sand and other ingredients in piles, and other supply areas in the manner that was quite common in glass plants.

This near disaster, and the fact that his business was growing in the East caused Kerr to make arrangements to have his Economy jar made in the East by Hazel Atlas as a second source of supply, from 1906 to 1909.

In February of 1909, Kerr purchased the closed glass factory at Altoona, Kan., rehired the former employees and started making glass under his own auspices as the Alexander H. Kerr & Company. The Kerr Glass Manufacturing Company was retained as the sales company, and remained in office in Portland, Ore., until 1912, when it was moved to Chicago, Ill., where it remained until 1915.

Kerr's one setback was the failure of the natural-gas supply at Altoona. (At that time there was no cross-country pipeline system.) By 1912 it had played out. He leased a factory in Sand Springs, Okla., transferred his operations, and began to plan a new plant there. In 1915 the offices were moved to Sand Springs and the new plant began operation. That same year, on August 31, Kerr was granted Patent No. 1,152,107, converting the Economy sealing principle into a metal lid with its flowed-in rubber compound as before, but adapted to the Mason jar by the use of a metal screw-band replacing the spring clip. The new assembly was given the name "Self Sealing." It would fit any Mason jar having the smooth machine-made top above the threads.

Kerr's Self Sealing proved to be a slow-moving revolution in the fruit-jar industry. It had followed two glass lid, rubber ring, and screw-band attempts to seal on the top of the jar finish of the new, machine-made Mason style. There were the White Crown Cap and the E D G Seal, both of which were too rigid to adapt to the often uneven tops. The more flexible metal lid, coupled with the heat-softening attached gasket met conditions of slight wave in the top better, and was destined to become almost the sole seal in practical use today.

It had many difficulties at first. Home canners had many thousands, perhaps hundreds of thousands, of "bust-off and grind" handmade jars in use, and the new cap, as well as the glass-lid type, could not be depended upon to make a good seal, both because of the ground area and because the grinding did not have to be level for the shoulder seal. These jars were still being made by the last of the hand shops. There were perhaps a dozen competing seal types then in use, and the housewife's stocks of them made their continued replacement the easiest course.

The efficiency of the seal depended upon smooth, machine-made, lips to provide a good sealing surface, but glassmaking machines were still in their infancy and left much to be desired. The major fault, so far as the Kerr seal was concerned, was the wavy top already mentioned, and there was no reason for the makers of the shoulder-seal Mason jars to improve this portion so long as the shoulder seal was of proper quality.

Further, the first of these seals had to be virtually hand assembled, in applying the rubber ring which was the first form of the heat-softening material, and then heat-bonding it to the lacquered metal disk.

Finally, a certain amount of prejudice on the part of the user had to be overcome. Long memories still associated metal contact with foods and corrosion and bad taste. People had to learn the effectiveness of modern lacquers, especially those people of New England, Canada, and upstate New York, long the stronghold of the glass lid.

The "cold pack" canning method then in vogue left a lot of air in the jar unless effectively exhausted while sealing or during the boil, and the new seal could not be left slightly loose as in the Mason shoulder seal, the Lightning, and the Safety Valve seals. Even the Economy would vent automatically under its spring clip—the Self Sealing jar seal was rigid in this respect. A narrow-topped finish could cut through the sealing compound. The screw-band rusted in place (and still does) if it is not removed when the jar has been cooled after processing.

The Kerr patent ran out, as patents do, and other manufacturers began to make their versions of the seal. Finish designs on the jar and the workmanship improved. Lacquers became even better perfected. The rubber compound was improved.

By World War II things had begun to brighten for the new seal. By the end of the war, helped perhaps by shortages of zinc and of rubber for solid rings, the two-piece metal lid and screw band must have accounted for nearly half of all home-canning seals. As time went on it even conquered Canada, New England, and upstate New York. Now, perhaps 90 to 95 per cent of all home-canning jars are closed with the Kerr-type seal, perhaps less than 1 per cent by the zinc cap, and the rest by the Lightning seal.

The home-canning closure revolution is over until someone comes along with a better seal.

Alexander H. Kerr died February 9, 1925, and his son, A. Thomas W. Kerr became president. When he died in 1930, Mrs. Rose (Alexander H.) Kerr assumed the office and held it until her death, as the only woman major top executive in American glass-making, taking her place alongside Lady Frances Erskine, who in 1750 founded the Alloa Glass Work, still operating, in Alloa, Scotland. But she was not alone in the fruit-jar industry, for nearly a dozen women have received fruit-jar and fruit-jar-seal patents. Her death in late 1967 closed over a half century of association with the industry.

Using the Jars

The history of how people in America learned to use jars for home canning is not so much tangled as it is obscure. Interest in canning must have started in America in 1812 with the New York publication of an English translation of Appert's book, of which more later. Commercial canning started in America soon afterward, actually in 1815, and the two phases of the canning industry carried on side by side. Enough people must have read Appert's book so as to create a demand for the jars. Only seventeen years later Thomas W. Dyott, of Philadelphia, was advertising "fruit jars," thus giving it a common name. Since I have found no further evidences of publications for many years, further spread of knowledge must have been by word of mouth as well as by this one book. That this was apparently successful is demonstrated by the continued growth of canning during those early years. This chapter is devoted to investigating the history of the changes in the canning operations.

Both commercial and home canning arose from a demand for the preservation of the more delicate foods—especially those which could not be sugared as preserves, or brined, or dried, or which, when so preserved, were so greatly changed as to be less flavorsome or less palatable, or so changed in taste as to be wholly a different food. The new industry arose largely from the initial efforts of one man, who revealed a method of canning to the French government in 1809 in fulfillment of a prize offer of fourteen years' standing—a method described to the world in a book published in 1810.

True: there was a heritage of information. Man had been preserving foods for many hundreds, and perhaps thousands, of years. Grains in Urasia and Africa were probably the first products of husbandry; corn and beans were added in the New World. These could be dried for long storage and later use. Man had even learned how to process foods, as in the making of beer and other alcoholic beverages, said to have arisen as one of the first accidental by-products of grain storage through fermentation of wet grains. Even the Bible records "wine and strong drink." Fire gave man the art of cooking. Some time later man began to purposefully ferment cabbage into sauerkraut, and to make pickles and yogurt. Salted and brined meats became the stand-bys of long sea voyages. Fish, and ham, bacon, and sausage were salted, smoked, dried, and brined. Root crops were stored in pits, and even today we see long barrows of covered root crops in our favorite Scotland, and in our own Ohio.

All these food products differ in taste, however, from their fresh counterparts. Kept submerged in brine and vinegar, sauerkraut and pickles keep a long time, but slowly change in taste and palatability, as I remember from my boyhood when these were made at home. Meat was reasonably edible, even if often not very palatable, soon after it was brined, but it slowly deteriorated. The last of the root crops began to spoil before spring. Apples had become a rarity by the time the January thaws had set in, while oranges were often considered only as a Christmas treat. In no manner could many of the fruits and vegetables be kept out of season at all, or in any way near their fresh-ripe condition of taste and appearance. One gorged himself during their times of plenty, and then waited until next year. Winter fare was more than monotonous.

For those products that could be preserved by the use of large amounts of sugar, as the jellies, conserves, and preserves of the day, there was a sealable package available during the 1700s in the form of bottles and jars that were corked, or protected by coverings of parchment or waxed paper often soaked in brandy, or impregnated with wax. The function of the closure was for cleanliness and to prevent evaporation or the growth of molds. The sugar content prevented bacterial decomposition. Some famous companies, as Crosse & Blackwell, had their start in those days.

The Canning Clan, by Earl Chapin May (The Macmillan Co., New York, 1937) tells a moving story of the work of Nicolas (François) Appert, born 1750 in Chalons-sur-Marne, France, who devised the first generally recognized method of preserving foods by "processing" in sealed glass containers in boiling water. Appert was a French chef, pickler, preserver, winemaker, brewer, confectioner, and distiller—a wonderful background for the fourteen years he spent in trial-and-error research after the French government, in 1795, offered a prize of 12,000 francs, worth about $4,000 in the values of that day, for the development of a method of preserving foods for the military forces.

Appert actually built his first canning plant in 1806. He was awarded the prize in 1809. In 1810 he published a book, reported as entitled *L'Art de Conserver les Substances Animales et Vegetables* with a sub-title generally translated "A Book for All Households." (The English translation of 1920 is called *The Art of Preserving.*) It was translated into English in London in 1811, and in New York in 1812 and again in 1920. Appert's first factory was destroyed in 1814, but he built anew in 1817, and continued to pack foods commercially until his death about 1841. The "House of Appert" still exists today.

The award took the form of a citation, dated "Paris, January 30, 1810" and is translated in a book by Dr. K. G. Bitting, published by The Glass Container Association in 1920. In flowery language it depicted the usefulness of the method in providing food for sea voyages, for hospitals, and in the domestic economy, cited the award of 12,000 francs, and required only that Appert deliver 200 copies of a description of the method to the Consulting Bureau of Arts and Manufactures of the Minister of the Interior.

In further translation, Appert described his method in these words:

1. To enclose in the bottle or jar the substances that one wishes to preserve;
2. To cork these different vessels with the greatest care because success depends chiefly on the closing;
3. To submit these substances thus enclosed to the action of boiling water in a water-bath for more or less time according to their nature and in the manner that I shall indicate for each kind of food;
4. To remove the bottles from the water-bath at the time prescribed.

In another portion of the book he described the bottles that must be used, since they must be strong—able to withstand the action of heating the bottle and contents and the force needed to drive the corks tightly into the necks—and since they must have larger openings than common to bottles of that day. He enjoined against filling the bottles too full, lest expansion burst the bottles. He described the folly of using cheap corks, describing those needed as "superfine."

After the cork had been driven to three-quarters of its length into the neck of the bottle, by means of a mallet, he secured it by tying with two crossed wires. After tying, the whole seal was luted with a mixture of quicklime. During the boiling process, each bottle was wrapped in sacking to prevent injury through bumping other bottles.

All the bottles were then arranged in a boiler, with fresh water added to a height up to their necks (but not completely covered). The boiler was covered and wet clothes placed over the cover to further seal it and to prevent evaporation. Then a fire was built under the boiler. When the water began to boil, it was kept boiling for a prescribed time, at the end of which the fire was extinguished. Fifteen minutes later the water was released through a valve; at the end of another half hour the boiler was uncovered, but the bottles were left in the boiler for another hour or two. (Appert took no chances on handling hot bottles, or subjecting them to sudden changes of temperature.)

When the bottles were dry Appert placed them for storage in a cool place. If they were to be sent to a distant place, he further tarred the closure—this probably applied to his commercial food-packing business.

Through much of his book Appert pointed out the necessity of great care in sealing and other handling. He stated that sometimes he did not have entire success in his operations, but he added: "But who is the worker who never makes a mistake?"

On August 30, 1810, Peter Durand was granted British Patent No. 3372 on "an Invention communicated to him by a certain foreigner residing abroad" of a method of "Preserving Animal Food, Vegetable Food, and other Perishable Articles." He went further into the alternate methods, mentioning bottles, pottery, tin (he was soon to receive a patent for the invention of the tinned iron can), or other metals or "fit materials." He stated that vegetable substances should be placed into the containers raw, but that meats were preferably half cooked, at least. He used a boiler, oven, stove, or steam bath for processing. He also provided for venting during the cook, and the later closing of the small aperture. Durand should be given much credit for expanding the tools of canning and making the art more practical.

Glass was not particularly suited for military transport. In 1810 Peter Durand patented a method of making cans from tin-coated iron in England, and he began to pack foods commercially. His work may have stemmed in part from a paper read at a session of the English Society of Arts in 1807 by a Mr. Saddington. This paper antedated Appert's book by three years, but Appert apparently had a factory by that time, and Saddington's paper seems to have attracted little attention.

Evidently the advent of tinned iron cans had an influence on glass containers, which were thereafter often referred to in patent applications as "glass cans" or "cans of glass and pottery." Both metallic and ceramic "cans" owe their name to an abbreviation of the word "canister," a military term for a cylindrical form of the charge for cannons. *Random House Dictionary* defines canning as, "the art of preserving foods in cans or jars."

The Columbia Encyclopedia notes this progress in commercial canning in the United States: "A patent was taken out in New England c. 1815 by Ezra Daggett for the canning of oysters, salmon, lobsters, pickles, jams, and sauces. In 1820 a Boston firm made pickles, jellies, and jam and canned some quinces, currents, and cranberries. About 1847 a large quantity of tomatoes were [sic] put up for the use of students at Lafayette College, Easton, Pa. During the Civil War considerable amounts of canned meat and of canned tomatoes and other vegetables were in use. The canning of sea food at Eastport, Maine, began in 1843. Salmon was canned on the Columbia river in 1866 and in Alaska in 1872."

In England, as reported by Colin Clair in *Kitchen and Table*, (Abelard-Schuman, London, 1964), processed meats were being used in the British Navy as "medical comforts" in 1830. By 1844 to 1852 that Navy had contracts with eight firms who supplied four million pounds of preserved meats and soups, but a scandal arose in 1852 when 5,000 cans out of a shipment of 6,000 spoiled. In 1857 the British Navy established its own canning factory.

The establishment of commercial canneries meant that there was another source of technical information besides Appert's book—the leakage of canning techniques from the canneries. From that time on, most of the transmission of information must have been orally and by example—but word-of-mouth and mother-to-daughter is not a reliable method for keeping technical details free from error. There must be an occasional reference to a standard. Canning required an exactness of control of temperature and of timing, especially timing, since during the first one hundred years of home canning only the boiling temperature could be used. Although large-size pressure cookers became available to the commercial canners about mid-century, the small sizes more suitable for home canning were not available until after 1900. That lack made no difference in fruit canning, but the time of processing in canning of meat and vegetables was long and very tedious, when boiling the jars at the common temperatures of boiling water at different elevations. Too long a cooking time meant softening, loss of color, and loss of flavor, discouraging to the canner. Too short a time gave incomplete sterilization; a "flat sour" decomposition of corn, for example, would make for a total loss; and botulism was possible in the food which could prove fatal.

Evidently the ladies' magazines of the day gave little attention to canning. Inspection of available copies of Godey's Lady's Book by Louis Antoine Godey revealed that long-time editor Sarah Josepha Hale did not consider the farm woman, presumably the most likely to can foods, among those whose causes she espoused. Her nearest approach to the farm was in one of the house plans (in the thirty years of "Godey's model homes"), billed as a country home—complete with Mansard roof, bay windows, Spanish towers, Gothic arches, Georgian portico, side verandas, and "carpenter gothic" fret work. Neither did the Ladies Illustrated Magazine, Graham's, Peterson's, nor Desmond's Family Magazine give information on canning.

Even those publications that should have been more reliable sometimes used out-of-date material that could have been written by a dyspeptic bachelor who was asked to fill space. Mildred Veley Hardcastle, writing in the Spinning Wheel on "Canning —Quick and Easy," April, 1968, quotes the American Agriculturist of 1861-62 as carrying a space-filler in total opposition to the use of glass jars with patent seals. Instead, a method of using the wax-luted, whittled cork stopper, probably used by Appert, was described, together with a method of improving the seal by inverting the corked jar over a dish of melted wax until the wax, dish and all, solidified and remained attached to the top of the jar. The reference did not state in any manner how the jar was filled or processed. The patented glass jars and seals were ridiculed. Mrs. Hardcastle goes on to show that four years later the *Agriculturist* had changed its attitude. The later references to glass jars were more favorable, but they sound very much like the "trade puffs" which were so fondly used by editors in favorable mention of a good advertiser, or a potential advertiser.

The patent applications of the mid-1860s and later could have been one source of information on how to can. Unlike today, when patents are quite technical documents, patentees of that day went beyond the rule of "complete disclosure" to add language on the use of jars. They seem as much an advertisement as an application for the protection of an idea. Some of them devoted much space to the praising of their idea—and to the disparaging of other ideas. It is quite possible that the copies of the patent were distributed to wholesalers, jobbers, and perhaps to some retail customers. The general tenor of the language followed Appert's method of heating the jar, filling it with boiling, or at least hot, food, sealing, and boiling for a length of time. At least one jarmaker, according to the patent claim, distributed canning directions with the jars he sold.

The problem of venting air from the capped jar was taken up by many patents, and shows the interest of the jarmaker in quality canned foods. Venting the air both minimized flavor loss from oxidation, and made possible higher vacuums. Some jar seals incorporated one-way valves, as Earle's Patent and the Valve Jar. Others furnished two notches on top of the cap; a central one on top to make a tight seal, and an intermediate one to make a seal loose enough to vent air and steam during the boiling process. These include the Safety Notch and Gilberds, the latter in the Improved form. The Safety Valve accomplished the same thing through a spring to hold the lid while boiling, and a cam lever to make the seal tight. The Mason Disk Protector Cap held the food below the liquid level by means of a perforated plate extending downward from the cap liner, and Ruth A. Gilchrist used a domed liner that displaced the air by going far enough into the jar to make the liquid overflow. Ella G. Haller filled a hollow glass stopper with syrup, which was drawn down into the jar when a vacuum formed on cooling. All these patentees explained the use of their ideas.

About 1880 cookbooks began to include canning directions. As will be seen, most of the directions followed closely upon Appert's method. For fruits, some did not think it necessary to boil the jars after sealing. Some even filled the jars with cold food, contrary to Appert's precooking instructions, then filled with hot syrup, sealed the jar and boiled it a little longer. Vegetables were generally cooked, or at least brought to a boil, placed hot into hot jars, filled with hot water, sealed and boiled. Sometimes the boiling times given are woefully inadequate. It will be seen that the Department of Agriculture repeated the same paths later. One is led to the conclusion that few of the cookbook authors canned foods, but let us look at a few of the books.

In *My Grandmother and the Kitchen,* by Helen Lyon Adamson (Crown Publishers, New York, 1965), methods of the 1880s are recounted. Generally the basic method was a departure from that of Appert in that the fruit was cooked, filled hot into jars that had been boiled thirty minutes with their lids, sealed, and allowed to cool without further boiling process. Solid fruits were cooked until clear and soft; berries and small fruits were merely brought to a boil before canning. Vegetables were not mentioned. This process was to return under the auspices of the United States Department of Agriculture (USDA) as the open kettle method, advocated, and then abandoned.

Mrs. S. T. Rorer, Principal of the Philadelphia Cookery School, edited a book, *How to Cook Vegetables,* published in 1891 for W. Atlee Burpee & Co., the Philadelphia, Pa., seed people. Her only change from *My Grandmother and the Kitchen* was to let fruit stand covered with sugar for from two hours to overnight before canning. Vegetables were packed cold, then the jars filled with hot water, sealed, and boiled as much as three hours. She cautioned about the need for handling in small quantities, two or three jars at a time.

About the same time, 1893, Emma Frances Voris compiled the *New Columbian White House Cookery* (John E. Potter & Co., Philadelphia, Pa.). She wrote a mixture of contradictions. In her *general* directions for fruits she describes a cold fill, first covering the jars without sealing and boiling them for twenty to twenty-five minutes. Since the lack of precooking caused shrinkage, she then used one jar in four to fill the others, sealed the full jars, and set them aside to cool without further processing. In the specific directions for individual fruits, however, she specified first boiling them in a kettle, filling hot fruit into hot jars (no shrinkage there), and setting aside to cool. For vegetables she again reverses herself, giving general directions to cook them until "done," filling hot into hot jars, sealing, and then boiling the jars for twenty to thirty minutes. But for peas, beans, and tomatoes (considered a vegetable?) as individual directions, she filled the jars with the cold vegetables, added water, sealed the jars, and then "Boiled as for corn." Somehow she failed to give any directions for canning corn! Mrs. Voris added a formula for wax used on wax sealers.

In 1897 the *Twentieth-Century Cook Book,* by Mrs. C. F. Moritz and Miss Adele Kahn, was published by M. A. Donohue & Co., Chicago, Ill. It gives some directions that would be questioned today. It calls for the fruit to be placed into the jars without precooking, boiled (not necessarily boiling) water is added and the jars sealed, followed by setting aside without further process of boiling the jars. Meats were placed in the jars raw and covered with hot lard, or cooked before filling the jars, and the jars filled with the hot juice. In neither method were the jars boiled after sealing. A concession is made for grapes—they are placed into the jars cold and boiling water is poured over them. After ten minutes the water is poured off and the jars are filled with hot syrup and set aside to cool.

The *White House Cook Book* appeared in 1908 under the editorship of Hugo Zieman, steward of the White House (at least he did not write about the lives of the inmates), and Mrs. F. L. Gillette (Saalfield Publishing Co., New York City). It follows generally the methods of the 1880s and 1890s, in cooking the food separately, filling the hot jars with the hot food, sealing, but without boiling the jars, when fruit is being canned. Long boiling is prescribed for vegetables, after a cold fill, but covering with hot water. Formulas are given for sealing wax, and the technique of its use including whittling the corks to fit, hammering them into the jar opening with a mallet (à la Appert a hundred years earlier), and brushing the top with hot wax before dipping the inverted jar into the melted wax. If this appears incongruous for 1908, let me add that this, and much of the rest of the book is a direct copy of the *New Columbian White House Cookery* by other authors and another publisher in 1893. I doubt that the White House did much canning.

In 1929 the Frigidaire Corporation published *Food Preservation in Our Daily Life* in which brief mention was made of canning, following Appert's method of hot fill, sealing, and boiling the jars in a water bath.

Variations in parts of the canning techniques exist today, with due regard to the needs of the differing processes, and with even other modifications than those mentioned so far. Even in very recent years there have been changes. Suppose we now take a look at the official government publications, in chronological order, beginning with the first USDA publication, issued in 1910, and the first of all such directions ever to be published under an official auspice.

Canning Peaches on the Farm

Farmers Bulletin 426, USDA, Dec. 10, 1910; revised Feb. 15, 1915.

Apparently this is the first bulletin issued by the United States Department of Agriculture. It covers the use of tin cans only, and ignores the glass jars that had already functioned for nearly a century, but this bulletin is slanted toward marketing the product rather than for home use. It was for a cold pack—the peaches were placed in the can without preheating, and filled with either hot or cold water, but the bulletin states: "Boiling water, however, is more commonly used."

The filled cans were next placed, uncovered, in boiling water reaching not quite to the top rim of the can, and held for five to seven minutes. This is to drive air from the plant tissues, and is generally called "exhausting"—in later bulletins for jars an equivalent process was "blanching." In more elaborate installations where steam was available, the process could be carried out in a steam chamber instead of in a water bath. After this the can lids were soldered in place and the cans immersed in boiling water for a time interval depending on the size of the can. At the end of this process, the cans are quickly cooled. The whole sterilizing treatment is generally known as "processing."

Pressure cooking is mentioned by the statement: "It is also possible to process by steam in a closed retort." Since the bulletin is concerned with farm operations, even in the orchard, steam was probably dismissed as generally unavailable in most instances. It is here worthy of note that J. H. Flickinger, who had his own jars with the monogram J H F blown on the side, labeled his products as "packed in the orchard."

Home Canning of Fruits and Vegetables

Farmers Bulletin 853, USDA, July, 1917; reprint May, 1918.

This World War I bulletin features a Lightning jar on its cover. Elsewhere it shows the Safety Valve, and a tall, tapered jar with a Kerr two-piece lid and metal screw-band, as well as a Weir pottery jar. The standard zinc cap Mason and the Improved Mason are not shown, but inferred from a discussion of the rubber seals.

Directions are given to boil the jars and lids, filling them with fruit "blanched" by a few minutes in boiling water followed by quenching in cold water, adding either hot or cold syrup, and then boiling the jars in a water bath for a stated length of time. Blanching not only drives out the air absorbed in the fruit tissue, but the quenching fills the space left by the air that could cause changes of taste in time. Since the blanching process leaves the fruit colder than the temperature of a hot cook, this is to be considered somewhere in between a hot pack and a cold pack. Vegetables are treated in the same manner as to blanching, but the jars are filled with either hot water or hot brine. There are two processing methods given for vegetables: long boiling in a water bath, or with an alternate timing for those who have a pressure cooker.

There is one interesting point that will be referred to in respect to succeeding bulletins. This bulletin specifies that the height of the water in the water bath be at least two inches *below* the tops of the jars. This is also the first departure from the cold pack except for the bulletin on *Canning Peaches on the Farm.*

Meats are not mentioned in this bulletin, the title of which does not include them.

Home and Farm Canning

University of California Circular No. 158, Revised April, 1923.

The jars shown in pictures are the Safety Valve, Lightning, Kerr Economy, Golden State, shoulder-seal Mason, and beaded neck Mason.

Almost all food products are blanched, with longer timing than in the USDA bulletin preceeding. Jars are filled with the food products as hot as they come from the blanching process and cold-water dip. Boiling syrup is added to the fruits after they are in the jars: boiling water or brine, and in many cases lemon juice or vinegar, to the vegetables. An alternate method of hot packing, direct from cooking in a separate kettle, instead of blanching, is also given for fruits. Jar lids are left loosely placed on the jars, except on the Economy and the Golden State, during the boil, to be tightened after the jars are removed from the water bath. Water level is two inches *below* the tops of the jars.

Vegetables are processed in the water bath, as for fruits, if they contain added lemon juice or vinegar. These lemon-juice or vinegar directions were rescinded in the next California bulletin, as requiring the attention of a skilled technician. Non-acid foods require pressure cooking.

Canning Fruits and Vegetables at Home

Farmers Bulletin No. 1471, USDA, May, 1926, revised May, 1933.

The jars pictured are the Lightning, beaded-neck Mason, Improved Mason, Kerr Economy, and Golden State.

The "open kettle" method is mentioned by that name for the first time. It entails the precooking of fruits and tomatoes in a separate vessel, filling hot into hot, sterilized jars, sealing with sterilized lids, and then setting aside to cool without boiling the jars. This gave a name, and official sanction, to a method that was being used as far back as in the 1880s.

Cold pack is also described for fruits and vegetables, which must first be blanched. Both fruits and vegetables from a cold pack must then, after sealing, be boiled in a water bath, and for varying lengths of time. The times are longer because the food is colder, even when the jars are filled with water, brine, or syrup at the boiling point, and this is stated as one of the disadvantages of the cold pack.

Hot pack is defined as by bringing the foods just to the boiling point in a separate vessel, as contrasted with complete cooking in the open-kettle method, because the hot-pack foods are not completely cooked. Since the foods are blanched by this method, they are filled into the hot jars direct from the heating vessel, filled with hot syrup, brine or water, sealed, and the jars boiled for a shorter time than for the cold pack. Jars are heated to prevent breakage, but not necessarily sterilized. This hot-pack method most closely approaches that of Appert.

Directions are given for the first time for testing the rubber bands used for sealing. The simplest test was to double the rings together and press the fold with the fingers. The rubber should not crack under this treatment. They should also stretch to twice their length and return without change of shape. USDA was to abandon this test later.

The water-bath method was now recommended only for fruits, and directions were that the jars should be *covered* by two inches of water in the water bath. The oven canning process is mentioned for the first time, with *no* warning that jars must not be sealed tightly, or that they should be handled with extreme care, lest they explode. It was recommended that all vegetables be pressure cooked, but if a pressure cooker was not available, some other method had to be used. In retrospect, USDA never followed California with respect to acidifying vegetables with lemon juice or vinegar and then boiling in a water bath as for fruits.

Home Canning

University of California Circular No. 276, March, 1924; revised August, 1942.

The jars pictured are the Lightning, Kerr Self Sealing, Kerr Economy, Golden State, Vacuum Seal, and the beaded-neck Mason.

The cold pack is mentioned for fruits, with its disadvantage of shrinkage and partial filling. The hot pack is preferred, with hot fill from the kettle in which the preliminary heating was made, and with liquid from that heating. Boiling times for the jars filled with fruit are given for the water bath. Only the timing for pressure cooking is given for vegetables. The oven-canning method is mentioned, pointing out that many housewives have the mistaken belief that jars of food heated in the oven reach the temperature of the oven. It adds: "The oven method of heating packed jars or cans of fruit is very unsafe and should not be used." The use of lemon juice or vinegar is recommended only for commercial canning, or for community, group, or club packing under the guidance of a qualified technician.

Home Canning of Fruits, Vegetables and Meats

Farmers Bulletin No. 1762, USDA, September, 1936; revised 1942.

This war-time revision does not have a picture or illustration of any kind. It does describe the Mason beaded-neck design, the Improved Mason, the Kerr Self Sealing jar, and the Lightning. It goes on to state that the Lightning jar has been discontinued "for the duration," but to my knowledge, as Chief of the Glass Container Division of the War Production Board, which controlled glass-container permitted designs in production, no such order was ever issued by my office.

Processing methods discussed are the boiling-water bath for acid foods, which include the fruits and tomatoes, and the steam pressure cooker for the non-acid foods, which include the vegetables and meats. Steamers and oven canning are also permitted for the acid foods. Precautions are voiced that in the oven method the containers should not be tightly sealed. In this respect USDA has not acted to ban the method as did California. Sealing rubber tests already given in Bulletin No. 1471 are repeated.

Considerable space is given the "so-called" open-kettle method of completely cooking the food in a separate kettle, filling hot into hot sterilized jars, capping with sterilized lids, and cooling without first boiling in the water bath. One disadvantage pointed out is that great attention must be paid to sterilizing the jars, lids, and rubber rings, and that sterile conditions must be maintained during handling and filling.

The stated water level in the water bath is now given as two inches *above* the jar tops.

Home Canning of Fruits and Vegetables

Home and Garden Bulletin No. 8, USDA, February, 1965.

Only two seals are illustrated, both for the same beaded-neck style Mason: the Kerr-type two-piece metal lid and metal screwband, and the shoulder-sealing zinc cap. As the zinc cap phases out, probably only the two-piece lid will survive for home canning.

Cold pack returns under a new name: Raw Pack. Together with Hot Pack, these are the only recommended methods of filling. Neither now includes blanching. With the Raw Pack the fruit or vegetable is placed into the jar cold, the jar filled with hot syrup, brine, or water, the jar sealed and processed. With Hot Pack the food is precooked, filled hot into hot jars with juices from the cook, the jars sealed and then processed. For some foods only the Hot Pack is recommended. Other foods may be packed either way. No foods are listed for Raw Pack only. All fruits and tomatoes are processed in a boiling-water bath, with Raw Pack given slightly longer time. All vegetables are processed in the pressure cooker with similar time differentials. The open-kettle method, so far as not processing after sealing is concerned, is now termed unsafe, and is not recommended. The oven method is called dangerous because of possible jar explosions. A reversal is made in regard to testing rubber bands by folding and stretching —instructions are *not* to do it.

Some interesting summaries may be made from the directions given in these government bulletins spanning over a half century. Suppose we first redefine the several methods that have come and gone, and trace their history.

Hot Pack

After much trial and error Appert adopted the hot-pack method in part. Foods were first cooked, or nearly completely cooked, in a separate vessel with the syrup, water, or brine appropriate to the food. The jars and lids were heated separately so that hot food could be ladled into the hot jar, with enough of the hot liquid to fill the voids. After sealing, or partially sealing to allow venting, the filled jars were boiled for lengths of time appropriate to the food.

Some foods, as corn, were given an intermittent boiling. In this, a three-day process, the jars were boiled for an hour to an hour and a half on each day, cooling overnight, with the object of killing the spore forms that would vegetate during the interval, because these spores were difficult to kill on a single heating, while their vegetative forms killed more easily.

Appert's water bath is unknown, but the family wash-boiler did double duty for canning in many an American home. Of late years the pressure cooker, with the lid applied loosely or the vent wide open, fills this need—we just do not boil clothes any more!

The hot-pack method survived unchanged during all these

years, even when threatened briefly by the early version of the open-kettle method in the 1880s, and by the cold pack in the 1920s. The only real change, and that is very important, is that equipment is better, vegetables and meats are now processed in the pressure cooker, timing and temperature are better controlled, and the fruit jars and their seals are vastly superior than Appert knew them.

Modified Hot Pack

When blanching began to be a part of home canning in order to remove air from food tissues, the foods were placed in boiling water for only a few minutes, then removed and plunged into cold water for a matter of seconds. The food would only be slightly hot when packed into the jars. Hot syrup, water, or brine was then used to fill the voids in the jars, after which they were sealed and placed in the water bath. Somewhat longer boiling times would be necessary than for hot-packed foods, but less than for the cold pack.

Blanching is no longer recommended, or, in most cases needed, since fruits are cooked more completely before canning, and vegetables are usually so cooked because it shortens the time in the pressure cooker.

Cold Pack

In the cold pack the food is cleaned and otherwise prepared, and then placed directly into the jars. Appert used it for fruits and vegetables. The jars are then filled with the proper liquid, either cold or hot but usually hot. After sealing, the jars must be boiled for somewhat longer time than in the other methods since the food must first be brought to the processing temperature.

The cold pack came into official being about 1920, but even by 1926 it began to meet with disfavor. Until 1942 it was only discouraged in the bulletins, but in 1965 it popped up again under a new name: Raw Pack. In its earlier days it was particularly recommended as a means of improving the flavor of peaches, pears, plums, prunes, and cherries.

Open Kettle

This method includes the complete precooking of the food, filling hot into hot, sterilized jars, sealing with heated lids, and setting aside to cool without further boiling of the jars. It came into vogue, without the dignity of a name, by the 1880s, was recognized with the tentative name in the 1920s, highly advocated in the 1930s and 1940s, and then condemned in the 1965 bulletin.

Low Temperature Packing of Certain Fruits

In 1923 the California Department of Agriculture recommended a method that allowed a much lower temperature for a longer heating time for certain very acid fruits, as peaches, pears, apricots, berries, and cherries. Heavy syrups were used. The fruits were packed into the jars cold, covered with the hot syrup, exhausted for five minutes at 150° F. without having the caps in place on the jars, sealed, and then processed at 175° F. for 45 minutes more. The object was to preserve more of the original flavor and texture, which would otherwise be greatly modified by boiling temperatures. It never became an important method, and was never mentioned in any other bulletin.

Acidified Vegetable Pack

For a time, California, in its 1923 bulletin, dwelt upon the merits of adding lemon juice or vinegar to vegetables during the precooking, or in the water added to the filled jars. It materially shortened the time necessary to sterilize the jars, making it possible to process vegetables in the same times as fruits. It materially improved the texture of vegetables, since they were generally overcooked otherwise, by the time they were safely sterile. The taste was quite tart, and it was necessary to add baking soda to them before using. Later bulletins limited the method to commercial packing, or to group, community, or club packing under the guidance of a technician who could control the acidity.

Another method of making vegetables more acid was to mix tomatoes with corn, peas, carrots, or the like, in equal proportions. The advent of the pressure cooker made the method unnecessary, and the method was never mentioned after the 1920s and 1930s.

Boiling-Water Bath

The boiling-water bath of Appert is still one of the two recommended processing methods for home canning. Any kind of vessel deep enough to hold the jars may be used; the wash-boiler was an old-time favorite. Today the pressure cooker does double duty as a water bath, leaving the lid ajar, or at least leaving the vent open and using a lower fire after boiling begins.

As already noted, early recommendations were to keep the water level two inches *below* the tops of the jars. Then came a period of indifference, to be succeeded by a recommendation that the water level be two inches *above* the jar tops.

Steaming

Steaming may be used instead of a water bath if the boiling of the small quantity of water is vigorous, circulation of steam good, and the cover tight enough to ensure that the steam blankets the jars well. The pressure cooker with the vent open is excellent. The method was included in 1936 directions, but omitted from later bulletins.

Oven Canning

Oven canning was first mentioned in 1926-33 bulletins, and without any warning that the jar lids must never be so tight that if steam was generated, that jars be unable to vent. There was considerable report of explosions following this. In 1942 oven canning was mentioned with strong reservations, and in 1965 it was condemned as unsafe and dangerous.

Pressure Cooking

The first Department of Agriculture bulletin of 1910 makes only a mention of pressure cookers. In 1918 it illustrated the crude form then available for home or small canner use. It was then given the status of an alternate to the water-bath boiling method. By 1923 the pressure cooker was the preferred method of canning process for all vegetables unless acidified, and after 1936 it became the sole and standard instrument for vegetable canning.

And so the pendulum has swung—from the side of faster canning timing, greater risks, and less tedium, to the side of slower canning cycles and with less risk; from one processing method, through a period of several methods, and back to two methods—one for fruit and the other for vegetables. Appert was as nearly correct in his beginning as the facilities of his time permitted. In the course of time the glass industry added a multitude of sealing devices and jars, and better glass technology in substance and manufacture. The jar has now crystalized into one modification of the MASON jar, so changed that Mason himself might not recognize it, particularly since his zinc cap probably seals less than 5 per cent of the jars now used. Better technology has provided better equipment: pressure cookers, temperature control, and better metals for processing equipment. Agriculture has provided better basic food materials through plant breeding and the development of new types and varieties, such as stringless string beans. Pasteur has explained the action and the role of micro-organisms —a study that did not start until fifty years after Appert had solved the problem pragmatically. All this has been the result of a century and a half of canning.

Statements have been made to the effect that "now that canning has disappeared one should collect fruit jars because they will be scarce." How ridiculous this is may be considered in the light of today's production of fruit jars. The volume has dropped off from the World War II peak, to be sure, but the average of the past ten years is about 60 per cent of that high. The 1967 production of eighty million home-canning jars was the highest in seven years. Besides those jars made and sold as home canners, there were available several times that many jars having the same thread design and capable of being used as fruit jars. Truly, the report of the death of home canning was somewhat premature and unfounded.

Dating the Fruit Jar

Every collector likes to feel that his jar is very old, and would like to date it to the earliest possible moment. Of course, every collector is sure that his jar was made during the very first year of the patent, and therefor, glassmakers must have had a wonderful *first* year of production. Some collectors, finding two patent dates on a jar, unhesitatingly quote the earlier of the two —it's like finding the date 492 B.C. on an ancient urn!

The best we can do is to bracket the dates. Sometimes these dates are very close together. Take, for example, a John M. Moore Co. jar, having the patent date, Dec. 3, 1861. Now, such a jar had to be made after that date, perhaps early in 1862 to allow time to get the notification that the patent had been granted, to make the molds, and finally to make the glass. Bear in mind here that few glass companies made their own molds but depended either upon itinerant moldmakers or a mold-supply house in some central city. (That is why different companies had very similar lettering styles.)

But John M. Moore took his brother, Dr. D. Wilson Moore, and another man into his firm in 1863, under the style of Moore Bros. & Co., and in 1864 the firm became simply Moore Brothers when the other man dropped out. Again, allowing for a delay in changing the lettering, it might be 1865 before the new company name might appear on the jar, as it was later changed to "Moore Bros. Patent." Thus the John M. Moore Co. jar would have been made during 1862, 1863, and possibly 1864. But this is a very satisfactory bracket of dates, and should satisfy almost any collector.

In general, I have relied upon patent dates, as "circa 1862" for the Moore jar, to indicate the earliest possible date of manufacture; and for some styles of sealing, a year or two must have spelled their doom, if indeed they "got off the ground" at all. Next would be dates for the manufacturer himself, but these may not be the true dates for the different styles and names of jars he made. For example, Cohansey started as a name in 1870 when the

387

Bodines incorporated. Cohansey brought out a "Cohansey" jar in 1872, so the finding of the jar and Cohansey's name would not date the jar back to 1870. But Cohansey continued the Airtight jar, which Bodine & Potter, one of the earlier owners of the Bridgeton (N.J.) Glass Works, had first brought out—hence, an Airtight jar bearing the name "Cohansey" could date from 1870.

Other dates can be broadly approximated from the styles of lettering as shown in another chapter. But this method is only a generality, and covers a wide range of years at the best. The use of the style should be used with caution for it points only to a period.

One point always bothers me—to hear a collector date jars on the basis that machine-made jars started in 1904, with the Owens machine, presumably on the stroke of midnight of December 31, 1903, and that any handmade jar must date before this time and any machine-made jar after this time. Any such statement is vastly incorrect since the transition period of from full hand blowing to full automatic blowing covered a span of perhaps fifty years.

Now, one *generally* true statement is that the mark of a machine-made bottle is the absence of the ground lip—except for the pressed laid-on-rings that were made as far back as the 1850s for the groove-ring wax sealer and other seals requiring a thick, heavy, and flat top or for those jar-lips which could be fire polished. We have to say "generally" because some of the first semi-automatic machine jars were hand finished after forming, but not for long, as they were merely development stages before neck rings became a reality. I would classify as semi-automatic those machines making jars (or bottles) whose finishes were pressed in neck rings along with the parison, or blank, and then the parison transferred to another mold for blowing to the finished shape, and including from the stages where all transfers were made by hand, until the stage just before the glass was automatically transferred from the furnace to the machine. It was the automatic transfer of glass from furnace to machine that made the difference between semi-automatic and automatic machine operation. That stage was from the first Ashley machines in England in 1886 until the developments of the Hartford-Empire feeders about 1915 made it possible to convert almost any of the semi-automatic machines in use at that time into automatics. While the Owens machine was first successful about 1904, and was supplied to franchised manufacturers within the next decade, only Ball Brothers, so far as I know, had a license to make fruit jars on it.

The Blue machine, a semi-automatic device developed by Charles E. Blue for the Hazel Glass Company and the Atlas Glass Co., was probably the first to be applied to wide-mouth fruit jars, and was developed in 1894. The Ball-Bingham machine came into being about 1907, although Ball did use the Blue machine for a few years. The 1906 version of the Ball machine was the first power-operated—the Blue machine was rotated into positions by hand. Other machine users making fruit jars have been mentioned elsewhere.

Even the invention of a semi-automatic machine or its purchase did not mean that hand operations were eliminated in any such factory. Naturally, each factory had its own transition period. At first there would be probably only one machine, working side by side with hand operations making the same jars. One glassmaker had to erect a wall between these two operations in order to prevent sabotage. There were cases where the opposition of the workers brought about the abandonment of the machine operations in the plant.

In the meantime, some companies never bought machines of any kind—and created a sad story of broken and bankrupt companies who could not compete price-wise and quality-wise with machine-made production. Many such companies went out of business between 1900 and 1915. But, in the meantime, they were making handmade jars carrying the ground lip. One cannot tell with certainty if a jar made during the period from 1905 to 1920 was made by semi-automatic machine or automatic machine. So do not date a bottle merely by the presence or absence of the ground lip—it is far from accurate.

The trade mark of a company, and especially the changes in the trade mark, can be very useful. The Illinois Glass Company, for example, used the simple initials, "I G Co," from shortly after its beginning in 1873 until about 1900. Then it put the "I G Co" in a diamond. For a few years, between about 1906 and about 1910, it used, at least on its fruit jars, a monogram of "I G Co." About 1914 it began to use the letter "I" alone in a diamond, and did so until it merged with the Owens Bottle Company. As Owens Illinois it simply placed a large "O" circling the "I" and intersecting the points of the diamond, and in 1956 took away the diamond, leaving an "O" circling the "I."

Sometimes a datum point is found when an old established company adopts a trade mark and places it on the jar. Hazel Atlas did not use its familiar "H over A" mark until some years after it had been using the mark on its fine pressed tableware in 1920. The Diamond Glass Company, established in 1888, did not use its plain diamond trade mark until it began machine production in 1924. So, when you have identified a trademark with a company, *next* find out when they started to use the trade mark before using it to fix the age of one of their jars.

Here is another example: As the "Hero Glass Works" that company for a time used an elaborate "H G W" monogram, probably about 1870 to 1875. Before that it used nothing. About 1880 it adopted the Hero cross (do not call it a Maltese Cross because each wing of the Maltese Cross is deeply indented—not the straight lines of the Hero cross). It was *not* lettered in the four wings. In 1884 the company changed its name to "Hero Fruit Jar Company," and lettered the wings in the cross with "H," "F," "J," and "Co." Hence we have three datum points for Hero: 1875, 1882, and 1884.

I have a historical flask lettered "F A & Co," for Fahnstock, Albree and Company, Pittsburgh, Pa. They leased the Lorenz plant for only two years, giving an excellent set of dates, 1861 to 1863. What more could I ask? My point is: using the combination of company names, trade marks, patents, and some idea of their history, some very satisfactory approximations as to the age of a jar can often be obtained. Doesn't some *factual* information about the jar give greater satisfaction in its ownership?

Changing Styles in Names and Decoration

In the early days of fruit-jar manufacture there was a simplicity of lettering and practically no decoration. Lettering was confined to one line, or at the most, two. Even though some later jars, as the Leotric, continued the style, in general one can "spot" an old jar by the kind of lettering used. Modern jars have clear-cut lettering, often intricate design, and excellent mold work.

In the beginning, also, there was a sense of formality. It was "The Gem," "The Hero," "The Queen," and "The Ball." Then it became simply, "Gem," "Hero," "Queen," and "Ball."

In 1871 the Consolidated Fruit Jar Company (note how early the word "fruit") started the fad of elaborate initials as a monogram, which lasted until about 1890. Their monogram was an intertwined "C F J Co." Hero Glass Works used a monogram of "H G W" until about 1880 or 1882, Ruth A. Gilchrist came along with "R A G" intertwined in 1895, Ball Brothers Glass Manufacturing Company, Buffalo, with "B B G M Co" intertwined in 1886 as the one with perhaps the most letters.

A rash of fanciful names, no doubt intended to entrance the housewife with their vigor and romance came along in the late '80s and '90s. Protector, Retentive, Safety, Sanety, Dandy, and Peerless are only a few. But the trend continued well into this century, with Double Safety, Magic, Sure Seal, Acme, Strong Shoulder, Premium, and Good Luck, to name only a few.

This century brought a trend toward the simplicity of just one or two initials in squares, triangles, diamonds, or other geometric figures. G, J, and P were in squares. D and I were in diamonds, and P and C in the two portions of a broken rectangle. The trend has grown, and is now the most common of marks.

Next to the simple letter in some kind of a geometric device is the one-word company name. Smalley, Ball, and Atlas no doubt started it, continuing with Schram, Knox, Pine, Port, and Swayzee, for example.

Mason started with the full wording "Mason's Patent Nov. 30th

1858," and continued it throughout his connection with the glass-making business. Later users, after the patents had expired, used the same wording unblushingly, or left out only the " 's." Then it became "Mason's Patent," without the date, or Mason Patent, and finally the one word "Mason." Even while Mason was active, the screw-capped jar was referred to in patents as the "Mason jar," or the "so-called Mason jar." Inventors Drey and Boyd also had jars named after them.

Shields, floating ribbons, stars, and elaborate scrolls came in about 1890 to 1900, and lasted to sometime in the 1920s. It was a time of elaborate decorations, and the Flaccus Steershead was about the most flamboyant of all. The Flaccus opal glass speci-men, with what appears to be an elk's head with branched antlers, is one of the most decorative of all jars—and it is reported to have been made as a catsup bottle!

It was all a matter of taste, or sometimes the lack of it. I have noted under its name in the Glossary of jars, one that had three types of lettering style, in three lines of differing direction on the jar, and nothing else. The styles were Old German, slanting script, and Gothic—perhaps the moldmaker was exhibiting his varying skills.

Early lettering was generally in Roman type, with every serif painstakingly cut in position in the metal. Soon the fact that these would fill up with "dope" and blow irregularly in glass, as well as adding to the moldmaking cost, brought about a general conver-sion to Gothic *sans serif*, or simple block lettering, which remains the preferred and usual lettering today. One of the Ball Brothers jars, the De Luxe, has letters so well cut in a prismatic form, and so beautifully blown up, that it almost sparkles on one's shelf.

These changing styles are interesting in themselves, and do serve to point out another field of interest for the fruit-jar col-lector. They do indicate a general period, but only approximately, and with numerous proved exceptions. The collector cannot es-tablish an approximate age on the style of lettering alone, but it does indicate a starting point.

The Shape of the Fruit Jar

Several collectors, in referring to Mason jars, have used the words "old style" and "new style." It is a good distinction only so long as everyone knows that they are referring only to the sealing position under the zinc cap. The distinction is between sealing on the shoulder or sealing on a bead blown in the neck. It is not a distinction between hand and machine blowing, as many believe. Also, it neglects entirely the top-seal, or "Improved," Masons.

It is true that all of the hand-blown Masons using the full zinc cap sealed only on the shoulder. But so did the early machine-made jars. Not until Hazel Atlas developed the bead sealing location for the sealing rubber on their Strong Shoulder, did machine-made Masons abandon the shoulder sealing locations for the full zinc cap. From the late 1860s and early 1870s, handmade jars, which came to be called the "Improved Masons," sealed on the top above the threads and under a glass lid—Mason was not the original inventor but he did coin the name, "Improved." There can be at least four distinctive styles for the Mason jar shape that followed in the course of sealing design.

1. Mason's patent of November 30th, 1858, which followed by one week his patent for a mold for that jar, sealed on the shoulder because he saw no practical way of sealing on the ground lip that would prevent air passage across the grinding. He blew the threads as part of the jar mold, included a space above the threads for a bulge that would enable the glass to be blown thinner and to be cracked off without much chance of involving the thread area, and then ground this "blow-over" down almost to the thread line, but not quite. Otherwise the sharp cutting edge of the end of the thread would cut the soft zinc cap, and endanger the hands of the user.

2. The top seal is generally credited to Imlay in 1865 (pre-dated to December 4th, 1864), but his seal was on the ground lip, while Rowley used a sealing ledge surrounding the ground lip in 1869. Imlay patented a closure with the same jar design, but with

a wire cage instead of a screw-band (the Valve Jar) in 1868, so this antedated Rowley. Lyman and Shaffer worked out versions of the idea in early 1869, also, with Mason following with his first top seal late the same year. Thus the progress in a seal employing an inverted-cup glass lid, which straddled the ground lip, and a screw-band or some other means, was rapid. The threaded portion was outside the diameter of the sealing surface, and below it on the jar.

SHOULDER (ORIGINAL)   TOP SEAL (IMPROVED)   BEADED (MODERN)

MASON SEALS   S denotes sealing points

3. Early semi-automatic and automatic machine operations, beginning about 1896, had to be content with making *either* a shoulder seal or a top seal. It was not until 1910 that an effort was made to make a seal directly on the lip of a *shoulder* seal jar. Glassmakers had difficulty in making the lip smooth enough for a good seal directly on the lip.

4. The machine jar, using a bead as a place to seal instead of on the shoulder came into being about 1915. One of the difficulties in using former jars for combination shoulder and top sealing was that the finish was somewhat apt to be distorted in grasping the jar to take it out of the mold. The bead was now a place to grasp the jar, and less distortion took place.

The specific sealing contour was not the only difference in style. Much of the traditional beauty of free-blown glass lies in its curving structure, and it is most fortunate that hand tooling and shaping of the piece on the blowpipe and pontil could not result in sharp cornered or prismatic design—that could be left to the engraver; engraving would not have been a part of a fruit-jar forming. Free-blown and engraved glass is for the beauty of the piece, which would never be subject to the stresses of heating, or abrasion, given "work-a-day" or reusable utility bottles and jars.

Mason's patent drawing for his November 30th, 1858, jar illustrates the difficulties in making a strong shoulder-seal jar. The area of the threads is a vertical wall. Below the threads the wall makes a sharp turn into the horizontal sealing area. Then it again turns into an almost vertical, accentuated in the pints in particular. Each right-angle bend would break more easily than a moderate radius. I have seen only one jar that resembles Mason's first patent—it is Nora and Dean Davenport's "fat 58," a half gallon, and it is probably very rare.

Many of these early jars had sharp angles where the body of the jar joins the bottom.

The fact that the half-gallon "fat 58" was too rounded at the shoulder for quarts, and certainly for pints (it probably led, also, to the small mouth used for the "midget" jars) led to making the sealing surface just as flat as could be withdrawn from the molds, and either narrow or with an even sharper angle into the shoulder. Some jars approached the sealing area with a slight taper. Some were made with a barrel-shaped body. Generally the square bottom angle was retained. There must have been breakage from heat shock at the bottom, and from mechanics (twisting, bumping, leverage of sticking caps) at the shoulder. I believe that breakage could have been one of the deterrents to early Mason success in the shoulder seal, together with the metallic taste imparted to the contents from the then-exposed inner area of the zinc cap. All this, in spite of the fact that the Mason shoulder seal was simple to make and could have undersold other jars of the time.

The top seal had no such strength handicap, and withall presents a much more graceful appearance. Every one of the drawings in the fifteen or twenty top-seal patents that followed show the side wall merging into the thread wall almost as a straight line, or a gradual curve. Rowley, in his patent that enabled him to place "NOV 26 67" on almost every Hero jar, actually patented the sweeping curve from body to finish (see Hero in Glossary) but everyone seems to have used the idea. This could be considered an "old style" of its own.

The top seal had a basic disadvantage that may have held down its use—the cost. The necessity of having the sealing surface outside the line of the ground lip made for a larger thread diameter. Since the cost of the metal was an important factor, this meant that top seals would require a larger diameter "blank" of metal—and the size changes with the square of the diameter, as does the cost. One could meet the added cost by making the diameter of the ground lip smaller—and thus displease the user.

One could also keep the diameter of the opening, use a larger and more costly metal screw-band—and again displease the user by the added cost. Most jarmakers had to compromise by making the thread diameter from one-fourth to three-fourths inch larger and try to reach a middle ground. This destroyed all hope of standardization. The only saving feature was the all-glass contact.

When machine blowing of the Mason jar came into being, the weak shoulder shape, or "old style" was kept for the next fifteen or twenty years. Thus we find the old shape persisting, but without the ground lip. The juncture between the neck and the shoulder was still at a sharp angle. In general, the neck parting line, which now comes into the picture as the mark left on the jar where the "neck rings" and body molds meet, is found almost, but not quite, in the corner where the thread section of the neck and the inside of the sealing area join. A few jars moved this parting line to just below the sealing flat area.

Then the bead seal came into being. It could be cut into the finish rings, above their juncture with the body mold; it could be cut half in the finish rings and half in the body mold; or it could be cut entirely in the body mold. The first position was favored for those glass-blowing machines that used the bead as part of the suspension in the neck ring during transfer from blank to finish mold. The middle position would be used in those machines in which the bead could be used to suspend the parison at the top of the finishing mold, by the bead.

By whatever reason, the bead replaced the shoulder as the primary point of seal when the zinc cap was used. The jar designer could now eliminate the sharp corners of the former shoulder. The result was a curving fillet from the neck to the body, and the shoulder became a smooth tangent into the neck area. This is what is generally meant as the "new style." I prefer to name them by their functions—the "shoulder seal" and the "bead seal."

That this contributed to the strength of the shoulder by permitting curving lines unencumbered by the necessity of flat sealing surfaces, was immediately capitalized upon by the Hazel Atlas Glass Company, in its Strong Shoulder jar.

These restrictions of the older shoulder-seal design were not felt by other types of seals, for only the Mason employed the shoulder location of the seal. The earlier wax sealers, the early glass tops, the Lightning, Queen, Haines, Millville, Smalley, and a host of others, whether or not they incorporated a bead at the top as some part of the lid-gripping system, were able to make the shoulder design free-flowing and rounded. The first Lightning, often referred to as the "old Lightning shape," could blow thin in the shoulder, but the newer designs substituted beads or other methods of holding the tie-wire and the lever, and thus, also, became stronger.

I have stated my belief that the slow acceptance of the Mason principle could have been due, in part, to the fact that there could have been a great deal of breakage in use. Only its relative cheapness as compared with other types of seals kept it in competition. Its greater freedom from being rendered useless by chipping the sealing surface no doubt had a bearing. The shoulder-seal Mason required no special tooling, only ordinary glassmaking dexterity, and it could be taken directly from the mold to the annealing oven. This eliminated the expensive "finishing" operation that required more skill in the making of other jars. The only finishing procedure was the grinding of the lip after annealing, and that was done by the cheapest of boy-labor. A glass company could get into the business of making Mason jars with only a mold and a grinding wheel. Caps were sold separately until about 1885 or 1890, and replacement caps were readily available in the stores. Hence the mushrooming companies that got into the Mason-jar business after 1885 could readily sell their product.

Because caps did have to be replaced when they became bent and damaged, collectors should be wary of dating their Mason jars by the caps they find on them, and not assume that the maker of the cap was also the maker of the jar. The same is not true of other jars, where the caps were not so standard. When these caps and lids were not readily available, the jar was unusable—a deterrent to the continued use of that design. The ready availability of replacement zinc caps of the standardized Mason design may have done much to keep the Mason jar in use.

Mason avoided the pitfall of attempting to make the seal on the ground surface of the lip. Many other inventors tried to seal in this fashion, and soon found that the rough surface of the ground area would allow air to pass. It has been interesting to note that many of these designs were later revised in other patents, and sometimes by other inventors, by changing the seal so that the rubber rested against a smooth glass surface.

Patent Chronology

This list is made up from many sources, including not only those dates found on jars, but many found while searching for such dates in the patent files, and by reference from other sources.

Many of the patents for the earlier years could not be found. Many such dates were suspected of being in error when the date proved to be a day of the week other than Tuesday, the issuance date of the *Patent Office Gazette,* whose publication on this day each week is the official date of the patent. In some instances it is thought that the jar date was in error because of a mistake in cutting the mold, when a true patent was found for a slightly changed date. Others in error could be the mistaken use of the date of application for the patent. Some could have been in order to claim a non-existent patent! At least one, the Victor, used the date as 1899 only, on the first production, possibly in anticipation of the patent being issued and in order to get into production early, while later Victor jars bear the date Feb. 20, 1900. Some patents cited only month, or even only the year.

Date	Pat. No.	Patentee	Jar name	Sealing type
1810				
Aug 30	3,372	British Patent	(Durand)	Method of sealing and heating
1854				
Jul 18	11,332	James Spratt		Wax sealer and screw-thread cover
1855				
Jan 2	12,153	Arthur	Many	Groove-ring wax sealer
1856				
Jan			Gem	Probably lid for wax sealer
Feb 12	14,245	Lewis	Hero?	Screw cap and wax seal

398

Date	Pat. No.	Patentee	Jar name	Sealing type
Feb			Gem; Pearl	Wax sealer lids
Mar 7		Mason	Hero; Gem	Metal spinning; probably lid for wax sealer
Dec 2	16,139	Bennett		Half groove in jar; half in lid; for wax sealing; cites screw-cap shortcomings
1857				
Oct 27	18,498	Chase		Screw cap without gasket
Nov			Gem	Wax sealer lid
1858				
Apr 13	19,964	Borden	Airtight	Potter & Bodine's wax sealer
Jun 16			Queen	Wax sealer
Sep 13			Economy	Wax sealer
Oct 19			Potter & Bodine	Glass lid; yoke; 2 or 3 lugs
Oct 19	21,831	Hartell	Hartell	All-glass cover cap
Nov 16	22,066	Dalbey	Dalbey's Fruit Jar	Neck collar with 3 thumbscrews
Nov 23	22,129	Mason	Mason	Mason-jar mold details
Nov 30	22,186	Mason	Mason	Shoulder seal; screw-cap Mason jar
Dec 28	22,433	Jenkins	Queen	Wax composition
1859				
Jan 4	22,535	Willoughby	Willoughby Stopple	Rubber ring squeezed between metal plates by thumbscrew
Feb 15	22,962	Martin & Nicholson		3 helical neck lugs
Mar 7			McCarty	Vacuum seal; unknown details
Jun 28	24,566	Ludlow		Helical lugs; metal lid; yoke
Oct 25	25,894	Fridley & Cornman	Burnham	Neck lugs; cast-iron lid
1860				
Aug 18			"Patent Aug 18, 1860"	Wax sealer groove-shaped on blowpipe
1861				
Jan 29	31,235	Gilbert		Cam lever; metal lid

Date	Pat. No.	Patentee	Jar name	Sealing type
Jun 18	32,594	Whitall	Whitall; Millville	Glass lid; spring clip; date used on Millville Atmospheric in error
Jun 20		Wilson	Moore's	Possibly application date
Jun 29			Gilbert	Error for Jan. 29 lettered on jar
Jul 9	32,805	Wilson	Moore	Thumbscrew and internal thread
Aug 6	33,002	Ludlow	Ne Plus Ultra	Glass lid; helical yoke; 3 neck lugs
Dec 3	33,870	Wilson	Moore	Glass stopper; yoke; thumbscrew
Dec 17	33,938	Gilbert	Eagle	Glass lid; spring yoke; neck bead

1862

Date	Pat. No.	Patentee	Jar name	Sealing type
Feb 15			Peerless	Yoke to helical neck lugs
May 20	35,286	Adams		Yoke; neck beads; ramps on lid
Jun 10			Worcester	Glass lid and spring clip
Jun 10	35,529	Lyman		Glass stopper
Aug 5	36,131	Zettle		Glass lid; beads; spring clip
Aug 5			W. W. Lyman	Metal lid side seal
Aug 19	36,264	Fisher		Friction side seal
Aug 19				Waxed paper under spring clip
Oct 7	36,612	Griffen	Griffen	Glass lid; helical yoke; lugs
Nov 4	36,835	Otterson	Millville Atmospheric	Glass lid; yoke; thumbscrew; correct date—*not* shown on jar
Nov 4			Hero; Pearl; Gem	Dates on glass lids
Dec 17			Hero; Gem	Dates on glass lids

1863

Date	Pat. No.	Patentee	Jar name	Sealing type
Feb 10	37,647	Spencer	Spencer	Stopper with attached rubber
Feb 15			Peerless	Iron yoke; screw threads; jars also show Feb. 15, 1862
Oct 27	40,415	Kline	A. R. Kline	Glass stopper side seal
Nov 10	40,556	Earle		Hole closed by cam and yoke

Date	Pat. No.	Patentee	Jar name	Sealing type
Dec 22	40,966	Earle		Venting by clapper valve

1864

Date	Pat. No.	Patentee	Jar name	Sealing type
	D1,656	Griffen	Griffen	Design patent for lugs
Feb 2	41,425	Earle	National Preserve	Spring replaced cam in yoke
Feb 9			Victory; Pacific; OK	Glass lid; screw-band; top seal
Feb 9	41,532	Parker		Rubber ring side seal
Feb 9			W. W. Lyman	Seal unknown
Feb 9	41,575	Harris	Eureka; Lafayette	Friction side seal
Mar 9			W. W. Lyman	Details unknown
Jun 21	43,232	Smith		Stopper and pump
Oct 26				Wax sealer
Dec 6	47,834	Imlay		Antedated from May 23, 1865
Dec 6			Hero	Details unknown
Dec 27	45,601	Griffen	Eureka; Lafayette	Friction side seal; thumb-hold tab on Mason rubber ring

1865

Date	Pat. No.	Patentee	Jar name	Sealing type
May 23	47,834	Imlay		Screw-band top seals
May 23		Rowley?	Hero	Seal unknown
Aug 8	49,256	Gillinder & Bennett	Dexter	Used for all-glass lid, but patent was for glass lid and screw-band

1866

Date	Pat. No.	Patentee	Jar name	Sealing type
Jan 2	51,844	Lyman		Stopper
Feb 6	52,379	Bennett	Bennett	Stopper
Feb 13	52,525	Bunnell	Empire	Yoke; lugs; cam lever
Mar 10			Vacu-top	Wire spring clip
Apr 3	53,659	Oliver	Stopper	Squeezed rubber ring like Willoughby Stopple
Jun 5	55,248	Dalbey	Magic	Yoke; cam and helical neck lugs
Jul 10	56,266	Johnson		Ramps on glass lid; yoke
Jul 17	56,390	Ells	Nonpareil	Flat metal lid, wax coated

1867

Date	Pat. No.	Patentee	Jar name	Sealing type
Ca. 1867-68			Protector	Lid and metal clip; neck lugs

Date	Pat. No.	Patentee	Jar name	Sealing type
Feb 12	61,921	Borden	Cohansey	Glass lid and clips
Mar 26	63,193	Wilcox	Wilcox	Glass lid and spring clip
Jun 18	65,844	Trissler		Lead vent tube to pump
Jun 22			Victory; OK	Glass lid; screw-band top seal
Jul 30	67,215	Purdy		Venting by mouth suction
Aug 27			Model	Details unknown
Nov 26	D2,840	Rowley	All Hero line	Basic jar shape—most quoted
Dec 10			Hero; Gem	Details unknown
Dec 17			The Gem	On bottom with other dates

1868

Date	Pat. No.	Patentee	Jar name	Sealing type
Jan 14		Whitmore?	Whitmore	Wire bail; notched lid
Jan 28	73,724	Imlay	All Right	Helical neck slots; spring clip
Jan 28	73,846	Spencer	Spencer	Notched lugs; metal lid; loops
Feb 11	74,249	Rowley	Hero; Gem	Helical lugs on neck
Mar 10	75,275	Imlay	Valve Jar; Cohansey; Potter & Bodine	Wire screw; glass lid; top seal
Mar 10			Pomona	Stopper-type finish
Apr 21	76,915	Hilton		Glass lid; yoke; ramps on lid
May 5	77,570	Batterson		Metal lid; helical neck lugs
Jun 9			Gem; Hero; Pearl	Lid design
Jun 16			Queen	Glass lid top seal; screw-band
Jun 16	78,976	Lehman		Lock for stopper
Jul 28	80,296	Lyman	W. W. Lyman	Metal lid; spring clip
Aug 18	81,296	Rohrbacher & Hormann	The Best	Internal thread stopper
Aug 31				Glass lid; yoke; thumb-screw
Sep 1	81,585	Betts		Plain neck lugs
Sep 1			Gem; Hero	Glass lid top seal; screw-band
Sep 1	81,856	Williams		Stopper held by rubber band
Sep 8			Hero; Gem; Pearl	Lid design

Date	Pat. No.	Patentee	Jar name	Sealing type
Dec 22			Hero; Gem; Pearl	Lid design
1869				
Jan 19	85,932	Hinman	Gem; Pearl	Rubber band holds top seal
Jan 19	86,089	Mason	Mason Improved	First Mason top seal, with glass lid and . screw-band
Jan 19	86,090	Mason	Mason	Top seal held by rubber band
Feb 23	87,274	Mason	Mason Improved	Glass lid top seal; screw-band
Mar 2	87,515	Rowley	Hero	Wire cage; screw top seal
Mar 30	88,439	Boyd	Mason Shoulder Seal	Glass cap liner (signed first name "Lewis")
May 11	89,845	Boyd	Mason Shoulder Seal	Glass cap liner (signed first name "Louis")
Jun 19			The Gem	Date appears on glass lid
Jun 29	91,871	Ripley		Metal lid; helical neck slots
Aug 31	94,452	Thompson		All-glass cap; metal thread liner
Oct 7		Griffen	Scranton	Glass lid; roller; spring bars
Oct 12	95,819	Lyman		Glass lid top seal; screw-band
Nov 2	96,400	Shaffer	The Queen	Glass lid top seal; screw-band
Dec 7	97,588	Bargis & Underwood		Floating top spacer inside jar
Dec 14	97,920	Holcomb	Dictator B	Wire clip; metal lid; wax
Dec 14	97,964	Rowley	Gem	Metal lid top seal; screw-band
1870				
Mar 1	100,306	Mason	Mason Improved	Glass lid top seal; screw-band
Mar 1	100,396	Haines	Haines	Ramps on lid; grooved sealing area contacts rubber ring
Apr 12	101,958	Woodward	Winslow Improved	Thumbscrew design

Date	Pat. No.	Patentee	Jar name	Sealing type
Apr 19	102,024	McCully	Paragon Valve	Glass lid; threaded neck; wire yoke gave spring valve action
May 10	102,913	Mason	Mason Improved	Glass lid top seal; screw-band
Aug 23			Pearl	Lid design
Nov 29	109,703	Woodward	Winslow	Glass lid; wire clip, double neck helix
Dec 20	D4,522	Biesenback	Kieffer No. 1	Ornamental 3-pronged lid holder
1871				
Feb 7	111,607	Bissel	Gem	Grinding top for glass lid fit
Jun 6	115,754	Mason	Mason	Shoulder seal cap with lug for wrench
Jul 18	117,236	Taylor & Hodgetts	Holz, Clark & Taylor; Salem	Glass lining for internal screw stopper
1872				
Jul 16	129,235	Imlays	Cohansey	Wire screw cage; glass lid
Sep 3	131,003	Howson	Hero; Gem	Glass lid in metal retainer, both held by screw-band
Sep 24	131,695	Mason	Mason Improved	Glass lid top seal; wrench; Mason's last patent
Dec 31	134,400	Rowley	Hero; Gem	Metal lid with glass liner
1873				
Feb 4	135,430	Howson	Hero; Crystal	All-glass lid
Feb 25	136,148	Gaskill	Winslow	Changed seal from ground lip of Nov. 29, 1870 patent
Feb 25	136,240	Haller		Glass screw stopper; hollow
1874				
Jul 28			Crystal	All-glass lid
1875				
Jan 5	158,406	de Quillfeldt	Lightning	Toggle linkage for bottles; basis of later fruit-jar seals
Apr 7				Cast metal; wire over top

Date	Pat. No.	Patentee	Jar name	Sealing type
Jun 22			Western Pride	Glass lid; bail; ramps on neck
Jun 22	164,663	Stevens & Lumley	Stevens	Ramps on lid
Jul 27	165,962	Stevens & Lumley	Tin Top	Lugs in groove; disk; wax seal
Nov 23	170,172	Hunt		Mason Disk Protector Cap (first)

1876

Jan 18	172,289	Young	Cohansey	Twin lugs for screw cap
Jun 27	179,231	Stevens	National	Diamond-shaped neck and cap lugs
Jun 27				3 lugs (like Cohansey)
Sep 12	182,119	Hunt		Mason Disk Protector Cap (second)

1877

Mar 6	188,135	Hipwell		Lightning-type beverage seal
Mar 20			Airtight	Cohansey wax sealer
Feb 27			Royal	Reason for patent unknown
Jun 5		de Quillfeldt	Lightning	First fruit-jar attempt fails
Jun 5	191,519	Darby		All-rubber stretch cap
Dec 18	198,439	Whitman		Hinged lid and toggle cover
Dec 25	198,528	Woodward	Almy	All-glass lid; screw thread

1878

Jan 16			Cohansey	
Dec 17			Crystal Jar	All-glass cap; 3 lugs
Dec 17	211,011	Harrison		Pressure locking cover

1879

Jul 1				Looped seal to high serrated glass lid

1880

May 25			Globe	Glass lid; cam lever hemispherical, on bail wire
Sep 18			Patent Sept. 18, 1880	A moldmaker's error for 1860
Nov 9		Stewert		Details not known

Date	Pat. No.	Patentee	Jar name	Sealing type
Nov 30	234,842	Andrew	Mason's Patent Nov 30th, 1880	Mason Disk Protector Cap (third)
1881				
May 3	241,095	Van Vliet	Van Vliet	Yoke; thumbscrew; full wire circling jar vertically
1882				
Apr 25	256,857	Putnam	Lightning	Metal plates replace wire loops as lever fulcrums
May 22		de Quillfeldt		Lightning details
Jul 11	260,850	de Quillfeldt		Lightning details
Jul 11	260,851	de Quillfeldt		Lightning details
Oct 24	266,375	Luger	Franklin-Dexter & Independent	All-glass hinged lid. Could not have been basis of Franklin-Dexter or Independent unless patent details changed in manufacture
1883				
Jul 31	282,188	Gilberds	Gilberds Jar	Single-notched glass lid held by wire circling jar vertically
1884				
Apr 15	297,082	Lyon & Bossard	Lyon & Bossard's Jar	Glass lid; clamp; clutch cam
Sep 2			Lafayette	Another date on Lafayette jar
Sep 2	304,449	Pietsch		Glass lid top seal; spring clip
Nov 25	308,571	Otterson	Woodbury	Solid stud; yoke
1885				
Mar 3	313,229	Otterson & Voorhies	Woodbury	Perforated stud; yoke. Some jars lettered March 30
Mar 17	314,109	Clarke	Clarke Jar	Glass lid; yoke; cam lever
Mar 24	314,322	Hannes	Wheeler	Glass lid; double wire lever
Mar 24	314,332	Gannaway		Stopper; double wax seal
Aug 4	323,636	Comly		Ramps on lid; internally held yoke

Date	Pat. No.	Patentee	Jar name	Sealing type
Sep 15			Economy	Wax sealer mislettered?
Oct 13	328,115	Gilberds	Gilberds; Dandy	Double-notched glass lid

1886

Date	Pat. No.	Patentee	Jar name	Sealing type
Mar 16	338,185	Otterson	Woodbury	Perforated stud; screw-band replaces yoke; glass lid retained
Mar 30	339,083	Buchholz	Brighton	A top toggle of Everlasting type
Apr 6	339,556	Johnston		Internal screw stopper
Apr 7		Smalley?	Royal	Lightning variation, wrong day
Apr 20	340,428	de Steiger		Ramp on lid (pre-Columbia?)
Apr 20			Imperial	Glass lid top seal; screw-band
May 4	341,341	McMillan		Clips to lugs on neck
May 27		Clarke	Clarke Jar	Glass lid; yoke; cam lever
Jun 29		Otterson	Woodbury	Details unknown
Jul 20	345,999	Somerville		Mason Disk Protector Cap (fourth); only form so far found made
Jul 27		Otterson	Woodbury	Details unknown
Oct 27		Kline	Kline	Mold error for Oct. 27, 1862
Dec 7	353,926	Darracott		Wax sealer; glass lid; clip
Dec 29			Columbia	Possibly premature or error

1887

Date	Pat. No.	Patentee	Jar name	Sealing type
Mar 29				Lightning-type jar
Mar 29	360,131	Ashby		Diaphragm top seal
Mar 29	360,165	LeCompte	Perfection	Glass lid, notched; two bails
Sep 15			Economy	Wax sealer (may be mold error)

1888

Date	Pat. No.	Patentee	Jar name	Sealing type
Feb 28		Howe	Howe-Scranton	Glass lid and spring-wire bail
Mar 27	380,091	Corey		Glass lid; wire clip to finish lug
Mar 30			Fruit-Keeper	Glass lid; wire hooks; cam lever. Not a patent issue date

Date	Pat. No.	Patentee	Jar name	Sealing type
1889				
Dec 31	418,266	Barker	Canton Domestic	Glass lid; spring-wire bail
1890				
circa		Lyon	Steershead	Lid: "Lyon Patent Allowed"
Apr 1	424,720	Monier & Monier	Sun	Glass lid; cam lever; yoke (rare)
1892				
Mar 1	469,985	Teamer	Weir	Glass lid; lever on bail
Jun 28	477,955	Patterson	Leader	Lever and bail
Jul 12	478,659	Thomas		Glass lid; clips; helical lugs
Dec 13			Smalley	Design details unknown
1893				
Feb 13			Fruit Growers Trade Co.	Seal details unknown
Apr 11	495,299	Calcutt	Calcutt	All-glass lid; lugs on neck
Jul 11	501,418	Guilleaume & Goltstein	Easy Vacuum; Vacuum Jar	Clip; side seal
Nov 7	D22,873	Calcutt	Calcutt	All-glass lid
1894				
Feb 27			Hero	Lightning-type seal
1895				
Jan 29	533,282	Dunkley	Dunkley	Top cam lever; glass lid
Jan 29			Hero	Lightning-type seal
Mar 12	535,549	Monier	Sun	Centering bar added (common)
Apr 2	536,870	Gilchrist	Gilchrist	Head-spacer dome insert
May 21	539,674	Dilworth	Safety Valve	Spring and cam lever
May 28	D24,337	Gilchrist	Gilchrist	Head-spacer dome insert
Jun 11	540,890	Amia	Whitall-Tatum	Yoke and thumb-wheel
1896				
Apr 7		Smalley?	Smalley	Rounded square shape. May be application date of Dec. 1, 1896, patent
May 5			Fruit Keeper	Glass lid; wire clamp; cam

Date	Pat. No.	Patentee	Jar name	Sealing type
May 5	559,564	Bonshire		Helical neck lugs; wire clip
Dec 1	572,281	Smalley	Smalley Jar	Rounded square shape; tabs
Dec 29	574,306	de Steiger	Columbia	Ramps on glass lid; yoke
1897				
Dec 13			Smalley	Date on jar
1898				
Apr 19	602,791	Wurzburg		Glass lid; spring clip circles jar except at center of bottom
Jun 14	605,482	Jaggard	J & B	Octagonal wrench; shoulder seal
Sep 20	610,897	Dunkley	Dunkley	Spring-band clip; glass lid
1899				
(1899)			Victor	Year date only; used prematurely
Jan 24			Pottery Mason	Ceramic shoulder seal
Feb 14	619,554	Fox	Sanitary Freezer	Neck slots; spring clip
Dec 19	639,559	Hansee	Palace Home	Top cam lever
1900				
Jan 2	640,182	Doolittle	Doolittle	Riveted wire side clips
Feb 14				Details unknown. Not an issue date
Feb 20	643,908	Meyer	Victor	Band cap circles top
Apr			Alston	Metal lid Lightning
Jun 12	651,500	Doolittle	Doolittle	Riveted cross-bar and side clips
Jul 10			Sanford	Glass lid top seal; screw-band
Jul 17	653,840	Brabrook		Friction side seal
1901				
(1901)			Schram	Automatic sealer
Apr 16	672,049	Weir	Weir	Lever changed from Mar. 1, 1892 patent
Apr 30	673,048	Dunkley	Dunkley	Glass lid; spring clip
Mar 19			Premier	Spring clip
Dec 3	687,710	Adams		Stopper
Dec 3		Doolittle	Doolittle	Change unknown
Dec 3	688,224	Bogart		Wrench for screw caps
Dec 3	D35,370	Greiner		Wrench for jar caps
Dec 24	689,543	Doolittle	Doolittle	Separate side clips
Dec ?				Details unknown

Date	Pat. No.	Patentee	Jar name	Sealing type
1902				
Jul 15	704,873	Fox	Sanitary Freezer	Spring wire vertical on jar
1903				
May 12	727,808	Knowlton	Knowlton	Venting screw-band top seal
Jun 9	730,500	Weir	Weir	Grooved sealing surface added
Jun 9	730,510	Beach		Slotted neck; boss on metal lid
Jun 9	730,760	Goltstein	Landsberger; Economy; Reiss & Brady	Lid and heat-softening rubber
Jun 23	731,509	Schonert		Metal disk stopper
Jun 23	731,690	Kraetzer		Glass lid; yoke; lever
Jun 23	731,793	Landsberger	Landsberger; Economy; Reiss & Brady	Spring metal clip to hold lid of Goltstein's June 9, 1903 patent
Aug 21				Details unknown. Not issue date
Oct 20	741,969	Keeffer		Notched neck ramp; wire clip
Nov 7			Calcutt	All-glass cap. Not an issue date
1904				
Jan 5	749,074	Martini		Venting diaphragm
Jan 5		Smalley?	Nu-Seal; Royal	Lightning-type closure
Jun 7	761,652	Brenzinger	"Goldie" seal	Band cap circles top
Jun 7	762,080	McConnel		Weir-type lever and bail
Nov 1	774,014	Wilson	Vacuum Seal	Helical neck lugs; metal lid
Nov 29	776,162	Abramson	Everlasting	Top toggle
1905				
Jan 5		Smalley?	Nu-Seal; Royal	Lightning-type closure; both 1904 and 1905 dates used on jars— 1904 correct year
Aug 22	797,711	Abramson & Bennett	Everlasting Improved	Changed to cam lever
Oct 24	802,381	Fenn	Sunshine	All-glass cap; threads in packing
Oct 24	802,382	Fenn		Similar; internal thread stopper
Oct 24	802,383	Fenn		Similar; metal cap
Dec 5	806,602	Uhl	Simplex	All-glass cap; beveled threads

Date	Pat. No.	Patentee	Jar name	Sealing type
1908				
Jul 14			Various	"Dimple" Lightning design
1909				
(1909)			Schram	Automatic sealer
Feb 23	913,214	Kilvan	Magic; Queen; Wears; others	Double side toggle
Aug 10	930,481	Kerr	Economy	Improved gasket composition
Aug 10	930,482	Kerr	Economy	Improved gasket composition
1910				
May 20			Golden State	Moldmaker's error for Dec. 20, 1910
Nov 22	976,623	Belles		Glass lid; yoke; helical neck groove
Nov 22	976,659	Keeran	White Crown Cap	Glass or metal lid; screw-band
Dec 20	979,183	Mackin	Golden State	Groove-top Mason seal
1912				
Oct 29	1,042,390	Brelle	Brelle Jar	Glass lid and clip
1913				
Oct 7			Thrift	Details not known
Nov 25		Keifer		4-notched glass lid
1915				
Aug 31	1,152,107	Kerr	Self Sealing	Economy adapted to screw-band
1920				
Sep 7	1,352,119	Drey & Hiett	Everseal	Lug pivots for Lightning lever
1921				
Jun 28	1,383,215	Kivlan	Magic; Victory	Double toggle improved
1929				
	1,702,795		Presto	Lightning-type
Apr 2	1,707,439	Kivlan	Victory	Side clips replace toggles
1930				
Aug 19	1,773,311	Killen	Vacuum Tite	Perforated glass lid; rubber dome seal

Fruit-Jar Seals

In the list of over eleven hundred names of fruit jars and variations within the same name as described in the Glossary, one thing stands out. It is the vast variety of sealing methods employed, and the many patents concerning them. There was no one simple seal that functioned without some drawback, and even the Mason shoulder-seal jar, which to many is seemingly synonymous with the fruit jar, is now so different from its beginning that only the name remains.

Much of this is due to the limitations of early glass-container manufacture in providing an opening that could be sealed hermetically. It either had to have a ground lip or a pressed lip. If pressed it could not have a screw-thread or indeed anything except some sort of spring or clamp. If ground, the sealing surface could not be the ground surface since that would leak and contaminate the contents. (Many tried to seal on the ground surface, however.) The best ways to cope with the ground surface was to straddle it with the cap, as in the Mason jar, and seal on the shoulder, or to straddle it with a glass or metal lid, or to form a stopper.

After the early waxed cork and other stoppers, modification started with the wax sealer with a metal or glass lid. Soon inventors were turning to other methods, in which some form of a helix—either a continuous thread (C.T.), helical neck lugs, helical yokes, helical ramps, or helical neck slots—was included as the chief form. Next came spring clips and spring bands, and also stoppers, bails or springs, thumbscrews, toggles, levers, and even rubber bands. Inventors also interested themselves in shapes for strength, for breakage avoidance, or for protection of the contents from metallic tastes, and in the design of wrenches to seal and to open the jars.

The object of this chapter is twofold. First, I wish to present a history of the growth in technical matters through a discussion of each general sealing type in chronology, with identification of the patents and the principles involved. Of equal importance, this chapter is intended to show collectors, by illustrations of important details from the patent drawings, what their incomplete jars looked like, so that they can be ever on the lookout for the cap that matches their jar—that greatest of satisfactions.

Early Cork Stoppers and Wax-Dipped Covers

There have been many kinds of closures for bottles, ever since glass and pottery have been used for container materials. Roman and Grecian containers used straw, rags, leather, and the like, luted with clay, resins, natural waxes, and other binders. Some of those newly discovered had their closures intact. I well remember the potato that closed the spout of the coal-oil can, and the pottery jug of something or other that grandfather kept hidden in the barn, stoppered with a corn cob.

When home and commercial preparation and packaging of preserves, jams, and jellies started in the early 1700s with the greater availability of sugar, one closure method was simply a cover of waxed paper, cloth, parchment, leather, or skin, stretched across the opening, tied, and shorn off just below the tie. It was usually then dipped into a hot wax. It was not paraffin, as some have stated, because paraffin had not yet been discovered. Neither was this hermetic sealing to preserve sterility—the products involved did not need such protection, nor had the principle of heat sterilization itself been discovered. All that was needed was to keep the contents from drying out, and to keep them clean, as from dust and other unwanted materials. The cover was crude, but even so, firms such as Crosse & Blackwell had their starts in the mid 1700s with just such closures.

These products did not need the more expensive, handcut, cork stoppers, and such closures were not immediately used. Traditionally the monk, Dom Perignon, cellerer and butler at the Benedictine Abbey at Hautvillers, France, from 1700 to 1715, is supposed to have started the use of whittled cork stoppers to hold the internal gas pressure of the wine that became known as champagne.

It was Nicolas (François) Appert—chef, pickler, preserver, winemaker, brewer, confectioner, and distiller in France about the turn of the nineteenth century—who discovered the principle of heat sterilization of foods in their containers. His fourteen years of study, ending with his being awarded a prize of 12,000 francs in 1809, were the beginnings of home canning. He found that the addition of some form of food acids, and salt, were beneficial. He turned to cork stoppers because they would withstand the action of boiling after sealing. He had to whittle them to fit, and that so tightly he pounded them in with a mallet. He learned that the cork either had to be dipped in tar, or luted with wax after "processing."

Appert had many failures in his studies, and it is possible that some of these failures may have been due to poor temperature, too short a time for heat penetration, lack of knowledge of bacterial action and control, and to the fact that the containers and closures he had to work with were very crude and did not give him a true hermetically sealed package. But remember that he was fifty years ahead of Pasteur and one hundred years before machine-made glassware.

The Wax Sealer

It was not long before home-canning container design had more or less settled down to glass or pottery containers with a bell-mouthed opening with an inner ledge. A cork could be pressed down to touch the ledge, leaving a cup-shaped depression on top so that wax could be poured in to fill the space above the cork. An alternate design was a knobbed cover of ceramic or glass that would rest on the ledge, as in the case of the cork, which would also leave room for a wax fill. My oldest fruit jar, made before 1850 because it has a discoloration due to the use of a bare iron pontil, is of this type.

1854, July 18

Patent No. 11,332 by James Spratt of Cincinnati, Ohio

We do not know whether this is the first of the groove-ring wax sealer patents, but it is the first that has been found. He is primarily concerned with the use of a wax seal as a replacement for soldering in tin cans, and his illustration shows both the seamed ends of the can and the use of a screw cap as a primary seal, further protected by sealing the skirt of the cap with wax.

Of primary importance is that he refers to the fact that glass jars are even then being sealed with wax. Just when that use started is therefore before 1854. It may have been some years before, since Dr. H. H. Holscher points out in "Hollow and Specialty Glass," *The Glass Industry,* June-November, 1965, that groove-ring construction *may* date from 1811 to 1835 for pottery jars, and *definitely* about 1840 to 1845.

1855, January 2

Patent No. 12,153 by Robert Arthur, of Washing, D.C.

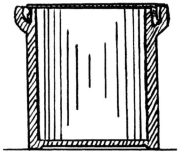

The patent illustrated tin cans and ceramic containers having the upper part including a moat for hot wax application. He described as essential the close fit of the metal lid, with its right-angled lip, and shows only the close vertical fit. Arthur is hailed as the inventor of the groove-ring jar in glass and pottery but I do not believe that this is true since he himself described as a bad condition the lack of close fit between container and cover *then on the market.* No glass container has been found with the lip vertical on the inside rise of the groove—they are always with a V-shaped groove. Hence, I believe that the use of the groove-ring antedates Arthur.

Arthur does describe how the moat in his device can be packed with waxed string, cloth, or even paper before the wax is added. It is also true that throughout the life of the grooved-ring wax sealer there was available on the market a prepared wax-dipped string for this purpose.

1856, January, February 12, and December

These dates appear on early Gem jars and others by Hero and may be for glass lids for use with grooved-ring wax sealers, giving the close fit deemed necessary by Arthur and achieved more completely by Darracott in 1886, below. See San Francisco Glass Co. in the Glossary.

1856, December 2

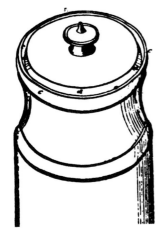

Patent No. 16,139 by Edwin Bennett of Baltimore, Md.

Bennett formed the groove in a simple manner. He pressed the jar finish so that there was a narrow flat area next to the opening, with half of the groove rising from, and outside, the flat. The lid was beveled at the edge. When the lid was placed on the jar the combination formed a groove. The jar was made in both glass and pottery, since Bennett was also a potter.

It is not known whether this is the December patent claimed by Hero.

1858, April 13

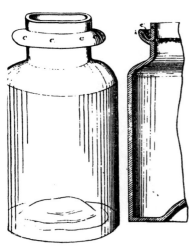

Patent No. 19,954, by Joseph Borden of Bridgeton, N.J.

Borden may have been employed by Potter & Bodine at their Bridgeton factory, since he assigned the patent to David Potter and Francis L. Bodine. The jar was blown in a mold having a large bulb, like the "blow-over" later patented by Mason and which Mason is supposed to have copied from William Brooke, which would be thin in glass cross-section. The resulting bulb on the jar was heated, compressed until it became a double-walled flange, and then the flange was tooled upward until it became a groove.

When the lip was ground off, the jar became a grooved-ring wax sealer, but without the pressing process used by others. It became Potter & Bodine's AIRTIGHT fruit jar.

1858, June 16

This date appears on the QUEEN jar, but must be in error since that date is not a Tuesday, on which all patents are issued.

1858, September 13

This date appears on the ECONOMY WAX SEALER, but the patent has not yet been found.

1858, December 28

Patent No. 22,433 by John K. Jenkins of Kingston, Pa.

This date also appears on the QUEEN and EAGLE jars. Patent for wax formula.

1862, August 19

Patent No. 36,264 by Henry S. Fisher of Newburg, Pa.

This called for a paper disk impregnated with beeswax, to be used as a seal. Such preparations were available even in recent times.

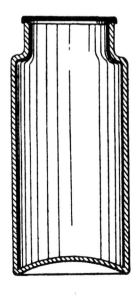

1866, July 17

Patent No. 56,390 by B. F. Ells of Dayton, Ohio

Ells anticipated the modern (1903) heat-softening sealing material by forty years, although his device was probably not very workable because he provided no means to hold the cap in place during any cooking process or until the contents cooled. He used a metal lid, turning it down around the rim, both to fit over the edge of the neck of the jar and, when inverted, to form a reservoir into which hot wax could be poured and allowed to "set" before use. In using the lid, it was placed over the jar and the wax would then soften by the heat of the jar contents.

1875, July 27

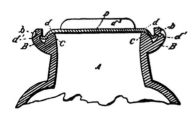

Patent No. 165,962 by David E. Stevens and Richard F. Lumley of Newark, Ohio

The pressed groove-ring was given two small inward curving lugs on the top. A metal lid, having a winged center by which it could be rotated slightly, also had a raised wing on either side, just small enough that they would catch under the lugs when the lid was rotated. This locked the lid to hold it tightly while wax was poured into the groove to make the seal. The patentees add, "If desired, a rubber gasket may be placed under the rim of the lid." The jar was known as TIN TOP.

1877, March 30

The patent was not found, but it appears as a date on a Cohansey AIRTIGHT fruit jar, no longer made by the April 13, 1858, technique.

1885, March 24

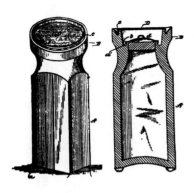

Patent No. 314,289 by Moning Rix Gannaway of Unionville, Tenn.

Gannaway did not believe in taking chances, for his jar had *two* wax seals. One was at the stopper that formed an inner seal deep in a cup-shaped opening. The second was in a normally formed grooved-ring with its metal lid. Both were to be used. Not only these two seals were provided, but Gannaway recommended that a cork be used under the inner metal lid to keep wax out of the food. Another improvement was at the bottom of the jar, which was square, and which had four wooden buttons, one at each corner, for the jar to rest upon so as to avoid breakage by the contact of the hot bottle with a cold surface.

1886, December 7

Patent No. 353,926 by George Darracott of Muncie, Ind.

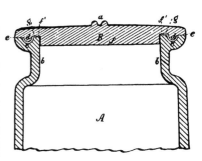

This grooved-ring wax sealer was rather advanced in technique. The groove was semicircular in cross-section, and the flat lid had a projecting ring of the same cross-section. The hot lid was to be pressed into the hot wax of the jar-groove and "worked" (rotated) until it drove all of the air out of the grooved space and cooled to "set." He provided two small buttons on top to center a wire clip, but did not provide the clip "or other means."

1887, September

This ECONOMY jar has been found with the date merely "Sept. 1887," which may be a mold-cutters error, for the original ECONOMY SEALER had a date of September 13, 1858. Note that this reference used the word ECONOMY only.

Stoppers

The stopper continued the trend started before the advent of the wax sealer. This group includes those seals which required either a bell-shaped opening within which the stopper fitted, or a depressed mouth within which the stopper was inserted. Stoppers marked one of the beginnings of mechanical action in sealing.

1859, January 4

Patent No. 22,535 by J. D. Willoughby of Carlisle, Pa.

The stopper that resulted from this patent is identified by the name, J. D. WIL-

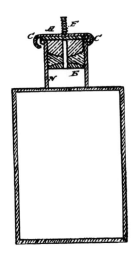

LOUGHBY STOPPLE, and the patent date. It consisted of a rubber disk held between two metal plates. When the plates were compressed by turning a thumbscrew, the rubber disk was squeezed outwardly against the wall of the jar neck. The stopple also carried a size designation—hence there must have been a variety for several sizes of jar necks. Several jars used this device, which was sold by A. R. Samuels, of Philadelphia, Pa., who also sold the KLINE stopper, differing from the Willoughby in having tapered sides.

1862, June 10

Patent No. 35,529 by W. W. Lyman of West Meriden, Conn.

This patent has sometimes been dated as January 10 due to the patent office use of script 'Jun' for June. This early Lyman stopper used a rubber ring in a grooved solid cap, with the rubber contacting the tapered mouth of the jar. Vacuum pulled the stopper down until seal was effected. A handle was provided for grasping to remove it.

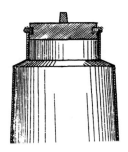

1863, February 10

Patent No. 37,647 by Charles F. Spencer of Rochester, N.Y.

The stopper was pressed to rest on a narrow ledge within a bell-shaped opening, and to hold so tightly that a ring-bolt was required to remove it. The material was metal, with the ring-bolt either cast with the stopper as one piece, and as a separate piece bolted through the stopper, giving metallic contact and possibility of leakage.

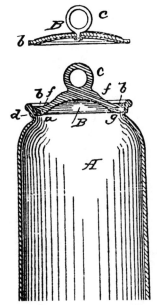

1863, October 27

Patent 40,415 by A. R. Kline of Philadelphia, Pa.

Kline's patent is sometimes confused with the Willoughby Stopple, but bottles made for the Kline have tapering side walls. The heavy glass stopper, also tapered, had a square rubber band that would slide on the stopper to the best fitting position. Removal would be difficult.

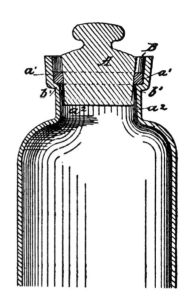

1864, without date

This appears on some VICTORY jars, and without either a name or a day no search could be made for the patent.

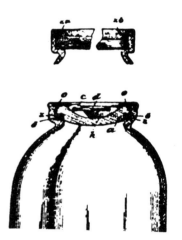

1864, February 9

Patent No. 41,532 by Samuel J. Parker of Ithaca, N.Y.

Parker used a bell-shaped mouth for his jars, except that about midway of the vertical wall of the bell there was a circular constriction on the inner side. The stopper had a core of fairly solid material, such as cork, encased with a rubber sheath, which had thicker walls around the rim. When the stopper was pushed into the opening, the constriction would cause it to snap into place. A ring was attached on the upper side for assisting in removal of the stopper.

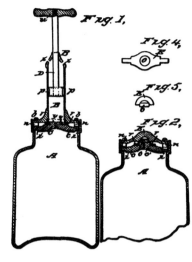

1864, June 21

Patent No. 43,232 by Harlow C. Smith of Chicago, Ill.

The stopper was incidental in Smith's invention. It is described as being of brass, slightly smaller than the opening so that a rubber gasket could be fitted around it before pushing the stopper into a slightly tapered opening in which it would become wedged when forced. The stopper had a rubber strap valve on top, to allow air to be pumped out, but not return. The key feature of the invention was a hand pump that would be temporarily fastened to the stopper in order to pump air out of the jar.

1865, May 23

Patent No. 47,834 by Charles G. Imlay of Philadelphia, Pa.

This patent covers so many matters that it will also be referred to in other places. In the present instance, it is to be noted that it shows a number of stopper designs, seating at the bottom of a cup-shaped opening having an inner ledge, and held with a screw-band. Other devices shown are glass lids seating on top of the ground lip, which would be questionable as to the sealing efficiency, and a glass cap.

1866, January 2

Patent No. 51,844 by W. W. Lyman of West Meriden, Conn.

The idea differs from that of Kline's patent of October 27, 1863, by having the cup made with vertical side walls, and placing the sealing rubber in a square-cut groove of the heavy glass stopper. He provided a deep groove in the stopper above the line of the finish lip so that a pry could be inserted to lift

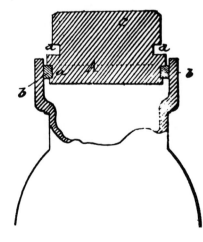

the stopper and break the vacuum for opening.

1866, February 6

Patent No. 52,379 by Edwin Bennett of Philadelphia, Pa.; but see also his 1856 wax-sealer
patent, from Baltimore, Md.

Bennett's stopper was of heavy glass, with
a screw thread on its tapered side, and two
glass knobs on top so that a lever could be
used for turning the stopper. The jar had a
similar tapered mouth, but it was without
screw threads. When the stopper was turned
within the rubber ring that formed the seal,
its threads would bury themselves in the
rubber and advance through it at the same
time, thus squeezing the rubber between the
stopper and inner mouth of the jar, until
jammed tight.

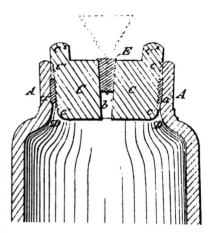

1866, April 3

Patent No. 53,659 by T. O. Oliver of New
York City

The action of this stopper was very similar
to the WILLOUGHBY STOPPLE, except
that the rubber ring was compressed by the
action of a cam lever instead of by a thumbscrew. It was slightly "dished" in contour so
that the lever was contained in the concave
side when in the closed position—thus the
jars could be stacked.

1868, August 18

Patent No. 81,296 by F. Rohrbacher and F.
Hormann of Philadelphia, Pa.

Used on THE BEST, the stopper was a
solid glass or metal piece, with lugs which
fitted into internal threads of the jar neck.
Not shown in the patent drawings are the
bosses on top of the lid, used for turning it.

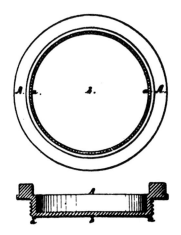

1871, July 18

Patent No. 117,236 by William Taylor and Charles Hodgetts of Brooklyn, N.Y.

The patent implies that there had been previously patented, or at least used, a metal stopper threaded to fit a jar having a thread inside of its opening, since the patent is not for such a device even though it illustrates it. The patent merely covers the facing of such a metallic cap with a liner that will not corrode. For this reason the patent is assigned to Louis R. Boyd, who had patented his inner liner for the Mason jar cap two years earlier, and had covered uses such as Taylor's. The jar concerned was the HOLZ, CLARK & TAYLOR and SALEM JAR.

1873, February 25

Patent No. 136,240 by Ella G. Haller of Carlisle, Pa.

The jar design was that of a large, bell-mouth, tapered opening, with two lugs blown in the glass below the tapered portion. The cap was a hollow glass, having a similar taper, a circular groove to take the round sealing rubber ring, and threaded below that to engage the two lugs in the jar mouth. It had an opening in the inside bottom.

In use, the hollow glass stopper was filled with syrup, then screwed into the jar opening by means of the lugs and its screw threads, until the round rubber ring was seated in the taper. After the cooking had been done, and during the cooling, the vacuum within the jar would pull syrup out of the hollow stopper and thus remain completely filled.

1885, August 4

Patent No. 323,636 by James Comly of Philadelphia, Pa.

This could be called an all-glass version of the WILLOUGHBY and OLIVER stoppers. One glass member fitted within the jar opening. Another rested on top of the finish. By means of a clutch cam rotated between the two members, a rubber ring was compressed within the neck of the jar. This device was used on one of the LAFAYETTE jars.

1886, October 27

This date, on a KLINE jar must have been a mold-cutter's error. The day is Sunday, on which no patents are issued. See, however, Kline's October 27, 1863, patent stopper, which was probably intended.

1890, circa

One of the STEERSHEAD jars has the words, on the stopper, "Lyon's Patent Allowed." No search could be made without more data.

1903, June 23

Patent No. 731,509 by Carl Schonert of Newark, N.J.

The idea concerns a jar made with a recess within the neck of the jar, into which a formed metal disk could be forced. The disk would expand into the recess and seal the jar. It would have been a single-use disk, and no method of removal was provided.

1901, December 3

Patent No. 687,710 by Olin Adams of Chicago, Ill.

This was the beginning of the familiar fiberboard plug cap for milk bottles, but the language of the patent would also cover the use of the idea for fruit-jar use.

1905, October 24

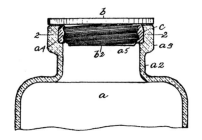

Patent No. 802,382 by William B. Fenn of Sheepshead Bay, N.Y.

The jar had a straight wall opening without screw threads. Into the bell shape was pressed a wax impregnated ring of fibrous material, having screw threads formed within the inner wall. The lid was of heavy glass or metal, and was provided with matching, but tapered, threads. When the lid was rotated to close the jar, its tapered threads would finally jam into the top portion of the threads on the fibrous ring and effect a seal.

Fenn received three patents on the same date. Patent No. 802,381 resulted in an all-glass screw cap, known as the SUNSHINE jar, and is discussed in the all-glass screw-cap section. No. 802,382 is the stopper seal discussed here. No. 802,383 was a screw thread and shoulder seal, discussed under that heading. Each was based on the inserted fiber-ring design.

The Helix and Its Forms as Sealing Tighteners

The helix (or coil), best known as the continuous thread, often abbreviated as "C.T.," accounts for many sealing styles. Not only is it used as the continuous thread for shoulder-seal jars, as in the Mason jar, and for top sealing, as in the later GEMS, but it also appears as short, slanting, helical lugs and slots on the neck of the jar, as plain lugs on the jar and helical lugs or threads in the cap, as sloping ramps on the top of caps and lids, and with yokes with helical-formed ends. These will be treated separately, even to the extent of having a separate entry for the all-glass cap, since its development should be apart from that of the continuous threads which most, but not all, of them used.

The beginning of the use of the helix in fruit-jar seals seems to have been lost. It was not Mason's patent which many deem the start of the screw thread. It antedated R. W. Lewis' patent of 1856, since he patented only an improvement of existing screw caps. Edwin Bennett, in his 1856 wax-sealer patent refers to the inefficiency of the screw caps then in use. Homer Brooke, who is quoted in the section about John Landis Mason in the chapter on "Men Who Made Fruit-Jar History," claims that his father had made screw-capped jars before 1855. Durand mentions screw caps in his British Patent No. 3,372 granted Aug. 30, 1810.

The history of the development of each kind will be taken up under the following groupings:

Continuous screw-thread shoulder seals
Continuous screw-thread top seals
Continuous screw-thread combination top and bead seals
The all-glass cap
Helical lugs on the jar neck
Helical slots in the jar neck
Helical ramps on the lid
Plain lugs with a helical yoke or cap

Continuous screw-thread shoulder seals

1857, October 27

Patent No. 18,498 by J. K. Chase of New York City

This patent is mentioned by Dr. H. H. Holscher in his "Hollow and Specialty Glass —Background and Challenge," which appeared serially in *The Glass Industry*, volume 46, from June to November, in 1965, who states that Chase took out a license from Mason later. It is a screw-cap design, but shows no sealing gasket. Hence, the Chase patent must have been ineffectual.

Chase did business in fruit-jar supplies, according to the advertisement reproduced in the *Mason Jar Centennial* of the Glass Container Manufacturers Institute, under the name of Williams & Chase, at 35 Park Place, New York City. The steaming device shown carries patent dates of 1867 to 1869, and the MASON'S IMPROVED jar shown was from the early 1870s.

1858, November 23

Patent No. 22,129 by John Landis Mason of New York City

The first patent allowed Mason, coming just one week before the date that he made famous by placing it on his jar, was for the details of a mold. It covered the details of the "vanishing thread," the "blow-over" that would make "cracking off" more uniform, and the venting of the bottom line of the threads so that the glass would fill the thread pattern. While it was more a mold patent than a jar patent, the jar is illustrated, and most of the jar claims of the November 30th patent were made here also.

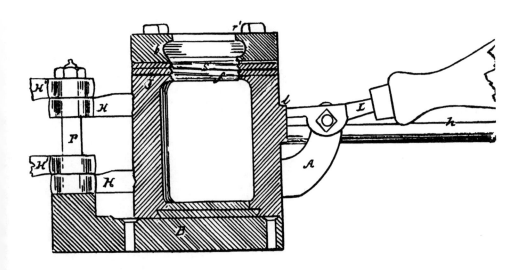

1858, November 30

Patent No. 22,186 by John Landis Mason of New York City

Coming after the patent for the mold on November 23, the patent for the Mason shoulder-seal jar merely repeats much of what was stated for the qualities of the mold. It seems strange that Mason does not illustrate the zinc cap and its details—it may have been because the screw-cap idea was already old and known to be unpatentable.

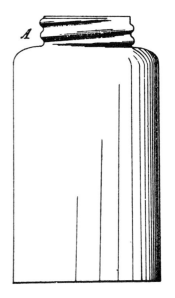

1864, December 27

Patent No. 45,601 by John F. Griffen of New York City

Griffen's patent covered two ideas. The first was for a tapered finish to hold a side-friction seal, and it led to the EUREKA and the LAFAYETTE jars. The second was for the thumb-tab on the rubber-ring gasket that went on the shoulder of the Mason jar. By pulling out on the tab the vacuum could be broken and the cap easily removed. That idea has remained unchanged through the years, even though all other details of the Mason jar and its closures have been greatly changed.

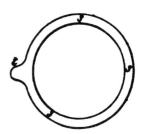

1869, March 30

Patent No. 88,439 by *Lewis* R. Boyd of New York City, and

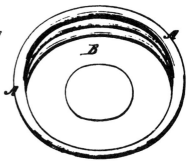

1869, May 11

Patent No. 89,845 by *Louis* R. Boyd of New York City

These two patents covered the lining of the zinc cap which had been blamed for imparting the metallic tastes to the contents of the Mason jar, and for the rise of glass-lidded competing jars. Boyd says in his application "To remedy this defect in metallic caps . . . a glass plate or partial lining, so arranged that the said glass shall be the only portion of the cap which at any time comes in contact with the contents of the jar."

The patent will also be mentioned in the section "Protection of Contents."

1896, December 1

Patent No. 572,281 by Albert G. Smalley of Chelsea, Mass.

While a portion of the patent covers the matter of the rounded-square shape and the limitations of the radii involved, of interest here is that Smalley also invented a tabbed rubber ring, but it did not replace the Griffen shape.

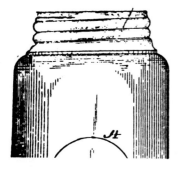

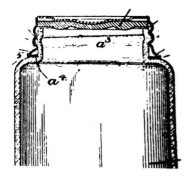

1898, June 14

Patent No. 605,482 by Samuel P. Jaggard of Blackwood, N.J.

The patent mainly concerns the use of an octagonal shoulder and an octagonal-topped zinc cap, both designed to receive octagonal wrenches by which the cap could be tightened and loosened. It was used on the J&B Fruit Jar.

1905, October 24

Patent No. 802,381 by William B. Fenn of Sheepshead Bay, N.Y.

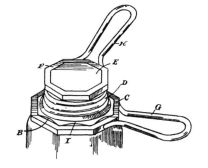

The threads on the jar were slightly tapered, narrow at the top. The cap was of solid construction, adaptable to either glass or metal, and without threads. It was lined with a wax-impregnated fibrous material which was threaded on the inside of the ring of this material. In use the cap would be rotated until the material was jammed in the jar threads and thus effect a seal. It was used on the SUNSHINE jar.

Variations of this patent, under other patent numbers, were proposed as a stopper seal and as a seal jamming into a deep groove. The latter follows. Fenn also patented a stopper and an all-glass cap.

1910 and after

With the development of machine jarmaking, followed by the bead seal, the shoulder seal was abandoned. See "Continuous screw-thread combination top and bead seals" which follows the next section on "Continuous screw-thread top seals."

Continuous screw-thread top seals

While the continuous thread idea was used before the first entry in this series, which in itself antedates Mason, no patent reference has been found. In actual use, the top seal lagged behind the shoulder seal in development, even though the number of patents in the top-seal field is very great. The entire problem was centered around methods of getting around the ground lip. The practical solution was that of straddling the ground lip with an inverted cup-like pressed-glass disk. The economic problem was that this method, which called for a thread diameter larger than the flat area devoted to the seal, called for more metal with which to make the cap and therefore a greater cost and selling price.

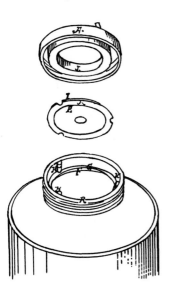

1856, February 12

Patent No. 14,245 by R. W. Lewis of Honesdale, Pa.

That this patent was not the first screw cap is attested by the fact that it is for a protective liner on an existing screw cap. The patent makes no claim for the screw cap, but only for the liner and a method of keeping it from rotating when the cap was turned. Note that this date is 33 months before the Mason Patent.

1863, February 15

The PEERLESS patent was not found. The jar has a continuous thread finish, uses a glass lid that straddles the ground lip, but instead of a threaded cap it uses a yoke whose ends are at an angle suitable for following the line of the thread helix when tightened. Peerless jars bear dates of Feb. 15, 1862 and 1863, neither of which is an official patent-issue date.

1864, February 9

This date appears on the VICTORY jar, made by both the Pacific Glass Company and the San Francisco Glass Company, crosstown rivals at San Francisco, Cal., who merged in 1876. It was also shown on the OK jar and PACIFIC GLASS WORKS jar. The jar also carries the date of June 22, 1867, often with the "22" backwards. Although other patents of this date were found, the VICTORY patent was not. It is a true top seal and clouds the statement that Imlay patented the first top seal.

1865, May 23 (Patent antedated December 6, 1864)

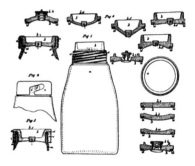

Patent No. 47,834 by Charles G. Imlay of Philadelphia, Pa.

Imlay's patent was a catch-all of ideas. It included an all-glass cap, a stopper of glass held by a screw-band, a slotted metal cap, and eleven top seals held by screw-bands. Three of the top seals were fitted with spring vents or threaded plug vents, five had rubber stoppers in the center of the glass lid for venting, and three lids had no provision for venting. It made no claim for the tapered jar top shown in the patent, so it was left to Rowley, of Hero, to "patent" this shape two years later. The antedating gives Imlay priority to 1864.

Sealing was made on top of the ground lip, so that sealing performance was questionable. It did introduce the screw-band, or screw-cap with a cut-out center.

1865, May 23

Hero shows this date on some of its jars. The Imlay patent was the only one found for the date claimed. It is quite possible that Imlay sold the patent, or leased it, to fellow Philadelphian Rowley, of Hero. Later Imlay seems to have done business with Potter & Bodine, the Bodine Brothers, and Cohansey.

1865, August 8

Patent 49,256 by Wm. T. Gillinder and Edwin Bennett, of Philadelphia, Pa.

While the DEXTER jar, which had the date as Aug. 6, 1865, also is found with an all-glass cap, this patent by the owners of the Franklin Flint Glass Co. is for a glass lid and metal screw-band. Its chief feature was a very flat glass disk, seating on the ground lip of the jar.

1867, June 22

This date has already been mentioned as being on the San Francisco glass lid and metal screw-band jar, along with the date of February 9, 1864. No details are known except that the glass lid differs from most in its being very tall above the screw-band.

1868, March 10

Patent No. 75,275 by William L. Imlay of Philadelphia, Pa.

While keeping the threaded jar neck, this device employed a coiled wire, shaped to follow the jar threads and having the top end of the wire curl over the jar lid and press on its center. The straddling of the ground lip is clearly shown. One of the witnesses was Charles G. Imlay, whose 1865-antedated 1864 patent has just been mentioned. The device became the VALVE JAR by the Valve Jar Company, of Philadelphia, Pa., who seem to be a subsidiary, or were absorbed by, either Hero or Cohansey. Hero seems likely since the patent shows the tapered rubber ring retention used by Hero. Jars have been found, however, with this seal and marked Potter & Bodine.

The Imlays joined in a patent for a jar using a helical lug in 1872, and sold it to Cohansey.

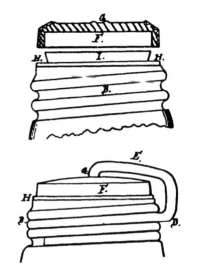

1869, January 19

Patent No. 86,089 by John Landis Mason of New York City

Mason's first venture into top seals called for a screw-band and a tall glass lid straddling the ground lip. The seal could be either on top or on the side of the finish, as it was so constructed that it mattered little at which point the lid touched first. It would be an expensive seal to make, partly because it called for both a flat rubber ring and a tube-like rubber ring. The inner contour as drawn would have been impossible to make, but it would not have influenced the sealing efficiency if not followed.

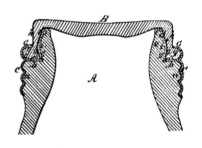

1869, February 23

Patent No. 87,274 by John L. Mason of New York City

This design was an improvement on the January 19 idea, in that it called for just one thick rubber ring, set into a groove on the side of the jar finish. The tall glass lid was

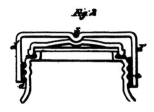

slightly tapered and came down along the outside edge of the rubber ring until it sealed.

1869, March 2

Patent No. 87,515 by Salmon B. Rowley of Philadelphia, Pa.

In this patent Rowley, of Hero, seems to have been trying to copy the Imlay simple coiled-wire top seal of William Imlay, Patent No. 75,275, which became the VALVE JAR. Rowley added stiffening members to the coil and carried these members over the top, to cross, and contact the glass lid in the very center. In doing so he lost the venting attributes of the VALVE JAR.

1869, October 12

Patent No. 95,819 by W. W. Lyman of Meriden, Conn.

Lyman was concerned with making a good seal on jars made with the minor imperfections of the sealing surface common to that day of hand blowing. He constructed the cap with serrations around the outer edge so that they would grip similar projections in the lid. When the screw-band was rotated in sealing, it would also rotate the lid, and, in his words "work" the sealing rubber so that it would fill the irregularities in the sealing surface.

1869, November 2

Patent No. 96,400 by H. E. Shaffer of Rochester, N.Y.

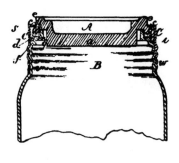

Shaffer used a very narrow rubber ring, which would tend toward less cost in making a full-sized opening, and so designed the glass lid and the finish that the ring was enclosed on all four sides before the metal screw-band was applied to tighten the assembly.

1869, December 14

Patent No. 97,964 by Salmon B. Rowley (Hero) of Philadelphia, Pa.

This could be the first well-engineered top seal. The sealing surface is at a slight slant, which would permit the molds to be opened without "dragging" the glass. The part above the sealing surface was tilted upward and outward so that the sealing rubber would be held in position. Like Lyman, in his October 12, 1869 patent just referred to, Rowley was concerned with the common irregularities of hand glassmaking. He solved the problem by using a thin metal cap which would flex to the waviness of the sealing surface. This placed him "out on a limb" with respect to his many glass-lid inventions, a position from which he quickly retreated, but only after leaving the door open for Mason to apply much the same construction using a glass lid.

1870, March 1

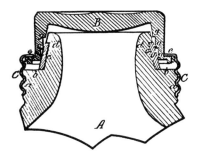

Patent No. 100,306 by John Landis Mason of New York City

Mason returned, here, to the steep slanting sealing surface and tubular rubber ring of his Patent No. 86,089 of January 19, 1869. In it he used a fairly thick rubber ring, and pressed the glass lid to form three squared steps inside, so designed that the pointed angles would dig into the rubber to make a tighter seal. The side groove which held the rubber tube on the finish was an almost impossible construction for the glassmaking of that day.

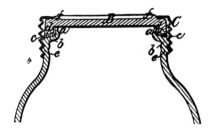

1870, May 10

Patent No. 102,913 by John L. Mason of New York City

This was an almost direct copy of Rowley's December 14, 1869, top seal, including the slanting surface for sealing, the slight angle above it to hold the sealing rubber in a fixed position, but with definite claim for a glass "or other vitreous material," for the lid construction. Mason had filled the Rowley loophole mentioned above.

It is interesting, and perhaps Mason used it as a smoke screen, that he mentioned a half dozen previous inventions in the field, and discussed the superiority of his device, but with no mention of Rowley. It is true that this is perhaps the best of Mason's top seals, and it is the one that he designated "improved."

1871, February 7

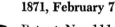

Patent No. 111,607 by Melville R. Bissell of Kalamazoo, Mich., and assigned to Salmon B. Rowley of Hero

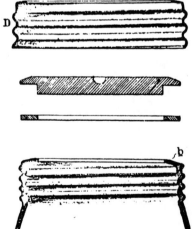

Bissell's idea was Rowley's December 14, 1869, idea in respect to the slanting sealing surface, but he ground down the rising rubber ring holding part until it was flat with the start of the sealing surface. To fix the rubber ring, he placed it on a circular under-projection of the lid, which was now back to glass in construction. Since the lid no longer had to straddle the ground lip, it was much thinner. It was held by the usual metal screw-band.

1871, June 6

Patent No. 115,754 by John L. Mason of New York City

Mason refers to this patent by number, but not by date, in his September 24, 1872, patent following. It introduced the small vertical bar on the zinc cap of the shoulder-seal and the top-seal jars. Its purpose was to serve as a grip for a wrench in opening and closing the jar.

1872, September 3

Patent No. 131,003 by Henry Howson, of Philadelphia, Pa., and assigned to S. B. Rowley of the same place (Hero patent)

This patent used the idea of a glass lid held in a metal cap, patented by S. B. Rowley on Dec. 31, 1872, as Patent No. 134,400, by showing how that assembly would be held on the jar by a metal screw-band as a top seal.

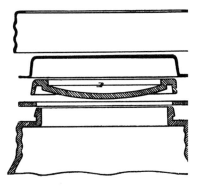

1872, September 24

Patent No. 131,695 by John L. Mason of New York City

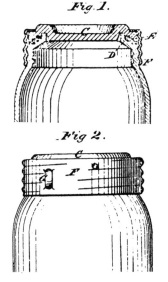

Fig. 1.

Here Mason returns to the use of a sealing surface composed of several steps in a slanting surface, with the idea that this would compress the rubber ring in concentric circles, and thus effect a better seal. He also showed an improved form of the bar on the zinc cap and the wrench that would be used to tighten and loosen the seal.

Fig 2.

Just as Rowley left the door open in his use of metal lids with his improved top seal and which Mason closed, Mason here left a door open by specifying a vertical bar—Rowley immediately came out with a horizontal bar.

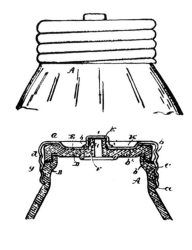

1886, March 16

Patent No. 338,185 by Thomas G. and John H. Otterson of Woodbury, N.J.

This was the final version of the Woodbury jar. The first two employed a yoke and helical lugs, and the second of them used the pierced knob for venting. The present patent converted the idea, still retaining the pierced knob, into a glass lid held by a metal screwband. The lid was less bulbous than the first two designs, and rested on a slanting sealing surface, with the rubber ring held by the portion rising to the ground lip, as the previous Hero and Mason designs of 1869.

This seems to be the first of such conversions to screw-bands. Others were the PREMIUM and the KERR. This became the IMPROVED WOODBURY.

1903, May 12

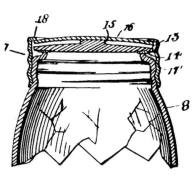

Patent No. 727,808 by Dallas Knowlton of Washington, D.C.

The patent shows a glass lid, sealing on the ground lip, and held by a circular piece of spring brass, resting on the center of the glass lid and developing its spring action by being pressed downward by the narrow ledge of a metal *screw-band*.

Then a funny thing happened to Knowlton on his way back from the Patent Office—he completely changed the sealing method when he came to manufacture the KNOWLTON jar. He changed to a cupped glass lid, resting on a ledge outside the rising part to the ground lip, eliminated the spring disk, and changed the cap to a full cap, in which six perforations gave it venting and some spring action. Before he was well along, he changed to machine-made jars. This is the design usually seen by collectors.

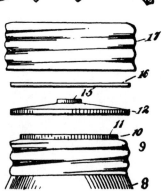

1905, October 24

Patent 802,383 by William D. Fenn of Sheepshead Bay, N.Y.

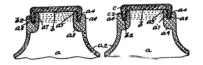

This is more a side seal than a top seal, but it has the aspects of both. The jar finish was threaded inside of a deep groove, tapering narrower at the bottom. The cap was a thin metal cup, holding a formed, wax-impregnated ring of fibrous material. The jar threads were of greater diameter near the bottom, but the threads formed in the fibrous disk were straight. When the cap was turned to tighten, the difference in thread diameter jammed the fibrous material, both on the threads and into the bottom of the groove.

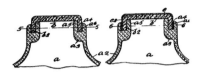

Fenn, on the same date, received two other patents, one of which was covered under "Stoppers" and the other will be covered in "All-glass screw caps" in a later section.

Further developments in the top seal are described in the next section, "Continuous screw-thread combination top and bead seals."

Continuous screw-thread combination top and bead seals

The advent of machine jarmaking eliminated the ground lip and made it possible to seal on the machine-made top surface. The old type of top seal, with the separate sealing ledge disappeared. About 1910 to 1915 the shoulder was eliminated in favor of a circular bead that served both as a sealing ledge for the shoulder seal, and as a "take-out" grip for mechanical removal of jars from the mold. Early top seals, employing a glass lid, were in some difficulty due to imperfections, such as waviness, of the top surface, but the advent of the metal disk and heat-softening sealing compound, together with better glassmaking, surmounted this difficulty.

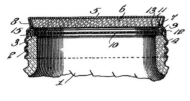

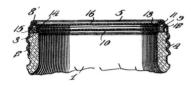

1910, November 22

Patent No. 976,659 by Charles R. Keeran of Bloomington, Ill.

The essence of Keeran's sealing method was a disk of metal which had a V-shaped groove around the edge, of the same diameter as the machine-made finish, and which held either a rubber ring, or a waxed fibrous ring which contacted the finish when inverted, groove side down, over the jar. It was held in place either by a specially designed glass insert in the usual metal jar cap, or by a cap without the insert, but having a similar groove, in matching position so that the cap groove fit over the disk groove when exerting pressure. Keeran preferred the waxed-fiber ring since it would flow to fit any irregularities in the finish when heated.

The date shown on the patent is that also shown on the WHITE CROWN CAP, and may have been changed in practice into the glass lid and metal screw-band of that cap. No other patent was found for that date.

Keeran was a jobber of fruit-jar and canning supplies, doing business as Keeran-Funk & Company, in Bloomington, Ill. Among his products was a wax-impregnated fiber disk, given to me along with a copy of Keeran's advertising folder, by Mr. Joe Wenger of Sabetha, Kan. It was inserted next to the glass liner of the usual zinc Mason jar cap and served as a seal in place of the rubber ring. Keeran claimed that it would seal without excessive tightening and would loosen as easily and that it could be used regardless of any bent or pinholed zinc cap since it did not seal on the shoulder.

1910, December 20

Patent No. 979,183 by Francis J. Mackin of San Francisco, Cal., and assigned to Ben Schloss of the same city

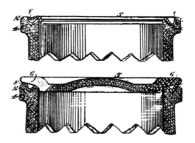

Like Knowlton, Mackin also changed his jar and cap design between patenting and actual manufacture. He started out with a groove on the top of the machine-made finish top, like a miniature grooved-ring wax sealer. The idea was that it would avoid the making of crizzles, or fine hair-line cracks across the sealing surface, which would leak air, destroy the vacuum, and spoil the product. He reasoned that while crizzles might form on the outer ridge of the groove, they would not form on the inner edge, and that would be where he would seal. He would crimp the edge of the metal cap around a small finish bead, or hold it with a clip. Before he was successful with his invention he had to change it to a metal cap held by very fine threads. Then he named it a "Mason" jar, even though there was little resemblance. The GOLDEN STATE jar.

1910-1915

So far as can be found the STRONG SHOULDER jar was not patented, but it was first made by Hazel Atlas about 1910-15. Its essential design was that of an ordinary Mason thread, with a bead replacing the shoulder as a place for the seal. It could also be sealed by the E D J SEAL invented by Hazel Atlas about 1910. Since it eliminated the abrupt angles at the normal shoulder seal, it gained much strength for the jar construction, hence the name.

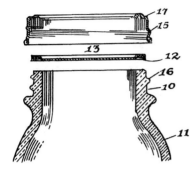

1915, August 31

Patent No. 1,152,107 by Alexander H. Kerr of Chicago, Ill.

This became the KERR SELF SEALING jar, but represented outwardly only one change over the ECONOMY jar, also by Kerr. That change was the use of a screw-thread metal band to replace the spring clip of the ECONOMY. The heat-softening compound, permanently adhered to the metal disk, was retained. The patent drawing shows the now-standard bead-sealing position of the STRONG SHOULDER jar, and permitted zinc caps to be used, with the rubber ring in place on the bead, but this was no part of Kerr's invention. Something of the difficulties faced by this type of seal is mentioned in the discussion of Kerr in the section "Men Who Made Fruit-Jar History."

To all practical purposes this invention ended further changes in the Mason jar, as it has become the standard type of seal in today's home canning.

All-glass screw caps

The all-glass screw cap was an ideal that glassmakers tried to achieve for a long time. Each had the same basic difficulty—that two equally hard surfaces, both unyielding, would, on sliding over one another under pressure, scratch and seize together, causing difficult removal and possible breakage. The nearest solution was Fenn's SUNSHINE JAR, which interposed the waxed sealing gasket between the two surfaces of glass.

1858, October 19

Patent No. 21,831 by Thomas R. Hartell of Philadelphia, Pa.

The patent is for the apparatus for the manufacture of the stopper. The stopper itself was for a top seal, with the sealing rubber within the cap and resting on the ground lip. Three helical lugs on the jar neck fitted matching lugs within the cap. It was lettered around the edge, "HARTELL'S GLASS AIR-TIGHT COVER."

1865, May 23

Patent No. 47,834 by Charles G. Imlay of Philadelphia, Pa.

One of the fourteen designs for caps in Imlay's patent was that of an all-glass cap for sealing on the ground lip, at the bottom of a deep groove, almost impossible either to make or of success in operation. It was probably never made into commercial glass.

1865, August 8

The patent claimed on the DEXTER fruit jar has not been found, so no details are available.

1869, August 31

Patent No. 94,452 by William S. Thompson of Rochester, N.Y.

Citing the by then well-known difficulties of glass to glass thread contact, Thompson threaded the neck of the jar as usual, but while he also threaded the inside of the cap, he placed a thin sheath of metal, conforming to the threads, within the cap and secured to it. Thus the metallic sheath turned with the cap and gave a metal-to-glass contact with the jar threads.

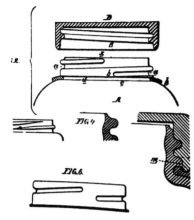

1873, February 4

Patent No. 135,430 by Henry Howson of Philadelphia, Pa., and assigned to Salmon B. Rowley of Hero

Howson laid considerable stress on the fact that his threaded jar appeared as though the threads were cut *into* a basic diameter the same as the greater thread diameter across the tops, as compared with Mason's threads, which appeared as though they projected from a basic diameter the same as the root diameter of the threads, and with the threads "vanishing" (in Mason's words) at each end. This enabled Howson to cut a groove below the threads, into which the rubber sealing ring could be snapped after stretching to go over the threads. His drawings show complete conformity of the threads with each other in glass cap and jar neck, a condition unattainable in the glassmaking practice of the day, and sure to seize with minor corrosion. Nevertheless it became the basis of Hero's CRYSTAL jar. No doubt it was modified in practice.

1873, February 25

Patent No. 136,240 by Ella G. Haller of Carlisle, Pa.

Mrs. Haller's stopper was a hollow glass receptacle for syrup, which would be drawn into the jar when it cooled. The stopper was fitted with grooved threads, which fitted two lugs in the throat of the jar. A rubber ring, held by a groove in the stopper, sealed on an inner ledge.

(Mrs. Haller does not say how she got the syrup into the small hole in the center bottom of the stopper.)

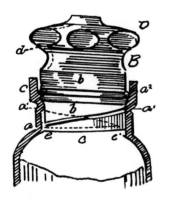

1877, December 25

Patent No. 198,528 by Theodore F. Woodward of Winslow, N.J., and assigned to Hay & Co. of the same place

Woodward's all-glass cap appeared on the IMPROVED WINSLOW jar. Its thread contact was "tight" and would have been difficult to make and to prevent "seizing" onto the jar.

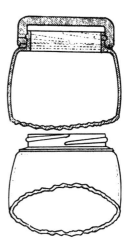

1878, December 17

This date is claimed on the CRYSTAL JAR all-glass lid, Consolidated's answer to Hero's CRYSTAL. The jar neck was threaded, but the cap had three internal lugs, instead of threads. Patent search for that date revealed, as a jar or closure patent, only that of George L. Harrison, Jr., of Philadelphia, No. 211,011, for an improvement in metallic cans in the form of a single-use closure not possible to use in glass containers.

1882, October 24

This date on the FRANKLIN-DEXTER and the INDEPENDENT all-glass lids could not be tied up with a proper patent. The only one of that date was that of Anton Luger, of Vienna, Austria, Patent No. 266,375, for a glass stopper-like lid, held by hinge on one side, and a snap lock on the other. It did not have a screw thread, and does not agree with the FRANKLIN-DEXTER details.

1886, April 6

Patent No. 339,556 by George Washington Johnston of Flemington, N.J.

While Johnston designed his stopper-type closure for clay and pottery, the design was subsequently used for glass, as attested by the date used on glass jars. Since no cap has been found, it is not known whether the cap fitting the jar was made of clay or glass.

1893, April 11 (patent found), and
1893, November 7 (patent not found)

Patent No. 495,299 by Reginald Boice Calcutt of Chicago, Ill.

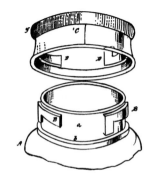

The jar and cap as seen do not agree with the April patent drawing. The April patent showed a cap with three helical lugs inside, and a jar with matching external lugs on the neck. All lugs were equipped with "stops" to halt rotation at the end of the helix. Jars as found had continuous screw threads, while the caps had lugs without stops. Possibly this was covered in the November patent. The CALCUTT CAP is quite commonly found.

1905, October 24

Patent No. 802,381 by William B. Fenn of Sheepshead Bay, N.Y.

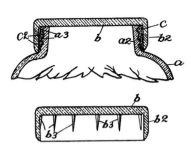

One of three patents issued to Fenn on the same day, this became the SUNSHINE JAR. It was an all-glass cap, but the cap was not threaded. Instead, it had vertical bosses to lock into place a thick gasket of waxed fibrous material. The inner side of the fibrous material had threads that tapered thicker toward the top of the cap, and as the cap was screwed into place, this thicker portion jammed on the jar threads until it became a tight seal.

The other patents covered a stopper-like all-glass closure of the same type (following), and a metallic-covered fibrous seal, and are discussed under "Stoppers" and "Screwthread shoulder seals."

1905, December 5

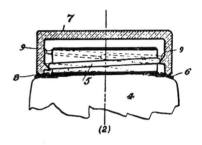

(2)

Patent No. 806,602 by Russel Uhl of Wilkes Barre, Pa., and assigned to the Perfection Glass Co., of Washington, Pa.

While both cap and jar had continuous threads, that of the cap was not rounded, but in the shape of an angular wedge which made only a line contact with the rounded jar threads. It became the SIMPLEX all-glass cap, and was more successful than most, even the almost equally good SUNSHINE JAR patented just six weeks earlier.

Helical lugs on the jar neck

The helix need not be a continuous thread to be effective in tightening a fruit-jar seal. Many jar and closure designs employed only portions of the helix, in the form of sloping lugs, slots, and ramps. Generally there were two or three such lugs, three being much better in providing a non-rocking basis for the yokes, but much compromised to two lugs because the yoke had only two ends. Four-lug designs found one lug generally superfluous, since the glassmaking of that day could not bring all four lugs into equal bearing at the same time—the result was always a tripod. This section deals with those closure designs in which two or more sloping protuberances, or helical lugs, on the jar neck are the chief means of identification.

1858, October 19

The patent was not found, but essentially the original design had two helical lugs on the jar, which held a yoke or spring clip passing over the glass lid. Other designs have been found with three lugs, and therefore

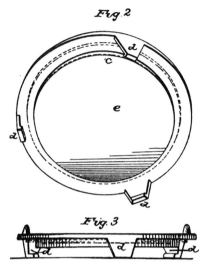

Fig. 2

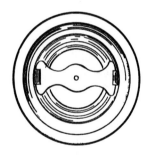

Fig. 3

using a three-pronged yoke or clip. Generally, but not always, the jar carried the POTTER & BODINE name.

1859, February 15

Patent No. 22,962 by James F. Martin and Henry C. Nicholson of Mount Washington, Ohio

The cap had three downward projecting lugs, formed in the same piece of metal as the lid. These engaged three long helical lugs on the body of the can or neck of the jar.

1859, June 28

Patent No. 24,566 by William D. Ludlow, of New York City

This, Ludlow's first patent of its kind, was for cans, but he shows this date on his glass jars made also to a later patent because the same principle applied—the springing of the metal yoke while rotating it under plain lugs on the jar or can.

1859, October 25

Patent No. 25,894 by Wm. Fridley and Frederick Cornman of Carlisle, Pa.

The patent was for a metal cap having helical threads matching the screw thread of the jar. The actual assembly was a very crude cast-metal cap, with lugs spaced to match the jar threads. A rubber disk was employed as the sealing medium, rather than a ring, in order to protect the contents of the jar from the metal. Some of the caps carry the spelling "FRIDLE."

1861, December 17

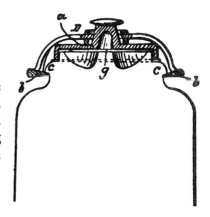

Patent No. 33,938 by N. S. Gilbert of Lockport, N.Y.

Gilbert employed two long sloping beads and a yoke (which he called a "bail") with four flexible legs, each of which hooked under the bead, and which brought spring pressure upon the center of the glass lid. A locking device for the yoke was included.

1863, February 15

Nothing could be found about the patent itself. The jar is well known, and has three spiral lugs, for a yoke and a glass lid. It is the PEERLESS. (The PEERLESS of 1861 used a Willoughby Stopple.)

1867, February 12

Patent No. 61,921 by Joseph Borden, of Bridgeton, N.J., and assigned to F. & J. Bodine, of Philadelphia, Pa.

This patent is probably that of the PROTECTOR jar, which bears no year date, but which was mentioned with criticism in D. I. Holcomb's Patent No. 97,920, of Dec. 14, 1869. It also fixes the Bodines as makers of the PROTECTOR jar. The jar neck had two helical lugs, on which the ends of a flat spring clip contacted. The drawing showed the clip as an integral part of the entire lid, but loose wire spring clips have also been found on the PROTECTOR jar.

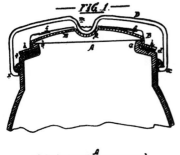

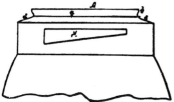

1868, February 11

Patent No. 74,249 by Salmon B. Rowley (Hero) of Philadelphia, Pa.

Rowley used a metal lid, held by a formed wire clip that contacted the lid in a depressed center, and rotated on two helical lugs on the jar. He used radial corrugations in the lid to give it strength against bending under central pressure.

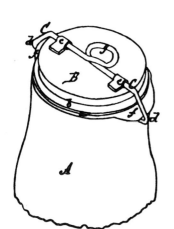

1868, May 5

Patent No. 77,570 by T. E. Batterson of Rochester, N.Y.

The two lugs were helical, but of opposite slope so that the wire clip, rotating in trunnions soldered to the metal lid would present its hooked ends on the same side of the jar, and be forced down the helix by a loop in the wire, on top of the metal lid, and which served as a spring.

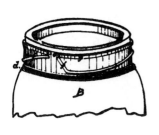

1870, April 19

Patent No. 102,024 by Robert McCully of Philadelphia, Pa.

McCully replaced the integral glass lugs on the neck with a spiral spring, held in a wide, flat groove. The cap had internal, button-like, lugs which tightened the cap when it was rotated.

1870, November 29

Patent No. 109,703 by Theodore F. Woodward of Winslow, N.J., and assigned to Hay & Co. of Philadelphia, Pa.

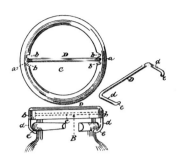

The yoke was of wire, crossing the top of the glass lid, and hooking under a bead-shaped pair of helical lugs. The chief different feature was that the lid was notched on opposite vertical sides to keep the wire from slipping off the lid. It was used on the first WINSLOW JAR.

1870, December 20

Design Patent No. D4,522 by Peter John Biesenbach of Rochester, N.Y.

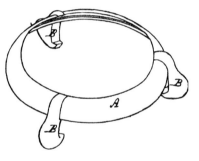

Biesenbach's intention was to design a fruit-jar sealing clamp of more graceful appearance, as well as being an efficient mechanical device. It consisted of an open ring, designed to cover the side of the lid, either glass or metal, extend slightly over the top edge, and exert downward pressure on the top through three rather graceful arms that hooked on three helical lugs on the jar. This tightened the lid when rotated. It was used on the KIEFFER'S NO. 1 JAR.

1872, July 16

Patent No. 129,235 by Charles G. and William L. Imlay of Camden, N.J. (previously of Philadelphia, Pa.)

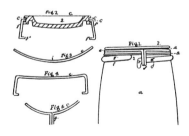

The glass lid was provided with a horizontal groove in its rim. A wire was bent to fill this groove and be permanently fastened to the lid. Two portions of the wire were bent downward to hook under twin helical lugs on the jar neck. Two features were that stops were provided, for the first time, at the lower ends of the lugs, and the lower sides of the lugs were slightly serrated as a holding device. COHANSEY used this patent.

1873, February 25

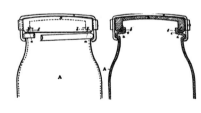

Patent No. 136,148 by Henry C. Gaskill of Mount Holly, N.J., and assigned to Hay & Co., of Philadelphia, Pa.

This patent is an improvement on the Theodore F. Woodward patent of November 29, 1870, which Hay & Co. also bought. The seal is no longer on the ground lip, the glass lid is more massive, and the centering of the wire clip against slippage is by a groove extending the full height of the lid. It was also used on the WINSLOW JAR.

1876, January 18

Patent No. 172,289 by John Young of Amsterdam, N.Y.

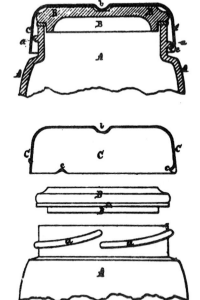

Young's closure would have presented a very modern appearance today with its smooth, unbroken cover cap, with its four "bumps" inward on the bottom edge. These inward turned lugs engaged four helical lugs on the glass jar neck. When rotated, the cap pulled down tightly on a glass lid. The latter, unfortunately, sealed on the ground lip of the jar, whose rough surface would not make a vacuum-tight seal. Another COHANSEY jar.

1876, June 27

Patent No. 179,231 by David E. Stevens of Newark, Ohio

Stevens' design is not a true helix, but is grouped with the helical lugs because its diamond-shaped lugs on the jar and the cap gave two sloping ramps which moved against one another to tighten for sealing, or for loosening. The primary design had the lugs on the inside of the cap and on the outside of the jar. A second design reversed these positions, as a stopper.

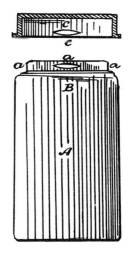

The NATIONAL fruit jar carried the date of June 27, 1876, and the Stevens' patent was the only one found. It has a radically different lug design than the Stevens', and if the Stevens' patent is meant by NATIONAL's dated jars, there was considerable liberty taken in changing the diamond-shaped lugs to NATIONAL's helical lugs. NATIONAL more nearly resembles POTTER & BODINE's 1858 patent that started this section.

1884, November 25

Patent No. 308,571 by Thomas G. Otterson of Philadelphia, Pa., and John H. Otterson of New York City

Thomas G. Otterson will be remembered as the inventor of the MILLVILLE jar. In the present patent, the first WOODBURY jar, they employed a glass lid with a small upward projection, threaded to take a retaining cap, a flat iron yoke with a hole in the center to slip over the retaining boss and to hook under two helical lugs, equipped with stops, on the neck of the jar. Note that the boss was not perforated as in later models.

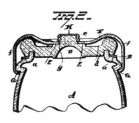

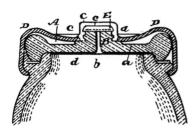

1885, March 3

Patent No. 313,229 by Thomas G. Otterson and Cornelius C. Voorhies of Woodbury, N.J.

The presence of Voorhies' name probably means that he was the one who suggested that if the boss in the original WOODBURY jar were perforated, and the small cap fitted with a sealing rubber, the jar would vent air on boiling if the small caps were to be left loosened for that purpose. This is the only change from the T. G. and J. H. Otterson patent of 1884, reviewed immediately above. It is the most common WOODBURY jar—the unvented boss is rare.

The final change of the WOODBURY jar, from a yoke and helical-lug design to a metal screw-band and continuous thread is covered in "Continuous screw-thread top seals" under the date of March 16, 1886. It is Patent No. 338,185 by Thomas G. and John H. Otterson, then residing in Woodbury, N.J.

1892, July 12

Patent No. 478,659 by Cassius D. Thomas of Moberly, Mo.

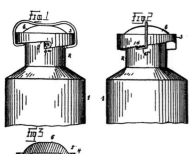

The design was somewhat crude and behind-times. The jar had a heavy pressed finish ledge, whose underside was sloping, and serrated below. The domed glass lid rested in a groove that was formed in the top of the finish, on a thin rubber sheet. A wire clip, very difficult to put into place and remove, crossed over the center of the glass lid, without any centering arrangement, and hooked under the finish ledge. The ends of the wire turned outward so that the round wire would take its place in the serrations.

1896, May 5

Patent No. 559,564 by Jacob Bonshire of
Yorktown, Ind.

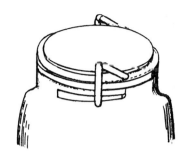

The feature is not the two helical neck
lugs, but the spring clip which is attached to
the lid by its own spring action and the fact
that it is circular to something over half the
diameter, and lies in a groove around the
upper part of the glass lid. It is shaped in
such a way that the two ends hook under the
lugs.

1903, October 20

Patent No. 741,969 by William Keefer of Gas
City, Ind.

A notch at the apex of opposing helical
lugs, the only patent with such a holding device, held the wire spring clip.

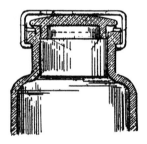

Helical slots in the jar neck

So far as the tightening function was concerned, it mattered
little whether the formation on the jar was a lug or a slot. What
mattered was that it was difficult glassmaking. Very few patents
of helical slots were found.

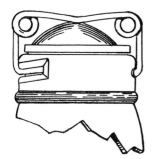

1868, January 28

Patent No. 73,724 by W. L. Imlay of Philadelphia, Pa.

The ALL RIGHT fruit jar had been considered to be a product of the Lockport, N.Y., factory purchased by Hero in 1869, but the finding of this patent by a Philadelphian, Hero's main factory town, proves it to be a Hero development. The jar as made differs in not having the domed top shown, and in minor details of design.

1869, June 29

Patent No. 91,871 by Daniel C. Ripley of Pittsburgh, Pa.

Ripley's patent was not strictly for fruit-jar use, as the lid could be fastened permanently. It is included because the design made a seal of the fruit-jar type possible.

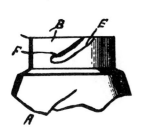

1903, June 9

Patent No. 730,510 by Henry B. Beach of Meriden, Conn.

Beach used a slanting slot, starting from the top of the finish. An internal metallic lug on the metal lid or cap followed the slot to tighten the cap.

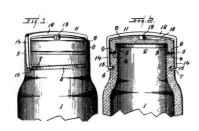

1910, November 22

Patent No. 976,623 by Francis Marion Belles of Shickshinny, Pa.

Two helical slots were placed on opposite sides of the rather thick neck wall. The glass lid had a slot from the side to the center, with a central enlargement into a circle. The rather heavy yoke, hooked at the ends to fit

the sloped slots, had a central boss, circular
except for sides flattened to fit the slot on the
glass lid, and was intended to be slipped into
place from the side, and then lock by its own
rotation.

A wrench was provided to turn the yoke if
needed.

Helical ramps on the lid

A small group of jars used the helix in the form of a sloping,
circular ramp on the lid of the jar. The lid was usually glass. By
rotating the jar to lift a yoke, or by rotating the yoke with the
lid in place, a tightening effect was produced.

1862, May 20

Patent No. 35,286 by John Adams of Pittsburgh, Pa.

This first ramp-lidded jar was very simple.
The one weakness in the Adams' patent was
in making the ramps too small—they were
close to the center of the glass lid, and described a circle hardly three fourths of an
inch in diameter, requiring steep ramp in-
clines and endangering slipping down the
ramp when the grip was loosened by the formation of a vacuum. The yoke was of heavy
flat metal, and hooked under a bead in the
finish of the jar. The bead was opened on
opposite sides so that the yoke could be lowered into place from the top.

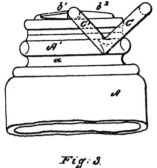

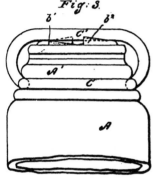

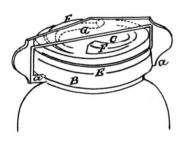

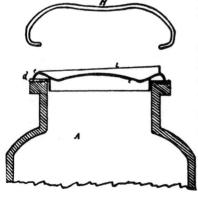

1866, July 10

Patent No. 56,266 by Josee Johnson of New York City

The ramp-circle was larger in this design, but still small, since the jar shown was almost a bottle, and the lid was a stopper. A groove ran around the jar at the finish. It fitted a large diameter wire yoke, which was placed in position across the low point of the ramps, and then lowered, using the position on the ramps as a fulcrum, until the ends of the yoke entered the groove. The yoke or the lid could then be turned until the yoke rode up the ramps and was tight. A feature was that the ramps rose from either direction, so that tightening could also be made in either direction.

1868, April 21

Patent No. 76,915 by Alexander J. H. Hilton of Boston, Mass.

Hilton's ramps described a wide circle on top of the lid. The yoke was of heavy sheet metal, cut quite squarely, and fitted under a square-cut finish bead.

1870, March 1

Patent No. 100,396 by Joel Haines of West Middleburg, Ohio

Haines started out with the grooved sealing surface that typifies his jars, but with a formed metal lid with a ramp on top. He soon changed to a glass lid. The yoke was first a wire, but that, too, was changed to a flat metal yoke. Both yokes hooked under the finish with its square ledge profile.

1875, June 22

Patent No. 164,663 by D. E. Stevens and R. F. Lumley of Newark, Ohio

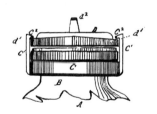

When the lid was rotated, the ends of two strap-like hooks fastened to the jar neck traveled up a sloping ramp on the lid, in either direction. The lid was notched to pass the hooks in applying the lid to the jar.

1886, April 20

Patent No. 340,428 by Joseph L. and Edward A. de Steiger of La Salle, Ill.

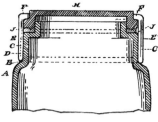

The de Steigers brought out the first and only ramp design in which the ramps were on the side of the lid. Their jar also was the only one in which the yoke did not extend over the top of the lid. Instead, its main body was a half circle that fitted into a circular groove around the neck of the jar, with two wings extending upward to where they hooked over the edge of the ramps.

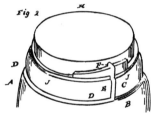

1896, December 29

Patent No. 574,306 by Joseph L. de Steiger of La Salle, Ill.

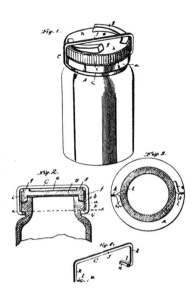

In this, the COLUMBIA jar, Joseph de Steiger returned the ramps to the top of the lid. The yoke, of wire square-shaped in cross-section, crossed over the top, down on two sides to below the beaded neck, then under the bead with a short length of wire along the bead to give better movement. The lid was knurled as a gripping feature.

Johnson & Johnson also used this jar for their sterile bandages for several years.

Plain lugs with a helical yoke or cap

Activity in this design was early—and short. It produced two of the most complicated, graceful almost to the point of being futuristic, and rarest closures in the fruit-jar field. One probable reason for the short life was the tendency to scratch the lugs, which would be difficult to blow thick in any event and which would break easily.

These remarks do not apply to the final entry in this group since it was designed for metal-to-metal contact, and came later in years.

1859, June 28

Patent No. 24,566 by William D. Ludlow of New York City

While adapted chiefly for cans, the principle could be used equally well on jars. The lugs were plain—the yoke was slanted on the ends.

1859, October 20

The BURNHAM jar, made to Fridley & Cornman's patent had a heavy cast-iron cap which had an inside screw thread which fitted two bulbous lugs on the neck of the jar. The seal was on the ground lip of the jar. There was no protection of the contents from the metal of the cap.

1861, August 6

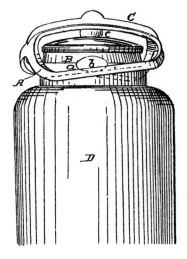

Patent No. 33,002 by William D. Ludlow of New York City

While the NE PLUS ULTRA jar of Bodine & Brothers of Williamstown, N.J., showed both this patent and that of Ludlow of June 28, 1859 (above), only the latter really applied. There were two plain lugs on the neck and a very graceful cage-like yoke holding the glass lid. The yoke crossed over the center of the glass lid, with a hollow fitting a raised portion of the lid. At the ends of this part of the yoke, two arms branched off to opposite sides. Each formed a slanting arm, joining the opposite yoke end with a long curving slant as a helix.

1862, October 7

Patent No. 36,612 by John F. Griffen of New York City

Griffen and Ludlow must have been associates, since Griffen's patent follows the details of the Ludlow patent with respect to jar lugs, most of the lid details, and the cage-yoke details with one exception. Instead of the cross-arm passing over the top of the glass lid, the yoke had from one to three short arms from the slanting portion toward the top of the lid. (The design pressed on the top center with a single arm rather than a yoke.) The object was to give a spring action in these arms and thus prevent glass breakage from too much pressure. Griffen freely refers to these shortcomings on the part of the Ludlow design with its single massive yoke.

1868, September 1

Patent No. 81,585 by Lewis F. Betts of Chicago, Ill.

The device was primarily designed for use with cans, being a metal top, open at the center for a helical-yoke-type stopper, which caught below two lugs at the opening. An alternate lid design was tapered for use with jars.

The Toggles

A toggle is an engineering term for a linkage of at least two elements, which present three fulcrums or centers of force. When these three centers are brought into proper alignment, they exert extreme pressure. By just passing centers, and with a design that prevents further movement, the toggle can be arranged to close securely, and lock, a device such as a fruit-jar seal.

Toggles were used in at least four types of fruit-jar seals: snap locks for hinged covers, the LIGHTNING closure series, the EVERLASTING jars of Abramson, and the twin toggles of KIVLAN.

The toggle with the hinged lid

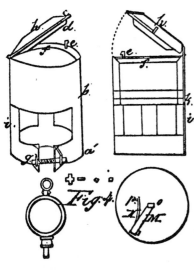

1868, June 16

Patent No. 78,976 by Leander Lehman of Harrisburg, Pa.

Strictly speaking, this first of the hinged lids was not a pure toggle, but it led to their use. Adapted first to beverage bottles, it consisted of a ring that was permanently fastened to the neck of the bottle. A hinge connected the ring or sleeve to the movable lid, and a spring catch snapped it in place. A rubber face on the lid sealed the contents, since the lid bore directly on the glass mouth of the bottle or jar.

1877, December 18

Patent No. 198,439 by William G. Whitman of Chicago, Ill.

The hinged lid was fastened to the jar by a heavy wire that was anchored in a slanting groove, so as to place its lower end well down on the neck. A smaller wire extended from the larger wire, acting as a hinge at the fastening, then crossed over the top of the metal lid, to which it was secured at the center, and across to the other side, where it served as a hinge for a short lever. The lever was hollowed at the end to fit over the low-placed neck wire, and when the lever was depressed to the bottom, it tightened the seal. The lever was locked in position by coming against the side of the jar.

1882, October 24

Patent No. 266,375 by Anton Luger of Vienna, Austria

This has already been mentioned as an all-glass lid. The strap metal bail was hinged on one side, secured to the glass lid by a bolt that went all the way through to the inside, and was held by a lever of strap metal on the other side.

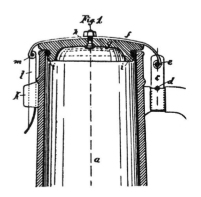

The LIGHTNING series of toggles

This not only includes the LIGHTNING closure itself and the jar which bore that name (both trade marked as such) but subsequent variations that left the principle unchanged. The references start with the beverage bottle from which the fruit-jar seal was modified.

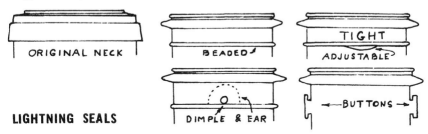

1875, January 5

Patent No. 158,406 by Charles de Quillfeldt of New York City

This patent covered all the basic details. The seal was composed of a neck tie-wire, a lever wire, and a bail. The bail passed through a hole in the metal, rubber faced, lid. The lever wire was hooked into loops in the heavy neck tie-wire on opposite sides of the

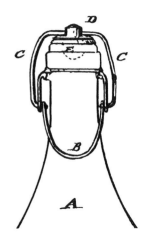

bottle. Movement of the lever wire past the line of centers of force was stopped by the neck of the bottle.

1877, July 5

A report that de Quillfeldt was issued a patent for a wide-mouth LIGHTNING, which became the fruit-jar seal, was not verified as being a patent date. However, it is known that LIGHTNING fruit jars were made about this time with the looped neck tie-wires, changed in the patent that follows, by Putnam.

1882, April 25

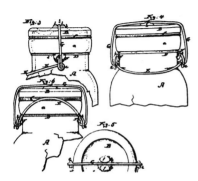

Patent No. 256,857 by Henry W. Putnam of Bennington, Vt.

Considered by many as the original LIGHTNING fruit-jar patent, this called for metal pieces to serve as fulcrums for the lever wire. The bail passed over the top of the glass lid and was centered by two raised dots.

1882, July 11

Patent No. 260,850 by Charles de Quillfeldt of New York City, and assigned to Henry Putnam of New York City

Putnam did not use this idea for fruit jars. The chief feature was a cam lever on a wire bail. The cam lever was on top of the seal, which was of rubber, and pressed downward.

1882, July 11

Patent No. 260,851 by Charles de Quillfeldt of New York City, and assigned to Henry Putnam of New York City

This patent for beverage bottles differs only slightly from Patent No. 260,850 of the same date.

1894, day unknown

Hero jars have been found with a modified Lightning seal. The date has been given as 1894 and 1895 but I have been unable to verify the date or the fact of a patent. The design differs in that the bail brings pressure in two places on the outside edge of the lip, instead of at the center. The lever wire was changed to a "squared" appearance. Canton also made this jar. Either Canton or Hero may have licensed the rights from the other.

1895, day unknown

This also has been quoted as a Hero Lightning date.

1908, July 14

The patent was not found. Ball and Hazel Atlas disclaim it. The change was the elimination of the neck tie-wire, and the substitution of a "dimple" or depression in the glass of the neck, into which the lever wire hooked. Other patents, in the hand-blowing days, had tried to use a dimple but in vain. Canton, in its DOMESTIC was the first to be successful, in the 1890s.

1910-15, circa

The ADJUSTABLE LIGHTNING seal was made about this time in Canada and by Smalley. The tie-wire was left loose on the neck so that it could be freely rotated on the neck. The tie-wire was placed below a bead which had a slight thickening on its lower side on opposite sides of the neck, identified by the word "TIGHT." When the fulcrums were turned to this point the distance to the top of the lid was greater and the seal would be tighter than when the fulcrums were elsewhere.

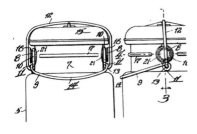

1920, September 7

Patent No. 1,352,119 by Leo A. Drey of St. Louis, Mo., and James L. Hiett of Sapulpa, Okla., assigned to Schram Glass Manufacturing Co. of St. Louis, Mo.

Drey and Hiett replaced the indented dimple with a knob (or buttons) on either side of the neck. The lever wire had a large loop that fitted into a groove in the boss.

The EVERLASTING toggles of Abramson

1886, March 30

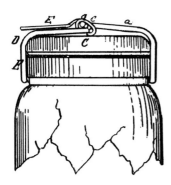

Patent No. 339,083 by Hermann Buchholz of Pittsburgh, Pa.

Although Edward Abramson is credited with the first of the "over-the-top" toggles, he was preceeded by another patent of similar form. The chief difference was that the looped wires were held at the neck of the jar by being hooked over squared lugs.

1904, November 29

Patent No. 776,162 by Edward Abramson of San Francisco, Cal.

This simple toggle had two hooked wire loops that fastened under the beaded finish, but rested on top of the glass jar lid. The lever had an eye on each end, looped to receive the hooked ends of one clamp end, and two more that received the hooks, about one third of the way up the lever, of the other clamp end. By pressure downward on the free end of the lever, the "line of centers" passed and locked the seal. When locked, the top profile was flat.

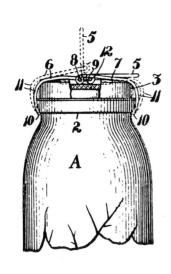

1905, August 22

Patent No. 797,711 by Edward Abramson and
Edward O. Bennett of San Francisco, Cal.,
with Bennett assigning his share to Abramson

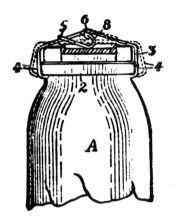

This is, strictly speaking, a cam lever and
not a toggle. The side clamps were hooked
into the cam lever at the same point. Moving
the cam lever raised the ends of the clamp
wires and tightened the entire assembly.
When locked, the profile was tent-shaped.

Abramson and Bennett, through the Illinois Pacific Glass Company, brought out an
IMPROVED EVERLASTING, with a ten-
sided pint and a fourteen-sided quart jar with
the new design, but since the lid was the
same and the clamping device interchangeable, all combinations of toggle or cam lever
with either jar are found. The interchangeable lids carried the first patent date in 1904,
and the 1905 date or both with the later design, so they must not be used as an identification of the patent used on any given jar.

The KIVLAN series of twin toggles

John L. Kivlan was issued three patents for very similar seals.
All were based on a neck tie-wire to which toggles or snap clips
were hinged. These elements rose to the edge of a glass lid,
over which they hooked. Since the lids are interchangeable, all
combinations are found by collectors.

1909, February 23

Patent No. 913,214 by John L. Kivlan of Boston, Mass.

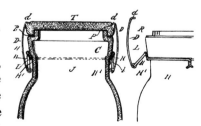

John L. Kivlan was a partner in Smalley,
Kivlan & Onthank. His first toggles had three
elements, the extra one serving only to space
the toggle outward from the bulge on the
neck that formed the finish and below which

the tie-wire anchored. The glass lid had a simple ledge over which the toggle hooked.

The jar finish was so near like the old LIGHTNING design that without toggles it could be mistaken for it. Furthermore, Smalley, Kivlan & Onthank could, and did, use the same jar for their LIGHTNING closure. Even the glass lids were exchanged. It is not unusual to find a LIGHTNING seal on a jar that has the Kivlan twin toggle patent date on the bottom. This Kivlan design was used on the QUEEN, MAGIC, and WEARS jars.

1921, June 28

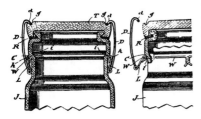

Patent No. 1,383,215 by John L. Kivlan of Boston, Mass.

This patent eliminated the extra member by using a smaller bead above the tie-wire. The outer member, now a wire loop, hooked into a groove on the top edge of the glass lid. Kivlan was now a senior partner in Kivlan & Onthank, successors to Smalley, Kivlan & Onthank in 1919. This design was used on MAGIC jars.

1929, April 2

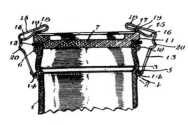

Patent No. 1,707,439 by John L. Kivlan of Roslindale, Mass.

In this patent, granted after Kivlan & Onthank had been dissolved, the toggle was replaced by a simple snap design. Jars with it have been found with the Crown Cork & Seal name on the bottom.

The VICTORY jar by Smalley, Kivlan, and Onthank, later by Kivlan & Onthank and finally by the Crown Cork & Seal Company used all three Kivlan patents, during its long life as a name.

Spring Bails

While a "bail" usually means a carrying handle, its use here is that of a simple wire member usually, but not always, fastened to the jar by some sort of trunnion or bearing that permits movement as though with a hinge. Exceptions are in three instances where the bail was secured to the jar by passing through a groove on the bottom of the jar. In fruit-jar sealing, the bail had the function, through spring action, of holding the glass or other lid in place.

1867, March 26

Patent No. 63,193 by B. B. Wilcox of New Haven, Conn.

Wilcox's bail was of heavy sheet metal, held to the jar by a split trunnion at the neck. It passed over a knob that was part of the glass lid. The knob was perforated, and a bit of rubber was placed between the knob and the rubber as a seal. Unfortunately, Wilcox sealed his jar on the ground lip, so that the seal would not hold a vacuum.

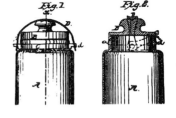

1883, July 31

Patent No. 282,188 by James Gilberds of Jamestown, N.Y.

This is the first of Gilberds' two patents in which the wire bail passed completely around the jar, being secured at the bottom by a groove across the bottom of the jar. The spring-wire bail was bowed slightly outward, so that it would stretch taut when applied. The glass lid had a single groove across the top to lock the bail. Gilberds also sealed on the ground lip. He also added a second bail for carrying.

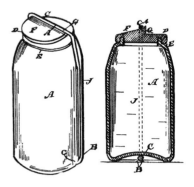

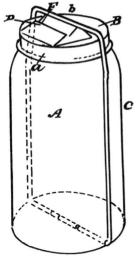

1885, October 13

Patent No. 328,115 by James Gilberds of Jamestown, N.Y.

Gilberds' second patent retained the bail just as in his first patent and in the same form. The change was the placing of a second notch on top of the glass lid, below the top notch, for the purpose of allowing easier venting during the boiling operation of canning.

A second part of this patent, using the same glass lid, was for a shorter bail which was to be hooked into two dimples, or non-perforated indentations into the side wall, about half way up the jar. This could not be made into glass, so Gilberds resorted to a neck band, similar in function to the LIGHTNING tie-wire, into which he hooked the ends of the bail. To compensate for the shorter radius he had to make a rising wing on the glass lid. He called this design THE DANDY.

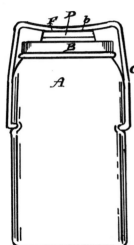

1887, March 29

Patent No. 360,165 by Lewis P. R. LeCompte of Portland, Ore.

The design used on the PERFECTION was very like THE DANDY except that there were two bails, parallel and about an inch apart. The rising wing over the glass lid was serrated instead of notched. The patent called for dimples in the neck, but again the inability of hand glassblowing to make them properly resulted in a change to a banded neck, with holes in the band serving as fulcrums for the bail.

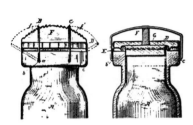

Jars have been found with the same construction, but with only one bail. A feature of the patent drawing was a circular sharp bead in the sealing surface, designed to give extra compression to the rubber ring.

1889, December 31

Patent No. 418,266 by David Barker of Canton, Ohio, assigned to the Canton Glass Company of the same place

This became the first successful dimple neck design. Its single bail had an ox-bow loop on each side in order to give it spring action. The glass lid had a high, raised wing, notched at the top only. The jar is known as the CANTON DOMESTIC.

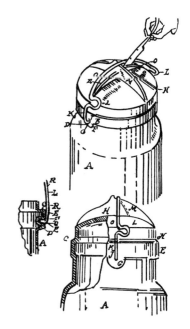

1902, July 15

Patent No. 704,873 by George H. Fox of Bangor, Me.

Not primarily for fruit-jar use, the design was an all-around-the-jar loop of wire as in the Gilberds jar, with a carrying handle. Two full loops, one on each side, gave spring action for tightening.

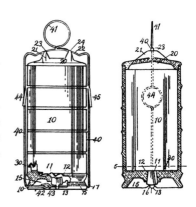

Spring Clips

The spring clip, either a wire or a narrow flat metal strip, was the simplest of all sealing methods after the stopper. All employed a loose lid, either of glass or metal, and all used a beaded neck, either rounded or with a squared edge, and usually continuously around the lip of the bottle without any suggestion of helix formation. Seal was made by sliding the spring clip into place, flexing it by hand in order to accomplish this. There were many versions of the spring clip, both in wire and flat metal.

1859, June 28

Patent No. 24,566 by William D. Ludlow of New York City

There were two lugs on the top of the can or jar, on opposite sides of the opening, with a notch or channel on the side toward the opening. The cap was in three pieces: a circular metal disk forming the top seal with a rubber ring following the circle of its circumference; a domed circle on top of it, serving in part as a spring and in part to equalize the downward pressure; and a rotatable spring yoke which had to be pressed down at the ends to enter the jar notches, thus giving pressure on the seal. The yoke was riveted to the dome at the center.

1861, June 18

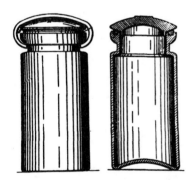

Patent No. 32,594 by John M. Whitall of Philadelphia, Pa.

The jar finish was a pressed lip with a squared groove on top for a rubber ring with a square cross-section. The glass lid was massive, and so was the spring clip which hooked under a rounded finish bead.

Whitall was senior partner in Whitall-Tatum & Co., of Millville New Jersey. They used this patent date on the MILLVILLE ATMOSPHERIC rather than the true date for the patent followed, thereby dating the jar a year earlier then it should have been. The MILLVILLE ATMOSPHERIC was made to Patent No. 36,853, of Nov. 4, 1862.

1861, December 17

Patent No. 33,938 by N. S. Gilbert of Lockport, N.Y.

The feature of this design was an elaborate yoke, of which each end split into two prongs curved down and under a beaded finish. The bead had two gaps through which the prongs of the yoke could pass when applying it into position. A lock above the center of the yoke, as part of the glass lid, held the yoke in place.

1862, August 5

Patent No. 36,131 by William Zettle of Cincinnati, Ohio

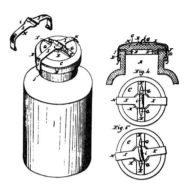

The spring yoke was a flat strap of metal, hooking under a squared-finish ledge. The center of the yoke was a domed arch. Two raised buttons on the glass lid served as safety catches—the yoke would be slid into place, in line with the buttons, then be given a slight turn so as to bring the buttons out of line with the dome.

1862, August 19

Patent No. 36,264 by Henry S. Fisher of Newburg, Pa.

The spring clip was hinged on one side, and held on the other like the clip on a safety pin.

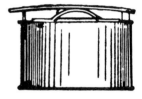

The first friction side seal covered by this same patent is discussed in the section "Friction-held Cover Caps."

1868, January 28

Patent No. 73,846 by Charles F. Spencer of Rochester, N.Y.

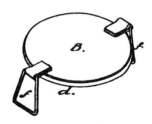

A loop fastened by a hinge on either side of the metal lid was sprung into place on a notched ear (almost impossible glassmaking) until it snapped into place. Advantages were claimed for sealing with rubber rings that were not uniformly thick, and on finishes not ground flat. This means that it sealed on the ground lip.

With a vacuum holding the lid tight, the loops could be turned upward to fit a bar or

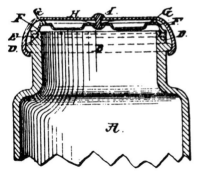

wrench so that extra pressure could be applied upwards from the top and break the vacuum.

1868, July 28

Patent No. 80,296 by W. W. Lyman of West Meriden, Conn.

Lyman used a metal cap, to the center of which was riveted a flat band-type spring clip. The ends of the clip hooked under the squared-finish bead.

1869, December 14

Patent No. 97,920 by D. Irving Holcomb of Henry County, Iowa

In contrast to the PROTECTOR, Holcomb used a loose spring clip, centered in place by the space between twin raised portions of the metal lip on opposite sides of the top of the metal lid. The lid fitted into a groove, and could be used either as a wax sealer or with a rubber ring for sealing. The jar was the McCully DICTATOR D.

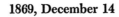
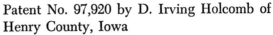

1884, September 2

Patent No. 304,449 by Herman Pietsch of Flatbush, N.Y.

The spring clip fitted the depressed top of the glass lid very similar to Dunkley's design of 1898 (14 years later). Probably the patentable differences were that the Pietsch design provided notches in the lid to prevent sidewise slippage and also provided a tabbed end to the clip for easy removal. Dunkley's design depended on sidewise slippage for removal. It became the successful jar.

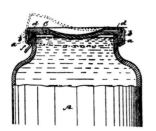

1886, May 4

Patent No. 341,341 by James McMillan of Allegheny, Pa.

McMillan's sealing device could be classified either as a spring clip or a friction side seal. [It is listed in "Friction-held Cover Caps" also.] The sealing portion of the neck is described as being a true vertical, with a flat groove to hold the rubber sleeve. The cap, either metal or glass as mentioned, is also formed with a true vertical at the seal. A clip is used to hold the two together during the cook and until a vacuum has been developed.

1888, March 27

Patent No. 380,091 by George D. Corey of Lowell, Mass.

The spring clip was a deformed loop that crossed over the center of the glass lid, being held in proper position by notches. The lower part of the loop wedged beneath the outwardly flared neck of the jar.

1893, July 11

Patent No. 501,418 by Franz Guilleaume and Ewald Goltstein of Bonn, Germany

The slightly sloping finish held a round rubber band in a groove. The lid could be either metal or glass, and fitted the same slope, stepwise at the rubber-ring contact, so as to deform the rubber for better seal. A wire spring clip, formed into three downward projections to clip under the squared finish, held the lid in place.

This patent became the EASY VACUUM. Goltstein appears again as the inventor of the heat-softening compound principle used in the ECONOMY jar.

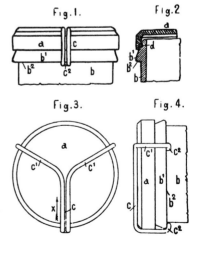

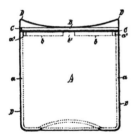

1898, April 19

Patent No. 602,791 by Ludwig Wurzburg of London, Eng.

Wurzburg's spring clip passed almost completely around the jar, clipping beneath the upwardly dished center of the bottom of the jar, but not crossing the center bottom. The strap then passed upward along the sides of the jar to a height above the edges of the glass lid, so that the center at the top could be bent downward to touch only the center-top of the lid.

1898, September 20

Patent No. 610,897 by Samuel J. Dunkley of Kalamazoo, Mich.

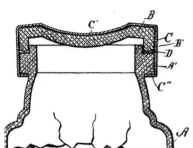

This design is notable chiefly by the reversed spring action required. Unattached, the spring flares outward. Since it fits the curve of the glass lid in such a way as to cause the lid to press upward in the center portion of the spring clip, this forces the ends of the clip inwardly, until they grip under the squared-finish bead.

This became the DUNKLEY JAR, used by the Dunkley Preserving Company, of Kalamazoo, Mich. The Illinois Glass Co. sold the DUNKLEY JAR in several versions as a general preserving jar, and under that name, about 1906.

1899, February 14

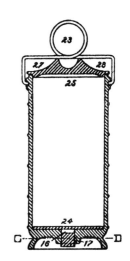

Patent No. 619,554 by George H. Fox of Bangor, Me.

A clip, looped at the top as a carrying handle, hooked into two slots in the neck of the jar. Fox probably abandoned this idea since the success of this ice-cream mold, which often appears in fruit-jar collections, depended on a smooth inner bore. Its 1902 replacement is classified as a fixed bail and spring.

1900, January 2

Patent No. 640,182 by Irvin P. Doolittle of Toronto, Ont., Canada

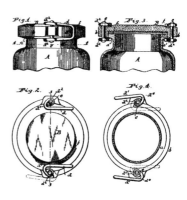

Two vertically pierced lobes extended horizontally on either side of the glass lid. A spring clip, like an enlarged paper clip, was secured to each ear by a pin that was riveted at each end. Moved toward the jar, they pinched the lid and beaded jar finish together as a seal, from either side.

In light of his several immediately following patents, this arrangements was not satisfactory—possibly because of breakage in assembly and in riveting.

1900, June 12

Patent No. 651,500 by Irvin P. Doolittle of Toronto, Ont., Canada

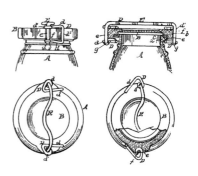

In his next patent, Doolittle tried a crossbar, turned down as a pin on either end. The clips hinged to the pin were the same as the previous patent. This eliminated two riveting points, but was still unsatisfactory.

1901, March 19

While the patent bearing this date, covering the PREMIER COFFEEVILLE, has not yet been found, the jar is new enough that many are found intact with their seals. It is seen as a spring clip, entering from the side of the covered jar, and so constructed that the clip holds the glass lid and the jar top together with a spring action. This allows the jar to vent during the cook, but holds the lid tightly enough that a vacuum will form and further hold the lid on the jar.

1901, April 30

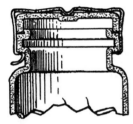

Patent No. 673,048 by Samuel J. Dunkley of Kalamazoo, Mich., was apparently not as successful as his Patent No. 610,897 of Sept. 20, 1898. It should have been easier to handle, since it had a small tab on one end of the spring clip, which would have facilitated removal. The patent shows three alternate forms for the spring clip, and as many for the glass lid.

Dunkley was a food packer with a bent for jar design, for he received several patents. The Illinois Glass Company, of Alton, Ill., was still advertising the Dunkley fruit jar in its 1906 catalog.

1901, December 3

Doolittle shows this date on his jars and lids, but the patent was not found.

1901, December 24

Patent No. 680,543 by Irvin Parker Doolittle of Toronto, Ont., Canada

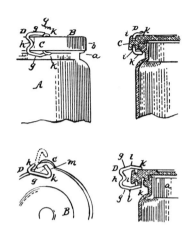

In this design, Doolittle abandons the riveted construction and, instead, merely squeezes the clips so that their ends enter the holes (now going only part way through the ears on the glass lid). The same method of using the clips is used as in the previous patents. In this last patent, Doolittle freely discusses the shortcomings of his earlier efforts: the weakening effect of the hole in the glass lid; the breakage in assembly; the cost of previous designs; and the detraction from good appearance.

1903, June 9

Patent No. 730,760 by Ewald Goltstein of Cologne, Germany, assignor to Julius A. Landsberger of Alameda, Cal.

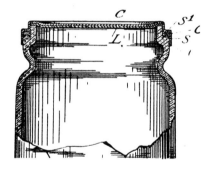

Goltstein here introduced the concept of a sealing compound that would soften under the application of heat, so that it would adapt itself to minor irregularities in the finish of the jar and, to some extent, flow down the side between the skirt of the cap and the side of the finish, so as to give some side grip. The jar cap was a metal lid, flat on top and with a small vertical flange around the edge. For some reason he did not include any means to hold the lid on the jar during the cook and while cooling, such as a spring clip as he did in the July 11, 1893, patent EASY VACUUM jar. Landsberger covered that in a patent applied for on the same date and granted two weeks later. (See below.)

Alexander H. Kerr secured the fruit-jar rights for this jar and named it the ECONOMY. Kerr also used the Landsberger patent following.

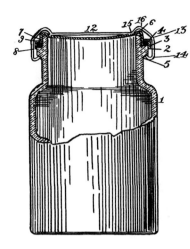

1903, June 23

Patent No. 731,793 by Julius A. Landsberger of Alameda, Cal.

Landsberger supplied the spring clip needed for Goltstein's patent of June 9, 1903. Together they supplied the design for Kerr's ECONOMY jar and Hazel Atlas' commercial jar of the same design.

1909, August 10

Patent No. 930,481 and Patent No. 930,482 by Alexander H. Kerr of Portland, Ore.

These patents covered the makeup of a heat-softening sealing compound for the ECONOMY jar; the first including Balata, a gum, and a compounding material, and the second including Balata and a compounding material.

1929, April 2

Patent No. 1,707,439 by John L. Kivlan of Roslindale, Mass.

This patent converted Kivlan's former toggles into a spring-clip design, but with little other change in the appearance.

The Levers

This group includes most of those sealing devices in which the movement of a lever applies pressure to hold a lid against the sealing surface, the exception being chiefly the levers of the toggles which have already been described. These lever-operated seals may be divided into three classes:

The CAM LEVERS, in which the lever has a rounded end, and which is off-center in respect to the axis of rotation. The cam slides along the face of the jar lid, usually glass, as the distance between axis and the working area of eccentric changes, thus changing the pressure against the lid since the cam axis is fixed by a bail of wire or a yoke. The cam axis is parallel to the plane of the jar lid. Friction is usually a sufficient lock against accidental movement of the lever.

The SIMPLE LEVERS, in which a bar, with an axis or fulcrum either in the center of the lever or at one end, is moved to change the amount of pressure exerted against a lid of glass or metal. The device usually locks in position by crossing a "line of centers." The axis is in a plane parallel to that of the lid.

The CLUTCH LEVERS, on which the axis of rotation is vertical to the plane of the lid. Movement is gained against the lid by a ramp-like structure in the lever, which moves the lever sidewise along the axis of rotation.

Cam levers

1866, February 13

Patent No. 52,525 by F. A. Bunnell of Syracuse, N.Y.

The device had several original features. The yoke was of heavy metal, with curving ends that hooked under a finish bead that was a helical ramp on its under side. The yoke was placed on the jar at the "loose" position on the helix, then rotated with respect to the jar until the helix brought the yoke into contact with the raised center of the lid. At this point the yoke had a simple cam lever which could be rotated on its axis, a pin through the yoke, until the seal was tight. Used on the EMPIRE jar.

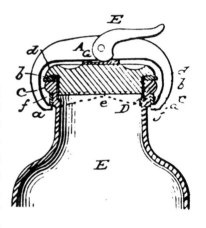

1866, June 5

Patent No. 55,248 by Reuben M. Dalbey of Springfield, Ohio

This seal embodied a yoke with the cam lever attached. The jar, with its helical yokes serrated on the under side, has been seen in several collections, but not with its perishable yoke and metal lid.

1880, May 25

The best-known early cam-lever seal is the GLOBE. The patent could not be found. The top of the glass lid had a hemispherical seat for a matching cam at the end of a short lever. The lever was held by a bail wire from a neck tie-wire. The hemisphere nicely solved the problem of sidewise movement or wobble.

1885, March 17

Patent No. 314,109 by William H. Clarke of Olean, N.Y., assignor of one half to Thomas W. Larsen of Bolivar, N.Y., and Mrs. M. A. Tack of New York City

The Clarke lever was of stamped, formed sheet-metal, one end of which was circular, with the axis of rotation near one side. The lever was held by a bail from a split trunnion around the neck. Pressure was against the center of the glass lid.

Clarke, who was manager of a store in Olean, N.Y., moved to Cleveland, Ohio, before the patent was issued and became manager of the Boston Store there. He built his factory in 1886 to make the fruit jar, but it lasted for only two years. The Cleveland City Directory indicates that he continued to manage the Boston Store while he also managed the factory, and continued to do so after it failed.

1892, June 28

Patent No. 477,955 by Robert I. Patterson of Muncie, Ind.

The design was very simple. The lever was a loop of wire over the lid, the ends of which described a half-circle, which was the cam, before being hooked into the "eyes" of the

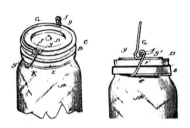

neck wire. The latter was a half-circle loop which was pushed under the squared-finish ledge, with the ends rising to the "eyes" at the level of the top of the jar lid.

When the lever was in the "open" position the glass lid could be slipped into its position from the side. Another method was to place the glass lid in position and then enter the wire assembly from the side. In either event, the seal was then tightened by rotating the lever wire from one side to the other so that it rode upward on its cam. The device was used on the LEADER fruit jar.

1895, January 29

Patent No. 533,282 by Samuel J. Dunkley of Kalamazoo, Mich.

This was Dunkley's first effort, and involved a double cam lever held by a wire yoke that hooked into dimples on the side of the neck. Since this was difficult to blow by hand, it was probably abandoned in favor of his spring-clip idea already described.

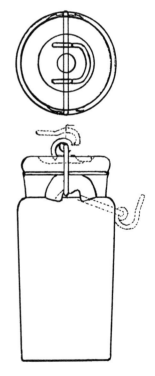

1895, May 21

Patent No. 539,674 by Henry C. Dilworth of East Orange, N.J.

The most famous cam lever was used on the SAFETY VALVE jar, which was made for about 35 years. It was also the most

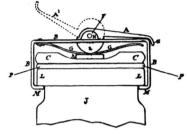

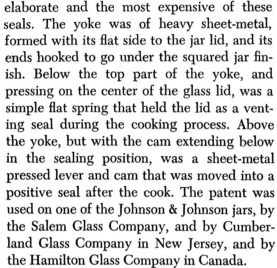

elaborate and the most expensive of these seals. The yoke was of heavy sheet-metal, formed with its flat side to the jar lid, and its ends hooked to go under the squared jar finish. Below the top part of the yoke, and pressing on the center of the glass lid, was a simple flat spring that held the lid as a venting seal during the cooking process. Above the yoke, but with the cam extending below in the sealing position, was a sheet-metal pressed lever and cam that was moved into a positive seal after the cook. The patent was used on one of the Johnson & Johnson jars, by the Salem Glass Company, and by Cumberland Glass Company in New Jersey, and by the Hamilton Glass Company in Canada.

1899, December 19

Patent No. 639,559 by Rimmon H. Hansee of Monticello, N.Y.

The HANSEE jar was sealed by a twisted wire yoke, held at the ends by a projection from a tie-wire around the neck. Unfortunately it sealed on the ground surface, which would not maintain a vacuum-tight seal.

1905, August 22

Patent No. 797,711 by Edward Abramson and Edward O. Bennett of San Francisco, Cal.

As stated under "Toggles" the original EVERLASTING toggle was changed to a cam lever after one year, as the IMPROVED EVERLASTING jar.

Simple levers

All of the simple levers were bent levers, with a pressure arm roughly at right angles to the handle of the lever. They are, nonetheless, levers. They were shaped to bring the handle in an appropriate position when sealed. Many of them sealed by a crossing of the "line of centers" as in a toggle, which they closely resembled.

1877, March 6

Patent No. 188,135, by Thomas Hipwell of Bridgeton, N.J., assignor to the Cohansey Glass Manufacturing Co. of the same place

Hipwell's was a beverage-bottle seal, but it is included because it foreshadowed the fruit-jar use. The stopper was closely like the LIGHTNING seal except for the lever action. This lever was secured near its center by a wire bail. The bent end pressed on the top of the lid when the lever was pressed down into contact with the neck of the bottle. At this location the position of the bent end of the lever was past the "line of centers" of force.

A feature of this invention was the hooking of the bail into any one of a series of holes in a metal strap-tie around the neck, and this may have influenced Putnam in his 1882 adoption of holes in small bits of metal for a similar purpose.

1885, March 24

Patent No. 314,332 by William F. Hannes of Oakland, Cal.

The Hannes' patent may have been the design for the WHEELER fruit jar made by the short-lived (two years) Campbell Glass Company, of Oakland, Cal. It had two spring-wire bent levers, rising from the neck tie-wire on opposite sides. They pressed on the high bead that was the circumference of the glass lid. Each lever had a hooked end. When the levers were depressed sufficiently, the hooks could be pushed under the opposing lever to secure the seal.

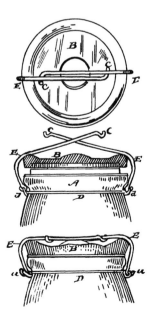

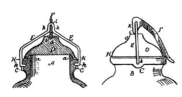

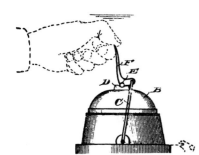

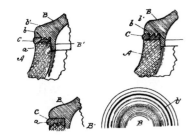

1892, March 1

Patent No. 469,985 by William Teamer (deceased; Rachel Teamer Administratrix), Evansville, Ind.

Teamers' seal was applied to the first WEIR jar in glass and pottery. The glass or ceramic lid had a high dome. A bail hooked into dimples or depressions in the neck held the lever. The pointed end pressed on the center of the lid when the lever was pressed down past the "line of centers" and against the wall of the neck.

1901, April 16

Patent No. 672,049 by William S. Weir of Monmouth, Ill.

Weir changed the lever greatly, probably because the older system of Teamer allowed wobbling on the point pressed against the center of the jar lid, thus making an uncertain seal which easily loosened. He changed the fulcrum, a hole through which the bail-wire passed, to one end. At the point of right-angle bend in the lever he passed a short bar, and rested its ends in two grooves on top of the lid. When the lever was pressed down to contact with the lid, the "line of centers" was passed, and the seal locked.

1903, June 9

Patent No. 730,500 by William S. Weir of Monmouth, Ill.

The only change in this over the preceeding patent was the incorporation of beaded surfaces, either in the sealing surface of the lid, or on the jar, or in both.

1903, June 23

Patent No. 731,690 by Edwin J. Kraetzer of Somerville, Mass.

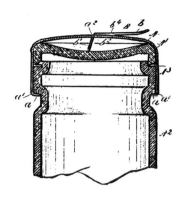

Kraetzer's invention was a bent simple lever of sheet-metal, affixed to a sheet-metal yoke. When moved to the sealing position it brought about pressure between the yoke and the center of the glass lid.

1904, June 7

Patent No. 762,080 by Hiram S. McConnel of New Brighton, Pa., assignor to Sherwood Brothers Company of New Brighton, Pa.

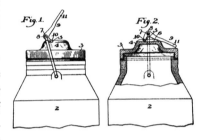

McConnel returned to the original lever design of Teamer in 1892. To stabilize the pointed end used by Teamer, he placed a bar across that end, similar to the Weir patent of 1901. In order to get clearance enough to insert the glass or pottery lid, he provided it with a high dome, grooved for the cross-bar.

Clutch levers

Only four designs used a lever in a horizontal position on an axis vertical to the top of the glass lid. The first was the earliest of all the levers, Gilbert's of 1861. The last two were by Monier in 1890 and 1895. They were remarkedly similar.

1861, January 29

Patent No. 31,235 by N. S. Gilbert of Lockport, N.Y.

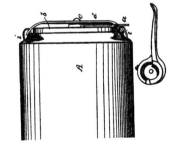

Gilbert used a flat metal yoke, secured at the neck of the jar. In the center of the yoke, secured by a pin, was a lever with a ramp that would move under the yoke in a manner to push it upward against the pressure of the under side of the lever in contact with the lid. The handle of the lever extended past the edge of the lid so that it could easily be moved to tighten or loosen the lid.

1884, April 15

Patent No. 297,082 by Phillip Lyon and Joseph H. Bossard of East Stroudsburg, Pa.

The feature of this patent was the clutch lever below the yoke, which, when rotated, would tighten the yoke against the lid when the yoke was compressed against the ramped disk of the wing-nut.

1890, April 1

Patent No. 424,720 by Fredrick and Elizabeth Monier of New Britain, Conn.

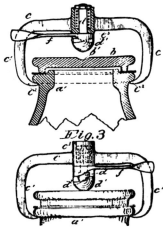

This very elavorate device, issued nearly thirty years after Gilbert's invention, had a heavy cast yoke, hooking under a finish bead. It had a central opening housing a spring-loaded and movable axle. It and the lever were fitted with matching ramps, so that moving the lever forced the axle, or ram, against the center of the glass lid. It was used on Barstow's SUN jar.

This construction is rarely found, as compared with the second Monier patent following.

1895, March 12

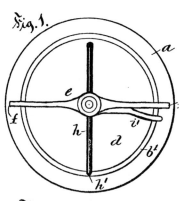

Patent No. 535,549 by Fredrick Monier, of New Britain, Conn., assignor to the Barstow Fruit Jar Company of New Jersey

The appearance and function is exactly like that of the 1890 patent just reviewed. The only change was the addition of a cross-bar which centered the yoke over the glass lid. This is the common jar found.

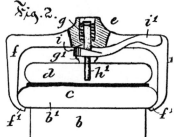

Friction-Held Cover Caps

This section is intended to include those patents and jars in which friction held the cap in place -aided by the vacuums produced on cooling after cooking. The greatest difficulty in the use of this idea was in keeping the cap in place while the jar held a slight positive pressure *during* the cook. Some inventors solved the problem by ignoring it.

This section does not include, by the use of the words "cover caps," that other area of friction sealing—the stopper, which is dealt with in its own section.

1862, August 19

Patent No. 36,264 by Henry S. Fisher of New-burg, Pa.

Among the several ideas covered by Fisher in one patent was a tapered cap and jar opening. He also provided the same cap with a thread in an alternate idea. Other ideas included spring yokes and clips more adaptable to cans.

1864, February 9

Patent No. 41,575 by Elbridge Harris of Boston, Mass., assignor to W. W. Lyman of West Meriden, Conn.

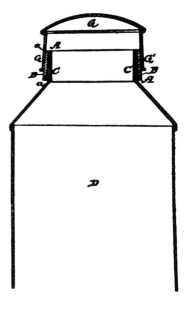

Harris' patent provides no other restraint than friction to hold the cap in place. The cap is shown as metal, dome-shaped, and with a very broad sealing surface on a tube-shaped ring of rubber.

In making the idea into glass, it was very important that the degree of taper and of roundness be carefully controlled. This was done by using a "dip mold" for the finish. After the jar was blown, the finish area was reheated, then thrust, neck first, into an iron mold which was perfectly round, and had the necessary taper. The jar was held there for a few moments until the glass conformed to the mold shape. The jar could be rotated if need be, and generally was.

The Harris patent has been found on some EUREKA and LAFAYETTE jars.

1864, December 27

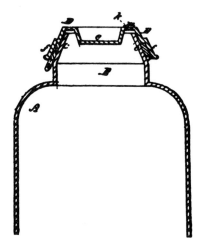

Patent No. 45,601 by John F. Griffen of New York City

This date has also been found on the EUREKA and LAFAYETTE jars. The patent drawing shows a greater angle, less adapted to friction holding, than in the Harris patent just described, and would have a greater tendency to pop off.

This patent is notable for one other idea, included elsewhere, under "Continuous screw-thread shoulder seals." This was the thumb-tab for grasping and removing the rubber sealing ring used in the Mason shoulder seal.

1886, May 4

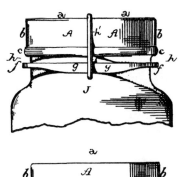

Patent No. 341,341 by James McMillan of Allegheny, Pa.

This seal has been described under "Spring clips" and is included here since it also was the only side-friction sealing device to have *vertical* side walls in the sealing area, a matter of which McMillan makes a strong point. It must have been impossible of venting during the cook—and what frustration in breaking the vacuum for its removal!

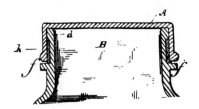

1900, July 17

Patent No. 653,840 by George Hale Brabrook of Taunton, Mass., assignor to the Reed & Barton Corporation of the same place

Essentially the closure was a domed metal lid, the outer circumference of which was turned back upon itself to form an annular groove, open toward the inside. Into this groove was placed the rubber ring or other sealing material. The lip of the jar was made slightly tapered as in the Harris and the Griffen patents.

1904, November 1

Patent No. 774,014 by Allen Furgason Wilson, of Clayton, N.J.

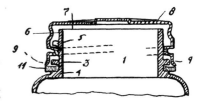

This invention was actually a combination of a friction side seal and lugs to hold the cap in place to prevent its "blowing off" during the cook.

Thumbscrews for Tightening Seals

The use of the thumbscrew as a device to tighten the seal on the fruit jar was a matter of a quick flurry, and then virtual disappearance, except for the cumbersome Van Vliet, and the revival as a museum jar by Whitall-Tatum.

1858, November 16

Patent No. 22,066 by Reuben M. Dalbey of Mount Washington, Ohio

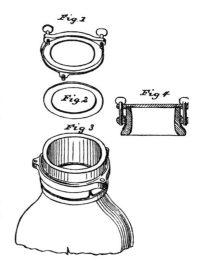

This first thumbscrew design actually used three screws. The lid was of metal, with three ears perforated for the screws. It held the rubber sealing ring, and sealed on the ground lip. A metal collar, with three matching ears threaded to receive the thumbscrew shanks, was slipped over the neck of the jar, and held in place by slipping a shim into a rounded depression, circular around the neck, in such a manner that the collar could not then be pulled off. It was used on the DALBEY jar.

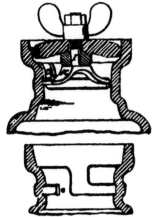

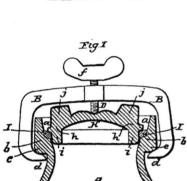

Fig. 1

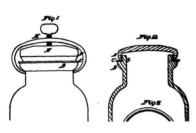

MOSPHERIC jar should be considered one year younger than the date on it. John M. Moore had already come out with his thumb-screw and stopper seal. Perhaps Whitall wanted some claim to priority.

The design was a close copy of the Moore design, except that the glass lid was a top seal. The yoke, carrying the thumbscrew at its center, hooked under a somewhat smaller bead on the lip of the jar. The jar finish was blown and ground instead of being pressed.

1870, April 12

Patent No. 101,958 by Theodore F. Woodward of Winslow, N.J., and assigned to Hay & Co. of Philadelphia, Pa.

Woodward's attempt to design a "yoke and thumbscrew" seal for the Winslow Glass Works has not been found in glass.

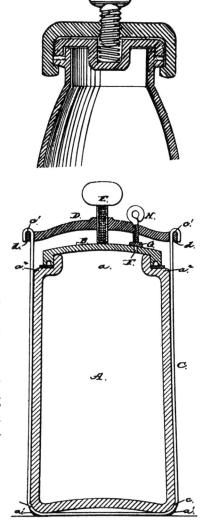

1881, May 3

Patent No. 241,095 by Warren R. Van Vliet of East Stroudsburg, Pa.

While this design introduced the use of a wire passing completely around the jar, being held in place at the bottom by a groove across the bottom, the tightening device was a yoke, fastened to the wire, and a thumb-screw. The lid differed from the MOORE by having two grooves to compress the sealing rubber. The jar was shown as having a metal lid, and a small vent-hole closed by a ring-headed thumbscrew.

1895, June 11

Patent No. 540,890 by Joseph Amia of Boston, Mass., assignor to the Whitall-Tatum Company of New York City (Millville, N.J.)

Amia's patent adapted the Otterson design to the use of ground surfaces as the seal.

Adaptations of this seal have also appeared as thumb-wheels, with the wheel below the yoke.

Rubber Bands as Fastening Devices

In addition to their use as a part of the hermetic seal itself, another use of rubber, in the form of small rubber bands, was that of holding the closure on the jar. In only one of the several such devices, a closure by John L. Mason, was the rubber band both a restraint on the seal and the seal itself, at the same time.

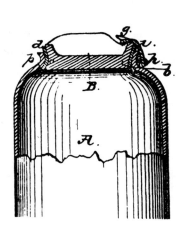

1868, September 1

Patent No. 81,856 by E. R. Williams of Rochester, N.Y.

Williams' closure was an unusual stopper. It hooked *under* the narrow part of the opening on one side, and down on that opening on the other. The hermetic seal was a rubber sleeve that was wide enough to cover the entire circular side of the slightly bowed-in stopper. The stopper had a hook on one side of the top—the jar had an opposing hook. A rubber band stretched between the hooks g and h held the stopper, while freely venting, from being blown out of place.

1869, January 19

Patent No. 85,932 by P. M. Hinman of Rochester, N.Y.

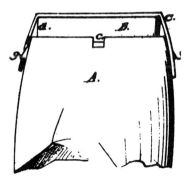

Hinman's use of rubber bands was simplicity itself. The jar had lugs to catch the rubber band on opposite sides of the neck. The rubber band c stretched from one lug g, over the glass lid top seal, and down to the other lug g. Another feature of the patent was that the inverted cup of the glass lid was placed into a deep groove, at the bottom of which was the sealing rubber. An opening into the groove on one side provided for breaking the vacuum with a pointed tool for easier opening.

1869, January 19

Patent No. 86,090 by John L. Mason of New York City

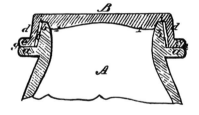

Issued the same day as Hinman's patent for a rubber-band lid holder, Mason employed the rubber sleeve as both seal and holding device, although he also used an internal rubber seal. The hermetic sealing rubber, g, was on a slanting surface almost as a friction side seal. The inverted cup of the lid, and a bead on the lip of the jar, matched each other in diameter and thickness. When a rubber sleeve was stretched to encircle them, its edges came back over the top of the ledge on the lid, and under the ledge on the jar. Since the entire assembly was on the jar during the process of sterilization, the outer rubber sleeve that held the lid and jar rim together would have sufficed, also, as a hermetic seal.

1877, June 5

Patent No. 191,519 by Catharine L. Darby of Fort Motte, S.C.

How to fit the rubber to the rest of the closure was no problem for Catharine L. Darby. She made the entire closure as one piece of rubber, stretched slightly for a tight fit, and extending over the mouth of the jar. The internal form of the rubber cap was molded as a hemisphere, forming a kind of stopper, held more tightly in place by the rest of the cap.

One-Use Seals

Two patents can best be classified as being for one-use or single-use sealing.

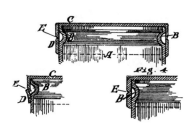

1878, December 17

Patent No. 211,011 by George L. Harrison, Jr., of Philadelphia, Pa.

The sealing compound was held in a groove. When the lid was placed over the groove and forced down, the skirt of the metal lid was deformed, entered the sealing compound, and locked into place.

1904, June 7

Patent No. 761,652 by Julius Brenzinger of New York City, assignor to the Max Ams Machine Co. of New York City

While this was for commercial canning, it could be used for home canning if the sealing machine were available. The closure consisted of a gasket and a metal lid. They were fastened by a partially preformed band which was placed in position and then secured by rolling down a flange that extended above the jar lid.

Protection of Contents

Most of the reasons for ideas for the protection of the contents of the jars arise from two causes—the taste that might be imparted by contact with metals, and the presence of air in the jar. In the case of air deterioration, venting was one answer, and holding the fruit or vegetables under the surface of the liquid was another.

Protection from metallic tastes

The earliest references were to metallic taste. Generally the answer was some kind of coating or the use of glass.

1856, February 12

Patent No. 14,245 by R. W. Lewis of Honesdale, Pa.

Lewis, in this first of all patents found concerning a screw cap, used two small plates of pure tin, covering the rubber sealing ring except where the rubber contacted the sealing surface.

1869, March 30

Patent No. 88,439 by *Lewis* R. Boyd of New York City, and

1869, May 11

Patent No. 89,845 by *Louis* R. Boyd of New York City (same man)

Boyd proposed a glass inner liner for the zinc cap used by Mason. It was gripped securely by rolling in the zinc at the top, so as to make the glass liner an integral part of the cap.

1871, July 18

Patent No. 117,236 by William Taylor and Charles Hodgetts of Brooklyn, N.Y., assignors to Louis R. Boyd of New York City

Taylor needed a liner for the Holz, Clark & Taylor screw-stopper fruit jar, but had to assign the patent to Boyd because of Boyd's patent.

1872, September 3 patent not found, and

1872, December 31

Patent No. 134,400 by Salmon B. Rowley of Philadelphia, Pa.

Using a glass inner lining, Rowley gave protection to the metal top-seal lid which he used interchangeably with the all-glass lid.

1877, June 5

Patent No. 191,519 by Catharine L. Darby of Fort Motte, S.C.

This device was a stretch cap of all-rubber, already mentioned under "Rubber bands as fastening devices."

1896, December 1

Patent No. 572,281 by Albert G. Smalley of Chelsea, Mass.

Smalley's patent concerned a glass liner for the zinc cap, which left a smaller space between the edge of the glass liner and the finish of the jar. At the same time he provided a vent to pass air through this space when opening, to break the vacuum.

Venting Air from the Jar

Most jars seals would vent air during the cook incidental to their primary function as sealing means. A few patents covered devices whose sole function was the removal of air. These are listed following.

1863, November 10

Patent No. 40,566 by Timothy Earle of Smithfield, R.I.

This first of three patents by Earle employed a lid perforated in the center, a "patch" and a yoke having on its under side a sort of clutch lever. When the yoke was rotated, with the patch in place over the vent, the clutch lever both tightened the cover on the jar, and sealed the opening.

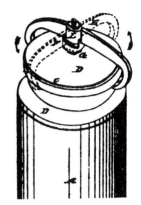

1863, December 22

Patent No. 40,966 by Timothy Earle of Smithfield, R.I.

In this idea, Earle used a clapper valve mounted on a metal cap. It was a slender spring, riveted to the cap at one end, and with the other end covering a small hole. A small rubber gasket allowed air to exit from the jar, as by the influence of heat, but not to return.

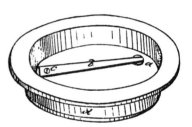

1864, February 2

Patent No. 41,425 by Timothy Earle of Smithfield, R.I.

This patent was similar to Earle's November 10, 1863, patent, except that a spring replaced the clutch lever, which Earle herein described as costly.

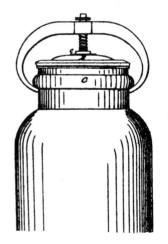

1864, June 21

Patent No. 43,232 by Harlow C. Smith of Chicago, Ill.

One of the more elaborate devices, the lid was a stopper. Its perforated center was covered by a rubber or leather flap valve. A hand pump could be applied to the top of the lid to pump the air out of the jar and create a vacuum.

1867, June 18

Patent No. 65,844 by W. H. Trissler of Cleveland, Ohio

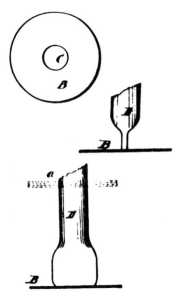

Trissler's was one of the most dangerous patents in the industry because he used lead in contact with food. He fastened a small lead tube over a hole in the top of the cap, then pumped the air out mechanically. When the vacuum was as complete as the pump could draw, he pinched the tube tightly near its junction with the lid, then cut the tube off, leaving a portion of the tube on the lid. Further, he claimed that by using his device the food need not be cooked!

1867, July 30

Patent No. 67,215 by Ebenezer Purdy of Ithaca, N.Y.

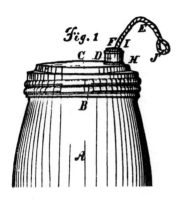

Fig. 1

In contrast to Trissler's dangerous device, Purdy's was only amusing. He provided a lid with a mouthpiece for *sucking* the air out. A short piece of string coming from the hole in the mouthpiece was connected to a cork or rubber stopper inside the jar. After sucking the air out, one was supposed to pull the string so as to wedge the cork into the opening from below. Purdy never solved the problem of taking hold of the string with one's hand while it was still in one's mouth, all the while sucking on the mouthpiece to maintain the small vacuum thus produced, nor the mechanics of wedging the stopper tightly enough to hold against the pressure of the atmosphere in the wrong direction!

1865, May 23, antedated December 6, 1864

Patent No. 47,834 by Charles G. Imlay of Philadelphia, Pa.

In Imlay's patent for one of the first, if not the first, top seal, he provided three versions of his seals with spring-loaded vents, and seven with small cork-sealed openings.

1904, January 5

Patent No. 749,074 by Hermann Martini of Riga, Russia

By far the most elaborate, and the most expensive, sealing device I have seen, Martini's method was to provide a diaphragm that would allow the jar to be completely filled with liquid. To maintain this condition, his valve, mounted in a dome on the top of the lid, would pass air outward, or even liq-uid, but would not pass air or liquid in-wardly. Several versions were shown, of which one had over a dozen separate parts.

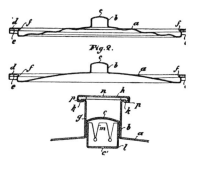

Fig. 2.

1930, August 19

Patent No. 1,773,311 by Dan Killen of Mil-waukee, Wis.

Killen used a perforated glass lid, whose attachment to the jar was immaterial to the patent, which he covered with a soft rubber "half-dome." Its action was one of slightly flattening against the glass lid as a vacuum developed within the jar as it cooled.

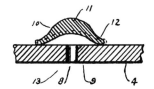

Protection from Air by Immersion

Anyone who has done home canning knows the dried-up and unwholesome appearance of fruit that has extended above the liquid level in the jar after it has been sealed and stored. The following devices recognized this condition early, and attempted to rectify it.

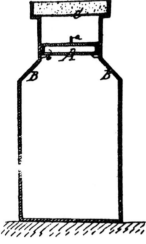

1869, December 7

Patent No. 97,588 by Thomas J. Bargis and John C. Underwood of Richmond, Ind.

The device was a simple round float of glass which could move within the straight-sided neck of the jar. It was prevented from dropping into the main body of the jar by ledges which were to be blown into the internal portion of the jar at the point where the straight neck joined the shoulder of the jar. It had just enough weight to sink slightly into the liquid, while holding the solid portion of the pack below the liquid line.

1875, November 23

Patent No. 170,172 by Elizabeth S. Hunt of Cleveland, Ohio

This first of two patents by Elizabeth S. Hunt, followed by one each by Andrew and Somerville, made up the Mason Disk Protector Cap as finally made by the Mason Fruit Jar Company after 1885. These patents represent the slow development of an idea.

In this first patent, the lid had a carrying arm fastened in the center of its under side. Hanging from it, but detachable, was another arm, with a plate of perforated metal of several designs, or shapes, which extended below the liquid level and forced the solid portion of the pack below the liquid level.

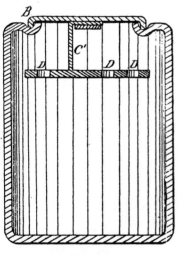

1876, September 12

Patent No. 182,119 by Elizabeth S. Hunt of Cleveland, Ohio

The second patent overcame the difficulties arising from the use of too much metal, by turning to ceramics. It was made from three parts: a ceramic disk that rested on the ground lip, the seal being on an external shoulder, a stem to connect this with the lower plate, and a lower plate that extended below the liquid level. The three were bolted together.

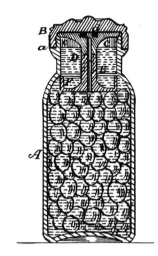

1880, November 30

Patent No. 234,842 by William E. Andrew of Jersey City, N.J.

This duplicated the second Hunt idea, except that it was of one piece, in ceramics or glass. It had an upper disk resting on the ground lip, a thin stem connecting the two disks, and a lower perforated disk. Its weakness was the long, small diameter stem which was easily broken.

In order to function, the disk had to be used with a jar having a long neck. This was accomplished by the use of a bead around the neck instead of on the shoulder, to serve as a sealing point for the Mason zinc cap. The bead idea did not work out with the hand blowing of that day, but reappeared on machine-made jars about 1910. The idea did result in the jar being lettered, when the Mason Fruit Jar Company began to make the jar, in the MASON PATENT NOV 30th 1880, considered by many to be a mistake in dating the mold.

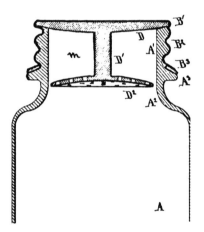

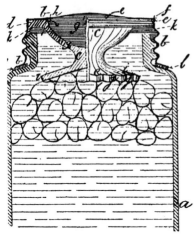

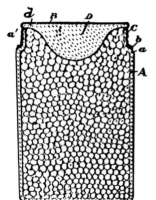

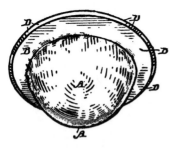

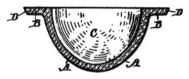

1886, July 20

Patent No. 345,999 by William Somerville of St. Louis, Mo.

This patent, still using the one-piece construction of Andrew, corrected the weakness of the long stem by making both plates in a domed form, leaving room for just a suggestion of a neck or stem. The whole design was dynamically rounded. The upper disk rested on the ground lip and the seal was on the usual Mason shoulder.

Evidently the Mason Fruit Jar Company, of Philadelphia, Pa., bought all four patents after they started business in 1885, since they show all four dates on the disk itself.

1895, April 2

Patent No. 536,870 by Ruth A. Gilchrist of Wilkes Barre, Pa., and

1895, May 28

Design Patent No. D24,337 by Ruth A. Gilchrist

Both patents cover the idea of an inverted dome, whose flanges replaced the usual position of the Boyd inner glass liner for the zinc Mason cap. In use, the dome entered the jar mouth far enough to displace the liquid upwards to overflowing, thus driving out all of the air, and at the same time keeping the solid contents of the jar totally immersed. It was perhaps the simplest, and most workable of all such designs, but unfortunately Mrs. Gilchrist lost an important suit over her alleged infringement on a jar design, and was bankrupted, together with the Elmer Glass Company, of Elmer, N.J., who had made her jar.

Wrenches

A variety of devices have been patented as wrenches that would be used to tighten or loosen a fruit-jar seal. Some of them are listed among the following.

1868, January 28

Patent No. 73,846 by Charles F. Spencer of Rochester, N.Y.

The earliest aid to opening a jar that has been found is that of Spencer, whose patent includes the use of two wire loops from the cap to hook under notched lugs on the finish of the jar. These loops could be turned upward, when freed for opening the jar, and a small bar placed between the arc of the loops could be used as a pry.

1871, June 6

Patent No. 115,754 by John Landis Mason of New York City

Mason here illustrates the shoulder-seal cap with a small lug of metal, extending vertically, on the side of the threaded lid. He describes it as a "thumb-piece" to assist in tightening or removing the cap, and makes no mention of the spanner wrench included later in his Patent No. 131,695 of Sept. 24, 1872. He does mention that he received Patent No. 17,437 on June 2, 1857, for a method of spinning metal into shapes and threads. This would credit Mason with at least nine patents.

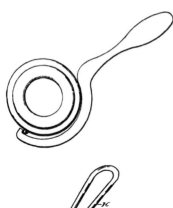

1872, September 24

Patent No. 131,695 by John Landis Mason of New York City

In Patent No. 131,695, in which Mason mentions his Patent No. 115,754 having the same device, Mason shows a vertical lug on the side of the zinc cap, and a spanner wrench fitting it, by which the cap could be both tightened and loosened. Rowley soon copied it with a horizontal lug.

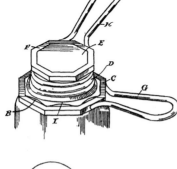

1898, June 14

Patent No. 605,482 by Samuel P. Jaggard of Blackwood, N.J.

This is the source of the J & B jar and cap. The top of the zinc cap is formed with an octagonal design, and the shoulder of the jar as well. Two octagonal wrenches were then used to tighten and to loosen the cap.

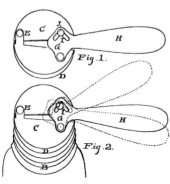

1901, December 3

Patent No. 688,224 by Henry W. Bogart of Cleveland, Ohio, assignor to Tarbox & Bogart Manufacturing Company of Cleveland, Ohio

The device is composed of two half-circles with a flange that fitted the upper part of the zinc cap. They were hinged on one side, and fitted with a lever on the opposite side. When the lever was pressed in the direction desired, either to tighten or to loosen, the half-circles closed on the top of the zinc cap and turned it in the direction desired.

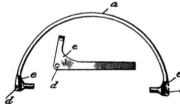

1901, December 3

Design Patent No. D35,370 by John M. Greiner of Monmouth, Ill.

On the same day as Bogart (above), Greiner was granted a design patent for a lever for a similar purpose.

1910, November 22

Patent No. 976,623 by Francis Marion Belles of Shickshinny, Pa.

The Belles jar had a heavy yoke moving in a helical neck slot. He also provided a spanner wrench by which the yoke could be rotated in the slot in either direction.

Patented Jar Shapes and Design Features

Only a few patents concerned the shape, or some other feature, of the jar itself.

1867, November 26

Design Patent No. D2,840 by Salmon B. Rowley (Hero) of Philadelphia, Pa.

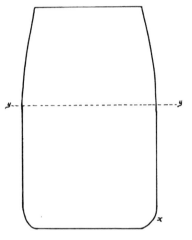

Rowley quickly took advantage of the fact that the screw-finish top seal would allow making a stronger jar because of the absence of the offset to form a shoulder-seal area. He patented the design of the tapering upper half of the jar that the top seal made possible. More important to the collector, he used this date, "NOV 26 67," on every Hero jar that he possibly could, even if it were the only patent listed. This gives a positive identification of any Hero-made jar on which it appeared.

1866-74, circa

Unknown if patented

The PENN jar, by Beck, Phillips & Co., of Pittsburgh, Pa., had three short legs on the bottom, giving a tripod on which the jar could stand. This was especially valuable when a hot jar was placed upon a cold, wet surface.

1885, March 24

Patent No. 314,289 by Moning Rix Gannaway of Unionville, Tenn.

This square-shaped jar went even farther than the PENN. It was blown with shallow holes at each corner, into which were inserted four wooden "buttons" to protect the hot bottle from chill shock.

1896, December 1

Patent No. 572,281 by Albert G. Smalley of Boston, Mass.

Smalley defined the radii at the corners of an otherwise squared jar, so that sufficient strength would be developed. This was the origin of the "rounded-square" jar shape.

1887, March 29

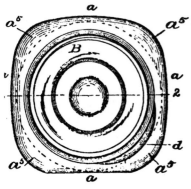

Diaphragms

Patent No. 360,131 by Delmer E. Ashby of San Francisco, Calif.

Ashby's idea was that by providing a thin diaphragm as the cover of the jar, it would protect the glass from breakage both from the expansion of the contents (if unvented or overfilled) while cooking, or from the gaseous fermentation that might take place on storage of a poorly processed jar. His jars would stack on each other because of their wide, flat tops.

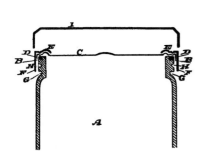

Since the diaphragm, by swelling upward on storage, would indicate spoilage, he states "if the fruit is not too far gone, these swells may be vented and recooked."

Compression Bands Circling Finish and Cap

A new principle of sealing was introduced in 1900, in which the lid and jar were held in contact by a band of metal tightened around both a flange of the jar finish and the lid, both of which had to be of the same diameter. The first of the following patents was applied by hand and used as a home-canning jar, under the name of VICTOR. The second required a capping machine for its operation, and generally was confined to use in commercial canning methods.

1900, February 20

Patent No. 643,908 by Ernst R. Meyer of Detroit, Mich.

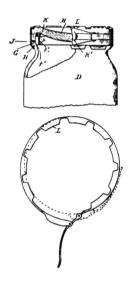

The importance of this as a new method is attested by the fact that it lay in the Patent Office for two years before it was granted. In design, the equal diameters of lid and finish ledge received a metal band that was tightened about them by means of a toggle lever. The upper contact area of the lid and the lower contact area of the finish ledge were beveled to the same bevel as about nine "fingers" extending inwardly on the upper and the lower edges of the band. When the band was tightened, these fingers drew the lid and jar top, with the intervening gasket, tightly together.

This became the VICTOR Jar. Some of these jars show that Meyer anticipated a little, in lettering them "PAT 1899," while later jars bear the full and true patent date.

1904, June 7

Patent No. 761,652 by Julius Brenzinger of New York City, and assigned to the Max Ams Machinery Company of New York City

Differing from the Meyer patent, this design employed a metal band whose edges, top and bottom, were at 90 degrees to the plane of the band around the finish. The band, therefore, embodied no action of pulling the lid and jar finish together. Instead, the machine pressed down on top of the lid and compressed the sealing gasket—then the band was placed on the jar, also by machine action, without the use of a toggle.

Fruit-Jar Manufacturers
and Their Jars

A

Acme Glass Co, Olean, N.Y., 1902-30
    ACME
John Agnew & Co., Pittsburgh, Pa., 1854-66, and
Agnew, Son & Co., Pittsburgh, Pa., 1866-76, and
Agnew & Co., Pittsburgh, Pa., 1876 to after 1886
    AGNEW
Anchor Hocking Glass Corp, Lancaster, Ohio, 1937 to date

ANCHOR HOCKING	ANCHOR HOCKING MASON
ANCHOR HOCKING	RATH'S
LIGHTNING	

Armstrong Cork Co., Lancaster, Pa., 1938 to date
    ELECTROLUX
Atlas Glass Co., Washington, Pa., 1896-1901, and
Atlas Glass & Metal Co., Wheeling, W. Va., 1901-2, and
Hazel Atlas Glass Co., Wheeling, W. Va., 1902-64

ATLAS	ATLAS IMPROVED MASON
ATLAS E – Z SEAL	ATLAS MASON'S PATENT

B

Baker Brothers, Baltimore, Md., 1853-1903 ?
    BAKER BROS., BALTO.
Ball Brothers Company, Muncie, Ind., 1888 to date

BALL	PERFECT MASON
BALL DELUXE JAR	QUICK SEAL
BALL JAR	RATH'S
BALL MASON	SAFE SEAL
BANNER	SANITARY SURE SEAL
CLIMAX	SCULPTURED PATTERN
ECLIPSE	SPECIAL MASON
IDEAL	STANDARD
IMPROVED MASON	SURE SEAL
MASON'S N	THE BALL
MASON'S PATENT	

Ball Brothers Glass Manufacturing Co., Buffalo, N.Y., 1886-87

"BUFFALO"	MASON'S PATENT
B B G M Co	PORCELAIN LINED
MASON	

Beaver Flint Glass Co., Toronto, Ont., 1897-1948
    BEAVER

Beck, Phillips & Co., Pittsburgh, Pa., 1866-74
  PET   THE PENN
Bernardin Bottle Cap Co., Cincinnati, Ohio, mid-1860s to date
  BERNARDIN
Bodine & Brothers, Williamstown, N.J., 1856-64
  NE PLUS ULTRA
Charles Boldt Glass Co., Cincinnati, Ohio, 1900-19, and
Charles Boldt Glass Manufacturing Co., Cincinnati, Ohio, and Huntington,
 W. Va., 1919-28
  BOLDT MASON JAR
Brockway Glass Co., Brockway, Pa., 1907 to date
  CLEAR-VU   SUR-GRIP
Buck Glass Co., Baltimore, Md., 1907-62
  THRIFT
Glashutte Bulach, St. Prex, Switzerland, modern
  BULACH
Burlington Glass Works, Hamilton, Ont., 1875-99
  THE BURLINGTON

C

Campbell Glass Co., West Berkeley, Cal., 1884-85
  WHEELER
Canton Glass Co., Canton, Ohio, 1883-93; Marion, Ind., 1893-1905
  CANTON DOMESTIC   FRUITKEEPER
  C G Co.
Chase Company No. 2, Milwaukee, Wis., 1880-81
 Also called Chase Valley Co., No. 2
  C C No 2 MILW
A. & D. H. Chambers, Pittsburgh, Pa., 1843-75
  MASON'S PATENT   UNION
Chattanooga Glass Co., Chattanooga, Tenn., 1901 to date
  C in a circle
Clarke Fruit Jar Co., Cleveland, Ohio, 1886-89
  CLARKE FRUIT JAR
Clyde Glass Works, Clyde, N.Y., 1868-86; 1895-1912
  C F J Co. MASONS   CLYDE
  THE CLYDE
Cohansey Glass Mfg. Co., Philadelphia, Pa., 1870-1900
  AIRTIGHT   JOHNSON & JOHNSON
  COHANSEY   LORILLARD
  FINKE & NASSE
Consolidated Fruit Jar Co., New Brunswick, N.J., 1869-82 (for bottles)
 Clyde is the only maker identified for this jobber
  C F J Co. MASONS   MASON'S IMPROVED
  CRYSTAL JAR   MASON'S PATENT
  D 446   PORCELAIN LINED
  IMPROVED BUTTER JAR
Consumers Glass Co., Toronto, Ont., 1917 to date
  CANADIAN JEWEL   CANADIAN SURE SEAL
  CANADIAN MASON   CORONA

JEWEL JAR   SAFETY SEAL
QUEEN   SURE SEAL
ROYAL   VICTORY
Craven Brothers Glass Co., Salem, N.J., 1879-96
    MASON'S C ?
Crowleytown Glass Works, Crowleytown, N.J., circa 1860
    First MASON jars
Cumberland Glass Co., Bridgeton, N.J., 1882-96, and
Cumberland Glass Manufacturing Co., Bridgeton, N.J., 1896-1920
    COLUMBIA   JOHNSON & JOHNSON
D. O. Cunningham Glass Co., Pittsburgh, Pa., 1882-1931
    D O C
Cunningham & Ihmsen, Pittsburgh, Pa., 1865-79
    CUNNINGHAM & IHMSEN   HEROINE
Cunninghams & Co., Pittsburgh, Pa., 1879-1909
    HEROINE   WAX SEALER

D

Diamond Flint Glass Co., Montreal, Que., 1901-13 (see also Diamond Glass Co., Montreal, and Dominion Glass Co. for other names of same company)
    SAFETY VALVE
Diamond Glass Co., Montreal, Que., 1891-1901
    CROWN   GEM
    DIAMOND
Diamond Glass Co., Royersford, Pa., 1885 to date
    ANDERSON
Dillon & Co. (or Dillon G. Co.), Fairmount, Ind., circa 1880s
    DILLON
Dominion Glass Co., Montreal, Que., 1913 to date
    BEE HIVE   IDEAL
    BEST   IMPERIAL
    CANADIAN KING   MASON FRUIT JAR
    CARROLL'S   PERFECT SEAL
    DYSON   SAFETY VALVE
    GEM   SCHRAM
Dominion Glass Co., Montreal, Que., 1886-98 (Note: different dates and different company)
    DOMINION   D G Co MONOGRAM
Dramsen's Glass, Norway, modern
    NORGE

E

East Stroudsburg Glass Co., East Stroudsburg, Pa., 1877-1920
    VAN VLIET ?
Elmer Glass Co., Elmer, Pa. circa 1890-1900
    GILCHRIST JAR   G J Co
    G J   R A G monogram

Empire Glass Co., Cleveland, N.Y., 1852-77
    EMPIRE   THE EMPIRE
Erie Class Works, Port Colbourne, Ont., 1895-98
    ERIE FRUIT JAR   ERIE LIGHTNING ?
Eureka Jar Co., Dunbar, W. Va., and Boston, Mass., 1864, again circa 1900
    EUREKA   EureKa (script, E and K large)
Edward H. Everett Glass Co., Newark, Ohio, 1882-1904
    Formed Ohio Bottle Co. in 1905; part of American Bottle 1905
    E H E   EVERETT
Excelsior Glass Co., St. Johns, Que., 1879; Montreal, Que., 1880-89
    E G Co monogram   IMPERIAL
    EXCELSIOR   SECURITY SEAL ?

F

Fahnstock, Albree & Co., Pittsburgh, Pa., 1860-62
    F A & Co   FAHNSTOCK, ALBREE & Co.
Fahnstock, Fortune & Co., Pittsburgh, Pa., 1866-68
    FAHNSTOCK, FORTUNE & Co. WAX SEALER
Fairmount Glass Co., Indianapolis, Ind., 1888 to date
    RELIABLE   SECURITY SEAL
Florida Glass Co., Jacksonville, Fla., 1929-48
    F G   TROPICAL CANNERS
Forster Glass Co., St. Helens, Lancs., England, 1902 to date
    FORSTER
Wm. Frank & Sons, Pittsburgh, Pa., 1866-76
    FRANK
Frank Glass Co., Wellsburg, W. Va., circa 1859
    McCARTY VACUUM
Franklin Flint Glass Co., Philadelphia, Pa., circa 1860s to 70s
    BENNETT'S No. 1   A. STONE & Co.
    BENNETT'S No. 2   THE BEST

G

John Gayner, Lessee of Holz, Clark & Taylor, Salem, N.J., 1879-1898
Gayner Glass Works, Salem, N.J., 1898-1957
    CLARK'S PEERLESS   GAYNER GLASS TOP
    ELECTRIC   LEOTRIC
    ELECTRIC FRUIT JAR
Glashutte Wauwil, St. Prex, Switzerland, modern
    WAUWIL
Glenshaw Glass Co., Glenshaw, Pa., 1894 to date
    GLENSHAW   MALLINGER
    G (in a square) MASON

H

J. T. & A. Hamilton, Pittsburgh, Pa., 1884-1944
    HOM-PAK

Hamilton Glass Works, Hamilton, Ont., 1865-93
See also Rutherford

CROWN	SAFETY VALVE
GEM	THE GEM
HAMILTON	

Hazel Glass Co., Wellsburg, W. Va., and Washington, Pa., 1886-1902, and
Hazel Atlas Glass Co., Wheeling, W. Va., 1902-64
See also Atlas

E D J SEAL	PERFECT MASON
E – Z SEAL	RATH'S
GOOD LUCK	REISS & BRADY
HAZEL	SINCLAIR
HAZEL ATLAS	SOCIÉTÉ
HORMEL	SPECIAL
IOWANA	STRONG SHOULDER
IVANHOE	T, with a number
MASON'S PATENT	VICTORY
M F A	WHOLEFRUIT

C. Hermann & Co., Milwaukee, Wis., 1854-86
HERMANN POTTERY MASON
Hermetic Fruit Jar Co., Portland, Ore., 1903
Name changed to Kerr Glass Manufacturing Co. the same year
ECONOMY
Hero Glass Works, Philadelphia, Pa., 1856-84, and
Hero Fruit Jar Co., Philadelphia, Pa., 1884-1909
Hero Metal Products Co., Philadelphia, Pa., 1909-18

ALL RIGHT	MASON'S IMPROVED
CRYSTAL	MASON'S S
GEM	NOV 26 67 (Patent date)
HERO	PEARL
HERO CROSS	PORCELAIN LINED
(lettered H F J Co.)	S MASON'S
HERO CROSS (unlettered)	THE GEM
H F J Co	THE HERO
H G W monogram	THE PEARL
IMPROVED GEM	

Glasfabrik Heye, Bremen, Germany, mid-1880s to date
ADLER
Hawley Glass Co., Hawley, Pa., 1872-1931
HAWLEY
Hitchen's Glass Works, Lockport, N.Y., 1840-69 (Lockport Glass Works)

ALL RIGHT ?	THE QUEEN

Holz, Clark & Taylor, Salem, N.J., 1860's-1879

CLARK'S PEERLESS	THE SALEM JAR
HOLZ, CLARK & TAYLOR	

I

Illinois Glass Co., Alton, Ill., 1873-1929, and
Owens Illinois Glass Co., 1929 to date

BOYD GENUINE MASON	BOYD PERFECT MASON

BOYD SUPREME MASON	I G Co monogram
BOYD MASON	I and O in a diamond
BOYD'S GENUINE MASON	PRESTO
GENUINE MASON	SUNSHINE JAR
GOOD HOUSEKEEPERS	SUPREME MASON
I in a diamond	VICTORY

Illinois Pacific Glass Co., San Francisco, Cal., 1902-30
Illinois Pacific Coast Co., San Francisco, Cal., 1930-32
Owens Illinois Pacific Coast Co., San Francisco, Cal., 1932-43
Owens Illinois Glass Co., Toledo, Ohio, 1929 to date

BOYD GENUINE MASON	GENUINE MASON
BOYD MASON	GOLDEN STATE
BOYD PERFECT MASON	GOOD HOUSEKEEPERS
BOYD SUPREME MASON	IMPROVED EVERLASTING
ENK SKELL Co.	PRESTO
EVERLASTING	SUPREME MASON

Independent Glass Co., Pittsburgh, Pa., 1876-1900
    INDEPENDENT   INDEPENDENT JAR

J

Jeannette Glass Co., Jeannette, Pa., 1889 to date
    J in a square   JEANNETTE HOME PACKER
Jefferson Glass Co., Toronto, Ont., 1913-25
    CROWN   PERFECT SEAL
    ERIE LIGHTNING ?

K

Kearns, Gorsuch Glass Co., Zanesville, Ohio, 1893-1929
    Started by Kearns in 1842; bought by Hazel Atlas in 1920
    K – G
Kearns, Henderson & Gorsuch, Zanesville, Ohio, 1876-93
    K H & G Z O
Kelley, Reed & Co., Rochester, N.Y., 1887-98
    Was Rochester Glass Co., 1865-87
    Became F. E. Reed Glass Co., 1898-1947, and
    Reed Glass Co., 1947-56
    THE SCHAFFER JAR
Kentucky Glass Works, Louisville, Ken., 1849-55
    See also Louisville Glass Works; Louisville Glass Co., Louisville, Ky.
    K Y G W   K Y G W Co
Kerr Glass Manufacturing Co., Portland, Ore. 1903-12; Chicago, Ill., 1912-15; Sands Springs, Okla., 1915-19; Los Angeles, Cal., since 1919
Alexander H. Kerr & Co., Altoona, Kan., 1912-15; rest as Kerr Glass Mfg. Co.

ECONOMY	KERR SELF SEALING
KERR ECONOMY	KERR WIDE MOUTH MASON
KERR GLASS TOP	

Kilner Brothers Glass Co., Thornhill Lees and Conisbrough, Yorks., England, 1863-73, and

Kilner Brothers, Ltd., same, 1873-1921
    K B G Co monograms   KILNER
    K B L   THE KILNER JAR
Kivlan & Onthank, Boston, Mass., 1919-25
    See also Smalley
    KIVLAN & ONTHANK   QUEEN
    MAGIC   VICTORY
Knox Bottle Co., Knox Pa., 1924-33, and
Knox Glass Associates, Knox, Pa., 1933-51
    KNOX
Knox Glass Bottle Co. of Mississippi, Palestine, Tex., plant, 1951 to date
    TEXAS MASON

L

Lamb Glass Co., Mt. Vernon, Ohio, 1921-63
    LAMB MASON
W. J. Latchford Glass Co., Los Angeles, Cal., 1921-38, and
Latchford Marble Glass Co., Los Angeles, Cal., 1938-56, and
Latchford Glass Co., Los Angeles, Cal., 1956 to date
    BERNARDIN   NEWMARK
    MISSION
Lindell Glass Co., date and place unknown
    LINDELL
Lockport Glass Co., Lockport, N.Y., 1900-33
    LOCKPORT IMPROVED   LOCKPORT MASON
    MASON
Lockport Glass Works, Lockport, N.Y., 1840-69
    Known also as Hitchen's Glass Factory when bought by Hero in 1869;
    sold to Alonzo Mansfield, 1872 (Mansfield Glass Works, 1872-1909)
    ALL RIGHT ?   EAGLE
Lorenz & Wightman, Pittsburgh, Pa., 1851-71
    L & W   RICE & BURNETT
Lynchburg Glass Co., Lynchburg, Va., 1920-27
    LYNCHBURG STANDARD
Lyndeboro Glass Co., Lyndeboro, N.H., 1866-86
    PUTNAM LIGHTNING ?

M

Macomb Pottery Co., Macomb, Ill., circa 1890-1910
    MACOMB POTTERY MASON   WEIR POTTERY
Manufactures des Glaces et Produits Chimiques de Saint Gobain, Chauney
    et Ciney, France, modern
    DUR FOR   L'IDEALE
Marion Fruit Jar & Bottle Co., Marion, Ind., 1890-1904
    M F J & B Co   THE MARION JAR
Mason Fruit Jar Co., Coffeeville, Kan., 1904-07
    M F J Co WAX SEALER
Mason Fruit Jar Co., Philadelphia, Pa., 1885-1900
    KEYSTONE (design)   "MASON"
    "MASCOT"   MASON DISK PROTECTOR CAP

McCully & Co., Pittsburgh, Pa., 1832-85
DICTATOR   MAGIC
DICTATOR D   STANDARD
Samuel McKee & Co., Pittsburgh, Pa., 1836-90
S. McKEE & Co.
Metro Glass Co., Jersey City, N.J., 1859-63
EASI-PAK
Michigan Glass Co., Saginaw, Mich., 1911-16
MICHIGAN
Midwest Glass Co., Winnepeg, Man., 1929-37
MIDWEST
Model Glass Works, Summitville, Ind., 1890's-1919
MODEL
John M. Moore & Co., Fislerville, N.J., 1859-63, and
Moore Brothers, Clayton (same town, name changed), N.J., 1863-80
MOORE BROS.   MOORE'S PATENT
MOORE BROS. MASON'S   J. B. WILSON'S PATENT
PATENT
Mutual Glass Co., Pittsburgh, Pa., dates unknown, possibly circa 1860-90
MUTUAL WAX SEALER

N

National Glass Co., Marion, Ind., circa 1900, but earlier elsewhere
NATIONAL ?
North American Glass Co., Montreal, Que., 1885-91
AMERICAN PORCELAIN   IMPERIAL
LINED   N A G monogram
CROWN
Northwestern Glass Co., Seattle, Wash., 1936 to date
N W ELECTROGLAS

O

Ohio Glass Products Co., Massilon, Ohio, 1924-25 only
OHIO QUALITY
Ohio Valley Glass Co., Bridgeport, Ohio, circa 1886
OVG Co
Olean Glass Co., Olean, N.Y., 1902-30
O G monogram
Owens Bottle Co., Toledo, Ohio, 1916-29
RATH'S
Owens Illinois Glass Co., Toledo, Ohio, 1929 to date
ELECTROLUX   PRESTO
ENG HUNG CHI   RATH'S
GENUINE MASON   RELIANCE
G G Co.   SUPREME MASON
GOOD HOUSE KEEPERS
Owens Illinois Pacific Coast Glass Co., San Francisco, Cal., 1932-43
See under Illinois Pacific Glass Co.

P

Pacific Coast Glass Co., San Francisco, Cal., 1925-30
    DOUBLE SEAL   PACIFIC MASON
    GOLDEN STATE   P C trade mark
    PACIFIC   SUEY FUNG YUEN Co.
Pacific Coast Glass Works, San Francisco, Cal., 1902-24
    Name changed from *Works* to *Company* in 1924
    P C G W
Pine Glass Co., Okmulgee, Okla., 1927-29
    PINE DELUXE   PINE MASON
    PINE DELUXE JAR
Port Glass Co., Belleville, Ill., 1902-10 or 13
    N MASON'S PATENT   PORT MASON'S PATENT
    PORT   PORT N MASON'S PATENT
    PORT MASON
Potter & Bodine, Philadelphia, Pa., 1855-63
    AIRTIGHT   VALVE JAR
    POTTER & BODINE
Premium Glass Co., Coffeeville, Kan., 1904-09
    PREMIUM   PREMIUM IMPROVED
Putnam Flint Glass Works, Putnam, Ohio, 1852-81
    HAINES   PUTNAM GLASS WORKS

R

Redfearn Brothers, Barnsley, Yorks., England, 1862 to date
    FLETT
Reid Bottle Co., Mansfield, Ohio, ?-1904
    MANSFIELD ?
Rochester Glass Works, Rochester, N.Y., 1865-87
    THE SCHAFFER JAR   WHITMORE'S ?
    SPENCER ?
Root Glass Co., Terre Haute, Ind., 1903-09
    ROOT   ROOT MASON
George Rutherford & Co., Proprietor, Hamilton Glass Works, Hamilton, Ont.,
    (1865-93) from 1873 to 1893
    GEM   THE GEM
    RUTHERFORD

S

Safe Glass Co., Bowling Green, Ohio, 1898-1905; Redkey, Ind., 1892-98;
    and Upland, Ind., 1898-1905
    MASON'S PATENT   S G Co. monogram
    RED KEY
Saint Gobain, Manufactures des Glaces et Produits Chimiques de: Chauney
    et Ciney, France, early 1800s to date, but modern jar
    DUR FOR   L'IDEALE

Salem Glass Works, Salem, N.J., 1895-1938

MASON'S	SAFETY VALVE
PETTIT	SANETY [sic]
PETTIT MASON PATENT	SANITARY
SAFETY	S W G monogram

San Francisco Flint Glass Co., San Francisco, Cal., 1865-69, and
San Francisco Glass Works, San Francisco, Cal., 1869-76

SAN FRANCISCO GLASS WORKS	VICTORY

San Francisco & Pacific Glass Works, San Francisco, Cal., 1876-98

EASY VACUUM	VACUUM JAR
GEM (under Hero license until 1885-86)	

Schram Glass Manufacturing Co., St. Louis, Mo., 1906-25

DREY	SCHRAM AUTOMATIC SEALER
DREY EVER SEAL	SCHRAM AUTOMATIC SEALER
DREY MASON	B
DREY SQUARE MASON	SCHRAM AUTO SEALER
IMPROVED MASON	SQUARE MASON
PERFECT MASON	

Albert G. Smalley & Co., Boston, Mass., 1872-1907, and
Smalley Jar Co., Boston, Mass., 1905-11, and
Smalley Fruit Jar Co., Boston, Mass., 1915-19, and
Smalley, Kivlan & Onthank, Boston, Mass., 1907-19, and
Kivlan & Onthank, Boston, Mass., 1919-25

DOUBLE SAFETY	ROYAL CROWN
KING	ROYAL NU-SEAL
MAGIC	ROYAL ROYAL
NU-SEAL	SMALLEY
PRINCESS ?	VICTORY
QUEEN	WEARS
ROYAL	

J. P. Smith & Co., Pittsburgh, Pa., circa 1860-70

J. P. SMITH

Southern Glass Co., Los Angeles, Cal., 1918-30

SOUTHERN

Standard Co-operative Glass Co., Marion, Ind., ?-1930

MASON	STANDARD MASON
STANDARD	

Star Glass Co., New Albany, Ind., circa 1960-1900

A. LEIBERSTEIN & Co.	STAR GLASS CO.
STAR	WEIR

Sterling Glass Co., Lapel, Ind., 1890-1950

STERLING

Swayzee Glass Co., Swayzee, Ind., 1890-1906

SWAYZEE MASON	SWAYZEE'S IMPROVED MASON
SWAYZEE'S FRUIT JAR	SWAYZEE'S MASON

Sydenham Glass Co., Wallaceburg, Ont., 1894-1913

CROWN	NEW GEM
GEM	WALLACEBURG GEM

T

Three Rivers Glass Co., Three Rivers, Tex., 1925-37
    Generally written "3 Rivers"
    CRYSTALVAC   3 RIVERS
Tigner & Co., Xenia, Ind., circa 1880-1900, or
Tigner G. Co., Xenia, Ind.
    TIGNER
Turner Glass Co., Terre Haute and Winchester, Ind., 1921-30
    T, in a bowed triangle

U

Upland Glass Co., Upland, Ind., 1911-22; Marion, Ind., 1922-29; and
Foster-Forbes Glass Co., Marion, Ind., 1929 to date
    FOSTER   RADER BROS. & LAMPKIN
    FOSTER SEALFAST   RONDEN & Co.
    P. A. NEILSON & SON   SEALFAST
Union Stoneware Co., Redwing, Minn., circa 1899-1910 for stoneware jars
    THE STONE MASON

V

Valve Jar Co., Philadelphia, Pa., circa 1860-70
    Possibly only a marketing jobber of their own patented jar, as made for
    them by Potter & Bodine
    THE VALVE JAR
Verrerie Cristalleric d'Arques, Arques, France
    TRIOMPHE
Verreries Hemain Frères, Rive-de-Gier, France
    LE PRATIQUE

W

Washington Glass Works, Williamstown, N.J. (Bodine & Bros.), 1839-1917
    NE PLUS ULTRA
Weir Pottery Co., Monmouth, Ill., circa 1890-1915
    WEIR
Whitall-Tatum & Co., Millville, N.J., 1857-1938
    MILLVILLE   MILLVILLE IMPROVED
    MILLVILLE ATMOSPHERIC   WHITALL-TATUM
Whitney Brothers, Glassboro, N.J., 1842-87, and
Whitney Glass Works, Glassboro, N.J., 1887-1918
    GLASSBORO   TELEPHONE JAR
    GLASSBORO IMPROVED   WIDE MOUTH TELEPHONE
    MASON JAR OF 1872   JAR
    MASON'S PATENT
Thomas Wightman & Co., Pittsburgh, Pa., 1871-?
    W & Co.   W (some with "L &" peened out
                                   from "L & W" from Lorenz &
                                   Wightman, after Lorenz' death)

Winslow Glass Co., Winslow, N.J., 1831 to after 1884
    Owned by Hay & Co., Philadelphia, 1866-84, when jars were made
    WINSLOW JAR
Woodbury Glass Works, Woodbury, N.J., 1882-1890
    W G W monogram   WOODBURY IMPROVED
    WOODBURY

Y

T. G. Yeoman, Walworth, N.Y., circa 1860
    YEOMAN'S FRUIT BOTTLE

Definitions and Terms

Jar Closures

Bail: Strictly speaking a "bail" is for carrying, and should not be used to describe any part of the sealing mechanism, unless attached permanently.

Yoke: Any flat, formed metal, part of a sealing device that crosses over the lid, that hooks or screws onto the finish of the jar, and that carries some device for applying pressure to the lid.

Clip: Any wire, or spring band, that crosses over the lid and hooks or snaps under some part of the finish, but which does not carry an auxiliary device for applying pressure to the lid.

Cap: Usually reserved to denote a cover for a jar that is complete in itself, which either screws or snaps into place. Example: zinc cap.

Lid: Usually reserved to denote a part of the closure that is a cover only, and which must be held in place by some mechanism. Example: glass lid.

Screw-Band: A metal cap whose center is almost completely cut out, so as to expose the glass or metal lid.

Perforated Cap: A metal cap which has a small hole or holes stamped out, and which depends on an inner lid for closing the jar. Example: Knowlton.

Stopper: Any closure that enters into, and seals within, the mouth of the jar, regardless of how it is held.

Jar Decorations

The glass industry uses the word "decorations" to include all designs, letters, numerals, or surface treatments (stippling, for example) cut into the mold.

Lettering

This includes both letters and numerals, and will be designated in the text by single quotation marks. Capital letters will be shown as such. Lower case will also be shown as such. If the lower case is in script, that will be noted, as well as italics or other lettering style.

Lettering Style

Almost all fruit-jar lettering is in Gothic, or block, print. Some used Roman characters, letters complete with serifs to embellish the ends of each stroke. A few were in Italics, and one or two in Old German.

Number of Lines

That part of the lettering that appears in one line will be enclosed in single quotation marks. Written: 'ALL,' 'RIGHT' (or 'ALL' and 'RIGHT') it means that the arrangement is:

ALL
RIGHT

Maker's (or Trade) Mark

A letter, or line of letters (usually initials), or a monogram, often included in some geometric device, such as a diamond, a triangle, a square, or other device, that indicates the maker of the jar, no matter what other name might appear.

Monogram

Old-time fruit-jar makers, and inventors, loved monograms. Many fanciful arrangements of letters appear on fruit jars. Some have been puzzling in deciding which letter comes first.

Glass Quality

Seeds or Bubbles: Actually almost a vacuum within the wall of glass, we arbitrarily call the object a seed if smaller than one sixteenth of an inch in longest dimension.

Blister: Also a vacuum, any such inclusion larger than one sixteenth of an inch in largest dimension. It is an arbitrary distinction based on size.

Whittle Marks: Popularly supposed to be the marks left on the surface of wood molds by whittling with a knife, this glass-making defect is in actuality the result of trying to blow into shape glass that was too cold for the purpose. As proof, it is a common "start-up" defect in modern glassmaking, and whittle marks were deliberately made in an experiment in modern, highly polished, molds by the simple expedient of allowing glass to be blown before the molds had warmed up.

Hand Glassmaking

Gather: Any portion of glass, of a size that will be used for or on one jar, that is removed from the furnace or pot on a blow-pipe, as for blowing, or on a pontil, as for laying-on a ring.

Gob: A portion of glass severed from the GATHER.

Laid-on-ring: An added portion of glass around the neck of a jar completely blown except for the tooling of the finish, formed by rotating the jar while a thin stream of glass is flowing from a small gather on a pontil. Generally speaking, fruit-jar laid-on-rings were at the lip only, but the laid-on-ring could be one or several such additions at various heights on the neck and for decorative purposes.

Applied Lip: An alternative term for laid-on-ring, but one which is not generally used in the glass industry. The term "laid-on-ring" both emphasizes that it is a complete ring, and that it is "laid" on, and not necessarily at the lip.

Laid-on-ring, Tooled: A laid-on-ring that is roughly shaped by using ordinary glass-shaping tools, as the pucella, pincers, or a single stick-shaped tool.

Laid-on-ring, Pressed: A laid-on-ring that is shaped with some sort of pressing tool in a single operation, and generally required when some standardization of shape or contour was necessary. Such pressing tools were variously described as hand presses, bench presses, side-lever presses, or foot-lever presses, according to their type.

Marver: A table of marble, other stone, or even iron, on which the gather on the blowpipe can be rolled in order both to shape it for better blowing and to chill the surface.

Blowpipe: A hollow tube on which glass is gathered at the slightly widened end, and through which air is mouth-blown in order to inflate the gather balloon-wise into a desired shape, with or without the use of a mold.

Pontil: A solid rod of iron, on which glass can be gathered at a slightly widened end, but on which the gather cannot be blown.

Bare Pontil: A more correct name than "graphite pontil" for the operation of sticking the pontil to the bottom of a bottle or jar without the use of a bit of hot glass as an intermediary. Leaves iron oxides on the bottom of the glass piece.

Gathering: The "glass-house" term for the operation of forming a gather on the end of a blowpipe or pontil, by placing the end in a pool of molten glass and slowly rotating it until the desired quantity, through the cooling action of the blowpipe, has gathered into a ball at the end of the pipe.

Parts of the Jar

Mouth: The opening at the top of the jar, including any conformation of the inside portions.

Lip: The terminal edge of the mouth—the very top of the jar.

Finish: That part of the jar that is contoured to fit whatever closure is being used. In hand glassmaking, it was the last part of the jar to be made or shaped—hence the jar was then "finished." In machine-making it is pressed into shape as part of the very first operation.

Neck: The narrow portion of the jar, if any, just below the finish.

Shoulder: Any widening part of the jar that joins the neck, or finish, to the wider portion, or body, of the jar.

Body: The main part of the jar, enclosing the contents.

Heel: The area that includes the curve, or corner, between the body and the bottom of the jar, as far as the bearing surface.

Bearing Surface: That part of the jar on which it rests when standing upright.

Bottom: The circle within the bearing surface.

Punt: An English term including heel, bearing surface, and bottom.

The Furnace

Pot Furnace: A furnace in which glass is made in, and withdrawn from, clay pots that are placed within the separate walls of the furnace, but each with a small opening to the outside.

Tank Furnace: A furnace in which the walls of the furnace are made from suitably fired clay blocks that hold the glass. The fire is in a separate side structure, so placed that the long flames will pass over the glass to be melted.

Day Tank: A furnace from which glass is intended to be drawn for blowing only during the daytime; during the night the melting and refining of the raw materials into glass takes place.

Continuous Tank Furnace: A furnace that is intended to be used for glass blowing "around the clock." In contrast with the day tank, which has small ports around all sides, if desired, for workman's use either for hand- or semi-automatic-machine glass blowing, the continuous tank has means for introducing the batch material at a slow and steady rate at one end, approximating the rate at which glass is withdrawn at the other end. Melting and refining go on continuously as the mixture flows from one end to the other.

Batch: The mixture of ingredients for glassmaking. In older days, measured by the shovelful, mixed on the floor by shovel, and shoveled into the pot or end of the day tank. Now measured electronically, mixed automatically, conveyed to the furnace by monorail hopper or continuous belt, and fed mechanically at a measured rate.

Machine Glassmaking

Operational Sequences: In order to understand what is meant by semi-automatic and by automatic machines, consider the following sequence of operation:

1. Removing a measured portion of glass from the furnace and placing it in the blank mold
2. Closing the blank mold
3. Turning on air or operating pressure plunger
4. Turning off air or retracting plunger
5. Opening mold
6. Transferring parison to finishing mold
7. Closing finishing mold
8. Turning on air pressure
9. Turning off air pressure
10. Opening mold
11. Removing bottle or jar

Semi-Automatic Glass-Blowing Machine: In the beginning, each of the above operations was done manually. Then, one by one, the operations were keyed into mechanically timed and performed operations. So long as any remained manual the machine was designated as "semi-automatic."

Automatic Glass-Blowing Machine: So long as glass had to be transferred from the furnace to the machine by hand, the operation could not be fully automatic. When this was finally accomplished, the operation was termed "automatic" even though the glass container had to be taken from the machine to the lehr by hand. This operation too, was soon automated.

Gob: Any portion of glass, of a size that will make one jar, that is transferred from the furnace to the machine by the operation of cutting a slowly moving stream of glass.

Blank Mold: The first of a series of two molds used to form a jar. The gob drops into this mold and a preliminary shaping, as well as the complete formation of the finish, takes place either by a blowing or by a pressing operation.

Parison: The shaped body of glass, not yet a jar, that comes from the blank mold. In other words, the blank mold converts the gob into a parison.

Blow or Finish Mold: The second of the two molds, in which the jar is blown into its final shape as a glass container. In other words, the finishing mold converts the parison into a glass container.

Jar: A glass container having a relatively wide mouth.

Bottle: A glass container having a relatively small mouth.

The distinction between bottle and jar is arbitrary, and there is no publicly established rule.

Press-and-Blow: A machine operation, in which the entire operation of the blank mold part of the sequence is by mechanical pressure, and the final blowing in the finishing mold by air pressure.

Blow-and-Blow: A machine operation, in which the entire operation of the blank mold part of the sequence is by air pressure, and the final blowing in the finishing mold by air pressure.

Neck Rings: In matching halves, that part of the mold assembly which shapes that part of the jar that holds the closure.

Body Mold: In matching halves, that part of the mold that shapes the main part of the jar.

Bottom Plate: In one piece, that part of the mold that shapes the bottom contour.

Plunger: A mechanically moving element that, in blow-and-blow operation, extends only enough into the mouth of the bottle

to determine the inside diameter at the opening, but in press-·
and-blow operation, extends well into the parison that it helps
form.

Cup Bottom: A mold construction in which the seam between the
bottom and the body is at the turn of the heel; so-called, because the depression in the bottom plate is deep and cup-shaped.

Post Bottom: A mold construction in which the seam between
the bottom plate and the body coincides with the bearing surface on the under side. The bottom plate resembles a plane
surface from which a post extends upward. Much favored in
hand glass blowing because it enabled a very simple centering
of the mold around the bottom plate post while the mold was
closed.

Seams and Parting Lines: Glassmakers seem to have distinguished
between vertical and horizontal mold lines on the glassware
by these two names.

Parting Line: Horizontal lines between mold parts of different
structure: i.e.,
Neck Parting Line between neck ring and body.
Bottom Parting Line between body and bottom.

Seams: Generally speaking, the juncture of the matching halves
of the same function, and which hinge outward to separate:
Side Seam between the two halves of the body mold.
Neck Seam between the two halves of the neck ring.

Plated Mold: A mold which has an opening, either round or oval
usually, into the side of the body mold, into which interchangeable "plugs" can be carefully fitted. By this means one side of
the body mold (single plate) can be altered in lettering or
design, or both halves (double plated) so that a full mold does
not have to be made for each customer who wants only a few
jars, and who is content with an otherwise stock design.

Glassmaking in Fruit Jars

Collectors who do not know glassmaking methods, or only know those that apply to modern bottles, will be able to understand better and appreciate the many differences in fruit-jar designs if they know something about glassmaking of a hundred years ago. They would understand the limitations of glassmaking techniques of that day and how they affected fruit-jar design, for it is very true that the progress of one industry is very dependent on the progress of another industry.

The great problem in fruit-jar design was in sealing, and this was the result of the final operation, or "finishing" the opening, so that the jar could be hermetically sealed. The opening could be flared with tools and fire-polished smooth at the furnace if it were intended to be sealed with a cork. Otherwise the roughened surface from the cracking-off had to be ground flat (and the ground surface would not seal hermetically), or it had to be made smooth by a hand tool, or by a hand-operated press. Let us take a look at the entire glassmaking operation of the 1850s when fruit-jar production began to be important.

So far as I have seen fruit jars, the wooden mold never played any part. Wood could be used only when the jar could be rotated in the mold while blowing (the so-called "turn mold") and this was impossible if the jar contained any lettering on the sides or bottom. Even in "turn mold" use, only up to a hundred jars or so could be made before the mold became oversize, or burned away. Therefore brass and iron were the mold materials. (Clay molds were used for carboys.) Iron came into greater use after 1840 when cast iron could be formed with some degree of freedom from internal cavities whose presence might ruin the mold while it was being cut although the first patent was in 1811 in England. Brass and bronze were used earlier. Later a method of chilling the iron reduced the chance of "blow holes." Before 1840 fruit jars were generally held on a pontil while the finishing operation took place, and during the 1840s some jars were held with the bare iron pontil, leaving a telltale mark of iron oxides on the bottom. During the 1850s a "snap" device, which held the bottom of the jar in shaped tongs, replaced the bottom-adhered pontil for these low-cost items. Remember that here was a use that particularly required low cost in production for those who would eke out a low income by preserving food for a winter's use. Every method that would enable a jar to be furnished at a price within the people's ability to pay would be used to bring up the volume of production in the glass plant.

Iron molds and the pressing operation were no strangers to the glass industry. Pressing the glass into a shape, as that of a plate, in an iron or brass mold, with a plunger operated by a hand lever had been developed in the 1820s, and the "laid-on-ring" to strengthen the lip and to give it the body required for pressing had dated for hand tools from the 1600s. The laid-on-ring gave the lip strength for the cork, and later the body size needed for pressing the groove-ring finish, almost the first of the fruit-jar special finishes. Since this finish was completed by a tin lid that had to fit the groove, this became an early matter of quality control and specification.

The logical place to start a description of glass blowing in the mid-1800s is with the furnace. The furnace may be considered to be an enormous fireplace, inside which are placed several clay "pots" in each of which could be placed from a hundred pounds to a ton, according to size of the pot, of glassmaking batch to be melted. Each pot would be enclosed entirely within the furnace except for an opening to the outside, through which it could be charged with batch materials or through which glass could be withdrawn for shaping. Anywhere from two to twenty pots might be placed in a circle within the furnace, according to the number of glass-blowing crews. Each crew might require from one to three pots. If one were used, it would be charged with new batch-making materials each evening, hoping that the glass would be formed by morning. Two pots for each crew would give more time for melting, and three would be used for the most bubble-free glass production. In this case, one pot would be melting, one "fining" and one being "worked."

Each pot, as has been said, was completely enclosed within the furnace. Pots for cheaper grades of glass would be open at the top, and be subject to all of the droppings of soot, ashes, and other material from the fuel and the furnace roof. For finer glass, for colored glass, and essential for "flint" or colorless glass, the pot had a cover, molded on and extended into the bricked furnace opening as a "boot," in order to keep out the unwanted contamination.

Much has been said about slight differences in color. The state of glass technology was such that little was known, except through hard-won trade secrets, about the coloring of glass. In the main, except for powders added by the proprietor, color was largely dependent upon the raw materials available in the immediate vicinity of the glass plant. A change in the stratum from which the sand was taken, or the mineral content of the earth in which the trees grew that were burned for "potash" might alter the color in the next pot—and back again. Generally the prevailing color was some shade of green, depending upon the amount of iron in the sand.

Little was known about the influence of the flame. A "reducing" flame, or one with less oxygen supplied for burning, might produce a bluish-green because the iron in the sand might then be reduced to one of the bluer iron oxides—an excess of air might make the more oxidized green iron oxides predominate. Early glassmakers knew little about this. Thus a fire banked for the night and with the air intake flues closed down, could produce quite blue glass for the morning's start, and change slowly during the day when the air vents were opened wide for a hotter flame.

Other than the "natural" greens most colors were made intentionally by adding specific oxides, or mixtures of oxides. Since these were generally trade secrets, the coloring material might be added by the manager by sprinkling the small quantity used, either over the batch ready to be shoveled into the opening, or into the pot itself, lest a workman moving on to another factory take the secret with him. Amber was made by adding some form of carbon as a reducing agent, together with some form of sulfur. In many ways the exact color produced was a matter of variance and chance.

What the collector often calls "white glass" or clear glass, or colorless glass, the glassmaker of today calls, equally erroneously, "flint." Originally "flint" glass was made in England from very pure quartz rock, of a variety called "flint," and very free of iron. This colorless glass was made directly without a decolorizer. Today's flint is made from very low-iron sand but with a decolorizer added to optically neutralize the color that would be present from even the low iron content.

Green color may be optically offset by some shade of pink. In earlier days the most commonly available source of pink was some form of manganese dioxide, or other source of manganese (not to be confused with magnesium oxide, a common ingredient of lime that was used in much greater quantity as part of the basic batch). The addition of manganese and its coloring by action of the sun was known before 1832, since a book of that year discussed its use. Neri discussed it in 1612.

Varying amounts of manganese dioxide would be necessary depending upon the amount of iron present, the purple sun-coloring of old glass today depends upon this amount. Sun-coloring is due to a chemical reaction that takes place between the iron and the manganese, changing the manganese to a purple oxide from the pink oxide, and the iron from a green oxide to a blue oxide. Thus both iron and manganese contribute to the purplish state. The color is much prized by collectors; but I am afraid that the "amethyst" color often reported for fruit jars may be a slightly sun-colored flint.

During World War I manganese dioxide, an import in part from Germany, was difficult to get, and makers turned to Canadian selenium. Notwithstanding the higher cost of selenium, the total amount required was so much less than of the manganese that the glass industry never went back to using manganese dioxide. Collectors may expect flint glass made before World War I to become purplish—that made after World War I to turn a smokey amber or grayish tint, if it changes at all. Acid washing and other treatment of sand has reduced the amount of iron contained in the sand so that even less decolorizer is now required.

Exposing a green glass of any age to the sun is probably a lost cause, since neither manganese dioxide or selenium would have been used.

I have noted that pots were refilled at the end of the shift, or when they became empty to the extent that the blowpipe would no longer reach the glass level. The filling was of batch materials brought to the pot opening in wheelbarrows, and shoveled in—so many shovelfuls of this and so many of that, with alternation for crude mixing. More often the batch materials were dumped together on the floor of the furnace room, and mixed by turning the pile over and over with shovels. The mixture was then shoveled into the pot, together with whatever was also lying on the floor.

The batch consisted of sand, soda-ash, or potash, and some form of lime. Whatever amount of broken glass that might be on hand from misblown bottles, breakage, or returned bottles was added. The glass sales agent often advertized for "cullet" or broken glass. Alumina and various other ingredients may have been added, but not in the earlier days. The decolorizer, already discussed, was also added at this time.

Melting times have been quoted from sixteen to thirty hours. Actually, the time depended upon the size of the pot, the amount of heat over it, to some degree upon the color because of different rates of absorption of heat, and to management policy. In the latter, as we shall see, the impatience of the manager or of the workmen to begin glass blowing played a part.

As the glass batch melted, the glass became filled with bubbles of entrapped gas. The chief source was the chemical release of carbon dioxide from the carbonates in the batch—the soda-ash, potash, and lime. The second source was the gas entrapped in the spaces between the particles of batch materials. During the later stages of the melting, usually called the "fining" or refining, the gas bubbles rose to the top, burst, and disappeared.

The speed with which fining took place depended much on the temperature of the melt. Lower temperatures retarded the refining by slowing the rate of rise of the bubbles to the top of the glass mass. It was common practice to bank the fires, keeping them low, during the night, and to fire the furnaces heavily an hour before glass blowing was to start. A lazy fireman could accomplish the same effect by allowing the fire to burn low. All this meant that the top layer of glass would be filled with bubbles.

Unfortunately for hand blowing, the blowpipe must be dipped into the upper area of molten glass, where the last of the bubbles still remained. With incompletely refined glass therefore the blowpipe will pick up many seeds and bubbles, large and small. The very act of inserting the blowpipe could drag large bubbles of air into the glass. The result would be many seeds and bubbles in the first production. Window-glass blowers using the cylinder process used to say that the first quarter of the pot was for bottles, the middle half for window glass, and the rest was trash. It is no wonder that many wndow-glass makers also made bottles, just to use up the seedy glass at the start of operations.

The fact that some collectors' jars from one company may generally be seedy may reflect only that company's policies, or the degree of supervision. Later in the day that same pot may be making seed-free glass. If the factory manager and the men had waited, or could have waited, it would have had fewer seeds at the start. The fact does not indicate a different glass in any event.

Now that we are beginning to take glass out of the pot as a "gather" on the blowpipe, let us follow it further. The amount that the glass blower, usually an assistant in the crew, or "shop," takes up is a matter of his own personal skill. Upon that skill will rest the weight of the jar, the thickness of the glass walls, and the capacity of the jar. When he thinks that he has gathered enough glass he takes it to the marvering table.

The marvering table is a flatbed of stone, usually marble (in French, *marvre*) or sometimes iron. The gather on the blowpipe is usually globular at the start. By rolling the gather on its side on top of the waist-high marver, the globular mass becomes cylindrical in shape, the length depending upon the temperature and the length of time it is rolled. It is now called a "parison," from the French word meaning "to prepare." Again, the skill of the operator takes a big part.

Contact with the marvering table cools the surface of the glass. This cooling area the glass worker calls "the skin" and it plays an essential part in glass blowing for it sets up not only a boundary, but also develops a condition in which the more fluid glass, the area where the air bubble blown by the glass blower progresses, is the center of the parison. Too little "skin" and uneven blowing will occur—too much, and the condition we call whittled glass (and which Pellatt called "ruffled" glass in 1849) results because the surface is too cold to expand evenly to the inner contour of the finishing mold.

When the marvered parison is judged ready for the final blowing it is passed, on the blowpipe, to the gaffer (literally, "grandfather") or chief glass blower of the "shop." He may manipulate the piece and blowpipe until he deems it ready and well shaped, sometimes swinging it in the air to further elongate the parison. He may also give it one or two "puffs" to start the "bubble." Eventually he lowers it into a mold which is being held open by a boy squatting at his feet.

Sometimes the gaffer lifts the parison in the mold in order to place it back more centrally—this is a cause of the double impression of the bottom lettering sometimes seen, for the rapidly chilling glass retains the first impression as well as the impression from the final blowing. When the gaffer is ready, the boy closes the mold and holds it closed during the blowing operation.

Here, again, skill plays a big part. Contact between hot glass and mold is longer in hand blowing, even though the glass temperature worked is generally lower. The molds may become too hot and need to be dipped into water. More often the time before the next jar is blown is over-long and the mold becomes over-cold. Both tend to destroy the rhythm of the "shop" as well as to produce variable ware. Pellatt tells how a boy would hold a gather of hot glass within the mold to keep it hot until the glassblower was ready to use it.

Several methods were employed for separating the blowpipe from the jar. In one, while the jar is still in the mold, the gaffer simply pulls up a little on the blowpipe, blows hard on the pipe so that the glass balloons out as a large bubble and bursts of its own thinness. This is the "blow-over" method. The mold is then opened and the jar removed with tongs. In other methods the mold is first opened, and the jar, still adhering to the blowpipe, removed to the "chair" which has large, level arms over which the blowpipe can be placed in a position to roll. The point to be severed may be a straight portion just above the threads, lugs, or other detail, or it may be a built-in "blow-over," a bulb cut in the mold at the correct point. In either case, placing a wet iron, or a wet board (called "wetting-off") causes the glass to snap free at the wanted position.

What happens next depends on the immediate processing for the jar. If it is to go to the lehr, to be annealed and then ground flat on the finish, the jar is apt to be caught in an asbestos basket,

picked up by a pair of tongs, placed on an asbestos covered pad-
dle, and carried to the lehr. If the jar is to be further handled as a
finishing process, it is more apt to be secured at the bottom, in
early days to a glass-tipped pontil, about 1845 to a bare iron
pontil, and for most times after 1855, by a snap tool that grasped
the jar by its bottom, all this before severing the piece from the
blowpipe.

Catching in the basket, and taking directly to the lehr, with the
intent of grinding the jar mouth flat later, was one of three routes
that the bottle could take from the mold to the finished piece.
That route was taken by all "ground-lip" finishes. Another route
was to reheat in a furnace opening, after trimming with a shears
if the break was ragged, followed by flaring or other manipulation
by hand tools. Cork-sealed jars were treated in this manner. The
reheating at the furnace remelted the lip and smoothed it out. A
third route was to reheat the finish, most often after adding a ring
of glass about the lip to thicken and strengthen it, and then mold
it to a desired shape by hand-held tools or by a hand press. This
was done to make almost the first patented sealing device known
—the groove-ring wax sealer, and on up almost to the abandonment of hand jarmaking.

A variation from the pressing method was to reheat the finish
portion of the jar, then press it firmly into a block of iron, which
had a circular hole with sides at an angle desired in the top half
inch or so of the jar. These were the friction seals, as in the
EAGLE and the LAFAYETTE, where a very precise taper was
desired.

After annealing, all but the jars intended to be ground on top
were ready to be packed and shipped. Those jars left with the
ragged glass lip for later grinding were merely ground flat, and
then shipped.

The ground lip was easy to make, but sealing could not take
place directly on it because its rough surface would not make a
hermetic seal. A few inventors ignored that fact, and their inventions presumably had a short life. The designing of the seal to
avoid the ground lip taxed the ingenuity of inventors for many
years, and produced a wide gamut of jar designs.

Mason solved the problem by making the seal on the shoulder
under a cover-all zinc cap. Putnam solved it for his LIGHTNING

by making an inverted cup-shaped glass lid to straddle the ground lip and seal on a flat area that surrounded it, just as Imlay and Rowley had done for screw-band top seals in the previous decade. Most of the spring clips, yokes, levers, and toggles followed in the same manner. It was not until the development of machine production that the straddle-cup could be abandoned, except with stoppers.

The grinding operation was a boy's job. The boys squatted around a horizontally rotating grinding wheel on which the abrasive of sand and water flowed from a central spout. Jigs and fixtures held the jars upright on the wheel, and the boys supplied the pressure necessary to hold the jar top firmly on the wheel.

The hours were long and any boy big enough to look about twelve years of age was employed. It was cold, wet, debilitating work, and a notorious child labor (but far from the worst of its day) that took its toll in health-wrecked men, if not an early demise of the boys. A boy was fortunate if he were transferred early enough to the job of "snapper-up" at the molds, or "carry-in" boy to the lehrs. One of my men retired at the age of sixty-five after fifty-three years in the glass business; he had started at the grind shop at twelve.

Automatic glass-blowing machines did not develop overnight; it was a matter of slow growth, through a stage of semi-automatic operation. The development of the Blue machine for Hazel Glass Co., for use at the newly built Atlas Glass Company plant at Washington, Pa., in 1894, and the F. C. Ball machine in 1898 played a great part in making these two companies the leaders that they became among the many fruit-jar makers of the earlier days.

Glassmakers had been groping in the direction of some sort of machine operation since the mid-1800s. Finally Phillip Arbogast laid down a guiding principle: let one mold do what the marvering table usually does, and another to do what the finishing mold does, in hand blowing, and place a part that would form the finish contour with the blank, or first mold. While at first the finish contour mold was cut into the blank mold, it quickly became a separate part, and could be used to lift the parison out of the blank mold and transfer it to the finishing mold. Arbogast received Patent No. 260,819 on July 11, 1882.

Try as he could, Arbogast was unsuccessful in getting his idea into practice. The Ripley Glass Co. bought the patent, but also failed. The E. C. Flaccus Glass Co. was successful. In England, in 1885, Ashley received his patent for a glassmaking machine, and it is believed that Ashley made the first bottles.

In practice, the very first semi-automatic machine was a collection of separate mold parts, grouped together, and little more. A gatherer still took what seemed to be the right amount of glass on a pontil (not the blowpipe this time). Holding the gather over the top of the blank, or first and parison-forming mold, he cut a gob free from the gather by a pair of shears. Of course, the mold was closed, with only the top open. Next he forced a plunger, usually mounted on a ram and actuated either by a hand lever, by air pressure, or by steam or water pressure, down into the opening so that glass was forced into all parts of the inner area of the mold, including the threaded or other closure-holding contour.

On withdrawing the ram and opening the mold halves, or pushing the parison up in a tapered mold fitted with a bottom plunger, the operator would transfer the parison from the blank to the finishing mold by a pair of tongs. Once in the finishing mold, he would cause a "blow head" to come down over the open top of the finishing mold. Next he turned on an air-pressure valve, held it until he thought the bottle had been blown, and then closed the valve. When the finishing mold had been opened the jar could be taken to the annealing oven, or lehr. All this came to be known as the "press-and-blow" system.

Another machine development had to be made for blowing bottles with narrower mouths. In these machines the plunger only entered the top opening of the bottle-to-be far enough to fix the finish contour. The inner volume of the blank mold had to be calculated so that it was entirely filled with glass, or the necessary pressure to "fill" the finish could not be developed. From this point operations were more like those of the first-described method for jars. This latter method would also be called "press-and-blow."

In a variation for either, and with a minimum plunger size, the mold for the parison would be placed upside down and the plunger pushed up from the bottom. Air pressure would be used to compact the glass about the finish contour. Such machines were called "blow-and-blow."

From its start as a mere assemblage of mold parts on a single frame with all operations manually controlled, improvements came fast. One by one the manual operations of opening and closing molds, actuating the plunger, opening and closing all valves, and transfer from blank to finishing mold were mechanized. Instead of a single blank and a single finishing mold, several were placed on a rotating table for greater speed in production. Power drive was added in the Ball-Bingham machine after 1900. Thus the semi-automatic machine came into being, and it was called semi-automatic until the vital operation of transferring glass from the furnace to the glassmaking machine could be accomplished with no hand work involved except to feed glass and to remove the jar. Owens did this by suction from the top of a molten glass tank in 1904—Homer Brooke (mentioned in connection with the history of John L. Mason) did much to accomplish the more difficult method of separating composite "gobs" from a flowing stream of glass, but Hartford Empire was most successful.

Besides the work of Hazel and Atlas together, and Ball, other fruit-jar makers developed semi-automatic machines. These included the machine by the Safe Glass Co., Redkey, Indiana; Cumberland Glass Co., Bridgeton, N.J.; Illinois Glass Co., Alton, Ill.; Swayzee Glass Co., Swayzee, Ind.; C. E. Flaccus Glass Co., Tarentum, Pa.; Marion Fruit Jar & Bottle Co., Marion, Ind.; and the Rochester Glass Co., Rochester, N.Y.

Some fruit jars were made by machine as early as 1896 at the Atlas Glass Co., Washington, Pa. (Handmade Atlas jars are known, in spite of the fact that Atlas was supposed to be an all-machine factory.) As other companies developed machines, or bought them, hand blowing went on through a long period of transition, side by side (but sometimes with a separating wall to prevent sabotage). Some factories never entered the machine age, and were to close because of the cost differential. Many companies failed, or were absorbed by companies using the machines, in the years that followed. Handmade fruit jars were still being made in 1915, or even later. For this reason, one cannot quote a single year-date as the close of hand blowing and the beginning of machine blowing.

Machine manufacture did much for the fruit-jar user. First, it enabled the manufacturer to reduce the price drastically. The early cost of from fifteen to twenty-five cents a jar was now from four to eight cents for a more durable jar. The jars were more uniform, and now favored the Mason-type of seal even more, because the Mason zinc cap was the cheapest to make and sell. An even more economical top seal was soon tried, since the lip, no longer ground, could be hermetically sealed. Soon the Mason shoulder seal gave way to sealing on a bead in the neck, making a stronger shoulder possible. The glass lid and metal screw-band top seals tried from 1910 on the still slightly uneven jar lips gave way in 1915 to the Kerr-developed metal lids in 1915, with their greater flexibility to conform to the top of the finish.

We still use the Mason name on a fruit-jar design that he would never recognize as his 1858 jar. Thus, as I stated near the beginning of this chapter, the progress of the use of the fruit jar was a part of the progress of the glass industry that made it.